Head First Ajax

Wouldn't it be dreamy if there was a book on web programming that wasn't a bunch of theory and fancy talk about Google Maps? But it's probably just a fantasy...

Rebecca M. Riordan

O'REILLY®

Beijing • Cambridge • Köln • Paris • Sebastopol • Taipei • Tokyo

SHROFF PUBLISHERS & DISTRIBUTORS PVT. LTD.
Mumbai   Bangalore   Chennai   Kolkata   New Delhi

Head First Ajax

by Rebecca M. Riordan

Copyright © 2008 O'Reilly Media, Inc. All rights reserved. ISBN-13: 978-0-596-51578-2
Originally printed in the United States of America.

Published by O'Reilly Media, Inc., 1005 Gravenstein Highway North, Sebastopol, CA 95472.

O'Reilly books may be purchased for educational, business, or sales promotional use. Online editions are also available for most titles (*safari.oreilly.com*). For more information, contact our corporate/institutional sales department: (800)998-9938 or *corporate@oreilly.com*.

Series Creators:	Kathy Sierra, Bert Bates
Series Editor:	Brett D. McLaughlin
Design Editor:	Louise Barr
Cover Designers:	Louise Barr, Steve Fehler
Production Editor:	Brittany Smith
Indexer:	Julie Hawks
Application Designer:	Fletcher Moore

Printing History:
August 2008: First Edition.

Sixth Indian Reprint: October 2011

ISBN 13: 978-81-8404-581-9

The O'Reilly logo is a registered trademark of O'Reilly Media, Inc. The *Head First* series designations, *Head First Ajax*, and related trade dress are trademarks of O'Reilly Media, Inc.

Many of the designations used by manufacturers and sellers to distinguish their products are claimed as trademarks. Where those designations appear in this book, and O'Reilly Media, Inc., was aware of a trademark claim, the designations have been printed in caps or initial caps.

While every precaution has been taken in the preparation of this book, the publisher and the authors assume no responsibility for errors or omissions, or for damages resulting from the use of the information contained herein.

No web pages were harmed in the creation of this book, although several were bent significantly out of shape. Several browser-server communications were interrogated, but only after their rights were carefully presented.

Published by **Shroff Publishers and Distributors Pvt. Ltd.** C-103, MIDC, TTC Industrial Area, Pawane, Navi Mumbai 400 705, Tel: (91 22) 4158 4158, Fax: (91 22) 4158 4141, e-mail: spdorders@shroffpublishers.com. Printed at Decora Book Prints Pvt. Ltd., Mumbai.

Author of Head First Ajax

Rebecca M. Riordan

With twenty years experience in the field, **Rebecca M. Riordan** has earned an international reputation for designing and implementing computer systems that are technically sound, reliable, and effectively meet her clients' needs. Her particular area of expertise is database design, and she is a five year Access MVP.

Rebecca has also authored several database books and served as a senior technical support engineer for Microsoft's database products. As a Microsoft employee in Australia, Rebecca was the Senior technical support engineer for Microsoft's database products.

Table of Contents (Summary)

Table of Contents (the real thing)

Intro

Your brain on Ajax. Here *you* are trying to *learn* something, while here your *brain* is doing you a favor by making sure the learning doesn't *stick*. Your brain's thinking, "Better leave room for more important things, like which wild animals to avoid and whether naked snowboarding is a bad idea." So how *do* you trick your brain into thinking that your life depends on knowing Ajax?

using ajax

Web Apps for a New Generation

Tired of waiting around for your page to reload?

Frustrated by clunky web application interfaces? It's time to give your web apps that slick, responsive desktop feel. And how do you do that? With **Ajax**, your ticket to building Internet applications that are *more interactive, more responsive,* and *easier to use.* So skip your nap; it's time to put some polish on your web apps. It's time to get rid of unnecessary and slow full-page refreshes forever.

I'm desperate... but I can't afford a more powerful server or a team of web experts.

Ajax pages only talk to the server when they have to... and only about what the server knows.

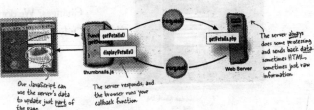

Our JavaScript can use the server's data to update just *part* of the page.

The server responds, and the browser runs your callback function.

The server *always* does some processing and sends back data... sometimes HTML, sometimes just raw information.

designing ajax applications
Thinking Ajaxian
Welcome to Ajax apps—it's a whole new web world.

So you've built your first Ajax app, and you're already thinking about how to change all your web apps to make requests asynchronously. But that's not all there is to Ajax programming. You've got to *think about your applications differently*. Just because you're making asynchronous requests, doesn't mean your application is user-friendly. It's up to you to help your users **avoid making mistakes**, and that means **rethinking** your entire application's **design**.

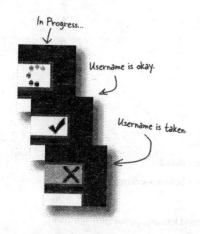

In Progress...

Username is okay.

Username is taken.

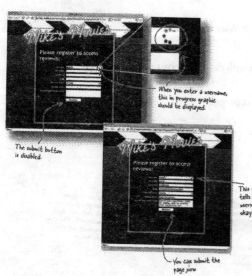

When you enter a username, this in progress graphic should be displayed.

The submit button is disabled.

This graphic tells you the username is okay.

You can submit the page now

3

javascript events

Reacting to your users

Sometimes you need your code to react to other things going on in your web application... and that's where **events** come into the picture. An event is *something that happens* on your page, in the browser, or even on a web server. But it's not enough to just know about events... sometimes you want to respond to them. By creating code, and registering it as an **event handler**, you can get the browser to run your handler every time a particular event occurs. Combine events and handlers, and you get **interactive web applications**.

Beginner

This is where you should start if you're new to yoga.

Intermediate

When the beginner course isn't a challenge, try this one.

Advanced

Very challenging!

4

multiple event handlers

Two's company

A single event handler isn't always enough.

Sometimes you've got more than one event handler that needs to be called by an event. Maybe you've got some event-specific actions, as well as some generic code, and stuffing everything into a single event handler function won't cut it. Or maybe you're just trying to build **clean, reusable code**, and you've got **two bits of functionality** triggered by the **same event**. Fortunately, we can use some **DOM Level 2** methods to assign multiple handler functions to a **single event**.

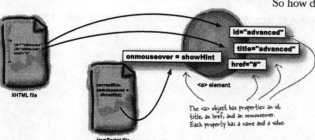

id="advanced"
title="advanced"
href="#"

onmouseover = showHint

XHTML file

JavaScript file

<a> element

The <a> object has properties: an id, title, an href, and an onmouseover. Each property has a name and a value.

asynchronous applications

It's like renewing your driver's license

Are you tired of waiting around? Do you hate long delays? You can do something about it with asynchrony!

You've already built a couple of pages that made asynchronous requests to the server to avoid making the user sit around waiting for a page refresh. In this chapter, we'll dive even deeper into the details of building asynchronous applications.

You'll find out what **asynchronous really means**, learn how to use **multiple asynchronous requests**, and even build a **monitor function** to keep all that asynchrony from confusing you and your users.

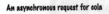

An asynchronous request for cola

Hey, Rufus, will you get me another cola?

Like before, you make a request to Rufus to GET you a cola. Except this time, you tell him he's an asynchronous dog.

I'm gonna ask for a pay raise. More chew toys.

Once again Rufus goes after your cola. But this time, Rufus is an ASYNCHRONOUS dog.

And that means you can do whatever you want while he's getting the cola. You're not stuck like you were when he was synchronous.

By the time Rufus gets back, you're on the 17th green. Perfect time for a break!

The result is the same: you get your cola. The difference is that you weren't completely stuck while you were waiting for it

the document object model
Web Page Forestry

6

Wanted: easy-to-update web pages. It's time to take things into your own hands and start writing code that updates your web pages on the fly. Using the **Document Object Model**, your pages can take on new life, responding to users' actions, and you can ditch unnecessary page reloads forever. By the time you've finished this chapter, you'll be able to find, move, and update content virtually anywhere on your web page.

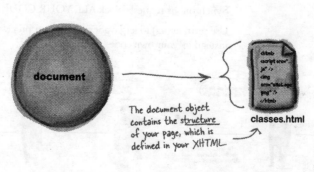

The document object contains the structure of your page, which is defined in your XHTML.

The style and even the code attached to your structure is also represented in the DOM.

manipulating the DOM

7 My wish is your command

Sometimes you just need a little DOM mind control.

It's great to know that web browsers turn your XHTML into DOM trees. And you can do a lot by moving around within those trees. But real power is **taking control of a DOM tree** and making the tree look like *you* want it to. Sometimes what you really need is to **add a new element** and some text, or to **remove an element**, like an <img>, from a page altogether. You can do all of that and more with the DOM, and along the way, **banish that troublesome innerHTML property** altogether. The result? Code that can do more to a page, *without* having to mix presentation and structure in with your JavaScript.

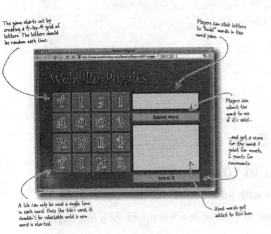

The game starts out by creating a 4-by-4 grid of letters. The letters should be random each time.

Players can click letters to "build" words in this word pane.

Players can submit the word to see if it's valid...

...and get a score for the word: 1 point for vowels, 2 points for consonants.

A tile can only be used a single time in each word. Once the tile's used, it shouldn't be selectable until a new word is started.

Used words get added to this box.

frameworks and toolkits

Trust No One

8

So what's the *real* story behind all those Ajax frameworks?

If you've been in Webville awhile, you've probably run across at least one JavaScript or Ajax framework. Some frameworks give you **convenience methods for working with the DOM**. Others make **validation** and **sending requests** simple. Still others come with libraries of pre-packaged JavaScript **screen effects**. But which one should you use? And how do you know what's really going on inside that framework? It's time to do more than use other people's code... it's time to *take control of your applications*.

Reasons to use a framework

Reasons NOT to use a framework

xml requests and responses

More Than Words Can Say

9

How will you describe yourself in 10 years? How about 20?

Sometimes you need **data that can change with your needs**... or the needs of your customers. Data you're using now might need to change in a few hours, or a few days, or a few months. With XML, the *extensible markup language*, your data can **describe itself**. That means your scripts won't be filled with ifs, elses, and switches. Instead, you can use the descriptions that XML provides about itself to figure out how to *use* the data the XML contains. The result: **more flexibility** and **easier data handling**.

Description: Pete Townshend once played this guitar while his own axe was in the shop having bits of drumkit removed from it.

Price: $5695.99

- http://www.thewho.com
- https://en.wikipedia.org/wiki/Pete_Townshend

Rob wants to add a price for each item.

Each item will have one or more URLs to find out more about the item.

json

SON of JavaScript

JavaScript, objects, and notation, oh my!

If you ever need to represent objects in your JavaScript, then you're going to love JSON, **JavaScript Standard Object Notation**. With JSON, you can **represent complex objects and mappings** with text and a few curly braces. Even better, you can **send and receive JSON** from other languages, like PHP, C#, Python, and Ruby.

10

JSON can be text AND an object

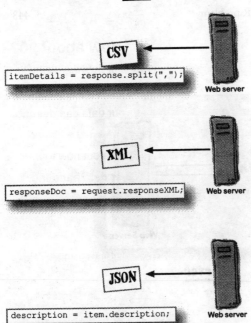

```
itemDetails = response.split(",");
```
CSV — Web server

```
responseDoc = request.responseXML;
```
XML — Web server

```
description = item.description;
```
JSON — Web server

forms and validation

Say what you <u>meant</u> to say

11

Everyone makes mistakes from time to time.

Give a human being a chance to talk (or type) for a few minutes, and they'll probably make at least one or two **mistakes**. So how do your web apps **respond to those mistakes**? You've got to **validate** your users' input and react when that input has problems. But who does what? What should your web page do? What should your JavaScript do? And what's the role of the server in **validation** and **data integrity**?

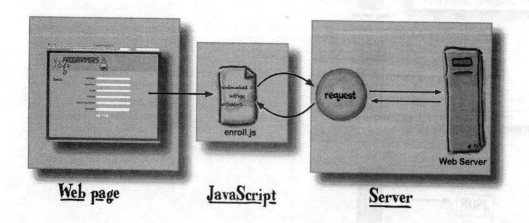

Web page **JavaScript** **Server**

12

post requests

Paranoia: It's your friend

Someone's watching you. Right now. Seriously.

Freedom of Information Act? Isn't that called the Internet? These days, anything a user types into a form or clicks on a web page is subject to **inspection**. Whether it's a network admin, a software company trying to learn about your trends, or a malicious hacker or spammer, your *information isn't safe unless you make it safe*. When it comes to web pages, you've got to **protect your users' data** when they click Submit.

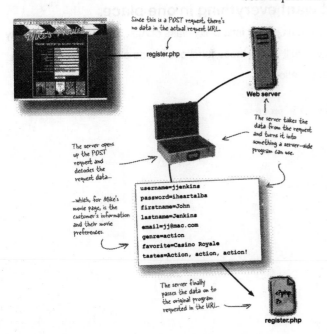

Since this is a POST request, there's no data in the actual request URL.

register.php

Web server

The server takes the data from the request and turns it into something a server-side program can use.

The server opens up the POST request and decodes the request data...

...which, for Mike's movie page, is the customer's information and their movie preferences.

```
username=jjenkins
password=iheartalba
firstname=John
lastname=Jenkins
email=jj@mac.com
genre=action
favorite=Casino Royale
tastes=Action, action, action!
```

The server finally passes the data on to the original program requested in the URL.

register.php

leftovers

The Top Five Topics (we didn't cover)

It's been a long ride... and you're almost to the end.

We can barely stand to let you go, but before you do, there's still a few things left to cover. We can't possibly fit everything about Ajax into one 600-page book. So we threw out everything you didn't really need to know and kept the last few important bits in this appendix.

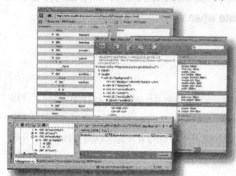

utility functions

Just Gimme the Code

Sometimes you just want everything in one place.

You've spent a lot of time using utils.js, our little utility class of Ajax, DOM, and event utility functions. Inside these pages, you'll get all those functions in one place, ready to put into your own utility scripts and applications.

how to use this book

Intro

In this section we answer the burning question: "So why DID they put that in a web programming book?"

Who is this book for?

If you can answer "yes" to all of these:

1 Do you know **HTML**, some **CSS**, and some **JavaScript**? (You don't need to be a guru or anything.)

2 Do you want to **learn**, **understand**, and *remember* Ajax, with a goal of developing responsive and usable web applications?

3 Do you prefer **stimulating dinner party conversation** to dry, dull, academic lectures?

this book is for you.

Who should probably back away from this book?

If you can answer "yes" to any *one* of these:

1 Are you **completey new** to HTML or CSS or JavaScript? (You don't need to be advanced, but you should definitely have some experience. If not, go get a copy of *Head First HTML and CSS*, today, and then come back and get this book.)

2 Are you a kick-butt Ajax or web developer looking for a *reference* book?

3 Are you **afraid to try something different**? Would you rather have a root canal than mix stripes with plaid? Do you believe that a technical book can't be serious if servers and web browsers are anthropomorphized?

this book is not for you.

[Note from marketing: this book is for anyone with a credit card.]

We know what you're thinking

"How can *this* be a serious book on web programming?"

"What's with all the graphics?"

"Can I actually *learn* it this way?"

We know what your *brain* is thinking

Your brain craves novelty. It's always searching, scanning, *waiting* for something unusual. It was built that way, and it helps you stay alive.

So what does your brain do with all the routine, ordinary, normal things you encounter? Everything it *can* to stop them from interfering with the brain's *real* job—recording things that *matter*. It doesn't bother saving the boring things; they never make it past the "this is obviously not important" filter.

How does your brain *know* what's important? Suppose you're out for a day hike and a tiger jumps in front of you, what happens inside your head and body?

Neurons fire. Emotions crank up. *Chemicals surge.*

And that's how your brain knows...

This must be important! Don't forget it!

But imagine you're at home, or in a library. It's a safe, warm, tiger-free zone. You're studying. Getting ready for an exam. Or trying to learn some tough technical topic your boss thinks will take a week, ten days at the most.

Just one problem. Your brain's trying to do you a big favor. It's trying to make sure that this *obviously* non-important content doesn't clutter up scarce resources. Resources that are better spent storing the really *big* things. Like tigers. Like the danger of fire. Like how you should never have posted those "party" photos on your Facebook page.

And there's no simple way to tell your brain, "Hey brain, thank you very much, but no matter how dull this book is, and how little I'm registering on the emotional Richter scale right now, I really *do* want you to keep this stuff around."

Your brain thinks THIS is important.

Your brain thinks THIS isn't worth saving.

Great. Only 500 more dull, dry, boring pages.

We think of a "Head First" reader as a learner.

So what does it take to *learn* something? First, you have to *get* it, then make sure you don't *forget* it. It's not about pushing facts into your head. Based on the latest research in cognitive science, neurobiology, and educational psychology, *learning* takes a lot more than text on a page. We know what turns your brain on.

Some of the Head First learning principles:

Make it visual. Images are far more memorable than words alone, and make learning much more effective (up to 89% improvement in recall and transfer studies). It also makes things more understandable. **Put the words within or near the graphics** they relate to, rather than on the bottom or on another page, and learners will be up to *twice* as likely to solve problems related to the content.

Use a conversational and personalized style. In recent studies, students performed up to 40% better on post-learning tests if the content spoke directly to the reader, using a first-person, conversational style rather than taking a formal tone. Tell stories instead of lecturing. Use casual language. Don't take yourself too seriously. Which would *you* pay more attention to: a stimulating dinner party companion, or a lecture?

Get the learner to think more deeply. In other words, unless you actively flex your neurons, nothing much happens in your head. A reader has to be motivated, engaged, curious, and inspired to solve problems, draw conclusions, and generate new knowledge. And for that, you need challenges, exercises, and thought-provoking questions, and activities that involve both sides of the brain and multiple senses.

Get—and keep—the reader's attention. We've all had the "I really want to learn this but I can't stay awake past page one" experience. Your brain pays attention to things that are out of the ordinary, interesting, strange, eye-catching, unexpected. Learning a new, tough, technical topic doesn't have to be boring. Your brain will learn much more quickly if it's not.

Touch their emotions. We now know that your ability to remember something is largely dependent on its emotional content. You remember what you care about. You remember when you *feel* something. No, we're not talking heart-wrenching stories about a boy and his dog. We're talking emotions like surprise, curiosity, fun, "what the...?", and the feeling of "I Rule!" that comes when you solve a puzzle, learn something everybody else thinks is hard, or realize you know something that "I'm a more senior programmer than you" Bob from the next cube over *doesn't*.

Why don't I just ask the guys to add a few lines to register.php? It's probably a good idea to let Mike's new customer know what they submitted, anyway.

This time, your page's code creates a special request object that the browser sends to the server.

request

Metacognition: thinking about thinking

If you really want to learn, and you want to learn more quickly and more deeply, pay attention to how you pay attention. Think about how you think. Learn how you learn.

Most of us didn't take courses on metacognition or learning theory when we were growing up. We were *expected* to learn, but rarely *taught* to learn.

I wonder how I can trick my brain into remembering this stuff...

But we assume that if you're holding this book, you really want to learn Ajax and web programming. And you probably don't want to spend a lot of time. If you want to use what you read in this book, you need to *remember* what you read. And for that, you've got to *understand* it. To get the most from this book, or *any* book or learning experience, take responsibility for your brain. Your brain on *this* content.

The trick is to get your brain to see the new material you're learning as Really Important. Crucial to your well-being. As important as a tiger. Otherwise, you're in for a constant battle, with your brain doing its best to keep the new content from sticking.

So just how *DO* you get your brain to treat web programming like it was a hungry tiger?

There's the slow, tedious way, or the faster, more effective way. The slow way is about sheer repetition. You obviously know that you *are* able to learn and remember even the dullest of topics if you keep pounding the same thing into your brain. With enough repetition, your brain says, "This doesn't *feel* important to him, but he keeps looking at the same thing *over* and *over* and *over*, so I suppose it must be."

The faster way is to do *anything that increases brain activity,* especially different *types* of brain activity. The things on the previous page are a big part of the solution, and they're all things that have been proven to help your brain work in your favor. For example, studies show that putting words *within* the pictures they describe (as opposed to somewhere else in the page, like a caption or in the body text) causes your brain to try to makes sense of how the words and picture relate, and this causes more neurons to fire. More neurons firing = more chances for your brain to *get* that this is something worth paying attention to, and possibly recording.

A conversational style helps because people tend to pay more attention when they perceive that they're in a conversation, since they're expected to follow along and hold up their end. The amazing thing is, your brain doesn't necessarily *care* that the "conversation" is between you and a book! On the other hand, if the writing style is formal and dry, your brain perceives it the same way you experience being lectured to while sitting in a roomful of passive attendees. No need to stay awake.

But pictures and conversational style are just the beginning…

Here's what WE did:

We used *pictures*, because your brain is tuned for visuals, not text. As far as your brain's concerned, a picture really *is* worth a thousand words. And when text and pictures work together, we embedded the text *in* the pictures because your brain works more effectively when the text is *within* the thing the text refers to, as opposed to in a caption or buried in the text somewhere.

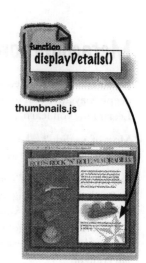

thumbnails.js

We used *redundancy*, saying the same thing in *different* ways and with different media types, and *multiple senses*, to increase the chance that the content gets coded into more than one area of your brain.

We used concepts and pictures in *unexpected* ways because your brain is tuned for novelty, and we used pictures and ideas with at least *some emotional* content, because your brain is tuned to pay attention to the biochemistry of emotions. That which causes you to *feel* something is more likely to be remembered, even if that feeling is nothing more than a little *humor*, *surprise*, or *interest*.

We used a personalized, *conversational style*, because your brain is tuned to pay more attention when it believes you're in a conversation than if it thinks you're passively listening to a presentation. Your brain does this even when you're *reading*.

We included more than 80 *activities*, because your brain is tuned to learn and remember more when you *do* things than when you *read* about things. And we made the exercises challenging-yet-do-able, because that's what most people prefer.

We used *multiple learning styles*, because *you* might prefer step-by-step procedures, while someone else wants to understand the big picture first, and someone else just wants to see an example. But regardless of your own learning preference, *everyone* benefits from seeing the same content represented in multiple ways.

We include content for *both sides of your brain*, because the more of your brain you engage, the more likely you are to learn and remember, and the longer you can stay focused. Since working one side of the brain often means giving the other side a chance to rest, you can be more productive at learning for a longer period of time.

And we included *stories* and exercises that present *more than one point of view,* because your brain is tuned to learn more deeply when it's forced to make evaluations and judgments.

We included *challenges*, with exercises, and by asking *questions* that don't always have a straight answer, because your brain is tuned to learn and remember when it has to *work* at something. Think about it—you can't get your *body* in shape just by *watching* people at the gym. But we did our best to make sure that when you're working hard, it's on the *right* things. That *you're not spending one extra dendrite* processing a hard-to-understand example, or parsing difficult, jargon-laden, or overly terse text.

there are no
Dumb Questions

We used *people*. In stories, examples, pictures, etc., because, well, because *you're* a person. And your brain pays more attention to *people* than it does to *things*.

Cut this out and stick it
on your refrigerator.

Here's what YOU can do to bend your brain into submission

So, we did our part. The rest is up to you. These tips are a starting point; listen to your brain and figure out what works for you and what doesn't. Try new things.

① Slow down. The more you understand, the less you have to memorize.

Don't just *read*. Stop and think. When the book asks you a question, don't just skip to the answer. Imagine that someone really *is* asking the question. The more deeply you force your brain to think, the better chance you have of learning and remembering.

② Do the exercises. Write your own notes.

We put them in, but if we did them for you, that would be like having someone else do your workouts for you. And don't just *look* at the exercises. **Use a pencil.** There's plenty of evidence that physical activity *while* learning can increase the learning.

③ Read the "There are No Dumb Questions"

That means all of them. They're not optional sidebars—*they're part of the core content!* Don't skip them.

④ Make this the last thing you read before bed. Or at least the last challenging thing.

Part of the learning (especially the transfer to long-term memory) happens *after* you put the book down. Your brain needs time on its own, to do more processing. If you put in something new during that processing time, some of what you just learned will be lost.

⑤ Drink water. Lots of it.

Your brain works best in a nice bath of fluid. Dehydration (which can happen before you ever feel thirsty) decreases cognitive function.

⑥ Talk about it. Out loud.

Speaking activates a different part of the brain. If you're trying to understand something, or increase your chance of remembering it later, say it out loud. Better still, try to explain it out loud to someone else. You'll learn more quickly, and you might uncover ideas you hadn't known were there when you were reading about it.

⑦ Listen to your brain.

Pay attention to whether your brain is getting overloaded. If you find yourself starting to skim the surface or forget what you just read, it's time for a break. Once you go past a certain point, you won't learn faster by trying to shove more in, and you might even hurt the process.

⑧ Feel something.

Your brain needs to know that this *matters*. Get involved with the stories. Make up your own captions for the photos. Groaning over a bad joke is *still* better than feeling nothing at all.

⑨ Practice writing web applications!

There's only one way to truly master web programming: **program web applications**. And that's what you're going to do throughout this book. Using Ajax is a skill, and the only way to get good at it is to practice. We're going to give you a lot of practice: every chapter has apps that we'll build. Don't just skip over them—a lot of the learning happens when you build these apps yourself. And definitely make sure you understand what's going on before you move on to the next part of the book.

Read Me

This is a learning experience, not a reference book. We deliberately stripped out everything that might get in the way of learning whatever it is we're working on at that point in the book. And the first time through, you need to begin at the beginning, because the book makes assumptions about what you've already seen and learned.

We assume you are familiar with HTML and CSS.

It would take an entire book to teach you HTML and CSS (in fact, that's exactly what it took: *Head First HTML with CSS & XHTML*). We chose to focus this book on Ajax programming, rather than rehash lots of markup and style that you could learn about in other places.

We assume you've at least seen JavaScript code before.

It would take an entire book to teach you... oh, wait, we've already said that. Seriously, JavaScript is a lot more than a simple scripting language, and we aren't going to cover all the ways you can use JavaScript in this book. You'll learn about all the ways that JavaScript is related to Ajax programming, and learn how to use JavaScript extensively to add interaction to your web pages and make requests to a server.

However, if you've never written a line of JavaScript, aren't at all familiar with functions or curly braces, or have never programmed in any language before, you might want to pick up a good JavaScript book and browse through it. If you want to plow into this book, feel free—but we will be moving fairly quickly over the basics.

We don't cover server-side programming in this book.

It's now common to find server-side programs written in Java, PHP, Ruby, Python, Perl, Ruby on Rails, C#, and a whole lot more. Ajax programming works with all of these languages, and we have tried to represent several of them in this book's examples.

To keep you focused on learning Ajax, though, we do not spend much time explaining the server-side programs used; we'll show you the basic inputs and outputs to the server, but that's as far as we go. We believe that your Ajax applications can be written to work with any kind of server-side program; we also believe that you're smart enough to apply the lessons learned from an example that uses PHP to one that uses Ruby on Rails or a Java servlet.

You can visit us online at **http://www.headfirstlabs.com/books/hfajax** to download sample server-side programs, so you can run these apps yourself.

We encourage you to use more than one browser with this book.

As much as it sucks, different web browsers handle your HTML, your CSS, and your JavaScript in completely different ways. If you want to be a complete Ajax programmer, you should always test your asynchronous applications on lots of modern browsers. All the examples in this book were tested on recent versions of Firefox, Opera, Safari, Internet Explorer, and Mozilla. If you find problems, though, let us know... we promise it's an accident.

We often use tag names for element names.

Rather than saying "the **a** element," or "the 'a' element," we use a tag name, like "the **<a>** element." While this may not be technically correct (because **<a>** is an opening tag, not a full blown element), it does make the text more readable.

The activities are NOT optional.

The exercises and activities are not add-ons; they're part of the core content of the book. Some of them are to help with memory, some are for understanding, and some will help you apply what you've learned. ***Don't skip the exercises.***

The redundancy is intentional and important.

One distinct difference in a Head First book is that we want you to *really* get it. And we want you to finish the book remembering what you've learned. Most reference books don't have retention and recall as a goal, but this book is about learning, so you'll see many of the concepts come up more than once.

The examples are as lean as possible.

Our readers tell us that it's frustrating to wade through 200 lines of an example looking for the two lines they need to understand. Most examples in this book are shown within the smallest possible context, so that the part you're trying to learn is clear and simple. Don't expect all of the examples to be robust, or even complete—they are written specifically for learning, and aren't always fully functional.

We've placed all the example files on the Web so you can download them. You'll find them at `http://www.headfirstlabs.com/books/hfajax/`.

The 'Brain Power' exercises don't have answers.

For some of them, there is no right answer, and for others, part of the learning experience of the Brain Power activities is for you to decide if and when your answers are right. In some of the Brain Power exercises you will find hints to point you in the right direction.

The technical review team

Bear Bibeault

Anthony T. Holdener III

Elaine Nelson

Not pictured (but just as awesome): Chris Haddix and Stephen Tallent

Pauline McNamara

Andrew Monkhouse

Fletcher Moore

Technical Reviewers:

Bear Bibeault is a Web Applications Architect responsible for an enterprise financial application used by the accountants that many of the Fortune 500 companies keep in their dungeons. He also delights clients with web applications he creates on the side (Ajax-powered, of course), and serves as a sheriff (senior moderator) at JavaRanch.com.

Anthony T. Holdener III is the Director of Information Technology for Korein Tillery, LLC, but was a web applications developer in his previous life as a programmer; he is also the author of *Ajax: The Definitive Guide* (O'Reilly).

Elaine Nelson has been designing websites for nearly 10 years. As she tells her mother, an English degree comes in handy everywhere. Elaine's current musings and obsessions can be found at elainenelson.org.

Pauline McNamara is involved in e-learning development and support at the Center for New Technologies and Education at Fribourg University in Switzerland.

Andrew Monkhouse is an administrator on JavaRanch, and a Java developer by day. He is currently working for PersonalShopper.com in the USA - a long way from his home in Australia.

Fletcher Moore did all our code samples and was indispensable to the project. He is a web developer and designer at Georgia Tech. In his spare time he's an avid cyclist, musician, gardener, and Red Sox fan. He resides in Atlanta with his wife Katherine, daughter Sailor, and son Satchel.

Acknowledgments

My support team:

Even beyond the fantastic technical reviewers, this book wouldn't have seen the light of day were it not for my own little technical support team. **Stephen Jeffries**, developer extraordinaire, helped out with the server-side code and reviewed all the samples before submission. **Michael Morrison** is the world's best sounding board for those middle-of-the-night, "Why does this code work everywhere but in this browser?" questions. And **John Hardesty** provided the basic algorithms for several of the games you'll be building. (He's also my brother, which I've always thought was pretty cool. But don't tell him I said so.)

My editor:

The greatest gift any editor can give a writer is to say, "This isn't working, this is why, and this is what I think you should do about it." **Brett McLaughlin** came through every damn time, and for that I will always be grateful.

Brett McLaughlin

The O'Reilly team:

Lou Barr

I'd also like to thank **Laurie Petrycki** for being the voice of reason in the always-insane world of technical publishing, and both **Louise Barr** and **Sanders Kleinfeld** for fielding even the wildest InDesign questions with patience and grace.

Sanders Kleinfeld

Safari® Books Online

 When you see a Safari® icon on the cover of your favorite technology book that means the book is available online through the O'Reilly Network Safari Bookshelf.

Safari offers a solution that's better than e-books. It's a virtual library that lets you easily search thousands of top tech books, cut and paste code samples, download chapters, and find quick answers when you need the most accurate, current information. Try it for free at http://safari.oreilly.com.

1 using ajax

Web Apps for a New Generation

I'll just take a little nap while I'm waiting for my web app to respond...

Tired of waiting around for your page to reload?

Frustrated by clunky web application interfaces? It's time to give your web apps that slick, responsive desktop feel. And how do you do that? With **Ajax**, your ticket to building Internet applications that are *more interactive, more responsive,* and *easier to use*. So skip your nap; it's time to put some polish on your web apps. It's time to get rid of unnecessary and slow full-page refreshes forever.

Web pages: the old-fashioned approach

With traditional web pages and applications, every time a user clicks on something, the browser sends a request to the server, and the server responds with a **whole new page**. Even if your user's web browser is smart about caching things like images and cascading style sheets, that's a lot of traffic going back and forth between their browser and your server... and a lot of time that the user sits around waiting for full page refreshes.

The user clicks something on your page.

The browser sends a request to the server.

The server sends back a whole new page, with all the changed information.

The user clicks something else.

The browser sends another request to the server.

Most of the time, only a single line or image is changing... but there's still a complete page refresh.

And the server sends back another whole page...

Web pages reinvented

Using Ajax, your pages and applications only ask the server for what they really need—just the parts of a page that need to change, and just the parts that the server has to provide. That means less traffic, smaller updates, and **less time sitting around** waiting for page refreshes.

With Ajax, the browser only sends and receives the parts of a page that need to change.

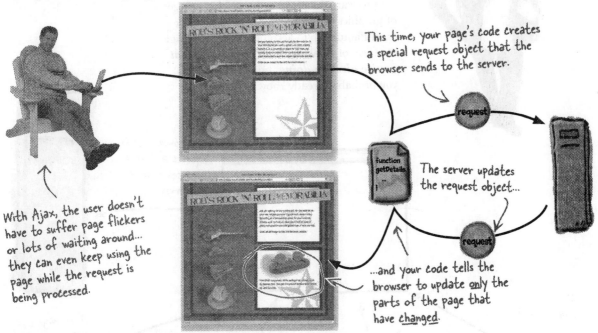

This time, your page's code creates a special request object that the browser sends to the server.

The server updates the request object...

With Ajax, the user doesn't have to suffer page flickers or lots of waiting around... they can even keep using the page while the request is being processed.

...and your code tells the browser to update only the parts of the page that have changed.

Sometimes the browser doesn't have to talk to the server at all.

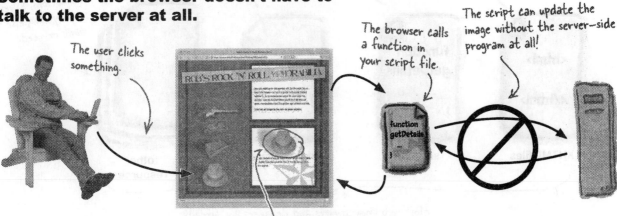

The user clicks something.

The browser calls a function in your script file.

The script can update the image without the server-side program at all!

The script tells the browser how to update the page... all without a page refresh.

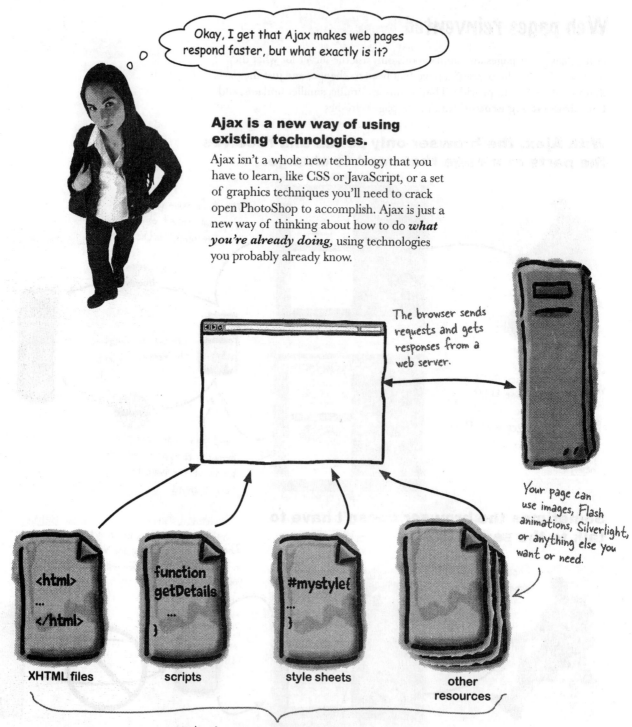

Okay, I get that Ajax makes web pages respond faster, but what exactly is it?

Ajax is a new way of using existing technologies.

Ajax isn't a whole new technology that you have to learn, like CSS or JavaScript, or a set of graphics techniques you'll need to crack open PhotoShop to accomplish. Ajax is just a new way of thinking about how to do *what you're already doing,* using technologies you probably already know.

The browser sends requests and gets responses from a web server.

Your page can use images, Flash animations, Silverlight, or anything else you want or need.

XHTML files

```
<html>
...
</html>
```

scripts

```
function
getDetails
...
}
```

style sheets

```
#mystyle{
...
}
```

other resources

Most web programmers and designers are already using some, or even all, of these technologies.

So what makes a page "Ajax"?

Ajax is a way of designing and building web pages that are as interactive and responsive as desktop applications. So what does that mean for you? You handle things at the client's browser whenever you can. Your pages make **asynchronous requests** that allow the user to keep working instead of waiting for a response. You only update the things on your pages that actually change. And best of all, an Ajax page is built using standard Internet technologies, things you probably already know how to use, like:

- **XHTML**
- **Cascading Style Sheets**
- **JavaScript**

Ajax applications also use a few things that have been around for a while but may be new to you, like:

- **The XmlHttpRequest**
- **XML & JSON**
- **The DOM**

> We'll look at all of these in detail before we're through.

An <u>asynchronous</u> request is a request that occurs <u>behind</u> <u>the scenes</u>.

Your users can <u>keep working</u> while the request is taking place.

---

there are no Dumb Questions

Q: Doesn't Ajax stand for "Asynchronous JavaScript and XML"?

A: Sort of. Since lots of pages that are considered "Ajax" don't use JavaScript or XML, it's more useful to define Ajax as a way of building web pages that are as responsive and interactive as desktop applications, and not worry too much about the exact technologies involved.

Q: What exactly does "asynchronous" mean?

A: In Ajax, you can make requests to the server without making your user wait around for a response. That's called an **asynchronous request**, and it's the core of what Ajax is all about.

Q: But aren't all web pages asynchronous? Like when a browser loads an image while I'm already looking at the page?

A: *Browsers* are asynchronous, but the standard web page isn't. Usually when a web page needs information from a server-side program, everything comes to a complete stop until the server responds... unless the page makes an asynchronous request. And that' what Ajax is all about.

Q: But all Ajax pages use that XMLHttpRequest object, right?

A: Nope. Lots do, and we'll spend a couple of chapters mastering XMLHttpRequest, but it's not a requirement. In fact, lots of apps that are considered Ajax are more about user interactivity and design than any particular coding technique.

Rob's Rock 'n' Roll Memorabilia

Meet Rob. He's put all his savings into an online rock n' roll memorabilia store. The site looks great, but he's still been getting tons of complaints. Customers are clicking on the thumbnail images on the inventory page, but the customers' browsers are taking forever before they show information about the selected item. Some of Rob's users are hanging around, but most have just stopped coming to Rob's online shop altogether.

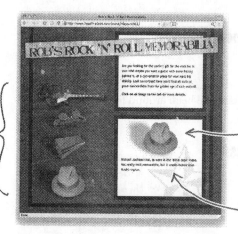

This pane contains thumbnails of the items Rob has for sale.

When the user clicks an item, a bigger picture of the image is displayed here...

...and the details about the item are shown here.

> I'm desperate... but I can't afford a more powerful server or a team of web experts.

Ajax pages only talk to the server when they have to... and only about what the server knows.

The problem with Rob's site isn't that his server is too slow, but that his pages are sending requests to the server *all the time*... even when they don't need to.

Sharpen your pencil

Here's what Rob's online store does right now. What's wrong with this picture?

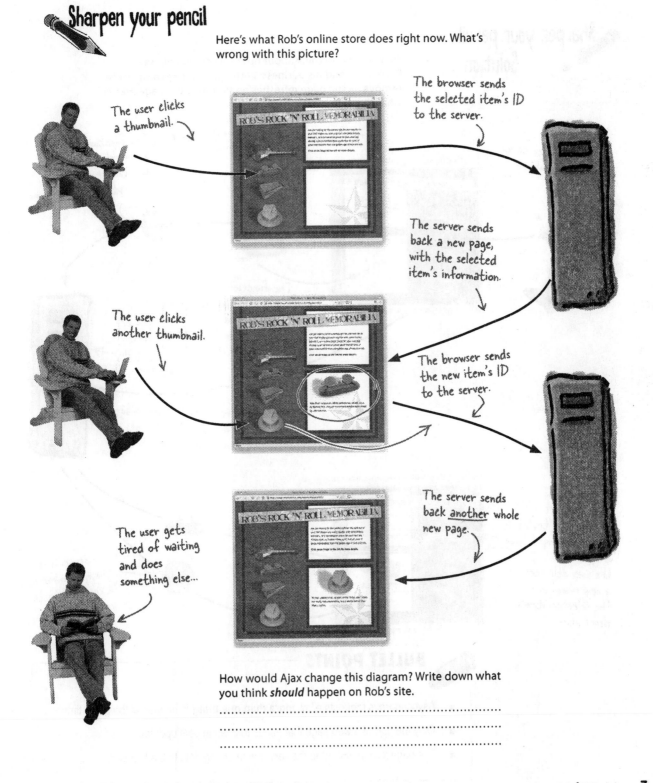

The user clicks a thumbnail.

The browser sends the selected item's ID to the server.

The server sends back a new page, with the selected item's information.

The user clicks another thumbnail.

The browser sends the new item's ID to the server.

The server sends back _another_ whole new page.

The user gets tired of waiting and does something else...

How would Ajax change this diagram? Write down what you think *should* happen on Rob's site.

....

....

....

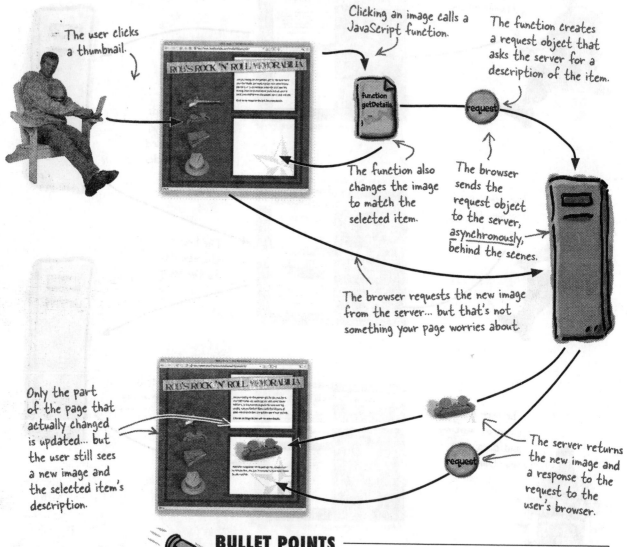

Sharpen your pencil
Solution

Your job was to think about how Ajax could help save Rob's site... and his business. With Ajax, we can **completely remove** all the page refreshes on his inventory page. Here's what that would look like:

The user clicks a thumbnail.

Clicking an image calls a JavaScript function.

The function creates a request object that asks the server for a description of the item.

ROB'S ROCK 'N' ROLL MEMORABILIA

function getDetails

request

The function also changes the image to match the selected item.

The browser sends the request object to the server, asynchronously, behind the scenes.

The browser requests the new image from the server... but that's not something your page worries about.

Only the part of the page that actually changed is updated... but the user still sees a new image and the selected item's description.

ROB'S ROCK 'N' ROLL MEMORABILIA

request

The server returns the new image and a response to the request to the user's browser.

BULLET POINTS

- Asynchronous requests allow **more than one thing** to happen at the same time.

- Only the part of a web page that needs to change gets updated.

- The page isn't frozen while the server is returning data to the browser.

Sharpen your pencil

Put a checkmark next to the benefits that you think Ajax can provide to your web applications.

☐ **The browser can request multiple things from the server at the same time.**

☐ **Browser requests return a lot faster.**

☐ **Colors are rendered more faithfully.**

☐ **Only the parts of the page that actually change are updated.**

☐ **Server traffic is reduced.**

☐ **Pages are less vulnerable to compatibility issues.**

☐ **The user can keep working while the page updates.**

☐ **Some changes can be handled without a server round-trip.**

☐ **Your boss will love you.**

☐ **Only the parts of the page that actually change are updated.**

BRAIN BARBELL

Not all pages will reap every benefit of Ajax. In fact, some pages wouldn't benefit from Ajax at all. Which of the benefits that you checked off above do you think Rob's page will see?

Sharpen your pencil
Solution

Remember, not every page is going to see all these benefits...

With asynchronous requests, you can make sure the browser works behind the scenes, and avoid interrupting your users with full-page refreshes.

☑ **The browser can request multiple things from the server at the same time.**

This is only true <u>sometimes</u>. The speed of a request and response depends on what the server is returning. And it's possible to build Ajax pages that are <u>slower</u> than traditional pages.

☑ **Browser requests return a lot faster.**

☐ **Colors are rendered more faithfully.** ← Color rendering is dictated by the user's monitor, not your app.

☑ **Only the parts of the page that actually change are updated.**

It's possible to make smaller, more focused requests with Ajax. Be careful, though... it's also easy to make a lot more requests—and increase traffic—because you can make all of those requests asynchronously.

☑ **Server traffic is reduced.**

Because Ajax pages rely on technologies in addition to XHTML, compatibility issues can actually be a <u>bigger</u> problem with Ajax. Test, <u>test</u>, <u>test</u> your apps on the browsers your users have installed.

☐ **Pages are less vulnerable to compatibility issues.**

Sometimes you <u>want</u> a user to wait on the server's response, but that doesn't mean you can't still use Ajax. We'll look at synchronous vs. asynchronous requests more in Chapter 5.

☑ **The user can keep working while the page updates.**

Handling things at the browser can make your web application feel more like a desktop application.

☑ **Some changes can be handled without a server round-trip.**

If you use Ajax in a way that helps your apps, the boss will love you. But you shouldn't use Ajax <u>everywhere</u>... more on that later.

☒ **Your boss will love you.**

☑ **Only the parts of the page that actually change are updated.**

Yes, this is the second time this shows up in the list. It's that important!

...but **Howard** said there's be much less traffic this way.

Well, yes, dear, unless **everyone** decided they'd try the same approach. Now look at the mess we're in! What a jam.

there are no Dumb Questions

Q: First you said Ajax was the web reinvented. Now it's increasing server traffic. Which is it?

A: Sometimes it's both! Ajax is one way to make requests, get responses, and build responsive web apps. But you've still got to be smart when deciding whether an asynchronous request or a regular synchronous request would be a better idea.

Q: How do I know when to use Ajax and asynchronous requests, and when not to?

A: Think about it like this: if you want something to go on while your user's still working, you probably want an asynchronous request. But if your user needs information or a response from your app before they continue, then you want to make them wait. That usually means a synchronous request.

Q: So for Rob's online store, since we want users to keep browsing while we're loading product images and descriptions, we'd want an asynchronous request. Right?

A: Exactly. That particular part of Rob's app—checking out different items—shouldn't require the user to wait every time they select a new item. So that's a great place to use Ajax and make an asynchronous request.

Q: And how do I do that?

A: Good question. Turn the page, and let's get down to actually using Ajax to fix up Rob's online store.

Ajax and rock 'n' roll in 5 steps

Let's use Ajax to fix up Rob's online store, and get his impatient customers back. We'll need to make some changes to the existing XHTML page, code some JavaScript, and then reference the script in our XHTML. When we're done, the page won't need to reload at all, and only the things that need to change will get updated when users click on the thumbnail images.

Here's what we're going to do:

1 **Modify the XHTML web page**

We need to include the JavaScript file we're going to write and add some `div`s and `id`s, so our JavaScript can find and work with different parts of the web page.

We'll group the thumbnails into a <div>, so our JavaScript can locate them on the page easily.

```
<html>
...
</html>
```
inventory.html

```
function
getDetails
...
}
```
thumbnails.js

We'll use a <script> tag to reference thumbnails.js in our XHTML page.

thumbnails.js will contain the JavaScript code we write for handling clicks on the thumbnail images and talking to Rob's server to get detailed information about each item.

2 **Write a function to initialize the page**

When the inventory page first loads, we'll need to run some JavaScript to set up the images, get a request object ready, and make sure the page is ready to use.

This tells the browser to run the initPage() function as soon as the page loads up.

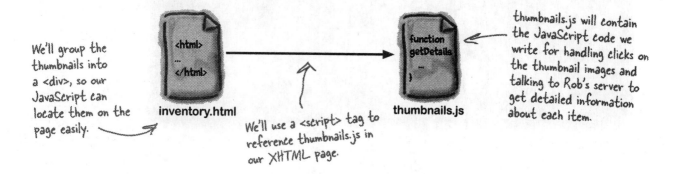

```
window.onload = initPage;
function initPage() {

  // setup the images
  // create a request object
}
```

We'll write code in initPage() to initialize all the thumbnail images, and set up onClick event handlers for each image.

```
function
getDetails
...
}
```
thumbnails.js

③ **Write a function to create a request object**

We need a way to talk to the server and get details about each piece of memorabilia in Rob's inventory. We'll write a function to create a request object to let our code talk to the server; let's call it `createRequest()`. We can use that function whenever a thumbnail is clicked to get a new request started.

onclick events trigger the getDetails() function.

getDetails() will call the createRequest() function to get a request object.

createRequest() is a utility function we'll use over and over. It creates a basic, generic request object.

function
getDetails()

thumbnails.js

request

function
createRequest()

thumbnails.js

createRequest() returns a request object for our onclick function to use.

④ **Get an item's details from the server**

We'll send a request to Rob's server in `getDetails()`, telling the browser what to do when the server responds.

function
getDetails()

thumbnails.js

request

The request object has information about what code should run when the server responds.

All we need to do to update the image is change that image's src property. The browser will handle everything else for us.

⑤ **Display the item's details**

We can change the image to display in `getDetails()`. Then, we need another function, `displayDetails()`, to update the item's description when the server responds to our requests.

function
displayDetails()

thumbnails.js

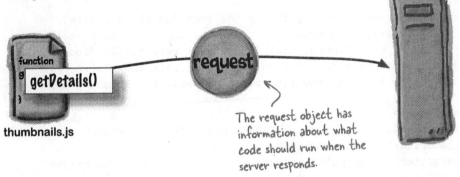

The event handler changes out the image...

...and another function we'll write can take the server's information and display it on the web page.

Step 1: Modify the XHTML

Let's start with the easy part, the XHTML and CSS that
create the page. Here's Rob's current version of the inventory
page with a few additions we'll need:

inventory.html

```
<!DOCTYPE html PUBLIC "-//W3C//DTD XHTML 1.0 Transitional//EN"
        "http://www.w3.org/TR/xhtml1/DTD/xhtml1-transitional.dtd">
<html xmlns="http://www.w3.org/1999/xhtml">
<head>
  <title>Rob's Rock 'n' Roll Memorabilia</title>
  <link rel="stylesheet" href="css/default.css" />
  <script src="scripts/thumbnails.js" type="text/javascript"></script>
</head>
<body>
  <div id="wrapper">
    <img src="images/logotypeLeft.png" alt="Rob's Rock 'n' Roll Memorabilia"
         width="394" height="91" id="logotypeLeft" />
    <img src="images/logotypeRight.png" alt="Rob's Rock 'n' Roll Memorabilia"
         width="415" height="92" id="logotypeRight" />
    <div id="introPane">
      <p>Are you looking for the perfect gift for the rock fan in your life?
         Maybe you want a guitar with some history behind it, or a conversation
         piece for your next big shindig. Look no further! Here you'll find all
         sorts of great memorabilia from the golden age of rock and roll.</p>
      <p><strong>Click on an image to the left for more details.</strong></p>
    </div>
    <div id="thumbnailPane">
      <img src="images/itemGuitar.jpg" width="301" height="105" alt="guitar"
           title="itemGuitar" id="itemGuitar" />
      <img src="images/itemShades.jpg" alt="sunglasses" width="301" height="88"
           title="itemShades" id="itemShades" />
      <img src="images/itemCowbell.jpg" alt="cowbell" width="301" height="126"
           title="itemCowbell" id="itemCowbell" />
      <img src="images/itemHat.jpg" alt="hat" width="300" height="152"
           title="itemHat" id="itemHat" />
    </div>
    <div id="detailsPane">
      <img src="images/blank-detail.jpg" width="346" height="153" id="itemDetail" />
      <div id="description"></div>
    </div>
  </div>
</body>
</html>
```

You need to add a reference to thumbnails.js. That's the script we'll be writing in this chapter.

This <div> holds the small, clickable images.

This <div> is where details about each item should go.

We'll put item details in here with our JavaScript.

Run it!

It's time to get the samples and get going.

Download the examples for the book at
www.headfirstlabs.com, and find the **chapter01**
folder. Now open the **inventory.html** file in a text
editor, and make the changes shown above.

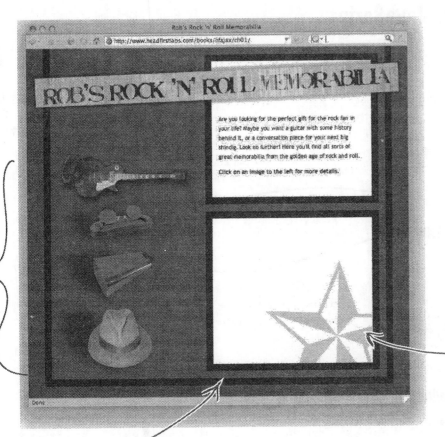

Here's a short version of the steps from pages 12 and 13 that we can use to work through Rob's page.

To Do

☑ **Modify the XHTML**
☐ Initialize the page
☐ Create a request object
☐ Get the item's details
☐ Display the details

Start out with no item detail and a blank area for the item's description to go in when something's selected.

This is the cascading style sheet for Rob's page. We'll use the id values on the <div> elements to style the page, and also later in our JavaScript code.

```
body {
  background: #333;
  font-family: Trebuchet MS, Verdana, Helvetica, Arial, san-serif;
  margin: 0;
  text-align: center;
}

p { font-size: 12px; line-height: 20px; }
a img { border: 0; }

#wrapper {
  background: #750505 url('../images/bgWrapper.png') 8px 0 no-repeat;
  border: solid #300;
  border-width: 0 15px 15px 15px;
  height: 700px;
  margin: 0 auto;
  ...etc...
```

There's a lot more CSS... you can see the complete file by downloading the examples from the Head First Labs web site.

#detail {
...
}

rocknroll.css

Step 2: Initialize the JavaScript

To Do

☑ Modify the XHTML
☐ **Initialize the page**
☐ Create a request object
☐ Get the item's details
☐ Display the details

We need to create the thumbnails.js file, and add a JavaScript function to set up the initial event handlers for each thumbnail image in the inventory. Let's call that function initPage(), and set it to run as soon as the user's window loads the inventory page.

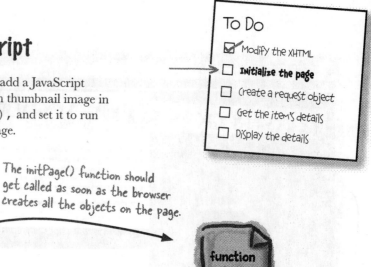

The initPage() function should get called as soon as the browser creates all the objects on the page.

function
initPage {
...
}

thumbnails.js

initPage() sets up the onclick behavior for each of the thumbnails in the inventory.

To set up the onclick behavior for the thumbnails, the initPage() function has to do two things:

① **Find the thumbnails on the page**
The thumbnails are contained in a div called "thumbnailPane," so we can find that div, and then find each image within it.

② **Build the onclick event handler for each thumbnail**
Each item's full-size image is named with the title of the thumbnail image plus "-detail". For example, the detail image for the thumbnail with the title FenderGuitar is FenderGuitar-detail.png. That lets us work out the name of the image in our JavaScript.

The event handler for each thumbnail should set the src tag for the detail image (the one with an id of "itemDetail") to the detail image (for example, FenderGuitar-detail.png). Once you've done that, the browser will automatically display the new image using the name you supplied.

Code Magnets

The code for the initPage function is all scrambled up on the fridge. Can you put back the pieces that fell off? Remember to set an event handler to run the initPage() function when the user's window loads, too.

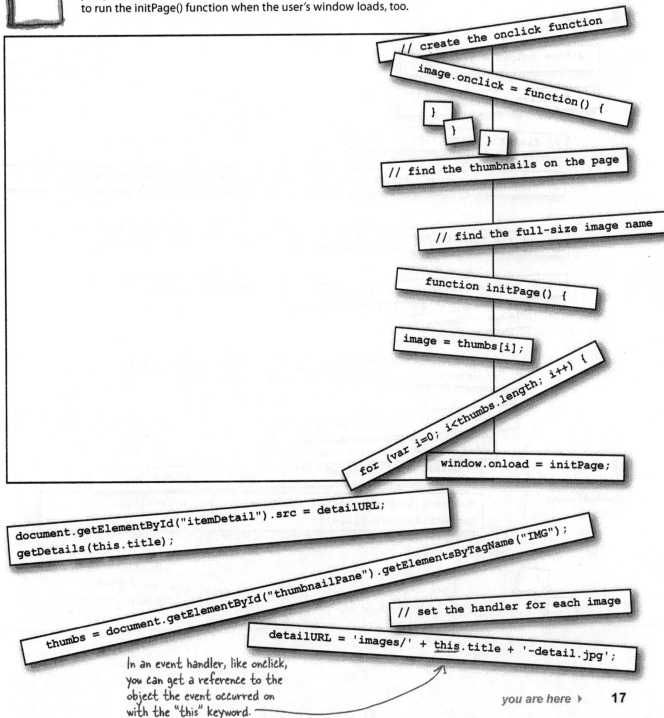

```
// create the onclick function

image.onclick = function() {

}

}

}

// find the thumbnails on the page

// find the full-size image name

function initPage() {

image = thumbs[i];

for (var i=0; i<thumbs.length; i++) {

window.onload = initPage;

document.getElementById("itemDetail").src = detailURL;
getDetails(this.title);

thumbs = document.getElementById("thumbnailPane").getElementsByTagName("IMG");

// set the handler for each image

detailURL = 'images/' + this.title + '-detail.jpg';
```

In an event handler, like onclick, you can get a reference to the object the event occurred on with the "this" keyword.

Code Magnet Solution

This sets initPage() up to run once the user's browser loads the page.

```
window.onload = initPage;
```

```
function initPage() {
```

Don't worry too much about this now... we'll talk about the DOM in detail a bit later.

All these "get..." functions use the DOM to look up something on the XHTML page.

```
// find the thumbnails on the page
```

```
thumbs = document.getElementById("thumbnailPane").getElementsByTagName("img");
```

These are the same ids we used in the CSS to style the page.

```
// set the handler for each image
```

We want to do this once for every thumbnail.

```
for (var i=0; i<thumbs.length; i++) {
```

```
image = thumbs[i];
```

```
// create the onclick function
```

JavaScript lets you define functions without giving them an explicit name.

```
image.onclick = function() {
```

When an image is clicked, that image's title is used to figure out the detail image's URL.

```
// find the full-size image name
```

This function is run whenever a thumbnail image is clicked.

```
detailURL = 'images/' + this.title + '-detail.jpg';
```

```
document.getElementById("itemDetail").src = detailURL;
getDetails(this.title);
```

```
}
```

```
}
```

```
}
```

Don't forget all the closing brackets, or your JavaScript won't run.

Clicking on a thumbnail changes the detail image's src attribute, and then the browser displays the new image.

TEST DRIVE

Create thumbnails.js, add the initPage() function, and give the inventory page a whirl.

Create a file named **thumbnails.js** in a text editor. Add the code shown on page 18, and then load inventory.html in your browser. initPage() should run when the page loads, and you're ready to try out the detail images...

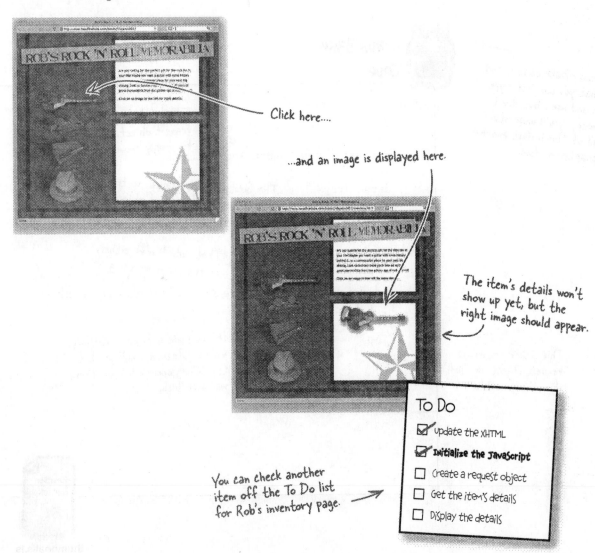

Click here....

...and an image is displayed here.

The item's details won't show up yet, but the right image should appear.

To Do
- ☑ Update the XHTML
- ☑ **Initialize the JavaScript**
- ☐ Create a request object
- ☐ Get the item's details
- ☐ Display the details

You can check another item off the To Do list for Rob's inventory page.

Step 3: Create a request object

When users click on an item's image, we also need to send a request to the server asking for that item's detailed information. But before we can send a request, we need to create the request object.

The bad news is that this is a bit tricky because different browsers create request objects in different ways. The good news is that we can create a function that handles all the browser-specific bits.

Go ahead and create a new function in `thumbnails.js` called `createRequest()`, and add this code:

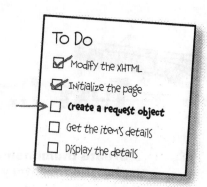

To Do
- ☑ Modify the XHTML
- ☑ Initialize the page
- ☐ **Create a request object**
- ☐ Get the item's details
- ☐ Display the details

Ready Bake Code

Ready Bake code is code that you can just type in and use... but don't worry, you'll understand all of this in just another chapter or two.

```
function createRequest() {
  try {

    request = new XMLHttpRequest();

  } catch (tryMS) {
    try {
      request = new ActiveXObject("Msxml2.XMLHTTP");

    } catch (otherMS) {
      try {
        request = new ActiveXObject("Microsoft.XMLHTTP");
      } catch (failed) {
        request = null;
      }
    }
  }

  return request;
}
```

This line tries to create a new request object, but it won't work for every browser type.

The first approach failed, so try again using a different type of object.

That didn't work either, so try one more thing.

If the code gets here, nothing worked. Return a null so that the calling code will know there was a problem.

This either returns a request object, or "null" if nothing worked.

thumbnails.js

Q: Am I supposed to understand all of this?

A: No, you're not. For now, just try to get a general idea of how all this looks and the way the pieces fit together. Focus on the big picture, and then we'll start to fill in the gaps in later chapters.

Q: So what's an XMLHttpRequest?

A: XMLHttpRequest is what most browsers call the request object that you can send to the server and get responses from without reloading an entire page.

Q: Well, if that's an XMLHttpRequest, what's an ActiveXObject?

A: An ActiveXObject is a Microsoft-specific programming object. There are two different versions, and different browsers support each. That's why there are two different code blocks, each trying to create a different version of ActiveXObject.

Q: And the request object is called XMLHTTP in a Microsoft browser?

A: That's the *type* of the object, but you can call your variable anything you'd like; we've been using request. Once you have the createRequest() function working, you never have to worry about these different types again. Just call createRequest(), and then assign the returned value to a variable.

Q: So my users don't need to be using a specific browser?

A: Right. As long as their browsers have JavaScript enabled, your users can be running any browser they want.

Q: What if they don't have JavaScript enabled?

A: Unfortunately, Ajax applications require JavaScript to run. So users who have JavaScript disabled aren't going to be able to use your Ajax applications. The good news is that JavaScript is usually enabled by default, so anyone who has disabled JavaScript probably knows what they're doing, and could turn JavaScript support back on if they wanted to use your Ajax app.

Step 4: Get the item's details

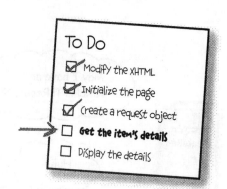

To Do

☑ Modify the XHTML
☑ Initialize the page
☑ Create a request object
☐ **Get the item's details**
☐ Display the details

Once a user clicks on an item in the inventory, we need to send a request to the server and ask for the description and details for that item. We've got a request object, so here is where we can use that.

And it turns out that no matter what data you need from the server, the basic process for making an Ajax request always follows the same pattern:

① **Get a request object**

We've already done the work here. We just need to call `createRequest()` to get an instance of the request object and assign it to a variable.

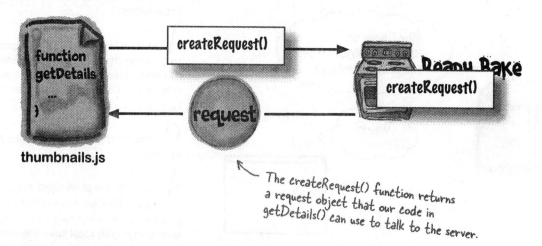

The createRequest() function returns a request object that our code in getDetails() can use to talk to the server.

② **Configure the request object's properties**

The request object has several properties you'll need to set. You can tell it what URL to connect to, whether to use GET or POST, and a lot more... you need to set this all up before you make your request to the server.

You can tell your request object where to make its request, include details the server will need to respond, and even indicate that the request should be GET or POST.

③ Tell the request object what to do when the server responds

So what happens when the server responds? The browser looks at another property of the request object, called `onreadystatechange`. This lets us assign a **callback function** that should run when the server responds to our request.

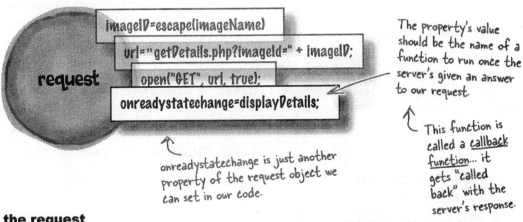

imageID=escape(imageName)

url="getDetails.php?imageId=" + imageID;

open("GET", url, true);

onreadystatechange=displayDetails;

The property's value should be the name of a function to run once the server's given an answer to our request.

This function is called a *callback function*... it gets "called back" with the server's response.

onreadystatechange is just another property of the request object we can set in our code.

④ Make the request

Now we're ready to send the request off to the server and get a response.

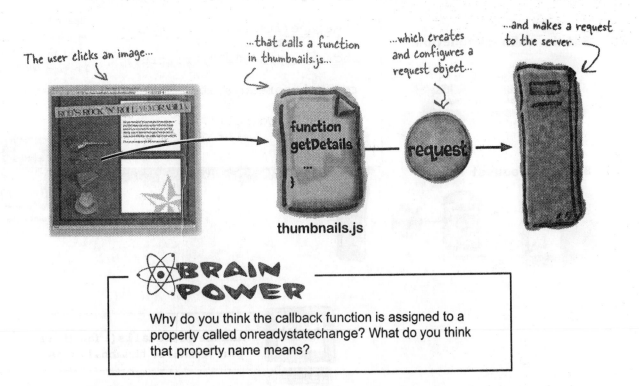

The user clicks an image...

...that calls a function in thumbnails.js...

...which creates and configures a request object...

...and makes a request to the server.

function getDetails ...

request

thumbnails.js

⚛ BRAIN POWER

Why do you think the callback function is assigned to a property called onreadystatechange? What do you think that property name means?

Let's write the code for requesting an item's details

Once we know what our function needs to do, it's pretty easy to write the code. Here's how the steps map to actual JavaScript in `thumbnails.js`:

The onclick handler for each inventory image calls this function and passes in the clicked img element's title attribute, which is the name of the item the image represents.

① **Get a request object**

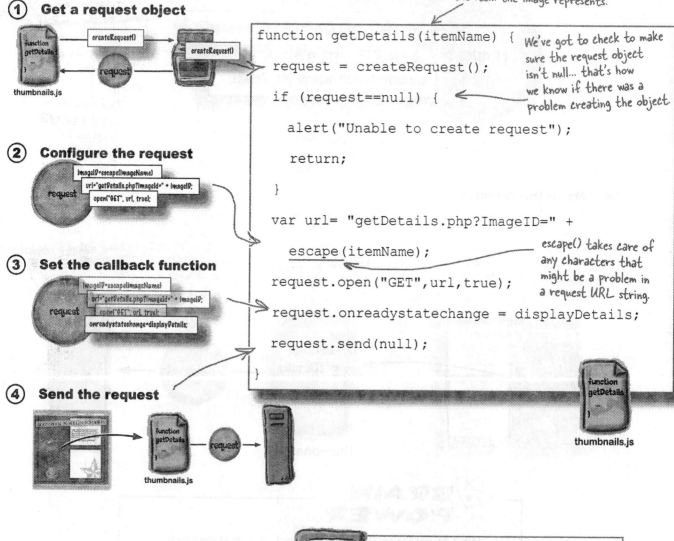

thumbnails.js

```
function getDetails(itemName) {

  request = createRequest();

  if (request==null) {

    alert("Unable to create request");

    return;

  }

  var url= "getDetails.php?ImageID=" +

    escape(itemName);

  request.open("GET",url,true);

  request.onreadystatechange = displayDetails;

  request.send(null);

}
```

We've got to check to make sure the request object isn't null... that's how we know if there was a problem creating the object.

escape() takes care of any characters that might be a problem in a request URL string.

② **Configure the request**

ImageID=escape(ImageName)
url="getDetails.php?ImageId=" + ImageID;
open("GET", url, true);

③ **Set the callback function**

ImageID=escape(ImageName)
url="getDetails.php?ImageId=" + ImageID;
open("GET", url, true);
onreadystatechange=displayDetails;

④ **Send the request**

thumbnails.js

thumbnails.js

> **Run it!**   Add the `getDetails()` function to your version of `thumbnails.js`

Always make sure you have a request object before working with it

The first thing `getDetails()` does is call `createRequest()` to get a request object. But you've still got to make sure that object was actually created, even though the details of that creation are abstracted away in the `createRequest()` function:

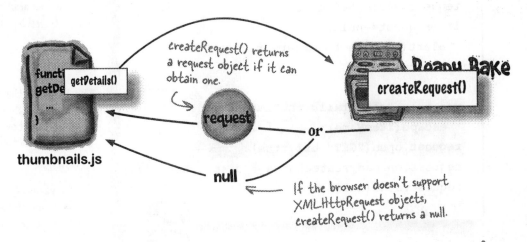

createRequest() returns a request object if it can obtain one.

Ready Bake createRequest()

request

or

null

If the browser doesn't support XMLHttpRequest objects, createRequest() returns a null.

And here's how that looks in our code...

This line asks for an instance of the request object and assigns it to the variable "request."

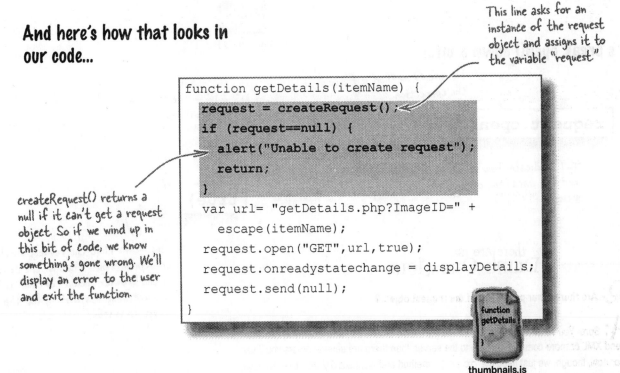

```
function getDetails(itemName) {
  request = createRequest();
  if (request==null) {
    alert("Unable to create request");
    return;
  }
  var url= "getDetails.php?ImageID=" +
    escape(itemName);
  request.open("GET",url,true);
  request.onreadystatechange = displayDetails;
  request.send(null);
}
```

createRequest() returns a null if it can't get a request object. So if we wind up in this bit of code, we know something's gone wrong. We'll display an error to the user and exit the function.

thumbnails.js

The request object is just an object

A request object is just a "normal" JavaScript object, and that means you can set properties on it and call methods. We can talk to the server by putting information in the request object.

To Do
- ☑ Modify the XHTML
- ☑ Initialize the page
- ☑ Create a request object
- ☐ **Get the item's details**
- ☐ Display the details

We're still working on getting the details for an item.

```
function getDetails(itemName) {
  request = createRequest();
  if (request==null) {
    alert("Unable to create request");
    return;
  }
  var url= "getDetails.php?ImageID=" +
    escape(itemName);
  request.open("GET",url,true);
  request.onreadystatechange = displayDetails;
  request.send(null);
}
```

This line tells the request object the URL to call. We send along the name of the item, so the server knows which details to send.

These parameters tell the request object how we want it to connect to the server.

function getDetails ... }

thumbnails.js

Let's break open() down a bit...

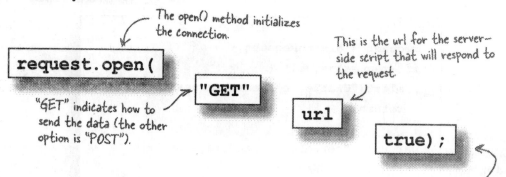

The open() method initializes the connection.

request.open(

"GET" indicates how to send the data (the other option is "POST").

"GET"

This is the url for the server-side script that will respond to the request

url

true);

This means that the request should be asynchronous. That is, the code in the browser should continue to execute while it's waiting for the server to respond.

there are no Dumb Questions

Q: Are there other properties of the request object?

A: Sure. You've already seen onreadystatechange, and when you need to send XML or more complicated data to the server, then there are several others you'll use. For now, though, we just need the open() method and onreadystatechange.

Hey, server... will you call me back at displayDetails(), please?

The properties of the request object tell the server what to do when it receives the request. One of the most important is the onreadystatechange property, which we're setting to the name of a function. This function, referred to as a **callback**, tells the browser what code to call when the server sends back information.

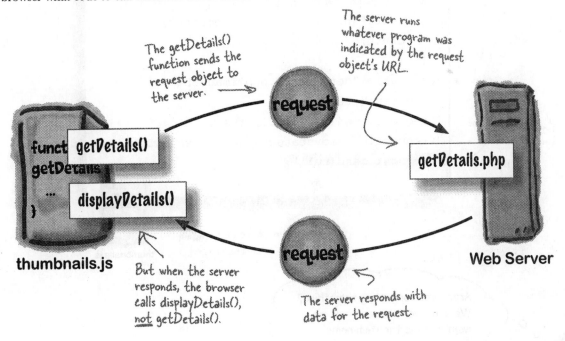

The getDetails() function sends the request object to the server.

The server runs whatever program was indicated by the request object's URL.

thumbnails.js

But when the server responds, the browser calls displayDetails(), not getDetails().

The server responds with data for the request.

Web Server

This is the line that tells the browser what code to call when the server responds to the request.

```
function getDetails(itemName) {
   request = createRequest();
   if (request==null) {
     alert("Unable to create request");
     return;
   }
   var url= "getDetails.php?ImageID=" +
     escape(itemName);
   request.open("GET",url,true);
   request.onreadystatechange = displayDetails;
   request.send(null);
}
```

thumbnails.js

This is a reference to a function, not a function call. So make sure you don't include any parentheses at the end of the function name.

Use send() to send your request

All that's left to do is actually send the request, and that's easy... just use the send() method on the request object.

```
function getDetails(itemName) {
  request = createRequest();
  if (request==null) {
    alert("Unable to create request");
    return;
  }
  var url= "getDetails.php?ImageID=" +
    escape(itemName);
  request.open("GET",url,true);
  request.onreadystatechange = displayDetails;
  request.send(null);
}
```

You're sending the request here...

...and this means you're not sending any extra data with the request.

function getDetails ... }

thumbnails.js

Aren't you forgetting something? We don't want to send null; we want to send the item name.

You can send data in your URL string.

The request object allows us to send all kinds of data in a variety of ways. In getDetails(), the item name is part of the URL string:

```
var url= "getDetails.php?ImageID=" +
  escape(itemName);
```

Since that's part of the URL sent to the server, we don't need to send anything else to the server in the send() method. Instead, we just pass null... which means "nothing."

Asynchronous apps make requests using a JavaScript object, not a form submit.

So what about the server-side code?

The server-side code is...
...on the server.

That sounds obvious, but lots of times, you don't have to (or even get to) write the code your web application is talking to. Instead, you work with an existing program, where you know the inputs and outputs, or tell another group what you need.

Not only that, but you might also have one server-side program that's written in PHP, and another in ASP.NET... and other than the URL, you don't have to change your JavaScript code at all. Take a look:

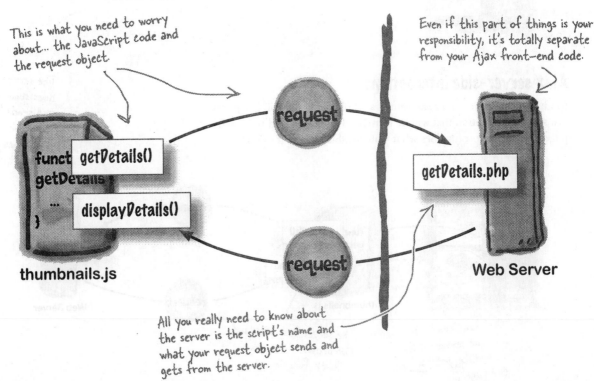

This is what you need to worry about... the JavaScript code and the request object.

Even if this part of things is your responsibility, it's totally separate from your Ajax front-end code.

request

funct getDetails()
getDetails
...
displayDetails()
}

thumbnails.js

getDetails.php

request

Web Server

All you really need to know about the server is the script's name and what your request object sends and gets from the server.

The server usually returns data to Ajax requests

In a traditional web app, the server always responds to a request from the browser by sending back a new page. The browser throws away anything that's already displayed (including any fields the user has filled in) when that new page arrives.

Traditional server-side interactions

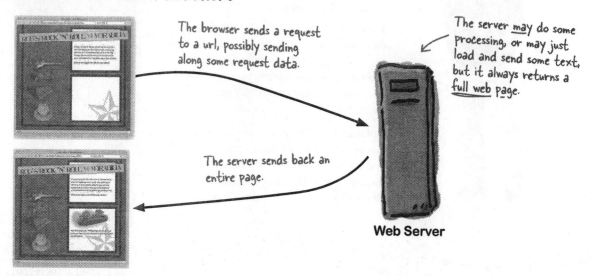

The browser sends a request to a url, possibly sending along some request data.

The server <u>may</u> do some processing, or may just load and send some text, but it always returns a <u>full web page</u>.

The server sends back an entire page.

Web Server

Ajax server-side interactions

In an Ajax app, the server can return a whole page, part of a page, or just some information that will be formatted and displayed on a web page. The browser only does what your JavaScript tells it to do.

The server <u>always</u> does some processing and sends back <u>data</u>... sometimes HTML, sometimes just raw information.

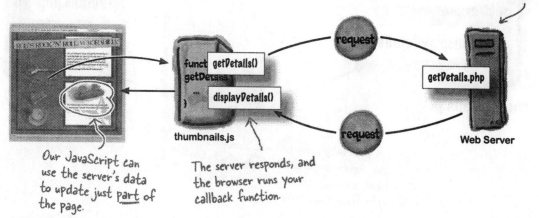

Our JavaScript can use the server's data to update just <u>part</u> of the page.

The server responds, and the browser runs your callback function.

Ajax is <u>server-agnostic</u>

Ajax doesn't require any particular server technology. You can use Active Server Pages (ASP), PHP, or whatever you need and have access to. In fact, there's no need to get into the details of the server-side technology because *it doesn't change how you build your Ajax apps*.

Here's all that Ajax really sees:

This is how Ajax sees server-side interactions.

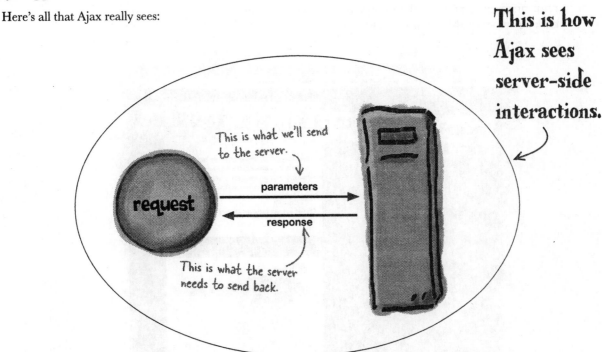

This is what we'll send to the server.

parameters

response

This is what the server needs to send back.

Sharpen your pencil

What parameter and response do we need for the interaction with the server for Rob's memorabilia page?

....

....

....

→ Answers on page 40.

Test Drive

Code getDetails(), and fire up your web browser.

Make sure you've got `getDetails()` coded in your
`thumbnails.js` file. Load up Rob's memorabilia page, and try
clicking on one of the inventory images.

BRAIN POWER

What happens? What's wrong with the page?
What do you need to do to fix the problem?

WHAT'S MY PURPOSE?

Below on the left are several properties of the request object. Can you match each property to what it does, or what information it contains?

readyState

    The status code message returned by the server, for example, "OK" for status 202.

status

    Contains information sent back by the server in XML format.

responseXML

    A status code returned by the server indicating, for example, success or that a requested resource is missing.

statusText

    Contains textual information sent back by the server.

responseText

    A number that represents the current state of the request object.

there are no Dumb Questions

Q: Can you explain what a callback function is again?

A: A callback function is a function that is executed when something else finishes. In Ajax, it's the function that's called when the server responds to a request object. The browser "calls back" that function at a certain time.

Q: So a callback executes when the server's finished with a request?

A: No, it's actually called by the browser *every time* the server responds to the request, even if the server's not totally done with the request. Most servers respond more than once to say that they've received the request, that they're working on the request, and then, again, when they've finished processing the request.

Q: Is that why the request property is called onreadystatechange?

A: That's exactly right. Every time the server responds to a request, it sets the readyState property of the request object to a different value. So we'll need to pay close attention to that property to figure out exactly when the server's done with the request we send it.

WHAT'S MY PURPOSE?
SOLUTION

Below on the left are several properties of the request object. Your job was to match each property to what it does, or what information it contains.

This one indicates that a request is finished, and it's now okay to process the server's results.

readyState

The status code message returned by the server, for example, "OK" for status 202.

status and statusText are different versions of the same information.

status

Contains information sent back by the server in XML format.

This is empty unless the server sends back data in XML format.

responseXML

A status code returned by the server indicating, for example, success or that a requested resource is missing.

Contains textual information sent back by the server.

statusText

A number that represents the current state of the request object.

responseText

This is empty unless the server sends back data as text (and not XML).

Use a callback function to work with data the server returns

TO DO

☑ Modify the XHTML

☑ Initialize the page

☑ Create a request object

☑ Get the item's details

☐ **Display the details**

How do we show the textual description for each item? Let's assume the server will send the details about an item as pre-formatted text in the `responseText` property of the request object. So we just need to get that data and display it.

Our callback function, `displayDetails()`, needs to find the XHTML element that will contain the detail information, and then set its `innerHTML` property to the value returned by the server.

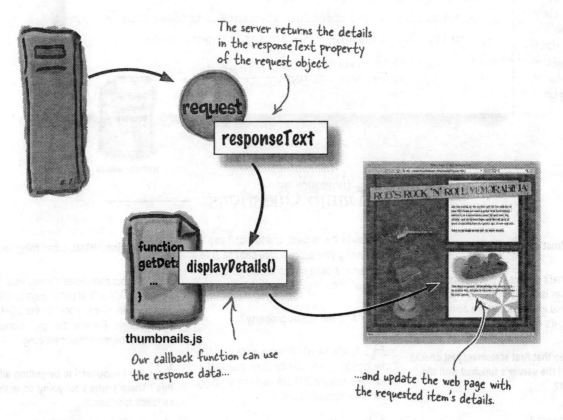

The server returns the details in the responseText property of the request object.

responseText

```
function
getDet...
   ...
}
```

displayDetails()

thumbnails.js

Our callback function can use the response data...

...and update the web page with the requested item's details.

there are no Dumb Questions

Q: So the server calls displayDetails() when it's finished with the request?

A: No, the **browser** actually does that. All the server does is update the `readystate` property of the request object. Every time that property changes, the browser calls the function named in the `onreadystatechange` property. Don't worry, though, we'll talk about this in a lot more detail in the next chapter.

Get the server's response from the request object's responseText property

The data we want is in the request object. Now we just need to get that data and use it. Here's what we need:

```
function displayDetails() {
    if (request.readyState == 4) {
        if (request.status == 200) {
            detailDiv = document.getElementById("description");
            detailDiv.innerHTML = request.responseText;
        }
    }
}
```

This line gets a reference to the XHTML element we'll put the item details in.

This line puts the XHTML returned by the server into that element.

It's okay if all of this isn't completely clear to you. We'll look at ready states and status codes in a lot more detail in the next chapter.

function display Details {
...
}

thumbnails.js

there are no Dumb Questions

Q: What's that readyState property?

A: That's a number that indicates where the server is in its processing. 0 is the initial value, and when the server's completed a request, it's 4.

Q: So that first statement just checks to see if the server's finished with the request?

A: You got it.

Q: Why do we have to check that every time?

A: Because the browser will run your callback every time the ready state changes. Since a server might set this value to 1 when

it receives the request, and to 2 or 3 as it's processing your request, you can't be sure the server's done unless `readyState` is equal to 4.

Q: And the status property?

A: That's the HTTP status code, like 404 for forbidden, and 200 for okay. You want to make sure it's 200 before doing anything with your request object.

Q: Why would the server set the ready state to 4 when the status code is something like 404?

A: Good question. We'll talk about that in the next chapter, but can you think of how a request could be complete and still have a status code that indicates a problem?

Q: Isn't innerHTML a bad thing to use?

A: It is, but sometimes it's also very effective. We'll look at better ways to change a page when we get more into the DOM in later chapters. For now, though, it works, and that's the most important thing.

Q: Am I supposed to be getting all this? There's sure a lot going on in that callback function...

A: For now, just make sure you know that the callback is where you can use the server's response. We'll talk about callbacks, ready states, and status codes a lot more in Chapter 2.

Test Drive

Code your callback, and test out the inventory page.

Add `displayDetails()` to your `thumbnails.js` file. You should also make sure that the server-side program with the inputs and outputs detailed on page 30 is running, and that the URL in your `getDetails()` method is pointing to that program. Then fire up the inventory page and click on an item.

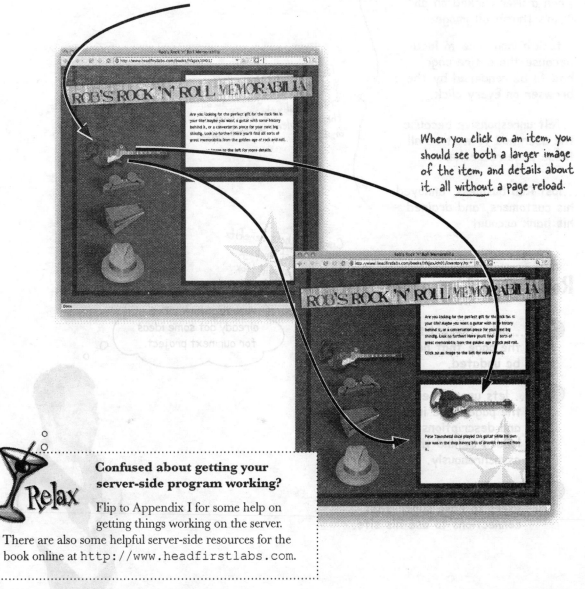

When you click on an item, you should see both a larger image of the item, and details about it.. all without a page reload.

Confused about getting your server-side program working?

Flip to Appendix I for some help on getting things working on the server. There are also some helpful server-side resources for the book online at `http://www.headfirstlabs.com`.

Goodbye traditional web apps...

Rob's page is working more smoothly now, customers are coming back in droves, and you've helped pair vintage leather with the next-generation web.

Rob's old, traditional web app:

- ...reloaded the entire page when a user clicked on an item's thumbnail image.

- ...took a long time to load because the entire page had to be rendered by the browser on every click.

- ...felt unresponsive because the user had to wait on all those page refreshes.

- ...lost Rob business, annoyed his customers, and drained his bank account.

These aren't problems that just Rob's having. Almost all traditional web apps have these problems in some form or fashion.

Compare these benefits with the list on page 10... they should look pretty similar.

Rob's new, Ajax app:

- ...only changed the part of the page that needed to be updated.

- ...lets users keep viewing the page while images and descriptions are loaded behind the scenes, asynchronously.

- ...reduced the need for his users to have super-fast connections to use his site.

> Amazing work... I've already got some ideas for our next project.

AjaxAcrostic

Take some time to sit back and give your right brain something to do. Answer the questions in the top, then use the letters to fill in the secret message.

This is the language you use to script Ajax pages.

—— —— —— —— —— —— —— —— —— ——
1   2   3   4   5   6   7   8   9   10

This type of function gets called when a process completes.

—— —— —— —— —— —— —— ——
11   12   13   14   15   16   17   18

This request object property tells us when the server has finished processing.

—— —— —— —— —— —— —— —— —— ——
19   20   21   22   23   24   25   26   27   28

If something goes wrong at the server, this property will tell us what.

—— —— —— —— —— ——
29   30   31   32   33   34

The browser will put text that the server returns in this property.

—— —— —— —— —— —— —— —— —— —— —— ——
35   36   37   38   39   40   41   42   43   44   45   46

If there's a problem, we can get a description of it in this property.

Use the letters from the blanks above to fill in these...

—— —— —— —— —— —— —— —— —— ——
47   48   49   50   51   52   53   54   55   56

—— —— —— ——   —— —— —— ——   —— —— ——
49 1 31 45   13 54 10 29   23 39 33

—— —— —— —— ——   —— —— —— —— —— —— —— —— —— ——
15 51 8 14 22   19 28 37 9 39 40 34 8 3 44

—— —— —— —— —— —— —— —— —— —— —— ——
31 9 38 14 8 6 26 46 8 39 40 24

Sharpen your pencil
Solution
From page 31

What parameter and response do we need to implement Rob's page?

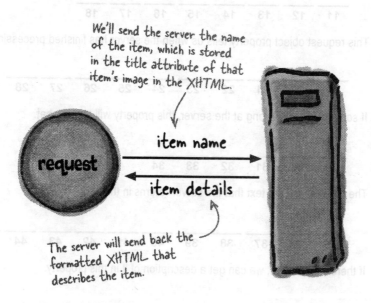

We'll send the server the name of the item, which is stored in the title attribute of that item's image in the XHTML.

item name

request

item details

The server will send back the formatted XHTML that describes the item.

AjaxAcrostic Solution

Take some time to sit back and give your right brain something to do. Answer the questions in the top, then use the letters to fill in the secret message.

This is the language you use to script Ajax pages.

J	A	V	A	S	C	R	I	P	T
1	2	3	4	5	6	7	8	9	10

This type of function get called when a process completes.

C	A	L	L	B	A	C	K
11	12	13	14	15	16	17	18

This request object property tells us when the server has finished processing.

R	E	A	D	Y	S	T	A	T	E
19	20	21	22	23	24	25	26	27	28

If something goes wrong at the server, this property will tell us what.

S	T	A	T	U	S
29	30	31	32	33	34

The browser will put text that the server returns in this property.

R	E	S	P	O	N	S	E	T	E	X	T
35	36	37	38	39	40	41	42	43	44	45	46

If there's a problem, we can get a description of it in this property.

S	T	A	T	U	S	T	E	X	T
47	48	49	50	51	52	53	54	55	56

A	J	A	X		L	E	T	S		Y	O	U
49	1	31	45		13	54	10	29		23	39	33

B	U	I	L	D		R	E	S	P	O	N	S	I	V	E
15	51	8	14	22		19	28	37	9	39	40	34	8	3	44

A	P	P	L	I	C	A	T	I	O	N	S
31	9	38	14	8	6	26	46	8	39	40	24

AjaxAcrostic Solution

Take some time to sit back and give your brain... hard something to do. Answer the questions, then use the letters to fill in the secret message.

This is the language you use to reply to pages.

J	Y	A	S	C	C	P	T
2	3	4	5	6	7	8	9	10

This type of function get called when a process completes.

C	A	L	L	B	A	C	K
11	12	13	14	15	16	17	18

This request object tells us when the service has finished processing.

R	A	D	Y	S	T	A	T	E
19	20	21	22	23	24	25	26	27	28

If something goes wrong at the server, this property will tell us what.

S	T	A	T	N	S
29	30	31	32	33	34

The browser will put text that the server returns in this property.

R	E	S	P	O	N	S	E	T	E	X	T
35	36	37	38	39	40	41	42	43	44	45	46

If there's a problem, we can get a description in this property.

47	48	49	50	51	52	53	54	55	56

A	J	A	X	L	E	T	S	Y	O	U	K
40	1	31	45	18	54	10	29	22	53	39	38

B	U	I	C	R	E	S	P	O	N	S	I	V	E
16	41	9	22	19	28	37	8	39	40	51	34	3	44

A	P	P	L	I	C	A	T	I	O	N	S
31	33	8	48	6	26	16	5	33	50	24

2 designing ajax applications

Thinking Ajaxian

> Doing two things at once with Ajax... gosh, it's the best! But I must admit, I have to think about things in a whole new way...

Welcome to Ajax apps—it's a whole new web world.

So you've built your first Ajax app, and you're already thinking about how to change all your web apps to make requests asynchronously. But that's not all there is to Ajax programming. You've got to *think about your applications differently*. Just because you're making asynchronous requests, doesn't mean your application is user-friendly. It's up to you to help your users **avoid making mistakes**, and that means **rethinking** your entire application's **design**.

Mike's traditional web site ~~sucks~~

Note from HR: Can we use a less offensive term? How about "consistently annoys every one of Mike's users"?

Mike's got the hippest movie reviews going, and he's taking his popular opinions online. Unfortunately, he's having problems with his registration page. Users visit his site, select a username, type in a few other details, and submit their information to get access to the review site.

The problem is that if the username's taken, the server responds with the initial page again, an error message... and none of the information the user already entered. Worse, users are annoyed that after waiting for a new page, they get nothing back but an error message. They want movie reviews!

Users shouldn't have to fill out eight fields to find out if the data in the first field is valid.

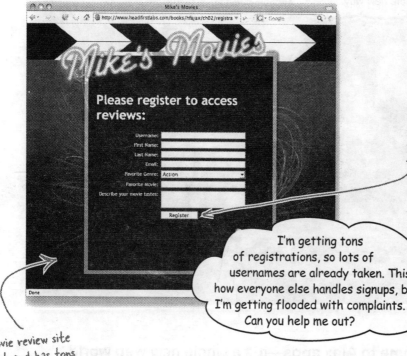

Right now the user fills out the form and clicks the "Register" button... and then waits, and hopes for the best.

I'm getting tons of registrations, so lots of usernames are already taken. This is how everyone else handles signups, but I'm getting flooded with complaints. Can you help me out?

Mike's movie review site looks great and has tons of terrific reviews... but only if users can get signed up and past the registration page.

Exercise

Mike's got real problems, but with one Ajax app under your belt, you should probably have some ideas about what Mike needs. Take a look at the diagram of what happens with Mike's app now, and make notes about what you think *should* happen. Then, answer the questions at the bottom of the page about what you'd do to help Mike out.

1 **A new user fills out the registration form**

2 **The form is submitted to a web server**

Web Server

3 **A server-side program verifies and validates the registration information...**

4 **...and returns a new web page to the user's web browser**

The server displays a Welcome screen...

←*or*→

...or it re-displays the screen with an error message.

Everything the user entered is gone... the fields are all empty.

What do *you* think is the single biggest problem with Mike's site? ....

....

....

What would *you* do to improve Mike's site? ....

....

....

Let's use Ajax to send registration requests <u>ASYNCHRONOUSLY</u>

Ajax is exactly the tool you need to solve the problem with Mike's page. Right now the biggest problem is that users have to wait for a full page refresh to find out their requested username is already taken. Even worse, if they need to select a different username, they've got to re-type all their other information again. We can fix both of those problems using Ajax.

Did you write down something similar to this as Mike's biggest problem?

We'll still need to talk to the server to find out whether a username has been taken, but why wait until users finish filling out the entire form? As soon as they enter a username, we can send an **asynchronous request** to the server, check the username, and report any problems directly on the page—all *without* any page reloads, and *without* losing the user's other details.

It's okay if you didn't think about sending the request as soon as the user types in their username... but bonus credit if you did!

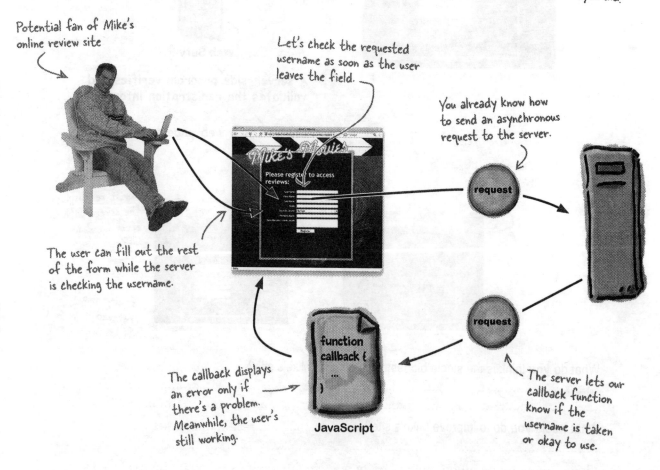

Potential fan of Mike's online review site

Let's check the requested username as soon as the user leaves the field.

You already know how to send an asynchronous request to the server.

The user can fill out the rest of the form while the server is checking the username.

request

request

function callback {
...
}

JavaScript

The callback displays an error only if there's a problem. Meanwhile, the user's still working.

The server lets our callback function know if the username is taken or okay to use.

> All this just so some movie buff doesn't have to retype their name and email address? Doesn't this seem like a bit of overkill?

Don't annoy your users... ever!

On the Internet, your competitors are only a click away. If you don't tell your users about a problem right away, or if you ever make them re-do something, you're probably going to lose them forever.

Mike's site may not be a big moneymaker (yet), or even seem that important to you... but it might to his fans. One day a user you're helping him not annoy may land him a six-figure income writing movie reviews for the New York Times. But Mike won't ever know if his site is hacking his users off. That's where your Ajax skills can help.

Important Ajax design principle

Don't annoy your users

If there's a problem with your web app, let your users know about it as quickly and clearly as possible. And you should never throw away anything the user has already done, even if something happened that they (or you) weren't expecting.

there are no Dumb Questions

Q: That design principle isn't really Ajax-specific, is it?

A: Nope, it applies to all web applications, ... in fact, to all types of applications. But with Ajax apps, especially asynchronous requests, lots of things can go wrong. Part of your job as a good Ajax programmer is to protect your users from all those things, or at least let them know what's going on if and when they do happen.

Exercise

It's time to get to work on Mike's site. Below are 5 steps that you'll need to execute to get his site working, but the details about each step are missing, and the ordering is a mess. Put the steps in order, and write a sentence or two about exactly what should happen on each step.

Create and configure a new request object

....
....
....

Set up event handlers for the web form's fields

....
....
....
....

Verify the requested username

....
....
....
....

Report any problems with the requested username

....
....
....

Update the registration page's XHTML and CSS

....
....
....
....

After you've got your steps in order, take a look at the two diagrams below that describe some of the interactions in an Ajax version of Mike's app. See if you can fill in the blanks so that the diagrams are complete and the annotations are accurate.

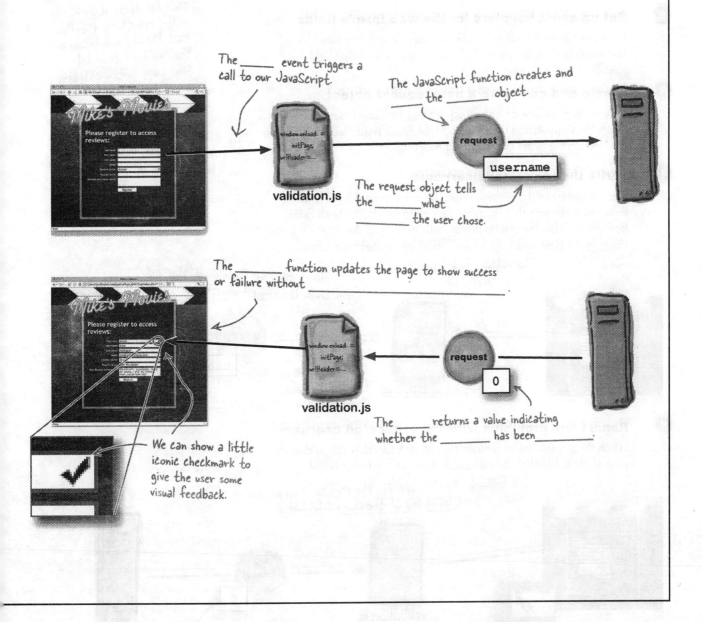

The _____ event triggers a call to our JavaScript.

The JavaScript function creates and the _____ object

The request object tells the _____ what _____ the user chose.

validation.js

request

`username`

The _____ function updates the page to show success or failure without _____

validation.js

request

`0`

The _____ returns a value indicating whether the _____ has been _____.

We can show a little iconic checkmark to give the user some visual feedback.

Exercise Solution

Your job was to order the steps to build an Ajax-version of Mike's movie review site, and fill in the missing descriptions of each step. You also should have filled in the missing words in the diagrams.

① Update the registration page's XHTML and CSS

We'll need to add <script> elements to the registration form to reference the JavaScript code we'll be writing.

Technically you can write the code for these steps in any order, but this is the flow that the app will follow and that we'll use to update Mike's app in this chapter.

② Set up event handlers for the web form's fields

We'll need some initiational code to set up an onblur event for the username field on the page. So when the user leaves that field, we'll start the request process.

③ Create and configure a new request object

We can use the same createRequest() function from Chapter 1 to create the request, and then we'll add the user's requested username to the URL string to get that over to the server.

We skimmed this function in the last chapter, but we'll look at it in detail in this chapter.

④ Verify the requested username

Once we've created a request object, we need to send it off to the server to make sure that the requested username hasn't been taken by someone else. We can do this asynchronously, so the user can keep filling in the page while the server's checking on their username.

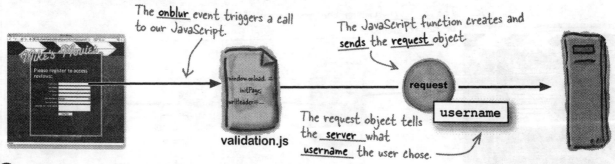

*The **onblur** event triggers a call to our JavaScript.*

*The JavaScript function creates and sends the **request** object.*

*The request object tells the **server** what **username** the user chose.*

validation.js

request
username

⑤ Report any problems with the requested username

When the request object returns, the callback function can update the page to show whether the username check succeeded or failed.

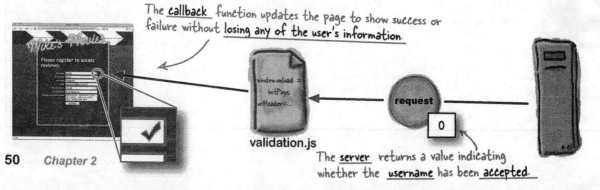

*The **callback** function updates the page to show success or failure without **losing any of the user's information**.*

validation.js

request
0

*The **server** returns a value indicating whether the **username** has been **accepted**.*

Update the registration page

The basic structure of Mike's registration page is already in place, so let's go ahead and add a `<script>` tag to load the JavaScript we'll write. Then, we can set up the username field on the web form to call a JavaScript function to make a request to the server.

Use an opening and closing `<script>` tag.

*Some browsers will error out if you use a self-closing `<script>` tag, like `<script />`. Always use **separate** opening and closing tags for `<script>`.*

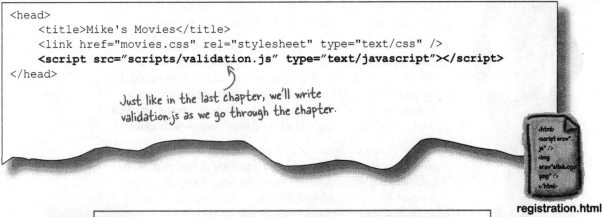

```
<head>
    <title>Mike's Movies</title>
    <link href="movies.css" rel="stylesheet" type="text/css" />
    <script src="scripts/validation.js" type="text/javascript"></script>
</head>
```

Just like in the last chapter, we'll write
validation.js as we go through the chapter.

registration.html

Make these changes in registration.html, Mike's registration page.

Download the registration page's XHTML and CSS.

If you haven't already done so, download the sample files for the chapter from **www.headfirstlabs.com**. Look in the Chapter2 folder for the file named **registration.html**, and then add the script tag shown in bold.

there are no Dumb Questions

Q: What's the big deal? This is all just like the rock and roll site from last chapter, isn't it?

A: So far, it is. But most Ajax apps start with a few `<script>` tags and some external JavaScript files.

Q: But we're still just sending a request and getting a response, right?

A: Sure. In fact, almost all Ajax apps can be described that simply. But as you'll see as we get into the registration page, there are actually two interactions possible: the one we're building to check a username, and the Submit button the user will press when they've filled out the form.

Q: What's the big deal about that?

A: What do you think? Can you see any problems with having two ways of making two different requests to a web server?

Hey, there's more to do in that XHTML. What about the onblur event handler on the username field? We want to run some code every time the user enters a username, right?

Separate your page's <u>content</u> from its <u>behavior</u>.

We could call the JavaScript directly from the XHTML by, for example, putting an onblur event in the username form field. But that's mixing the content of our page with its behavior.

The XHTML describes the **content** and **structure** of the page: what data is on the page, like the user's name and a description of the movie review site, and how it's organized. But how a page reacts to the user doing something is that page's **behavior**. That's usually where your JavaScript comes in. And the CSS defines the presentation of your page: how it looks.

Keeping content, behavior, and presentation separate is a good idea, even when you're building a relatively simple page all by yourself. And when you're working on complex applications that involve a lot of people, it's one of the best ways to avoid accidentally messing up somebody else's work.

Separate your page's content, behavior, and presentation.

Whenever possible, try to keep your page's content (the XHTML) separate from its behavior (JavaScript and event handlers) and its presentation (the CSS look-and-feel). Your sites will be more flexible and easier to maintain and update.

BRAIN BARBELL

How do you think separating the content of a site from its presentation and behavior makes it easier to change?

You'll hear some people refer to this principle as *unobtrusive JavaScript.*

Event Handlers Exposed

**This week's interview:
Where are you really from?**

Head First: It's good to have you with us, Event Handler. We've got some really interesting questions for you this week.

Event Handler: Really? I'm always eager to respond to questions.

Head First: Actually, there's this one question that everyone's been asking. Where exactly are you from?

Event Handler: Well, I hail from the land of ECMA, which was—

Head First: Oh, no, I mean, where are you *called* from?

Event Handler: Hmm... Well, I think the ECMA folks might want their story told, but if you insist... I usually get called from an XHTML form field or a button, things like that. Sometimes from windows, too.

Head First: So you're called from XHTML pages?

Event Handler: Most of the time, that's right.

Head First: That's what I thought. Well, that settles the dispute. You all heard it here first—

Event Handler: Wait, wait! What dispute?

Head First: Well, we had JavaScript calling in, swearing he could call you. Something about behavior calling behavior... it was really just nonsense.

Event Handler: Oh, you must be talking about assigning me programmatically. Very smart, that JavaScript...

Head First: Programmatically? What does that mean?

Event Handler: You see, I'm really just a property at heart—

Head First: Uh oh, is this more about ECMA?

Event Handler: —that can be set with JavaScript. No, now listen. You know about the DOM, right?

Head First: Well, not really... isn't that a later chapter?

Event Handler: Never mind. Look, everything on a web page is just an object. Like fields and buttons, they're just objects with properties.

Head First: Okay, sure, we've met some fields before. Nice folks. But Button, he never would return our calls...

Event Handler: Well, anyway, events like onblur or onload are tied to me through those properties.

Head First: You mean, like in XHTML when you say onblur="checkUsername()" on an input element?

Event Handler: Exactly! It's just a property of the input field. You're just telling the browser what function to run... you know, how to handle that event.

Head First: I'm totally lost...

Event Handler: Well, you can use JavaScript to assign a value to a property of an object, right?

Head First: So you're saying that you don't have to just assign event handlers from an XHTML page?

Event Handler: Right! You can do it directly in JavaScript code... and keep your content and structure separate from your behavior.

Head First: Well, this is quite surprising. But how do you get your JavaScript to run in the first place to assign an event handler?

Event Handler: Well, that's the trick. Any ideas?

Head First: I'm not sure. Let's ask our audience...

How can you get an initial piece of JavaScript to run *without* referencing a function in your XHTML page?

....

....

....

Set the window.onload event handler...
PROGRAMMATICALLY

We want some JavaScript code to run when the registration page loads, and that means attaching that code as the event handler on one of the first page events, `window.onload`.

And we can do that programmatically by setting the `onload` property of the `window` object. But how do we do that? Let's look at exactly what happens when the registration page is requested by a user visiting Mike's movie review site:

First, a user points their browser at Mike's registration page.

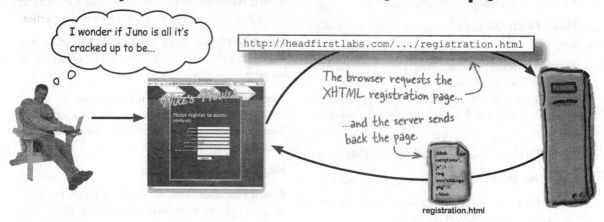

I wonder if Juno is all it's cracked up to be...

`http://headfirstlabs.com/.../registration.html`

The browser requests the XHTML registration page...

...and the server sends back the page.

registration.html

Then, the browser starts parsing the page, asking for other files as they're referenced.

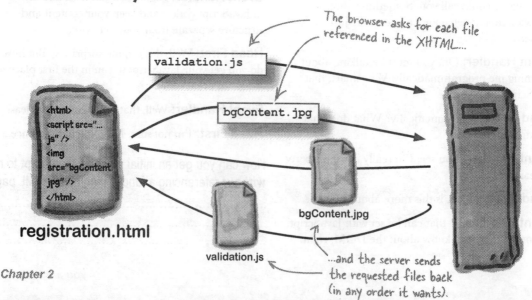

The browser asks for each file referenced in the XHTML...

`validation.js`

`bgContent.jpg`

```
<html>
<script src="...
js" />
<img
src="bgContent.
jpg" />
</html>
```

registration.html

bgContent.jpg

validation.js

...and the server sends the requested files back (in any order it wants).

If the file is a script, the browser parses the script, creates objects, and executes any statements not in a function.

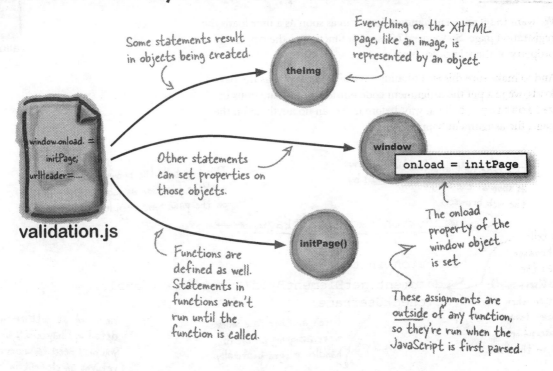

Some statements result in objects being created.

Everything on the XHTML page, like an image, is represented by an object.

theImg

validation.js

window.onload = initPage; urlHeader=....

Other statements can set properties on those objects.

window

onload = initPage

The onload property of the window object is set.

Functions are defined as well. Statements in functions aren't run until the function is called.

initPage()

These assignments are outside of any function, so they're run when the JavaScript is first parsed.

Finally, after all referenced files are loaded and parsed, the browser triggers the window.onload event and calls any function that's registered to handle that event.

All of this happens before you can actually use the page... so it's lightning fast!

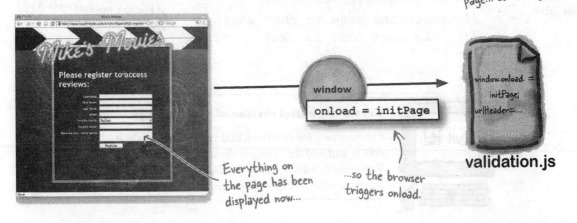

Please register to access reviews:

window

onload = initPage

validation.js

window.onload = initPage; urlHeader=....

Everything on the page has been displayed now...

...so the browser triggers onload.

Code in your JavaScript <u>outside</u> of <u>functions</u> runs when the script is read

validation.js

We want to set an event handler up to run as soon as a user loads the registration page. So we need to assign a function to the `onload` property of the `window` object.

And to make sure this event handler is assigned as soon as the page loads, we just put the assignment code outside of any functions in `validation.js`. That way, before users can do anything on the page, the assignment happens.

This code isn't in a function... it runs as soon as the script file is read by the web browser.

This line tells the browser to call the initPage function as soon as the elements on the page have been loaded.

```
window.onload = initPage;
```

This tells the browser to call the checkUsername() function when the user leaves the username field on the form.

```
function initPage(){
    document.getElementById("username").onblur =
        checkUsername;
}
```

Here's another case where we're assigning an event handler programmatically.

We'll look at getElementByID in detail in Chapters 5 and 6. For now, you only need to understand that it returns an element in the XHTML page with the specified id.

This is the function that will create and send the request object. We'll build this a little later.

```
function checkUsername() {
    // get a request object and send
    //    it to the server
}
```

```
function showUsernameStatus() {
    // update the page to show whether
    //    the user name is okay
}
```

This will update the page after the browser gets a response from the server.

Run it!

Create the initial version of validation.js.

Create a new file called **validation.js** in a text editor, and add the function declarations shown above. Remember to assign the `initPage()` function to the `window` object's `onload` property!

What happens when...

There's a lot going on in this step. Let's go through it to make sure everything's happening exactly when we want it to.

First...

When the browser loads the XHTML file, the `<script>` tag tells it to load a JavaScript file. Any code that's outside of a function in that script file will be executed *immediately*, and the browser's JavaScript interpreter will create the functions, although the code inside those functions won't run yet.

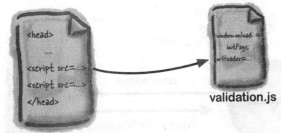

registration.html

validation.js

...and then...

The `window.onload` statement isn't in a function, so it will be executed as soon as the browser loads the `validation.js` script file.

The `window.onload` statement assigns the `initPage()` function as an event handler. That function will be called as soon as all the files the XHTML refers to have been loaded but before users can use the web page.

Even though these happen in sequence, ALL of this occurs before users can interact with the web page.

window.onload

initPage()

validation.js sets window.onload to call initPage() when the onload event occurs.

validation.js

Both the window.onload assignment and the initPage() function are in validation.js.

...and finally...

The `initPage()` function runs. It finds the field with an id of "username." Then, it assigns the `checkUsername()` function to the `onblur` event of that field.

This is the same as putting `onblur="checkUsername()"` in the XHTML. But our way is cleaner because it separates the code (the JavaScript function) from the structure and content (the XHTML).

initPage() sets up the link between the username input field and an event handler.

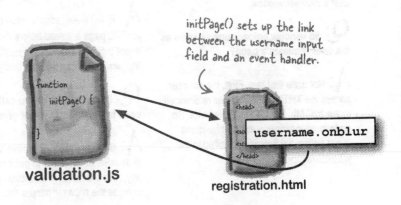

username.onblur

validation.js

registration.html

And on the server...

Before we can test out all our work on Mike's registration page, we need to check out the server. What does the server need to get from our request? What can we expect from the server?

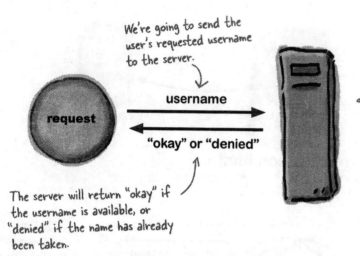

We're going to send the user's requested username to the server.

username

It doesn't matter if the server's running PHP, ASP, or something else, as long as it responds to our requests in the same way.

"okay" or "denied"

The server will return "okay" if the username is available, or "denied" if the name has already been taken.

Server-side help is online.

Remember, you can get sample server-side scripts and help with installing them online at **http://www.headfirstlabs.com**.

there are no Dumb Questions

Q: What's that window object again?

A: The window object represents the user's browser window.

Q: So window.onload runs as soon as the user requests a page?

A: Not quite that fast. First, the browser parses the XHTML and any files referenced in the XHTML, like CSS or JavaScript. So code in your scripts outside of functions is run before the function specified in the window.onload event.

Q: And that's why I can assign a function to window.onload in my script file?

A: Exactly. Any scripts referenced in your XHTML page are read *before* the onload event triggers. Then, after onload triggers, users can actually use your page.

Q: I thought you had to call JavaScript code to get it to run. What gives?

A: Good question. You have to call code in JavaScript *functions* to get it to run. But any code that's *not* in a function gets run as soon as the browser parses that line of code.

Q: But we should probably test this and make sure it works, right?

A: Right. Always test your application designs before you assume they're working.

Q: But nothing happens in this code. How do I test it?

A: That's another good question. If you have code that doesn't produce a visible result, you may want to resort to the trusty alert() function...

TEST DRIVE

Take the new registration page for a spin.

Make sure you've made all the changes to registration.html and validation.js, and then load the registration page up in your browser. Doesn't look much different, does it?

The initPage() function doesn't do anything visible, and checkUsername() function doesn't do anything at all yet... but we still need to make sure checkUsername() is actually called when users enter a username and go to another field.

It's a bit of a hack, but let's add some alert() statements to our code to make sure the functions we've written are actually getting called:

```
window.onload = initPage;

function initPage(){
  document.getElementById("username").onblur = checkUsername;
  alert("Inside the initPage() function");
}

function checkUsername() {
  // get a request object and send it to the server
  alert("Inside checkUsername()");
}

function showUsernameStatus() {
  // update the page to show whether the username is okay
}
```

Now try things out!

validation.js

http://headfirstlabs.com

Inside the initPage() function

http://headfirstlabs.com

Inside checkUsername()

OK

The alert() function gives us some visual feedback... now we know initPage() is getting called...

...as well as checkUsername() when you enter a username and leave the form field.

Some parts of your Ajax designs will be the same... every time

We've already used `window.onload` and an `initPage()` function twice: once for Rob's rock and roll store, and again for Mike's registration page. Next up is creating a request object that works the same for the registration page as it did for Rob's rock and roll site.

In fact, lots of things in Ajax apps are the same. Part of your job, though, is to build code so you don't have to write those same bits of code over and over again. Let's see how creating and using a request object looks in Mike's movie review site:

Good application designers look for <u>similarities</u> and find ways to reuse code from other designs and applications.

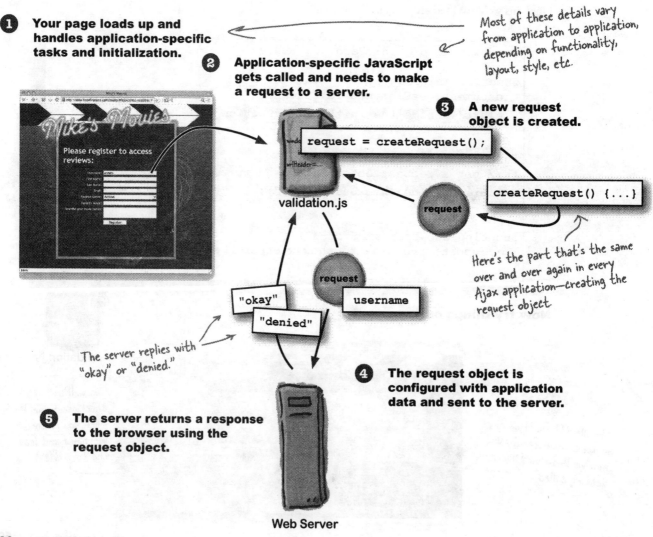

1 **Your page loads up and handles application-specific tasks and initialization.**

Most of these details vary from application to application, depending on functionality, layout, style, etc.

2 **Application-specific JavaScript gets called and needs to make a request to a server.**

3 **A new request object is created.**

`request = createRequest();`

`createRequest() {...}`

validation.js

request

Here's the part that's the same over and over again in every Ajax application—creating the request object

request

username

"okay"

"denied"

The server replies with "okay" or "denied."

4 **The request object is configured with application data and sent to the server.**

5 **The server returns a response to the browser using the request object.**

Web Server

createRequest() is always the same

We need a function to create a request object in almost every Ajax application... and we've already got one. It's the `createRequest()` function you saw back in Chapter 1, in fact. Let's take a closer look at how this function creates a request in all types of situations, with all types of client browsers.

IE 5 on the Mac still doesn't work, even with this browser-independent code. *Watch it!*

For this to be reusable, it can't depend on a certain browser or application-specific details.

```
function createRequest() {
  try {
    request = new XMLHttpRequest();
  } catch (tryMS) {
    try {
      request = new ActiveXObject("Msxml2.XMLHTTP");
    } catch (otherMS) {
      try {
        request = new ActiveXObject("Microsoft.XMLHTTP");
      } catch (failed) {
        request = null;
      }
    }
  }

  return request;
}
```

This handles lots of browsers and, therefore, lots of different users.

Remember, we have to keep trying until we find a syntax that the browser understands.

This line sends the request back to the calling code.

there are no Dumb Questions

Q: So what is this request object thing really called?

A: Most people call it an XMLHttpRequest, but that's a real mouthful. Besides, some browsers call it something different, like XMLHTTP. It's really easier to simply refer to it as a request object, and avoid being too browser-specific. That's how most everyone thinks about it anyway: as a request

> Wait... If it's exactly the same code as before, why can't we just copy and paste?

Copy and paste is <u>not</u> good code reuse.

The `createRequest()` function for Mike's movie site is identical to the `createRequest()` function from Rob's site in Chapter 1. And copying that code from the script you wrote in Chapter 1 into your new validation.js is a bad idea. If you need to make a change, you'll now have to make it in two places. And what do you think will happen when you've got ten or twenty Ajax apps floating around?

When you find code that's common across your apps, take that code out of application-specific scripts, and put it into a reusable utility script. So for `createRequest()`, we can pull it out of `validation.js` in the movie site and create a new script. Let's call it `utils.js` and start putting anything that's common to our apps into it.

Then, each new app we write can reference `utils.js`, as well as a script for application-specific JavaScript.

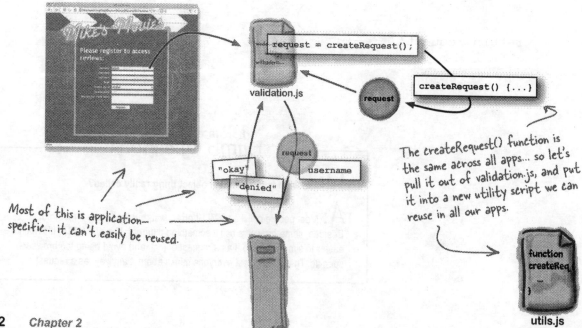

request = createRequest();

validation.js

request

createRequest() {...}

"okay"   request   username

"denied"

Most of this is application-specific... it can't easily be reused.

The createRequest() function is the same across all apps... so let's pull it out of validation.js, and put it into a new utility script we can reuse in all our apps.

function createReq
...
}

utils.js

☐ Create a new file and name it `utils.js`. Add the `createRequest()` function from the last chapter, or from page 61, into the script, and save your changes.

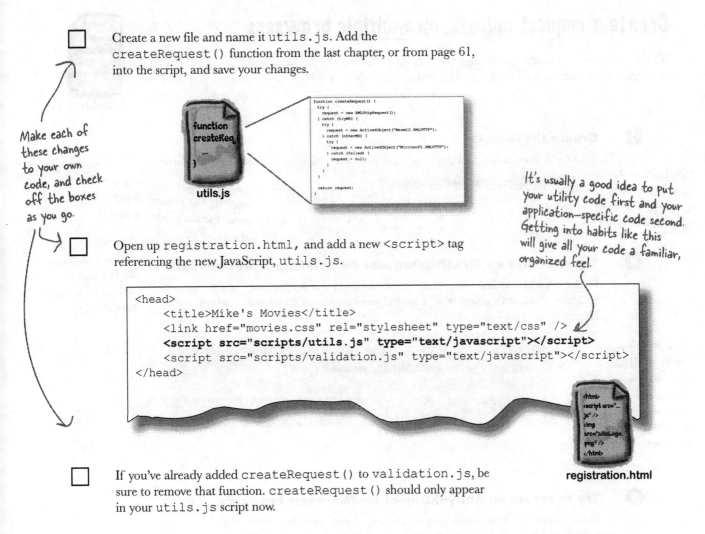

Make each of these changes to your own code, and check off the boxes as you go.

utils.js

```
function createRequest() {
  try {
    request = new XMLHttpRequest();
  } catch (tryMS) {
    try {
      request = new ActiveXObject("Msxml2.XMLHTTP");
    } catch (otherMS) {
      try {
        request = new ActiveXObject("Microsoft.XMLHTTP");
      } catch (failed) {
        request = null;
      }
    }
  }

  return request;
}
```

It's usually a good idea to put your utility code first and your application-specific code second. Getting into habits like this will give all your code a familiar, organized feel.

☐ Open up `registration.html`, and add a new `<script>` tag referencing the new JavaScript, `utils.js`.

```html
<head>
    <title>Mike's Movies</title>
    <link href="movies.css" rel="stylesheet" type="text/css" />
    <script src="scripts/utils.js" type="text/javascript"></script>
    <script src="scripts/validation.js" type="text/javascript"></script>
</head>
```

registration.html

☐ If you've already added `createRequest()` to `validation.js`, be sure to remove that function. `createRequest()` should only appear in your `utils.js` script now.

there are no Dumb Questions

Q: Why did you reference utils.js ahead of validation.js?

A: Lots of times your application-specific code will call your utilities. So it's best to make sure the browser parses your utility code before it parses any code that might call those utilities. Besides, it's a nice way to keep things organized: utilities first, application-specific code second.

Q: But I still don't understand how createRequest() actually works. What gives?

A: Good question. We've identified `createRequest()` as reusable and moved it into a utility script. That's a good thing, but we've still got to figure out what all that code is actually doing.

Separate what's the same across applications, and turn that code into a reusable set of functions.

Create a request object... on **multiple** browsers

It's time to break into JavaScript and figure out exactly what's going on. Let's walk through exactly what each piece of createRequest() does, step by step.

utils.js

❶ Create the function

Start by building a function that any other code can call when it needs a request object.

This function can be called from anywhere in our application.

```
function createRequest() {
    // create a variable named "request"
}
```

No matter what syntax we use to get it, the request object will behave the same once we have an instance of it.

This insulates the calling code from all the messy details of browser compatibility.

❷ Try to create an XMLHttpRequest for non-Microsoft browsers

Define a variable called request, and try to assign to it a new instance of the XMLHttpRequest object type. This will work on almost all browsers except Microsoft Internet Explorer.

XMLHttpRequest works on Safari, Firefox, Mozilla, Opera, and most other non-Microsoft browsers.

```
function createRequest() {
    try {
        request = new XMLHttpRequest();
    } catch (tryMS) {
        // it didn't work, so we'll try something else
    }
}
```

❸ Try to create an ActiveXObject for Microsoft browsers

In the **catch** block, we try to create a request object using the syntax that's specific to Microsoft browsers. But there are two *different* versions of the Microsoft object libraries, so we'll have to try both of them.

Most versions of IE support this syntax...

All of this code here...

...goes in here.

```
try {
    request = new ActiveXObject("Msxml2.XMLHTTP");
} catch (otherMS) {
    try {
        request = new ActiveXObject("Microsoft.XMLHTTP");
    } catch (failed) {
        // that didn't work either--we just can't get a request object
    }
}
```

...but some of them require a different library.

④ **If all else fails, return null**

We've tried three different ways of obtaining a request object. If the parser reaches this request block, that means they've all failed. So declare `request` as null, and then let the calling code decide what to do about it. Remember, `null` is the object you have when you don't have an object.

This goes in the final catch block.

```
request = null;
```

Returning null puts the burden on the calling code, which can decide how to report an error.

⑤ **Put it together, and return request**

All that's left is to return `request`. If things went okay, `request` points to a request object. Otherwise, it points to `null`:

```
function createRequest() {
  try {
    request = new XMLHttpRequest();
  } catch (tryMS) {
    try {
      request = new ActiveXObject("Msxml2.XMLHTTP");
    } catch (otherMS) {
      try {
        request = new ActiveXObject("Microsoft.XMLHTTP");
      } catch (failed) {
        request = null;
      }
    }
  }
  return request;
}
```

For non-Microsoft browsers

For the Internet Explorer fans out there

We could generate an error here, but we'll let the calling code decide what to do if we can't get a request object.

No matter what, something's returned even if it's just a null value.

BULLET POINTS

- Different browsers use different syntax to obtain a request object. Your code should account for each type of syntax, so your app works in multiple browsers.

- No matter what syntax you use to get an instance of the request object, the object itself always behaves the same way.

- Returning a null if you can't get an instance of the request object lets the calling code decide what to do. That's more flexible than generating an error.

Ajax app design involves both the web page **AND** the server-side program

Even though there was already a web form for Mike's registration page, we've got to interact with that form to get the user's username, and later on, to update the page with an error message if the selected username's taken.

And even though we're letting someone else worry about writing the server-side code, we've still got to know *what* to send to that code... and *how* to send that information.

Take a look at the steps we need to perform to check a username for validity. Most of these steps are about interacting with either the web form or a server-side program:

This is what the call to createRequest() does.

Remember, createRequest() doesn't handle errors, so we'll need to do that ourselves.

1 Try to get a request object

2 Show an alert if the browser can't create the request ←

3 Get the username the user typed into the form ← *This interacts with the web form.*

4 Make sure the username doesn't contain problematic characters for an HTTP request

5 Append the username to server url ← *These have to do with getting the username to the server.*

6 Tell the browser what function to call when the server responds to the request

7 Tell the browser how to send the request to the server *This is the "callback." We'll write it in a few pages.*

8 Send the request object

Now we're through until the request returns, and the browser gives it to the callback.

Here's more server interaction.

Good Ajax design is mostly about **interactions**. You've got to interact with your users via a web page, and your business logic via server-side programs.

Code Magnets

Most of the code for the checkUsername() function is scrambled up on the fridge. Can you reassemble it? The curly braces fell on the floor, and they were too small to pick up. Feel free to add as many of those as you need.

```
function checkUsername() {




}
```

validation.js

```
request.send(null);
```

```
alert("Unable to create request");
```

```
var theName = document.getElementById("username").value;
```

```
if (request == null)
```

```
} else {
```

```
request.open("GET", url, true);
```

```
request.onreadystatechange = showUsernameStatus;
```

```
request = createRequest();
```

```
var username = escape(theName);
```

```
var url = "checkName.php?username=" + username;
```

Code Magnet Solutions

Most of the code for the checkUserName() function is scrambled up on the fridge. Your job was to reassemble the code into a working function.

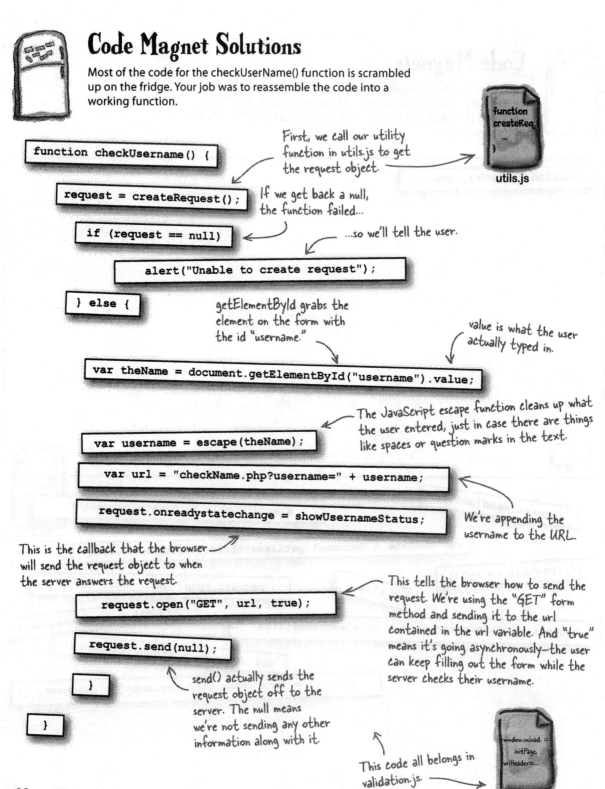

utils.js

```
function checkUsername() {
```

First, we call our utility function in utils.js to get the request object.

```
    request = createRequest();
```

If we get back a null, the function failed...

```
    if (request == null)
```

...so we'll tell the user.

```
        alert("Unable to create request");
```

```
    } else {
```

getElementById grabs the element on the form with the id "username."

value is what the user actually typed in.

```
    var theName = document.getElementById("username").value;
```

The JavaScript escape function cleans up what the user entered, just in case there are things like spaces or question marks in the text.

```
    var username = escape(theName);
```

```
    var url = "checkName.php?username=" + username;
```

```
    request.onreadystatechange = showUsernameStatus;
```

We're appending the username to the URL.

This is the callback that the browser will send the request object to when the server answers the request.

This tells the browser how to send the request. We're using the "GET" form method and sending it to the url contained in the url variable. And "true" means it's going asynchronously—the user can keep filling out the form while the server checks their username.

```
    request.open("GET", url, true);
```

```
    request.send(null);
```

```
    }
```

send() actually sends the request object off to the server. The null means we're not sending any other information along with it.

```
}
```

This code all belongs in validation.js.

validation.js

What we've done so far...

Now we've got everything ready to make a request to the server when a new username is entered in.

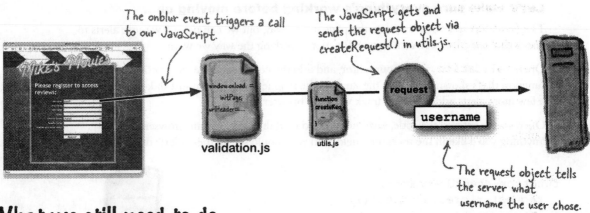

The onblur event triggers a call to our JavaScript.

The JavaScript gets and sends the request object via createRequest() in utils.js.

validation.js

utils.js

username

The request object tells the server what username the user chose.

What we still need to do...

Now we're just about ready to actually have the server respond to our request:

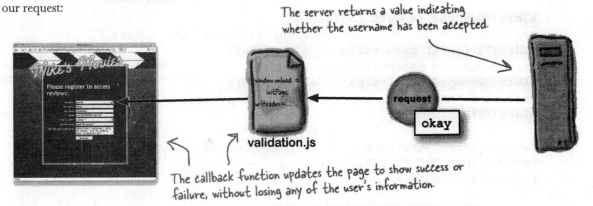

The server returns a value indicating whether the username has been accepted.

validation.js

okay

The callback function updates the page to show success or failure, without losing any of the user's information.

there are no
Dumb Questions

Q: What does that getElementById() thing do exactly?

A: We'll talk about getElementById() a *lot* when we look at the DOM in Chapters 5 and 6. For right now, all you need to understand is that it returns a JavaScript object that represents an XHTML element on a web page.

Q: And "value"? What's that?

A: The getElementById() function returns a JavaScript object that represents an XHTML element. Like all JavaScript objects, the object the function returns has properties and methods. The value property contains the text that the element contains, in this case, whatever the user entered into the username field.

TEST DRIVE

Let's make sure everything's working before moving on...

The JavaScript still doesn't update the page in any way, but we can use a few more alerts to check that our checkUsername() function's working the way we want.

Open validation.js in your editor, and add the code inside the checkUserName() function that's shown below. It's the same as the magnet exercise you just did, but there are a few more alerts added to help track what the browser's doing.

Once you've entered the code, save the file, and load the page in your browser. Enter anything you'd like in the username field, and you should see all these alerts displayed.

```
function checkUsername() {
  request = createRequest();
  if (request = null)
    alert("Unable to create request");
  else
  {
    alert("Got the request object");
    var theName = document.getElementById("username").value;
    alert("Original name value: " + theName);
    var username = escape(theName);
    alert("Escaped name value: " + username);
    var url = "checkName.php?username=" + username;
    alert("URL: " + url);

    request.onreadystatechange = userNameChecked;
    request.open("GET", url, true);
    request.send(null);
  }
}
```

validation.js

These alerts are like status messages or debugging information... they let us know what's going on behind the scenes.

You should see an alert indicating the request is created, configured, and sent.

http://headfirstlabs.com
Got the request object.

http://headfirstlabs.com
Original name value: s-stills$21

http://headfirstlabs.com
Escaped name value: s-stills%2421

http://headfirstlabs.com
URL: checkName.php?username=s-stills%2421

OK

Wait a sec... this is supposed to be real application design? A bunch of alert() statements and popup windows?

Asynchronous apps behave differently than traditional web apps, and your debugging has to account for that.

Asynchronous applications don't make you wait for a server's reply, and you don't get an entire page back from the server. In fact, most of the interactions between a web page and a server in asynchronous apps are completely invisible to a user. If the user's web browser runs into a problem when it executes some JavaScript, most of the time it will just stop, and you'll have no idea what happened.

Alerts are a good way to track down problems the browser doesn't tell you about. Alerts show you what the *browser* sees. They let you know what's going on in the background while your users are happily typing away.

You'll want to take out all these alerts once you've tracked down any problems.

You can't usually rely on a server to tell you there's a problem in asynchronous apps. It's **<u>YOUR</u>** job to figure out if there's a problem, and respond to it in a useful manner.

The request object connects your code to the web browser

All we have left to do is write the code that the browser will call when the server responds to the request. That's where the request object comes into play. It lets us tell the browser what to do, and we can use it to ask the browser to make a request to the server and give us the result.

But how does that actually happen? Remember, *the request object is just an ordinary JavaScript object*. So it can have properties, and those properties can have values. There are several that are pretty useful. Which do you think we'll need in our callback function?

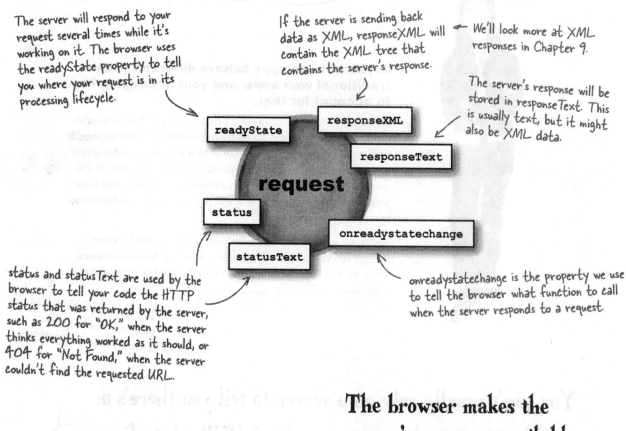

The server will respond to your request several times while it's working on it. The browser uses the readyState property to tell you where your request is in its processing lifecycle.

If the server is sending back data as XML, responseXML will contain the XML tree that contains the server's response.

We'll look more at XML responses in Chapter 9.

The server's response will be stored in responseText. This is usually text, but it might also be XML data.

status and statusText are used by the browser to tell your code the HTTP status that was returned by the server, such as 200 for "OK," when the server thinks everything worked as it should, or 404 for "Not Found," when the server couldn't find the requested URL.

onreadystatechange is the property we use to tell the browser what function to call when the server responds to a request.

The browser makes the server's response available to your code through the properties of the request object.

You talk to the <u>browser</u>, not the server

Although it's easy to talk about your code "sending a request object to the server," that's not exactly what happens. In fact, you talk to the web browser, not the server, and the browser talks to the server. **The browser sends your request object to the server,** and **the browser translates the server's response** before giving that response data back to your web page.

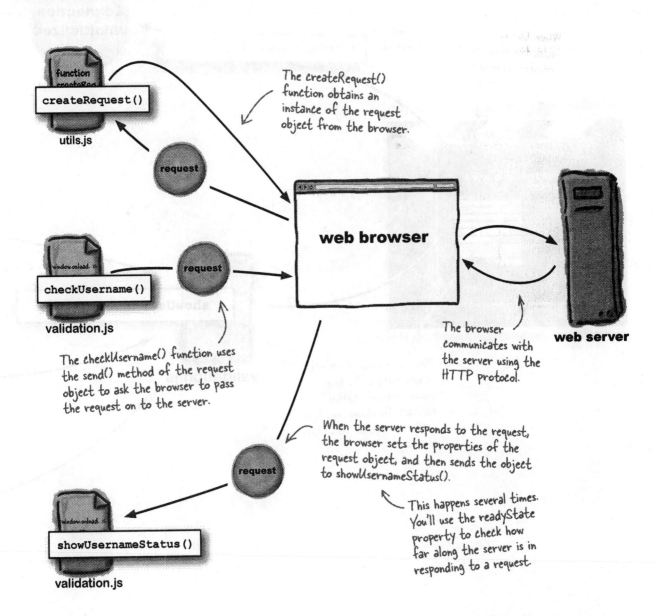

The createRequest() function obtains an instance of the request object from the browser.

The checkUsername() function uses the send() method of the request object to ask the browser to pass the request on to the server.

The browser communicates with the server using the HTTP protocol.

When the server responds to the request, the browser sets the properties of the request object, and then sends the object to showUsernameStatus().

This happens several times. You'll use the readyState property to check how far along the server is in responding to a request.

Ready states up close

The browser uses the `readystate` property of the request object to tell your callback function where a request is in its lifecycle. Let's take a look at exactly what that means.

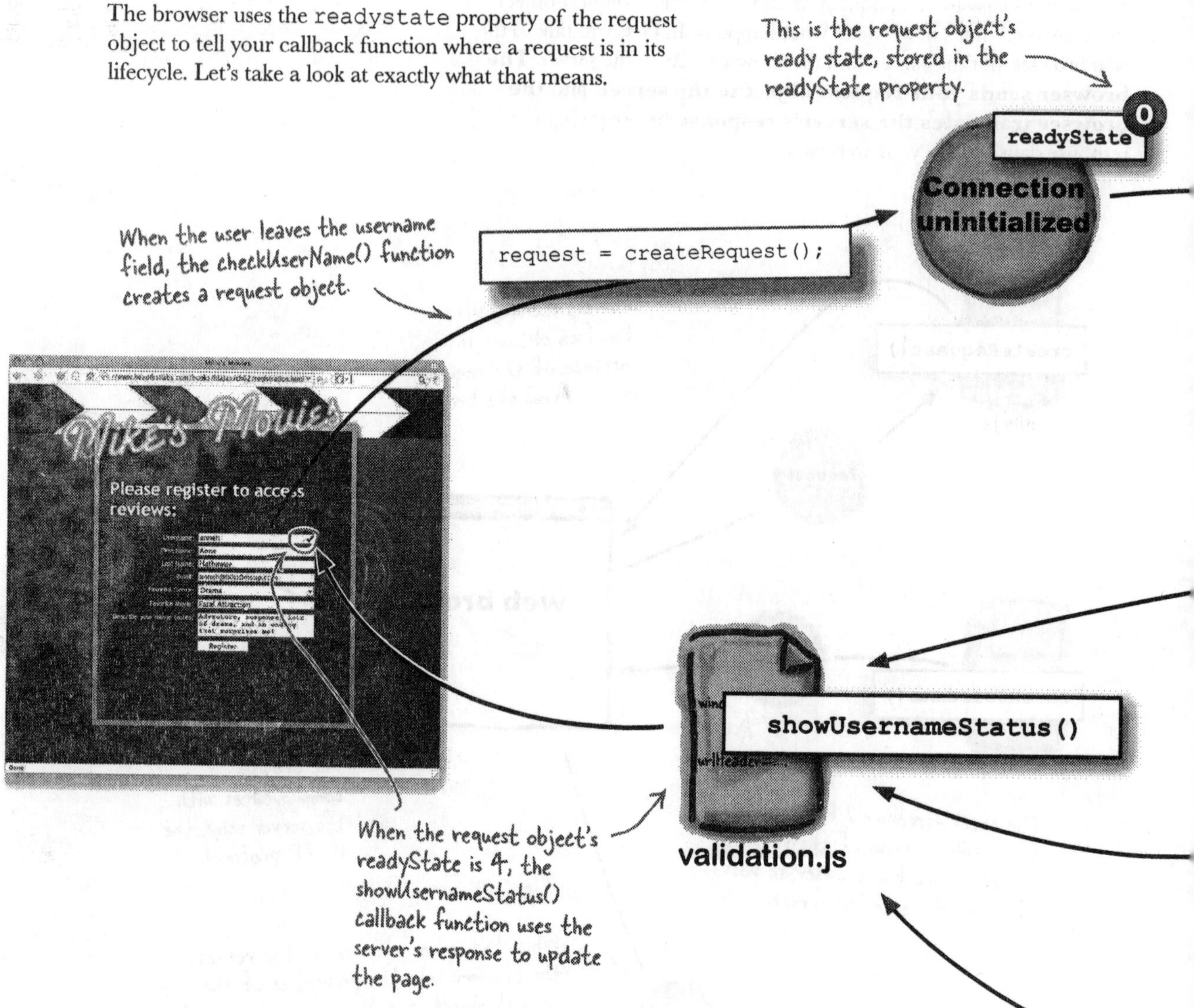

This is the request object's ready state, stored in the readyState property.
0
readyState
Connection uninitialized
When the user leaves the username field, the checkUserName() function creates a request object.
request = createRequest();
Please register to access reviews:
showUsernameStatus()
validation.js
When the request object's readyState is 4, the showUsernameStatus() callback function uses the server's response to update the page.

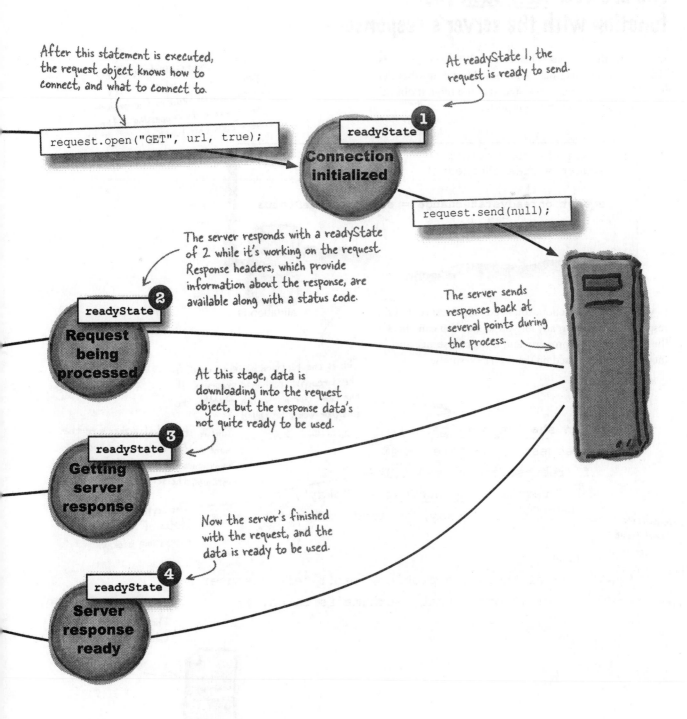

After this statement is executed, the request object knows how to connect, and what to connect to.

```
request.open("GET", url, true);
```

At readyState 1, the request is ready to send.

readyState ①

Connection initialized

```
request.send(null);
```

The server responds with a readyState of 2 while it's working on the request. Response headers, which provide information about the response, are available along with a status code.

readyState ②

Request being processed

The server sends responses back at several points during the process.

At this stage, data is downloading into the request object, but the response data's not quite ready to be used.

readyState ③

Getting server response

Now the server's finished with the request, and the data is ready to be used.

readyState ④

Server response ready

The browser <u>calls</u> <u>back</u> your function with the server's response

Every time the response object's `readyState` property changes, the browser has to do something. And what does it do? It runs the function assigned to the request object's `onreadystatechange` property:

Every time the ready state of the response changes — which is every time the server updates the browser on the request its processing — the browser calls this function.

```
function checkUsername() {
  request = createRequest();
  ...
  request.onreadystatechange = showUsernameStatus;
  ...
}
```

validation.js

In your callback function, you need to make sure that the response is actually ready for you to use. You can check the `readyState` property and the server status, and then take action based on the server's response:

This is the function name we used for the onreadystatechange property. If the name doesn't match exactly, the function won't be called.

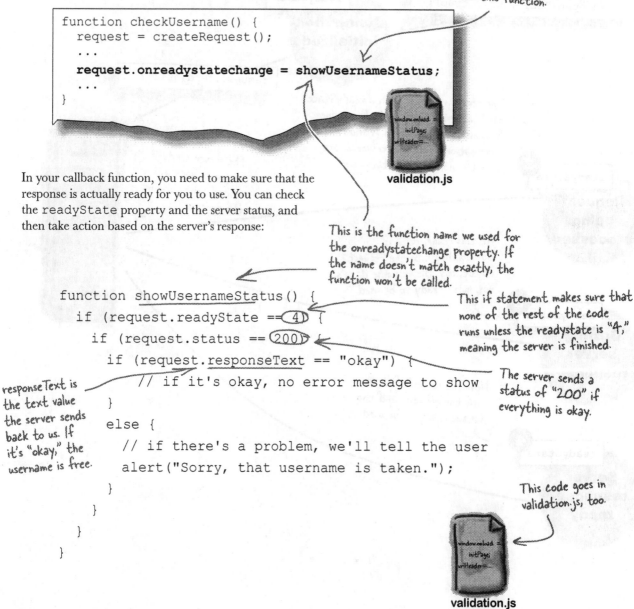

```
function showUsernameStatus() {
  if (request.readyState == 4) {
    if (request.status == 200) {
      if (request.responseText == "okay") {
        // if it's okay, no error message to show
      }
      else {
        // if there's a problem, we'll tell the user
        alert("Sorry, that username is taken.");
      }
    }
  }
}
```

This if statement makes sure that none of the rest of the code runs unless the readystate is "4," meaning the server is finished.

The server sends a status of "200" if everything is okay.

responseText is the text value the server sends back to us. If it's "okay," the username is free.

This code goes in validation.js, too.

validation.js

Test Drive

Add the showUsernameStatus() function to validation.js, and load the registration page in your browser.

Try entering any username except "bill" or "ted." Your browser should display all the alerts we added to test the initPage() and checkUsername() functions.

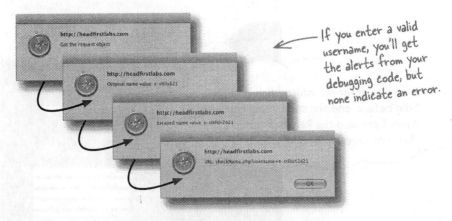

If you enter a valid username, you'll get the alerts from your debugging code, but none indicate an error.

Now try entering "bill" or "ted" as the username. You should get the error message that's displayed by showUsernameStatus().

This message should be displayed if you enter "bill" or "ted," and then leave the username field. Someone with that username is already registered.

Once you're sure everything's working, go ahead and remove all those alert statements in checkUsername() that you added to test the code. The only alerts that should be left are to report that a request can't be created, in checkUsername(), and to report a username's already taken, in showUsernameStatus().

Now that you're sure the interaction between your code and the server works, you don't need those alert() debugging statements anymore.

Show the Ajax registration page to Mike...

Everything works. But when you give all your code to Mike, and he goes live with the new improved registration page, there are still some problems:

> I tried to enter my information just like I did before, and the same thing happened. When I pressed the Register button, the browser threw away all my work!

What happened? Did all the work you put into the registration page get lost? Ignored?

What do YOU think?

The web form has **TWO** ways to send requests to the server now

Suppose a user does just what you expect: they enter a username, and while an asynchronous request is going to the server and getting handled by the browser, your callback is running, and the user's filling out other information on the form. Everything works great—just like you planned.

But suppose the user's so eager to get to Mike's review of Iron Man that they put in their username, ignore everything else on the form, and click "Register." What happens then?

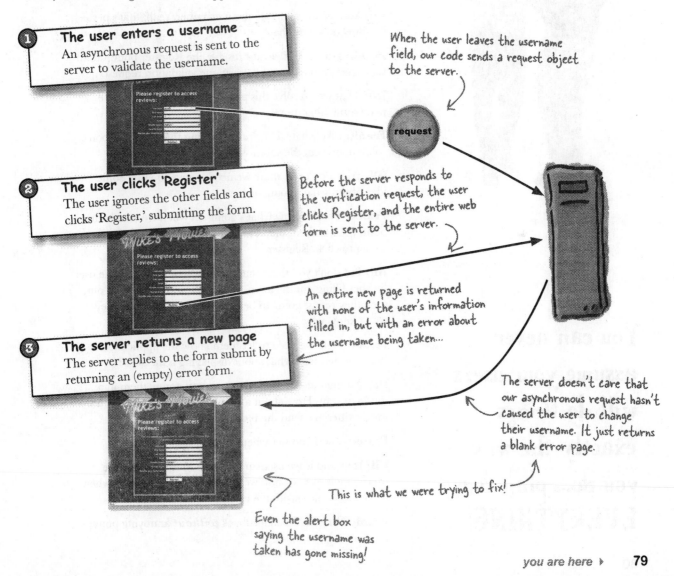

1 **The user enters a username**
An asynchronous request is sent to the server to validate the username.

When the user leaves the username field, our code sends a request object to the server.

2 **The user clicks 'Register'**
The user ignores the other fields and clicks 'Register,' submitting the form.

Before the server responds to the verification request, the user clicks Register, and the entire web form is sent to the server.

An entire new page is returned with none of the user's information filled in, but with an error about the username being taken...

3 **The server returns a new page**
The server replies to the form submit by returning an (empty) error form.

The server doesn't care that our asynchronous request hasn't caused the user to change their username. It just returns a blank error page.

This is what we were trying to fix!

Even the alert box saying the username was taken has gone missing!

But we never thought about users ignoring all of the other fields. How do we keep users from doing that?

Frank

Jill

You can never assume your users will do things exactly the way you do... plan for EVERYTHING!

Frank: Well, we can't keep users from skipping over fields, but maybe we can keep them from getting ahead of our request.

Jill: You mean validating the username? Yeah, that's perfect, but how do we do that?

Frank: How about we just disable the Register button until the server responds to the username validation request.

Jill: That would solve this problem, but it seems like we need something more.

Frank: Like what? They're submitting the form too soon, so if we prevent the submission, the problem's solved.

Jill: Well, don't you think we need to give the user some idea about what's going on?

Frank: They'll know what's going on when we enable the button. Until then, they should be filling out the form, not trying to click 'Register.'

Jill: But don't you think that might be confusing? If the user finishes filling out the form, or doesn't want to fill it all out, then they're just going to be sitting there, stuck, and they won't know why.

Frank: Well, we need to let them know the application is doing something. What about displaying a message?

Jill: Another alert? That's just going to annoy them in a different way. How about a graphic? We could display an image when we send the request to the browser...

Frank: ...and another when their username's verified.

Jill: Hey, and if we used an image to show whether the username is okay or not, we could get rid of the alert when there's a problem with the username, too.

Frank: Perfect! Visual feedback *without* annoying popups. I love it!

☐ **Display an "In Progress" graphic during verification requests**

When we send a request to the server to verify a username, we'll display a graphic next to the username field, telling the user what's going on. That way, they'll know exactly what's happening as they work through the form.

getElementById is probably starting to look familiar. It lets you access an element on an XHTML page.

Make each of these changes to your own code, and check off the boxes as you go.

```
function checkUsername() {
    document.getElementById("status").src = "images/inProcess.png";
    request = createRequest();
    ...
}
```

Displaying this image tells the user something's going on.

validation.js

☐ **Display a status message upon verification**

Once the request object returns, we can display another graphic in our callback function. If the username is okay, the graphic indicates that; otherwise, we'll show an error icon.

```
function showUsernameStatus() {
    ...
    if (request.responseText == "okay") {
        document.getElementById("status").src = "images/okay.png";
    }
    else {
        alert("Sorry, that user name is taken.");
        document.getElementById("status").src = "images/inUse.png";
        ...
    }
    ...
}
```

This graphic is displayed if the server says the username is okay.

We can ditch the alert popup in favor of a nicer graphical icon.

This graphic is shown if the username is taken.

validation.js

BRAIN POWER

What do you think about this approach? Does it follow the principle of separating content from presentation? Would you change anything?

> If we're changing the image in our JavaScript, aren't we mixing in our presentation with our behavior?

Try and keep your presentation in your CSS, and your behavior in your JavaScript.

Your XHTML stores structure and content. Your CSS should handle presentation, like images, colors, and font styles. And your JavaScript should be about what your page does: the page's behavior. Mixing those means that a designer won't be able to change an image because it's in your code. Or a programmer will have to mess with a page author's structure. That's never a good thing.

It's not always possible, but when you can, keep your presentation in your CSS, and use JavaScript to interact with the CSS rather than affecting the presentation of a page directly.

Let's create CSS classes for each state of the processing...

Instead of changing an image directly, let's put all the image details in our CSS. Open up `movies.css` and add the following CSS selectors:

This first class just sets up the location for the process icons...

...and these other three classes change out the image in that location.

```
... existing CSS ...
#username { padding: 0 20px 0 2px; width: 198px; }
#username.thinking { background: url("../images/inProcess.png"); }
#username.approved { background: url("../images/okay.png"); }
#username.denied { background: url("../images/inUse.png"); }
```

Add these four lines to your CSS.

`#detail {`
`...`
`}`

movies.css

These are the same images that we used in our JavaScript, but now they're in the CSS with the rest of the presentation.

...and change the CSS class with our JavaScript

Now our JavaScript doesn't need to know any image names, paths, or anything about **how** the process icons are being shown. Instead, we just need to know the three CSS classes that represent each stage of processing.

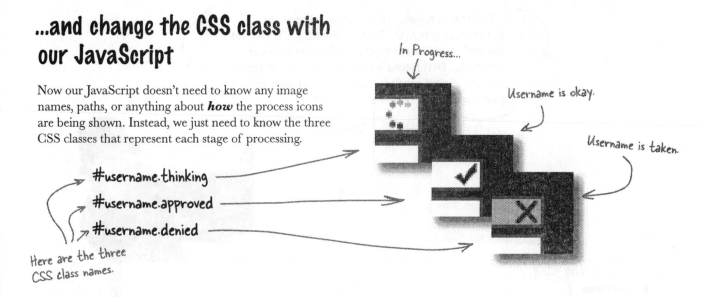

In Progress...

Username is okay.

Username is taken.

#username.thinking

#username.approved

#username.denied

Here are the three CSS class names.

Now we can update our JavaScript (again). This time we'll just change the CSS class instead of directly changing an image:

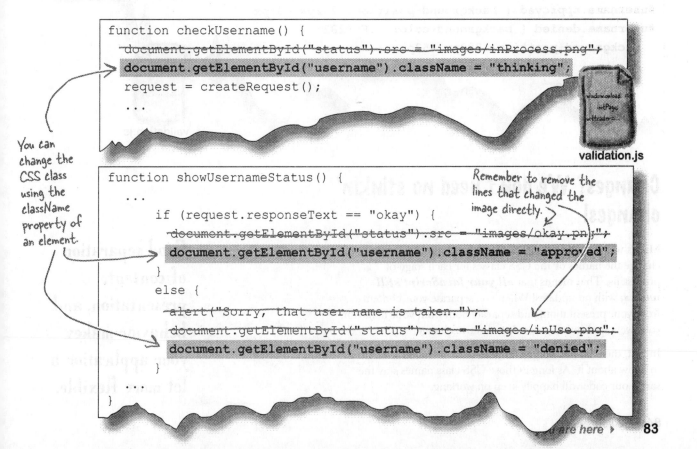

```
function checkUsername() {
  document.getElementById("status").src = "images/inProcess.png";
  document.getElementById("username").className = "thinking";
  request = createRequest();
  ...
```

validation.js

You can change the CSS class using the className property of an element.

```
function showUsernameStatus() {
  ...
    if (request.responseText == "okay") {
      document.getElementById("status").src = "images/okay.png";
      document.getElementById("username").className = "approved";
    }
    else {
      alert("Sorry, that user name is taken.");
      document.getElementById("status").src = "images/inUse.png";
      document.getElementById("username").className = "denied";
    }
  ...
}
```

Remember to remove the lines that changed the image directly.

So, listen. I'm going to use a single image for the process indicator. Then, in the CSS, I'll just set the different classes to show different parts of the image. That means less image loading and faster changes. Sound good? Do whatever you need to do to your code to get this to work, okay?

All of this CSS changed. Now there's just one image being moved around with the CSS.

Mike's web designer is always full of new ideas.

```css
... existing CSS ...
#username {
  background: #fff url('../images/status.gif') 202px 0 no-repeat;
  padding: 0 20px 0 2px; width: 198px; }
#username.thinking { background-position: 202px -19px; }
#username.approved { background-position: 202px -35px; }
#username.denied { background-color: #FF8282;
  background-position: 202px -52px; }
```

validation.js

Changes? We don't need no stinkin' changes!

Mike's web designer made lots of changes... but she didn't change the names of the CSS classes for each stage of processing. That means that **all your JavaScript still works,** with no updates! When you separate your content from your presentation, and separate both from your behavior, your web application gets **a lot** easier to change.

In fact, the CSS can change anytime, and we don't even need to know about it. As long as those CSS class names stay the same, our code will happily keep on working.

Good separation of content, presentation, and behavior makes your application a lot more flexible.

Only allow registration when it's _appropriate_

With process indicators in place, all that's left is to disable the Register button when the page loads, and then enable the button once a username's okay.

That involves just a few more changes to validation.js:

▢ **Disable the Register button**

When a user first loads the page, the username hasn't been checked. So we can disable the Register button right away in our initialization code.

> By setting the disabled property to true, the user can fill in the fields, but they can't press the submit button until we're ready.

```
function initPage() {
    document.getElementById("username").onblur = checkUsername;
    document.getElementById("register").disabled = true;
}
```

validation.js

▢ **Enable the Register button**

If the username is okay, the user's ready to register, so we need to enable the Register button. But if there's a problem with the username, they need to try again, so we should keep the Register button disabled. And just to make things easier for the user, let's move them back to the username field if their username is rejected:

```
function showUsernameStatus() {
    ...
        if (request.responseText == "okay") {
            document.getElementById("username").className = "approved";
            document.getElementById("register").disabled = false;
        }
        else {
            document.getElementById("username").className = "denied";
            document.getElementById("username").focus();
            document.getElementById("username").select();
            document.getElementById("register").disabled = true;
            ...
        }
    ...
}
```

> If the username is okay, enable the Register button.

> This moves the user back to the username field.

> If the username's taken, make sure the Register button stays disabled.

validation.js

TEST DRIVE

Make sure you've updated validation.js and mpovies.css, and load up Mike's registration page. Try it out to make sure everything's behaving like it should.

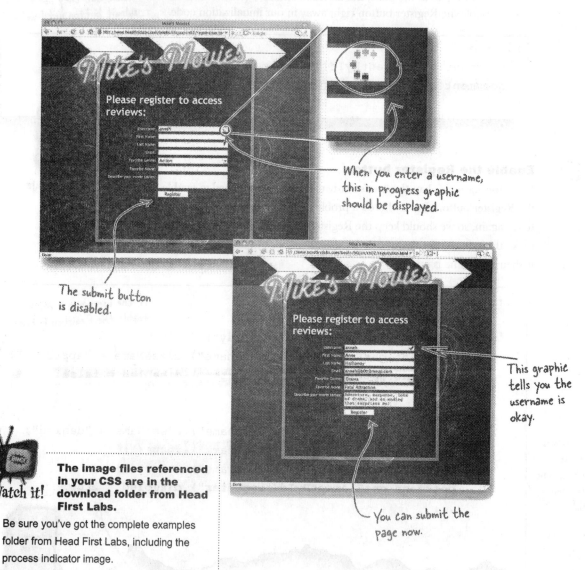

When you enter a username, this in progress graphic should be displayed.

The submit button is disabled.

This graphic tells you the username is okay.

You can submit the page now.

The image files referenced in your CSS are in the download folder from Head First Labs.

Watch it!

Be sure you've got the complete examples folder from Head First Labs, including the process indicator image.

That's what I'm talking about... satisfied users and a much cooler registration page.

Please register to access reviews:

Sweet! It's as good as it looks...

Cool... I'll avoid that one and save twenty bucks on tickets.

Mike's happy...

...and now his fans can get to his movie reviews.

Now Mike's page...

✳ ...lets users keep working while their requested usernames are verified by Mike's server.

✳ ...prevents user mistakes by disabling buttons that aren't safe or appropriate to use, and enables those buttons when they _are_ useful.

✳ ...doesn't annoy his users with intrusive popups, but still gives them useful visual feedback.

Along the way you started thinking about application design in an entirely new way... going beyond a traditional request/wait/response model.

Word Search

Take some time to sit back and give your right brain something to do. It's your standard word search; all of the solution words are from this chapter.

```
X A R S M O K E J U D H E
A C T I V E X O B J E C T
A V I O R S M A L T R S V
Q S L H O C L V J A R S L
J U Y O R U H A E A H A R
A M N N O N T L Y H E R A
Z O E U C S T F I D N E S
H P T K A H P I N L O L N
G E Y C C E R L O X L B R
A N I A H R E O A U D G R
O U N B E D Q B N R E A K
I N G L F A U R L O N S A
N D C L R I E F R I U D Y
A R E A D Y S T A T E S D
J E R C I C T H R I Z A R
```

Word list:

ActiveXObject
Asynchronous
Ajax
Cache
Callback
Null
Open
Readystate
Send
URL
XMLHttpRequest

Label Magnets

All the labels describing what's going on in the new-and-improved registration page fell to the ground. Can you place the labels in the right place on the diagram?

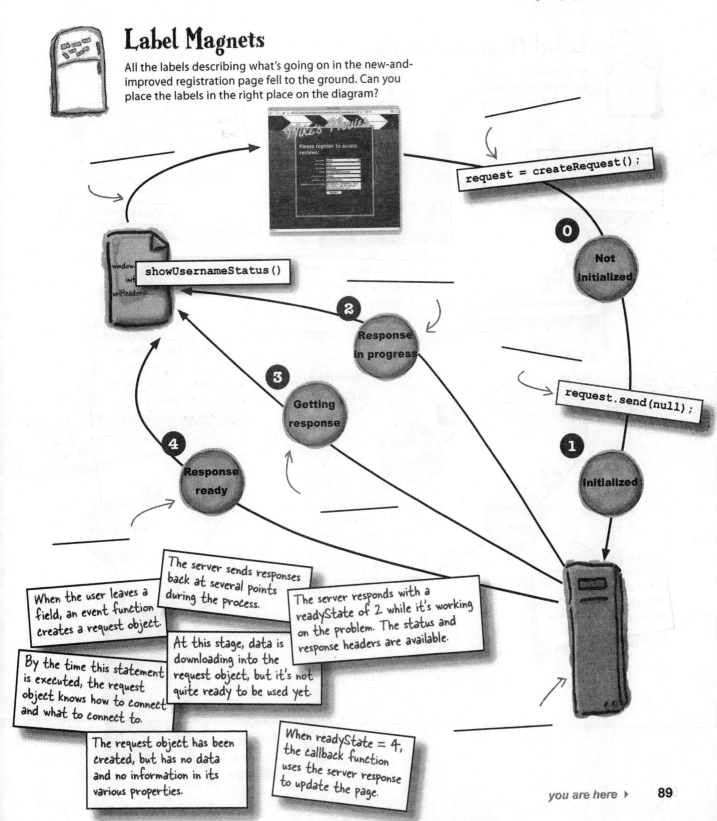

```
request = createRequest();
```

0 Not Initialized

`showUsernameStatus()`

2 Response in progress

3 Getting response

```
request.send(null);
```

4 Response ready

1 Initialized

The server sends responses back at several points during the process.

When the user leaves a field, an event function creates a request object.

The server responds with a readyState of 2 while it's working on the problem. The status and response headers are available.

At this stage, data is downloading into the request object, but it's not quite ready to be used yet.

By the time this statement is executed, the request object knows how to connect and what to connect to.

The request object has been created, but has no data and no information in its various properties.

When readyState = 4, the callback function uses the server response to update the page.

Label Magnets Solution

All the labels describing what's going on in the new-and-improved registration page fell to the ground. Can you place the labels in the right place on the diagram?

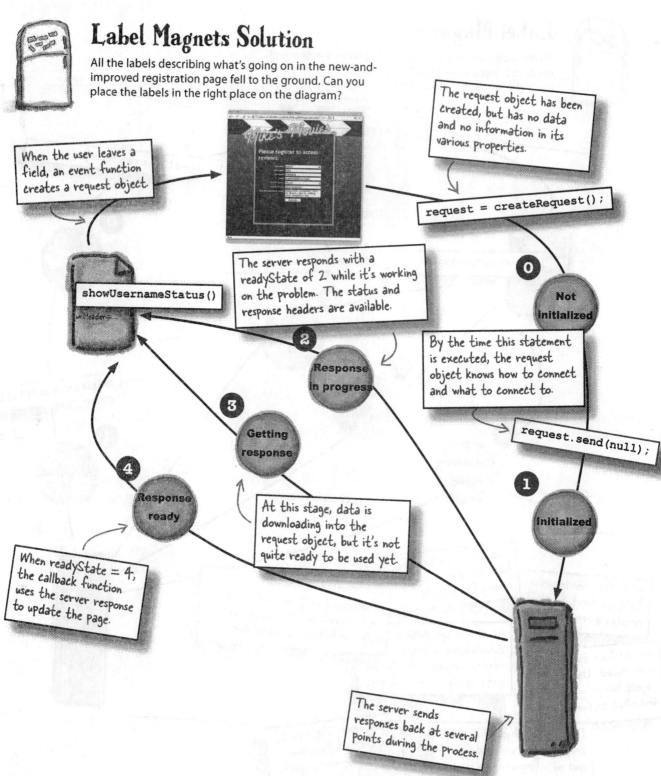

When the user leaves a field, an event function creates a request object.

The request object has been created, but has no data and no information in its various properties.

`request = createRequest();`

0
Not initialized

`showUsernameStatus()`

The server responds with a readyState of 2 while it's working on the problem. The status and response headers are available.

By the time this statement is executed, the request object knows how to connect and what to connect to.

2
Response in progress

`request.send(null);`

3
Getting response

1
Initialized

4
Response ready

At this stage, data is downloading into the request object, but it's not quite ready to be used yet.

When readyState = 4, the callback function uses the server response to update the page.

The server sends responses back at several points during the process.

Word Search Solution

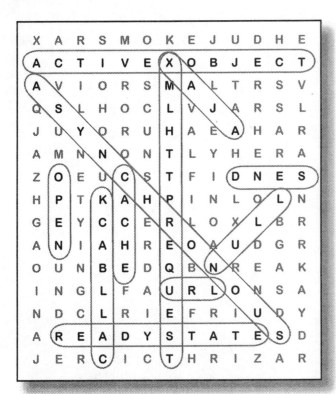

Word list:

- ~~ActiveXObject~~
- ~~Asynchronous~~
- ~~Ajax~~
- ~~Cache~~
- ~~Callback~~
- ~~Null~~
- ~~Open~~
- ~~Readystate~~
- ~~Send~~
- ~~URL~~
- ~~XMLHttpRequest~~

3 javascript events

Reacting to your users

So he said, "Hey,"
and then I said, "Ho," and then
he said, "Hey" again, and then I
said... well, you get the idea. I just
felt so **alive** reacting to him...

Sometimes you need your code to react to other things going on in your web application... and that's where **events** come into the picture. An event is *something that happens* on your page, in the browser, or even on a web server. But it's not enough to just know about events... sometimes you want to respond to them. By creating code, and registering it as an **event handler**, you can get the browser to run your handler every time a particular event occurs. Combine events and handlers, and you get **interactive web applications**.

It all started with a downward-facing dog...

Marcy's just opened up a new yoga studio that caters to programmers and techies. She wants a website that shows the different levels of classes she offers, the times they're available, and provides new customers a way to enroll in a class... all in a cool, intuitive package. But she doesn't have a clue how to build that kind of site.... that's where you come in.

To give you an idea of what she's looking for, Marcy worked up a quick sketch of what a page on her site needs to show her customers:

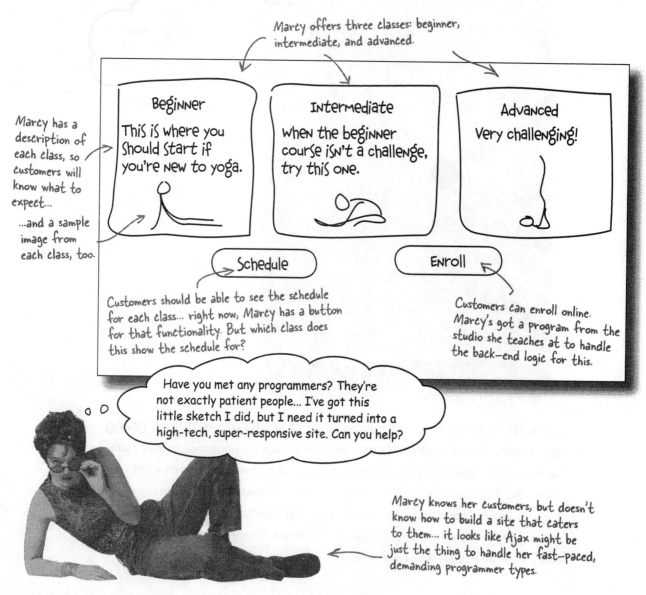

Marcy offers three classes: beginner, intermediate, and advanced.

Beginner
This is where you should start if you're new to yoga.

Intermediate
When the beginner course isn't a challenge, try this one.

Advanced
Very challenging!

Marcy has a description of each class, so customers will know what to expect...

...and a sample image from each class, too.

Schedule

Enroll

Customers should be able to see the schedule for each class... right now, Marcy has a button for that functionality. But which class does this show the schedule for?

Customers can enroll online. Marcy's got a program from the studio she teaches at to handle the back-end logic for this.

Have you met any programmers? They're not exactly patient people... I've got this little sketch I did, but I need it turned into a high-tech, super-responsive site. Can you help?

Marcy knows her customers, but doesn't know how to build a site that caters to them... it looks like Ajax might be just the thing to handle her fast-paced, demanding programmer types.

Design Magnets

It's time to turn Marcy's rough design into something you'd like to see in your own web browser (you're a programmer too, remember?). At the bottom of the page are lots of magnets representing parts of a potential web page. It's your job to arrange these on the web browser in a way that looks great. Also, see if you can design the site so when a customer clicks on a class level, the description and a picture of *just the selected class* is displayed.

← In the rest of this chapter, you'll build this site, so think about what Ajax lets you do: change parts of the page in real-time, talk to the server asynchronously, etc.

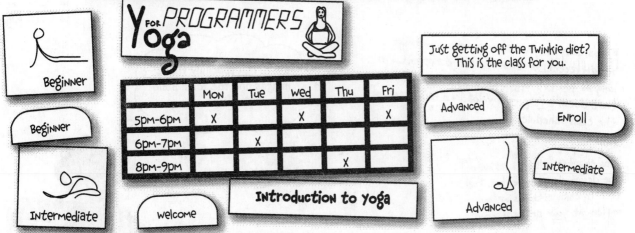

	MON	Tue	wed	Thu	Fri
5pm-6pm	X		X		X
6pm-7pm		X			
8pm-9pm				X	

Beginner

Beginner

Intermediate

welcome

Introduction to yoga

Yoga for PROGRAMMERS

Just getting off the Twinkie diet? This is the class for you.

Advanced

Enroll

Intermediate

Advanced

Our Design Magnet Solution

Your job was to arrange the design magnets onto the web browser in a way that looks great. Also, you should have designed the site so that when a customer clicks on a class level, the schedule, description, and a picture of *just the selected class* is displayed.

Here's where the Ajax came in... can we change out parts of the page without a reload? Of course...

These images will display a description of the class when the user rolls the mouse over them.

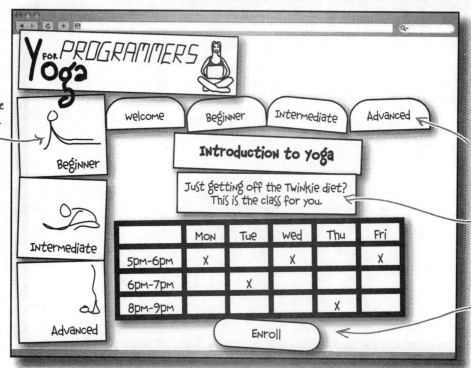

The "tabs" contain the class schedule. We'll get that on demand using a request object.

...and a description of the class will be displayed here.

When the schedule is displayed, clicking the Enroll button will take the user to a new page.

✳ It's okay if you came up with something a bit different, or even A LOT different... as long as you put together a dynamic design that doesn't require a reload to show each of the class schedules.

This chapter will be working off the design shown here, but feel free to change things up and implement your design instead...

I love it, especially those images and the tabs! Build it just like that.

Exercise

Suppose you want to build the website shown on page 96. In the space below, make notes about what should happen when customers click on different buttons, and what interactions you think you'll need between Marcy's web page and the server.

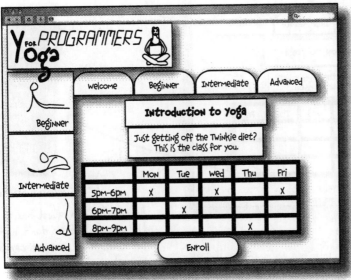

Web page

Web server

The studio Marcy teaches at has server-side programmers that can build whatever we need... but we've got to tell them what to build. What sort of server-side programs will we need? ....
....
....
....
....
....

Exercise Solution

Your job was to make notes about what should happen when customers click on different buttons, and what interactions you think you'll need between Marcy's web page and the server.

There's a tab for each class. When users click on a tab, it shows the description and schedule for that class.

Do we need to talk to the server for this?

Each tab updates the content part of the page.

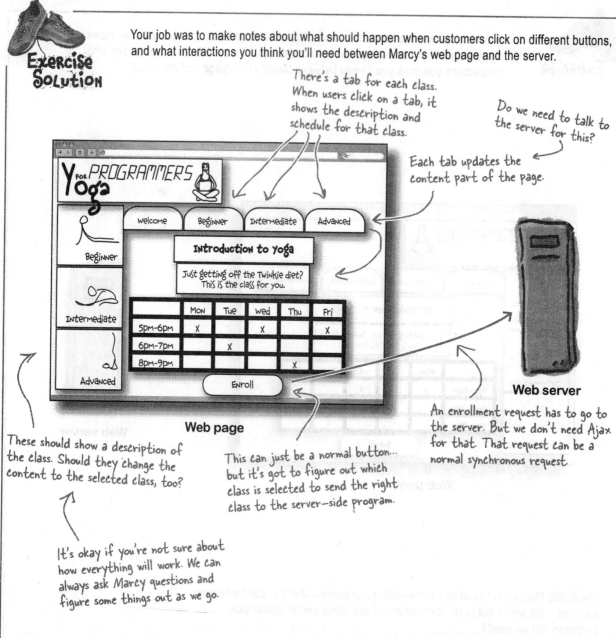

Web page

Web server

An enrollment request has to go to the server. But we don't need Ajax for that. That request can be a normal synchronous request.

These should show a description of the class. Should they change the content to the selected class, too?

This can just be a normal button... but it's got to figure out which class is selected to send the right class to the server-side program.

It's okay if you're not sure about how everything will work. We can always ask Marcy questions and figure some things out as we go.

The studio Marcy teaches at has server-side programmers that can build whatever we need... but we've got to tell them what to build. What sort of server-side programs will we need? We need a program that takes a class name... and brings up some sort of enrollment form. It sounds like Marcy's got the form, so when users click a button, we send a request to the server for enrollment in the selected class.
And what about the different class pages? We might need to request those from the server. Although something seems funny about that... I'm not sure what yet...

there are no
Dumb Questions

Q: I came up with something totally different for my solution. Is that okay?

A: It is as long as you figured out that you need to make a request to the server to enroll for each different yoga class, and realized that each tab should bring up a class schedule and description. But some details are still fuzzy. What do those buttons on the left do? And do we need an asynchronous request to get information about each class?

Q: Are those tabs along the top of that drawing?

A: They sure are. Tabs are a great way to let users not only see different options, but easily click on each option to find out more.

Q: XHTML doesn't have a tab control. Do we have to buy a third-party tool or something?

A: No, we'll do it all using graphics, some nifty client-side JavaScript, and a request object to fetch the schedule from the server.

Q: But there are some toolkits that do that stuff for you, right? Why don't we just use one of those?

A: Toolkits are great, but it's much better to know what's going on underneath something like script.aculo.us or mootools. In this chapter, you'll build a simple tabbed control on your own... and then when you want to use a toolkit, you'll know what's going on, instead of depending on someone else to figure out your JavaScript for you.

And of course, when the toolkit you're using doesn't do just what you want, you'll be able to change it or write your own controls.

script.aculo.us and mootools are two popular JavaScript toolkits for visual effects, among other things.

Q: This doesn't look like much new... didn't we do something similar with the movie review site already?

A: That's right, you did. Although in that case, there was a lot less interactivity on the web page. Users signed up, and the page and your code did everything else. On this site, we've got a lot more going on: dealing with several different button presses, figuring out *which* button was pressed... loads of new interactivity issues. That's what most of this chapter focuses on, in fact: **events** and **interactivity**.

> **Try not to rely on any toolkit unless you understand the code behind that toolkit.**
>
> **That way, when things don't work the way you want, you can fix the problems yourself.**

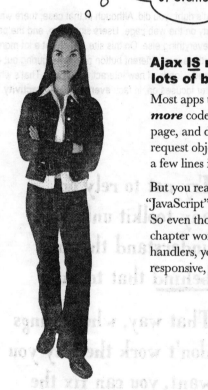

Hang on a second... half of this is web design and plain old JavaScript. I thought we were supposed to be learning about Ajax, not a bunch of events and boring scripting.

Ajax IS mostly JavaScript, events, and lots of boring scripting!

Most apps that use asynchronous requests have a lot *more* code that deals with web pages, objects on that page, and doing basic JavaScript tasks. The actual request object code may only be a callback function and a few lines in an event handler.

But you really can't break an application up into "JavaScript" and "Ajax" and "CSS." It all works together. So even though you'll be spending a lot of time in this chapter working with XHTML and CSS and event handlers, you're really building Ajaxian applications: responsive, user-friendly, modern web apps.

The more you know about JavaScript, XHTML, and CSS, the more effective and usable your Ajax apps will be.

Ajax apps are more than the sum of their parts

Ajax apps are really just a combination of lots of pretty simple technologies:
XHTML, CSS, JavaScript, and things like the DOM, which you'll get to in a few
chapters. In fact, if you take a close look at Marcy's app, **most** of the work is
not Ajax-specific. It's XHTML, CSS, and JavaScript... with a little asynchronous
requesting added in just when it's needed.

Assembling Marcy's page involves
XHTML and CSS... and sometimes,
some really complex CSS, especially
for positioning elements on the page.

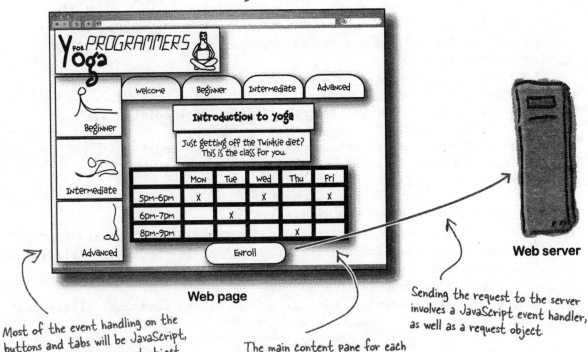

Web page

Web server

Most of the event handling on the
buttons and tabs will be JavaScript,
and it won't need a request object.

The main content pane for each
class is XHTML. We'll get that
XHTML with an asynchronous
request, but the response from the
server is just more XHTML.

Sending the request to the server
involves a JavaScript event handler,
as well as a request object.

The XHTML is styled by CSS. So
there's more presentation to deal
with.

Here's Marcy's XHTML...

Below is the XHTML for Marcy's page... it's already got a few references to the JavaScript files we'll need and several `<div>`s representing the different parts of the page. Go ahead and download this page, along with the rest of the Chapter 3 examples, from the Head First Labs web site.

```
<html>
<head>
  <title>Yoga for Programmers</title>
  <link rel="stylesheet" href="css/yoga.css" type="text/css" />
  <script src="scripts/utils.js" type="text/javascript"></script>
  <script src="scripts/schedule.js" type="text/javascript"></script>
</head>

<body>
  <div id="schedulePane">
    <img id="logo" alt="Yoga for Programmers" src="images/logo.png" />
    <div id="navigation">
      <img src="images/beginnersBtn.png" alt="Beginners Yoga"
        title="beginners" class="nav" />
      <img src="images/intermediateBtn.png" alt="Intermediate Yoga"
        title="intermediate" class="nav"/>
      <img src="images/advancedBtn.png" alt="Advanced Yoga"
        title="advanced" class="nav"/>
    </div>

    <div id="tabs">
      <img src="images/welcomeTabActive.png" title="welcome" class="tab" />
      <img src="images/beginnersTabInactive.png" title="beginners" class="tab" />
      <img src="images/intermediateTabInactive.png"
          title="intermediate" class="tab"  />
      <img src="images/advancedTabInactive.png" title="advanced" class="tab" />
    </div>

    <div id="content">
      <h3>Click a tab to display the course schedule for the selected class</h3>
    </div>
  </div>
</body>
</html>
```

utils.js is the utility file we created in Chapter 2 with createRequest().

We'll be adding a few new functions to utils.js in this chapter.

schedule.js will store the application-specific JavaScript.

The working section of the page is wrapped in the "schedulePane" div.

This div contains the images on the left side of the page.

This div contains the four graphics that represent the "tabs."

Here's where we need to update the class information and display a schedule for each class.

classes.html, along with yoga.css and the images used by the Yoga web page, are all online at the Head First Labs web site.

classes.html

Test Drive

See what Marcy's page looks like pre-Ajax.

Download the examples for Chapter 3 from the Head First Labs web site. Go ahead and open up `classes.html`, and see what Marcy's page looks like. There's no interactivity yet, and you may get a message letting you know that `schedule.js` can't be found. That's okay, we'll get to all that soon.

These are just images that look like tabs. It's all just XHTML and CSS.

○ ○ ○   Yoga for Programmers

http://www.headfirstlabs.com/books/hfajax/ch03/classes.html

Yoga FOR **PROGRAMMERS**

| welcome | beginners | intermediate | advanced |

Click a tab to display the course schedule for the selected class

Here's where a description of each class should appear.

BEGINNERS

INTERMEDIATE

ADVANCED

Waiting for www.headfirstlabs.com...

These really do look like buttons... we'll have to make sure they react like users expect them to.

This looks a lot like the sketch on page 96. Now we just have to figure out the interactivity part.

Events are the key to interactivity

Marcy's page needs to react to her customers. She wants a different schedule and description to appear when a customer clicks on a class, and we could even highlight a menu item by using <u>context-specific graphics</u>.

All this adds up to an **interactive web page**. In programming terms, "interactive" means that your page responds to specific **events**. And events are just things that happen. Those things can be triggered by the user, your code, the browser, or even a server:

<u>Context-specific graphics</u> is just a fancy term for changing a graphic when the customer moves their mouse over a menu option.

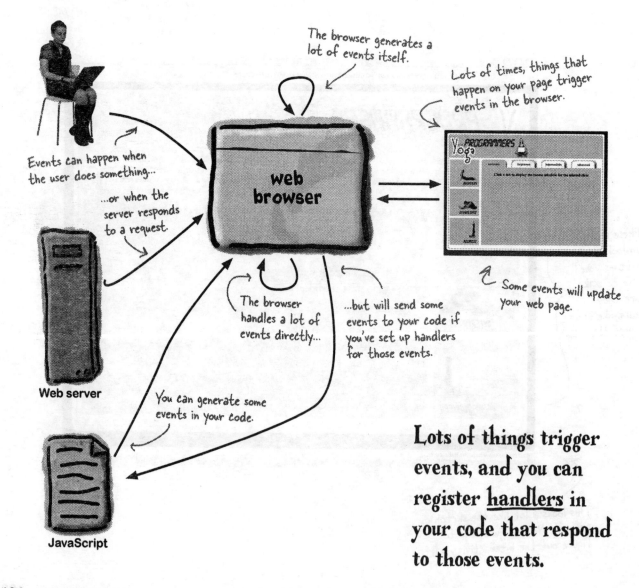

The browser generates a lot of events itself.

Lots of times, things that happen on your page trigger events in the browser.

Events can happen when the user does something...

...or when the server responds to a request.

Some events will update your web page.

The browser handles a lot of events directly...

...but will send some events to your code if you've set up handlers for those events.

Web server

You can generate some events in your code.

JavaScript

Lots of things trigger events, and you can register <u>handlers</u> in your code that respond to those events.

WHO DOES WHAT?

The names of most events give you a pretty good idea what they do.
Can you match the events to what they might be used for?

onclick

onfocus

onblur

onload

onmouseover

onmouseout

onsubmit

onresize

onerror

Use me when you want to validate a form before its contents are processed by a server-side program.

Use me when you want to provide audio feedback when a user has images disabled.

Use me when you want to scroll in on a portion of an image when a user clicks a certain spot of the image.

Use me when you want to let users know that increasing the width of the browser window could reduce their viewing experience.

Use me when you want to hide a submenu when the user moves away from a menu item.

Use me when you want to let a user know about the input format for a selected text field.

Use me when you want to change the color of a menu item when a user hovers over the item.

Use me when you want to give the user popup instructions for a form before they start using the form.

Use me when you want to validate a particular field every time data is entered into that field.

WHO DOES WHAT?
SOLUTION

The names of most events give you a pretty good idea what they do.
Your job was to match the events to what they might be used for.

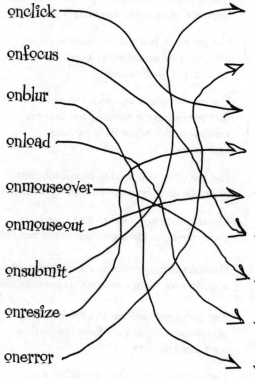

onclick

onfocus

onblur

onload

onmouseover

onmouseout

onsubmit

onresize

onerror

You want to validate a form before its contents
are processed by a server-side program.

You want to provide audio feedback when an
image can't be loaded.

You want to scroll in on a portion of an image
when a user clicks a certain spot of the image.

You want to let users know that increasing the
width of the browser window could reduce
their viewing experience.

You want to hide a submenu when the
user moves away from a menu item.

You want to let a user know about the
input format for a selected text field.

You want to change the color of a menu
item when a user hovers over the item.

You want to give the user popup instructions
for a form before they start using the form.

You want to validate a particular field
every time data is entered into that field.

Connect events on your web page to event handlers in your JavaScript

You've already used the `window.onload` event to trigger lots of setup work on web pages, and the `onclick` event to handle users clicking on an image. We can use these events, as well as the `onmouseover` event, to connect different parts of Marcy's yoga page to JavaScript functions we'll write.

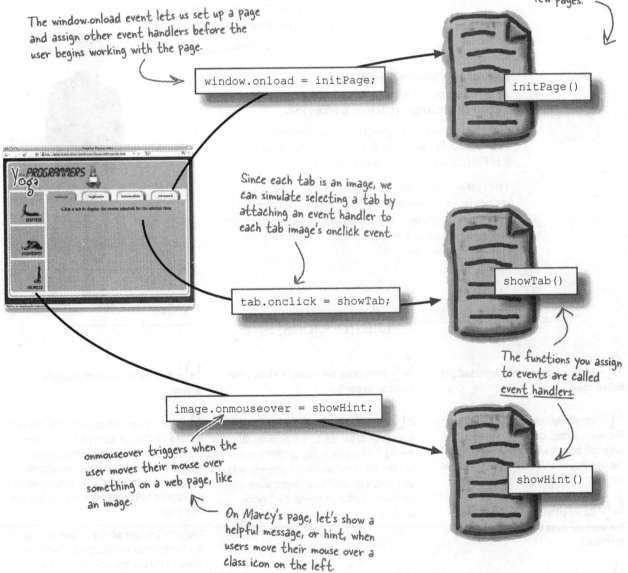

All of these functions will go in our schedule.js script... which we'll start on in just a few pages.

The window.onload event lets us set up a page and assign other event handlers before the user begins working with the page.

```
window.onload = initPage;
```

`initPage()`

Since each tab is an image, we can simulate selecting a tab by attaching an event handler to each tab image's onclick event.

```
tab.onclick = showTab;
```

`showTab()`

The functions you assign to events are called __event__ __handlers__.

```
image.onmouseover = showHint;
```

onmouseover triggers when the user moves their mouse over something on a web page, like an image.

On Marcy's page, let's show a helpful message, or hint, when users move their mouse over a class icon on the left.

`showHint()`

Use the window.onload event to initialize the rest of the interactivity on a web page

You've already used `window.onload` twice to initialize a page. We need to do the same thing in Marcy's yoga page because...

> Because
> we want to keep our behavior and
> content separate, right? We don't
> want our XHTML to have things like
> onclick="showTab()", yeah?

Assigning event handlers programmatically is one more way to separate content from behavior.

Anytime you can keep your JavaScript separate from your XHTML, you should. The same goes for XHTML and CSS: keep them separate.

The best way to assign event handlers is by using properties of the elements in your XHTML page, and doing that assignment in a function that runs before the user gets control of a page. `window.onload` is the perfect event for just that.

there are no
Dumb Questions

Q: So when does window.onload get called again?

A: Actually window.onload is an event. The event occurs, or fires, once the XHTML page has been read by the browser and all the files that XHTML references have been loaded.

Q: So when window.onload fires, the browser runs that event's handler function?

A: Exactly.

Q: How does the browser know what function to call?

A: The browser will call the function that you assign to the `onload` property of the `window` object. You set that property just like any other JavaScript property: with an equals sign. Just be sure you leave any parentheses off the name of the function:
`window.onload = initPage;`

Q: And we assign that property where?

A: The browser will run any code that isn't inside a function as soon as it encounters that code. So just put the window.onload assignment at the top of your JavaScript, outside of any function, and the assignment will happen before the user can interact with your page.

Then, the browser will fire onload and run the function you just assigned. That's your chance to set up the web page's other events.

JavaScript Magnets

You need to initialize Marcy's yoga page. Each left-side image and tab should display information about the rolled-over class. Additionally, clicking on a tab should select the class that's clicked. See if you can use the magnets below to build initPage(), as well as placeholders for the other functions referenced. For now, the placeholders can just display alert boxes.

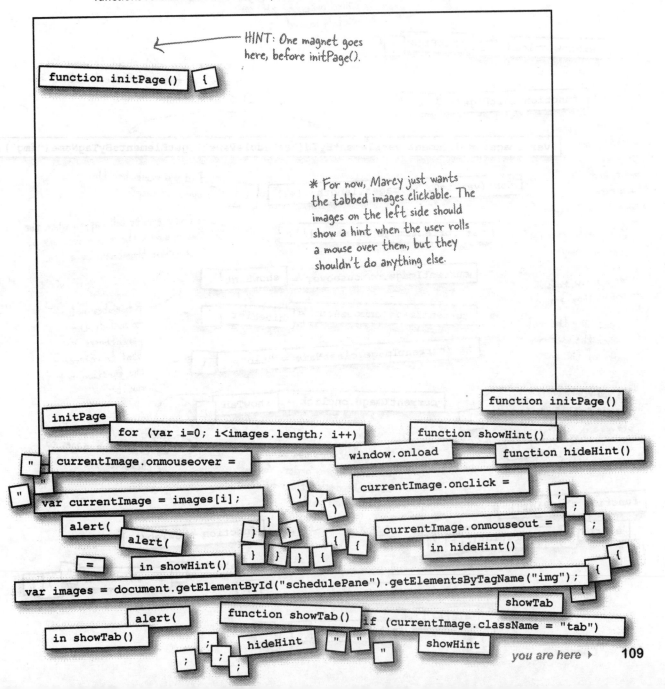

HINT: One magnet goes here, before initPage().

`function initPage()` `{`

* For now, Marcy just wants the tabbed images clickable. The images on the left side should show a hint when the user rolls a mouse over them, but they shouldn't do anything else.

`function initPage()`

`initPage`

`for (var i=0; i<images.length; i++)`

`function showHint()`

`window.onload`

`function hideHint()`

`currentImage.onmouseover =`

`"`

`currentImage.onclick =`

`;` `;`

`"` `"`

`var currentImage = images[i];`

`)` `)` `)`

`alert(`

`}`

`currentImage.onmouseout =`

`;`

`alert(`

`}` `}`

`{` `{`

`in hideHint()`

`=`

`in showHint()`

`}` `}` `}` `{`

`{` `{`

`var images = document.getElementById("schedulePane").getElementsByTagName("img");`

`showTab`

`alert(`

`function showTab()`

`if (currentImage.className = "tab")`

`in showTab()`

`;` `;`

`hideHint`

`"` `"`

`"`

`showHint`

`;` `;`

JavaScript Magnet Solution

Using the steps on page 16 and what you've learned about how events work in JavaScript, can you re-create the initialization code for Marcy's page?

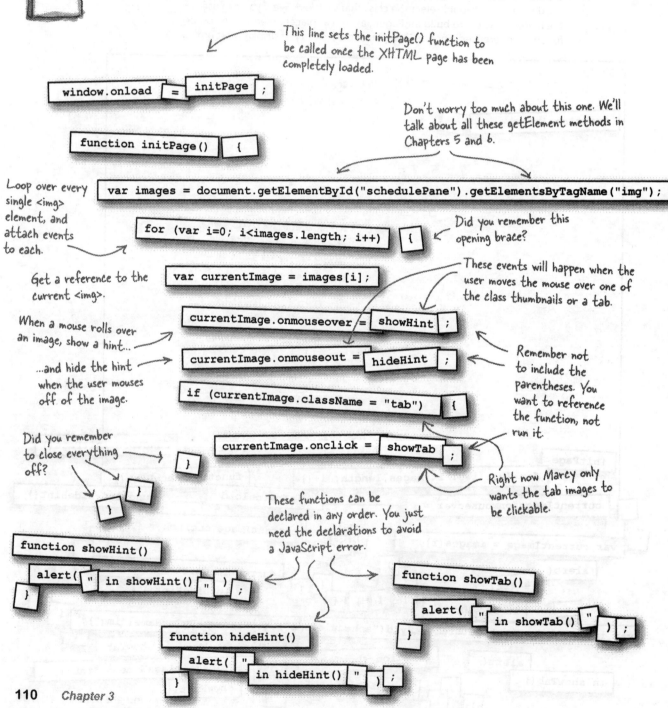

This line sets the initPage() function to be called once the XHTML page has been completely loaded.

```
window.onload = initPage ;
```

Don't worry too much about this one. We'll talk about all these getElement methods in Chapters 5 and 6.

```
function initPage ()  {
```

Loop over every single <img> element, and attach events to each.

```
var images = document.getElementById("schedulePane").getElementsByTagName("img");
```

```
for (var i=0; i<images.length; i++)  {
```

Did you remember this opening brace?

Get a reference to the current <img>.

```
var currentImage = images[i];
```

When a mouse rolls over an image, show a hint...

```
currentImage.onmouseover = showHint ;
```

These events will happen when the user moves the mouse over one of the class thumbnails or a tab.

...and hide the hint when the user mouses off of the image.

```
currentImage.onmouseout = hideHint ;
```

```
if (currentImage.className = "tab")  {
```

Remember not to include the parentheses. You want to reference the function, not run it.

Did you remember to close everything off?

```
}
```
```
}
```
```
}
```

```
currentImage.onclick = showTab ;
```

Right now Marcy only wants the tab images to be clickable.

These functions can be declared in any order. You just need the declarations to avoid a JavaScript error.

```
function showHint ()
  alert( " in showHint() " ) ;
}
```

```
function showTab ()
  alert( " in showTab() " ) ;
}
```

```
function hideHint ()
  alert( " in hideHint() " ) ;
}
```

TEST DRIVE

Create schedule.js, and add the functions shown on the last page. Don't forget to assign initPage to the window.onload event, too. Then, test things out in your web browser.

Roll your mouse over a tab. You should see an alert for showHint(), and then hideHint(). Try and click on a tab, too. Do you get a showTab() alert? What about clicking on an image on the left? Nothing should happen there right now.

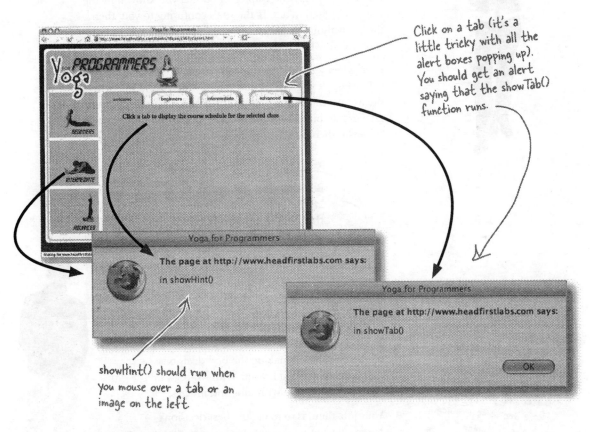

Click on a tab (it's a little tricky with all the alert boxes popping up). You should get an alert saying that the showTab() function runs.

showHint() should run when you mouse over a tab or an image on the left.

How do you like this user interface? Is there anything you would change?

Look, you can say what you want, but I still think those images over on the left look like buttons. Navigation's almost always on the left. Are we just going to ignore like a hundred years of web design?

If a web page is confusing to <u>YOU</u>, it will almost certainly be confusing to your users.

When you design and implement a site, you know how the site is supposed to act. If the site's confusing to you, then users—without the benefit of the information you have—will probably be even more confused.

Even when you don't get to control the design of a site, like with Marcy's yoga page, you should still try and make the site as unconfusing as possible. If that means turning some images into buttons to avoid users clicking on those images endlessly, then do it!

But isn't that confusing, too? If the images are clickable, then you've got two forms of navigation: tabs and images.

Sometimes you have to make a choice between okay and better.

This can even happen when you design a site that a customer loves. Later on, you realize there are some problems, but the customer doesn't want to make any changes because they like what they've already seen. →

If you're not in control of a site's design, you're often stuck making the best decisions based on an existing layout. With Marcy's site, she liked the design with tabs and images.

Your job, then, is to make the best decisions based on what you've got. In this case, that means two forms of navigation to avoid user-confusion. Otherwise, non-clickable images on the left might be construed as buttons.

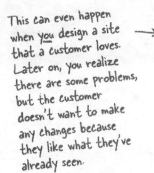

Change those left-side images to be clickable

It's a piece of cake to make the images on the left-hand side of Marcy's page clickable. In fact, all we need to do is *remove* code:

```javascript
function initPage() {
  var images =
    document.getElementById("schedulePane").getElementsByTagName("img");
  for (var i=0; i<images.length; i++) {
    var currentImage = images[i];
    currentImage.onmouseover = showHint;
    currentImage.onmouseout = hideHint;
    if (currentImage.className=="tab") {
      currentImage.onclick = showTab;
    }
  }
}
```

We don't want just the tabs to be clickable... we want all images, including the left-hand ones, to be clickable.

Don't forget to remove the closing brace.

schedule.js

window.onload = initPage; writeHeader=

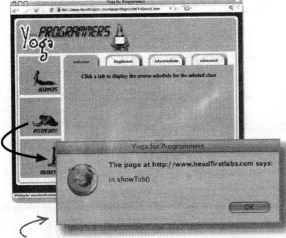

Try it out... each image should call showTab() now.

Good web pages aren't confusing

A good web page is as intuitive as possible. If something looks like a button, make it a button. And if part of a site is confusing to you, the web programmer, it's probably even more confusing to a user.

Use your XHTML's content and structure

showHint() is called when a user rolls their mouse over a tab or image.
But how do we know which tab or image is being rolled over? For that, we
need to take another look at Marcy's XHTML:

```
... XHTML for page head and body...
  <div id="schedulePane">
    <img id="logo" alt="logo" src="images/logo.png" />
    <div id="navigation">
      <img src="images/beginnersBtn.png" alt="Beginners Yoga"
        title="beginners" class="nav" />
      <img src="images/intermediateBtn.png" alt="Intermediate Yoga"
        title="intermediate" class="nav"/>
      <img src="images/advancedBtn.png" alt="Advanced Yoga"
        title="advanced" class="nav"/>
    </div>

    <div id="tabs">
      <img src="images/welcomeTabActive.png" title="welcome" class="tab" />
      <img src="images/beginnersTabInactive.png" title="beginners" class="tab" />
      <img src="images/intermediateTabInactive.png"
           title="intermediate" class="tab" />
      <img src="images/advancedTabInactive.png" title="advanced" class="tab" />
    </div>
```

Each image has a title attribute that identifies the class level.

The tab graphics use the same titles.

classes.html

Every XHTML element is accessible in your JavaScript code as an object

You've been using getElementById() to access the images in
Marcy's XHTML page. That works because each element in the
XHTML is represented by the browser as an object you can manipulate
in your JavaScript.

Even better, all the attributes on an element are stored as properties on
the JavaScript object that represents that element. Since Marcy's images
have titles, we can use those titles to figure out which image or tab was
selected and show the right hint.

<img>

title = "advanced"

The title attribute becomes a property of the JavaScript object that represents the <img> element.

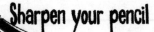

Sharpen your pencil

showHint() should display a short hint-style message about each class when a user rolls their mouse over an image. But the hint should only appear if the welcome tab is selected; if one of the classes is selected, hints are disabled. Your job is to complete the code for showHint() that's started below.

```
var welcomePaneShowing = ................;
```

← This is a global variable: it's outside any functions. It should indicate if the welcome pane is showing, which is the only time we want to show hints.

```
function showHint() {

  alert("in showHint()");

  if (!.............................. ) {

    return;

  }


  switch (this...................) {

    case " ...................... ":

      var hintText = "Just getting started? Come join us!";

      break;

    case " ...................... ":

      var ............ = "Take your flexibility to the next level!";

      break;

    case " ...................... ":

      var hintText =

        "Perfectly join your body and mind with these intensive workouts.";

      ....................

  ................ :

      var ............ = "Click a tab to display the course schedule for the class";

  }

  var contentPane = ...............................("content");

  ..................innerHTML = "<h3>" + ............ + "</h3>";

}
```

Sharpen your pencil
Solution

Your job was to complete the showHint function to display a hint based on the title of the image.

```
var welcomePaneShowing = ....true....;
```

When the page loads, the welcome pane is showing. So we start out with this set to true.

Make sure this variable is declared outside of initPage(), showHint(), or any other function.

```
function showHint() {
    alert("in showHint()");

    if (! welcomePaneShowing ) {

        return;

    }
```

If we're not on the welcome page, don't do anything. Just return.

"this" refers to whatever object called this function. That's the image that the user rolled over.

"title" is the attribute of the XHTML page we want to check... so we access it with the "title" property of the image.

```
    switch (this. title ) {

      case " beginners ":

        var hintText = "Just getting started? Come join us!";

        break;

      case " intermediate ":

        var hintText = "Take your flexibility to the next level!";

        break;

      case " advanced ":

        var hintText =

            "Perfectly join your body and mind with these intensive workouts.";

        break;
      default :

        var hintText = "Click a tab to display the course schedule for the class";

    }

    var contentPane = getElementById ("content");

    contentPane .innerHTML = "<h3>" + hintText + "</h3>";

}
```

For each different class level, we want to set some hint text

It's always good practice to have a default in your switch statements. Our default can just be a generic instruction message.

All that's left is to get the <div> where the content is shown, and show the hint text.

window.onload...
initPage;
writeHeader: ...

schedule.js

Add the code for hideHint(), too

The code for hideHint() is simple once showHint() is done. You just
need to grab the content pane, and set the hint text back to the default:

```
function hideHint() {
  alert("in hideHint()");
  if (welcomePaneShowing) {
    var contentPane = document.getElementById("content");
    contentPane.innerHTML =
      "<h3>Click a tab to display the course schedule for the class</h3>";
  }
}
```

This is basically the reverse of showHint(). The function grabs the content <div> and sets the text to the default message.

schedule.js

TEST DRIVE

**Update schedule.js. Add a welcomePaneShowing variable, and update
the showHint() and hideHint() functions. Then try everything out.**

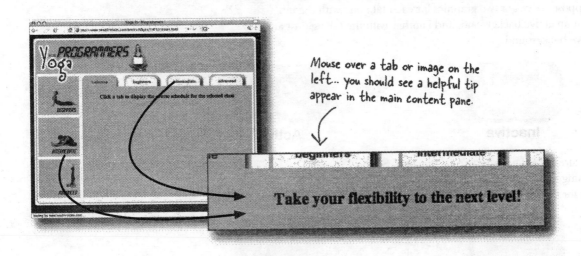

Mouse over a tab or image on the left... you should see a helpful tip appear in the main content pane.

Take your flexibility to the next level!

Tabs: an optical (and graphical) illusion

Marcy likes the look and feel of tabs on her yoga page. While there are lots of fancy toolkits that let you create tabs, a simple graphical trick is all we need.

On the yoga page, we've got a main content pane that's dark green. So that color basically becomes the "active" color. The Welcome tab starts out that color, and the other tabs are a lighter color, the "inactive" color:

These tabs are inactive... they're a lighter color.

The Welcome tab is active: it's a darker color.

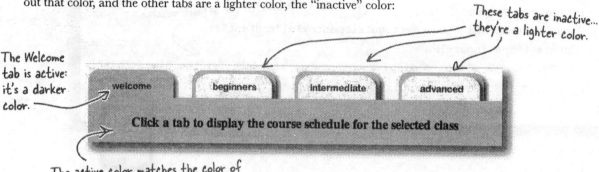

The active color matches the color of the main content pane.

To make a tab active, we need to change the tab's background to the "active" color

All we need to do to make a different tab active is change it to the active color. Then, we can make the old active tab inactive by changing it to the inactive color.

So suppose we've got two graphics for each tab: one with the tab against an active background, and another with the tab against an inactive background:

This is the inactive tab.

Here's the same tab in an active version.

Inactive   **Active**

We've already got a `showTab()` function. So the first thing that function should do is change the tab image for the clicked-on tab.

Inactive   **Active**

Use a for... loop to cycle through the images

You've already used the `title` property of the image objects in `showHint()` to change the hint text. We need to do something similar in `showTab()`: figure out which tab should be active, and change that tab to the active image. For all the other tabs, we just want the inactive image.

```
function showTab() {
  alert("in showTab()");
  var selectedTab = this.title;

  var images = document.getElementById("tabs").getElementsByTagName("img");
  for (var i=0; i<images.length; i++) {
    var currentImage = images[i];
    if (currentImage.title == selectedTab) {
      currentImage.src = "images/" + currentImage.title + "Top.png";
    } else {
      currentImage.src = "images/" + currentImage.title + "Down.png";
    }
  }
}
```

O

O

> You're kidding, right? What happened to all that business about separating behavior from presentation?

This event handler has a **LOT** of presentation-specific details.

`showTab()` now works directly with image names, and it actually builds those image names dynamically! So not only does `showTab()` mix behavior with presentation (the images), but it actually is depending on the content of the XHTML page—the title of each image—to figure out what presentation to use.

There's a real problem here. But what would **you** do to fix the problem? Think about how you would separate content, presentation, and behavior **before you turn the page.**

CSS classes are the key (again)

Marcy likes the look and feel of tabs on her yoga page. While there are lots of fancy toolkits that let you create tabs, a simple graphical trick is all we need.

For each tab, there are two possible states: active, which is the darker color that matches the content pane, and inactive, which is the lighter, unselected color. So we can build two CSS classes for each tab: one active, and one inactive.

Open up `yoga.css` in your app's `css/` directory, and add these lines:

```
#tabs a#welcome.active {
  background: url('../images/welcomeTabActive.png') no-repeat;
}

#tabs a#welcome.inactive {
  background: url('../images/welcomeTabInactive.png') no-repeat;
}

#tabs a#beginners.active {
  background: url('../images/beginnersTabActive.png') no-repeat;
}

#tabs a#beginners.inactive {
  background: url('../images/beginnersTabInactive.png') no-repeat;
}

#tabs a#intermediate.active {
  background: url('../images/intermediateTabActive.png') no-repeat;
}

#tabs a#intermediate.inactive {
  background: url('../images/intermediateTabInactive.png') no-repeat;
}

#tabs a#advanced.active {
  background: url('../images/advancedTabActive.png') no-repeat;
}

#tabs a#advanced.inactive {
  background: url('../images/advancedTabInactive.png') no-repeat;
}
```

Each tab has an active class with the active image...

...and an inactive class with the inactive tab image.

There are two classes for each tab.

This CSS can go anywhere in yoga.css. It's up to you.

```
#tabs {
...
}
```

yoga.css

Ummm... but the tabs aren't <a>'s !

Did you notice what element the CSS is styling? #tab indicates a <div> with an id of "tab." That's okay. But then, the CSS indicates it's styling <a> tags, with ids of "welcome," "beginners," and so on. That doesn't match Marcy's XHTML page at all.

But that's no big deal... we can change all the images on the XHTML page to <a> tags to separate one more layer of content from presentation.

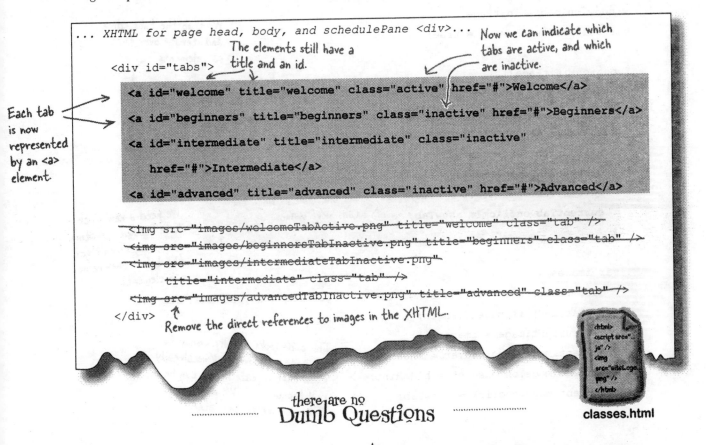

... XHTML for page head, body, and schedulePane <div>...

Now we can indicate which tabs are active, and which are inactive.

The elements still have a title and an id.

```
<div id="tabs">

  <a id="welcome" title="welcome" class="active" href="#">Welcome</a>

  <a id="beginners" title="beginners" class="inactive" href="#">Beginners</a>

  <a id="intermediate" title="intermediate" class="inactive"

    href="#">Intermediate</a>

  <a id="advanced" title="advanced" class="inactive" href="#">Advanced</a>
```

Each tab is now represented by an <a> element.

```
  <img src="images/welcomeTabActive.png" title="welcome" class="tab" />
  <img src="images/beginnersTabInactive.png" title="beginners" class="tab" />
  <img src="images/intermediateTabInactive.png"
       title="intermediate" class="tab" />
  <img src="images/advancedTabInactive.png" title="advanced" class="tab" />
</div>
```

Remove the direct references to images in the XHTML.

classes.html

there are no Dumb Questions

Q: Why is the href set to "#"?

A: # references the current page. We don't want the tabs to take the user anywhere else, although later we'll write code so that clicking on a tab shows the selected class's schedule.

Q: If we're not taking the user anywhere, why use <a> elements?

A: Because the tabs are ultimately links. They link to each class schedule, even if it's in a slightly non-traditional way. So the best XHTML element for a link is <a>.

On the other hand, there are usually at least two or three ways to do something on the Web. You could use a <span> element, a <div>, or even an image map. It's really up to you. As long as you can attach event handlers to the element, you're good to go.

This broke our JavaScript, too, didn't it?

We've got a nice, clean XHTML page and some CSS that truly controls the presentation of the page. But now all that JavaScript that depended on <img> elements isn't going to work. That's okay, though, because even though it worked before, it mixed images in with behavior... a real problem.

Let's fix up our script, and separate all that presentation from the behavior of the yoga page.

```javascript
window.onload = initPage;
var welcomePaneShowing = true;


function initPage() {
  var tabs =
    document.getElementById("tabs").getElementsByTagName("a");
  for (var i=0; i<tabs.length; i++) {
    var currentTab = tabs[i];
    currentTab.onmouseover = showHint;
    currentTab.onmouseout = hideHint;
    currentTab.onclick = showTab;
  }

  var images =
    document.getElementById("schedulePane").getElementsByTagName("img");
  for (var i=0; i<images.length; i++) {
    var currentImage = images[i];
    currentImage.onmouseover = showHint;
    currentImage.onmouseout = hideHint;
    currentImage.onclick = showTab;
  }
}


function showHint() {
  // showHint() stays the same
}

function hideHint() {
  // hideHint() stays the same
}
```

We grab the tabs <div>, and iterate over the <a> elements.

This isn't much different... the events and handlers are the same as when the tabs were images.

We need a new block here because iterating over images won't get the tabs... they're now <a> elements.

This code looks awfully similar to the code up above, and we already know that repeated code can be a real trouble spot. We might need to come back to this later.

```
function showTab() {
  var selectedTab = this.title;
```

> This is the same loop as in initPage(). We want all the <a> tags in the tabs <div>.

```
var tabs = document.getElementById("tabs").getElementsByTagName("a");
for (var i=0; i<tabs.length; i++) {
  var currentTab = tabs[i];
  if (currentTab.title == selectedTab) {
    currentTab.className = 'active';
  } else {
    currentTab.className = 'inactive';
  }
}
}
```

> No image names. Now we just change out the CSS classes. Much better!

schedule.js

TEST DRIVE

You've got a lot of changes to make. Update classes.html, yoga.css, and schedule.js. Then, see if those tabs work... try clicking on each.

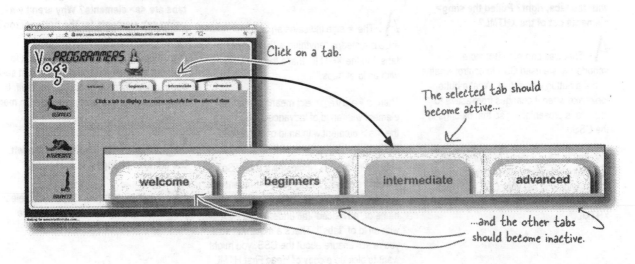

Click on a tab.

The selected tab should become active...

...and the other tabs should become inactive.

> Wow, so it takes a lot of work to separate content from presentation and behavior, especially if you don't do things that way from the beginning.

The earlier you separate your content from your presentation and behavior, the easier that separation will be.

With Marcy's site, we didn't really think about content or presentation early on, and it's only when we were a few functions into our behavior (the JavaScript) that we saw problems. If we'd planned from the start to keep images out of our code, and let our CSS handle all the presentation, we'd have fewer changes to make to our JavaScript.

Still, even if you find problems late in the process, it's almost always better to do the work to really separate out content, presentation, and behavior. Your app will be a lot better for the work you put into it.

there are no Dumb Questions

Q: So should I never have images in my XHTML? That's basically what we did with the tabs, right? Pulled the `<img>` elements out of the XHTML?

A: That was part of it. But more importantly, we used CSS to control whether or not a button was active. What a button looks like when it changes from active to inactive is presentation, so that belongs in the CSS.

It's okay to have images in your XHTML; just make sure that if those images are tied to behavior, you get your CSS and code involved, and keep those details out of your XHTML.

Q: That CSS confused me. What does "#tabs a#advanced.inactive" mean?

A: The # sign indicates an id. So `#tabs` means "anything with an id of 'tabs'." In the XHTML, that's the `<div>` with an id of "tabs."

Then, `a#advanced` means "for an `<a>` element with an id of 'advanced'." So that's the `<a>` element with an id of "advanced" nested within a `<div>` with an id of "tabs."

And finally, the "`.`" indicates a class. So `a#advanced.inactive` means the `<a>` element with an id of "tabs" and a class name of "advanced" (all under a `<div>` with an id of "tabs"). That's a mouthful, so if you're still unsure about the CSS, you might want to pick up a copy of Head First HTML with CSS & XHTML to help you out.

Q: Isn't it sort of weird that all the buttons on the left are images, but all the tabs are `<a>` elements? Why aren't we using `<a>` elements for the buttons, too?

A: Good question. We'll come back to that, but anytime you notice things that seem out of place, jot down a note to yourself. It might be something worth looking at in more detail.

Q: When I click a button on the left, the tab also changes. Is that right?

A: What do you think? When you select the "advanced" button, do you think the "advanced" tab should become active?

Sharpen your pencil

We've gotten a lot done, but showTab() is still incomplete. We've got to show the schedule for a selected class when a tab is clicked on. Assume the schedule is an HTML description and a table that shows the days of the week that the selected class is available. There will also probably be an "Enroll button."

How should we store the details and schedule for each class? In an HTML file? In the JavaScript? Why did you choose the format you did? ....

....

....

....

How would you replace the main content pane with the schedule and details for a selected class? ....

....

....

....

Does your solution:

☐ Separate the content of your page from its presentation?

☐ Separate the content of your page from its behavior?

☐ Separate the behavior of your page from its presentation?

Ajax is all about INTERACTION. Your page can interact with server-side programs, elements within itself, and even other pages.

> Well, the first part's easy. If the schedule and description is HTML, we should store that as an HTML page.

Jill: You mean *X*-HTML, right?

Joe: Well, yeah.

Frank: As an entire page? That's no good... we don't want to recreate all the tabs and stuff for each class, do we?

Joe: Well, then how about an XHTML fragment. Like, just the elements and text for the actual schedule and class description.

Jill: Yeah, because there's no way we want all that content in our JavaScript. And if we use XHTML, we can use the same CSS styles as in the main page.

Frank: But how do we load up that... what? XHTML fragment—

Joe: Sure.

Frank: —okay, right. So how do we load it?

Joe: Well, the tabs are `<a>` elements. Maybe we put the fragments in the `href` attributes instead of those # symbols?

Frank: But that would replace the entire page. That's no good. Besides, it seems sort of slow...

Jill: Guys, what about using a request object?

Joe: What do you mean?

Jill: What if we use a request object to get the XHTML fragment, and just set the content pane's `innerHTML` to the returned page?

Frank: Can you even do that?

Jill: Why not? Instead of requesting a server-side program, we'll just request the XHTML fragment we want.

Joe: And we can do it asynchronously, so there's no waiting or page refreshing!

Use a request object to fetch the class details from the server

The server doesn't need to do any processing for Marcy's page, but we can still use a request object to grab the XHTML fragments for each class. This is a request to the server, but it's just for a page rather than a program. Still, the details are the same as you've already seen.

We'll build the code the same way we always do, using the `createRequest()` function from `utils.js` and a callback to display the results in the content pane. Here's what we need:

schedule.js

```
function showTab() {
    var selectedTab = this.title;

    // set each tab's CSS class

    var request = createRequest();
    if (request==null) {
        alert("Unable to create request");
        return;
    }
    request.onreadystatechange = showSchedule;
    request.open("GET", selectedTab + ".html", true);
    request.send(null);
}

function showSchedule() {
    if (request.readyState == 4) {
        if (request.status == 200) {
            document.getElementById("content").innerHTML =
                request.responseText;
        }
    }
}
```

This is the part of the showTab() function that you've already written.

This is the same request creation code we've been using for talking to server-side programs

This time we're sending the request object to a page URL. So we need to name the fragments beginner.html, intermediate.html, and advanced.html.

he showSchedule() allback function s called when the equest returns.

The XHTML in the file is available in responseText. We can display the XHTML using the innerHTML property of the content page.

⚛ BRAIN POWER

Make these changes to schedule.js, and try out the improved web page. Is everything working? Are there any changes you'd make?

Be careful when you have two functions changing the same part of a web page

There's a bug! Class schedules show up okay, but mousing over another tab or button image hides the class schedule and replaces the content pane with hint text. That doesn't seem too intuitive...

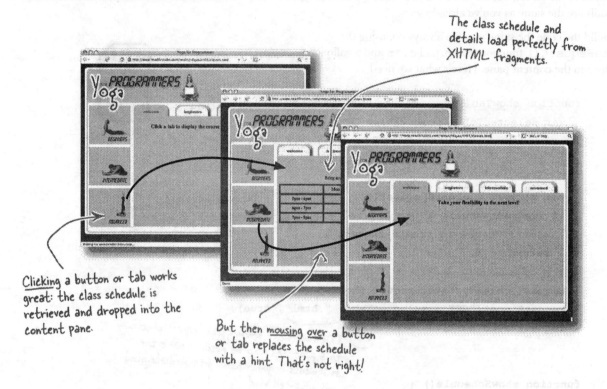

The class schedule and details load perfectly from XHTML fragments.

Clicking a button or tab works great: the class schedule is retrieved and dropped into the content pane.

But then mousing over a button or tab replaces the schedule with a hint. That's not right!

Make sure you have the class XHTML fragments.

XHTML fragments for each class are included in the examples download from Head First Labs. Make sure they're named `beginner.html`, `intermediate.html`, and `advanced.html`. They should be in the same directory as your main page, `classes.html`.

Sharpen your pencil

It's time to finish up Marcy's page. You need to change the JavaScript so that hints only show when the welcome tab is active. If a class is selected, no hints should appear. Mark up, cross out, and add to the code below to finish up schedule.js. To help you out, we've only shown the parts of the script that you need to change or add to, and parts that are relevant to those changes. Good luck!

```javascript
var welcomePaneShowing = true;

function showHint() {
  if (!welcomePaneShowing) {
    return;
  }
  // code to show hints based on which tab is selected
}


function showTab() {
  var selectedTab = this.title;

  var tabs = document.getElementById("tabs").getElementsByTagName("a");
  for (var i=0; i<tabs.length; i++) {
    var currentTab = tabs[i];
    if (currentTab.title == selectedTab) {
      currentTab.className = 'active';
    } else {
      currentTab.className = 'inactive';
    }
  }
  var request = createRequest();
  if (request == null) {
    alert("Unable to create request");
    return;
  }
  request.onreadystatechange = showSchedule;
  request.open("GET", selectedTab + ".html", true);
  request.send(null);
}
```

Sharpen your pencil
Solution

Your job was to finish up the code so that tabs selected classes and turned off hints. Hints should only appear when the Welcome tab is active.

```
var welcomePaneShowing = true;
```

This is the key variable. This should indicate if the welcome pane is showing. If it's not, we don't want to show any hints.

```
function showHint() {
  if (!welcomePaneShowing) {
    return;
  }
  // code to show hints based on which tab is selected
}
```

We've already got a check in showHint() for the welcome pane... so we just need to make sure this variable is set correctly.

```
function showTab() {
  var selectedTab = this.title;
```

Here's the new code. First, we need to see if the selected tab is the Welcome tab.

```
  if (selectedTab == "welcome") {
```

If so, we should update the welcomePaneShowing variable.

```
    welcomePaneShowing = true;

    document.getElementById("content").innerHTML =
```

You get bonus credit if you figured this out. If the welcome pane is selected, we need to overwrite any class schedule with the welcome message...

This really is a hack... we're putting presentation in our JavaScript! You'll learn a way to avoid this when you get into the DOM in Chapters 5 and 6.

```
      "⁰⁰h3⁹⁹Click a tab to display the course schedule for the class⁰⁰/h3⁹⁹";

  } else {

    welcomePaneShowing = false;

  }
```

...otherwise, the welcome pane will have a class schedule, and it won't even be clear which class is showing!

If any other tab is selected, update welcomePaneShowing to false. Now no hints will show because of the if statement in showHint().

```
  // everything else stayed the same!
}
```

there are no
Dumb Questions

Q: What if I didn't catch the bit about changing the content pane back to the welcome message when the Welcome tab is selected?

A: That's okay. Make sure you add that code to your copy of schedule.js, though. One way you can avoid missing things like that in the future is to always test your code. Load up the yoga class page, and click and move the mouse around... does anything look funny? If so, then make whatever changes you need to fix that problem.

Test Drive

Make sure you've got the XHTML fragments, the updated CSS, the clean XHTML class page (with no presentation!), and your completed copy of schedule.js. Load up Marcy's web page, and give it a spin.

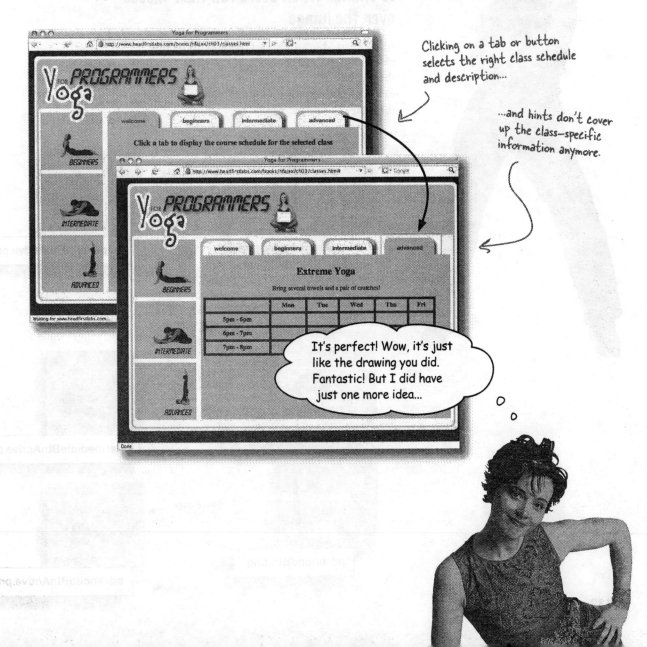

Clicking on a tab or button selects the right class schedule and description...

...and hints don't cover up the class-specific information anymore.

It's perfect! Wow, it's just like the drawing you did. Fantastic! But I did have just one more idea...

> I have more images of the different yoga classes. Wouldn't it be cool if when you moused over one of those left-hand images, the image changed?

Marcy wants the images on the left to change when users roll their mouse over the image

It's too bad Marcy didn't let us know about this earlier, but this still shouldn't be too hard. So when the page loads, the images should look one way, but each time a user rolls their mouse over the button, the image should change.

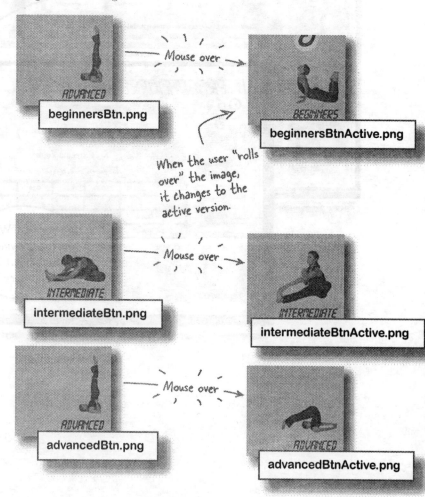

beginnersBtn.png

Mouse over

beginnersBtnActive.png

When the user "rolls over" the image, it changes to the active version.

intermediateBtn.png

Mouse over

intermediateBtnActive.png

advancedBtn.png

Mouse over

advancedBtnActive.png

When you need to change images in your script, think "change CSS classes" instead

Here's another case where separation of presentation and behavior can be a big issue. Before changing any code, think, "Is this a case where I'm going to have to mix my behavior (my code) and my presentation (like images)?"

If it is, it's time to restructure some things. The image buttons are really just like the tabs. They just look like buttons instead of tabs. So let's add some new CSS classes for both button states: the normal button and the active button.

```css
#navigation a {
  display: block;  float: left;
  height: 0;  margin: 0 0 10px 0;
  overflow: hidden;  padding: 140px 0 0 0;
  width: 155px;  z-index: 200;
}
```

These rules apply to all the <a>'s and handle positioning and sizing.

```css
#navigation a#beginners {
  background: url('../images/beginnersBtn.png') no-repeat;
}
```

By default, buttons use one image...

```css
#navigation a#beginners.active {
  background: url('../images/beginnersBtnActive.png') no-repeat;
}
```

...and when a button is active, it uses a different image.

```css
#navigation a#intermediate {
  background: url('../images/intermediateBtn.png') no-repeat;
}

#navigation a#intermediate.active {
  background: url('../images/intermediateBtnActive.png') no-repeat;
}

#navigation a#advanced {
  background: url('../images/advancedBtn.png') no-repeat;
}

#navigation a#advanced.active {
  background: url('../images/advancedBtnActive.png') no-repeat;
}
```

```
#tabs {
...
}
```

yoga.css

Just like with the classes for the tabs, these can go anywhere in your CSS.

Links in XHTML are represented by \<a\> elements

Here's another place where we can make some improvements to our
XHTML. Currently, the images are represented by \<img\> tags, but
they really are functioning as linking buttons: you can click on one to
get a class schedule.

Let's change each button to an \<a\>, which better represents
something you can click on to get to a different destination, in this
case a class schedule and description.

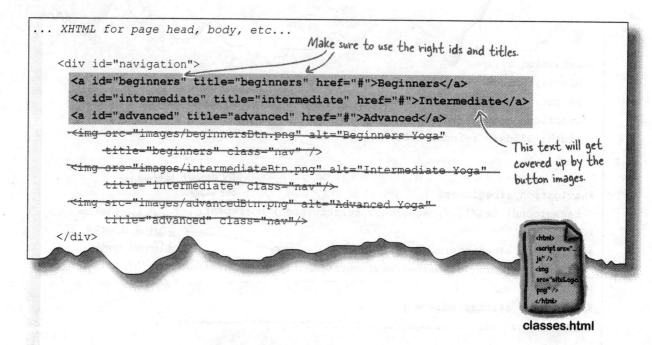

Make sure to use the right ids and titles.

```
... XHTML for page head, body, etc...

    <div id="navigation">
        <a id="beginners" title="beginners" href="#">Beginners</a>
        <a id="intermediate" title="intermediate" href="#">Intermediate</a>
        <a id="advanced" title="advanced" href="#">Advanced</a>
        <img src="images/beginnersBtn.png" alt="Beginners Yoga"
            title="beginners" class="nav" />
        <img src="images/intermediateBtn.png" alt="Intermediate Yoga"
            title="intermediate" class="nav"/>
        <img src="images/advancedBtn.png" alt="Advanced Yoga"
            title="advanced" class="nav"/>
    </div>
```

This text will get covered up by the button images.

classes.html

there are no Dumb Questions

Q: With the tabs, we had an inactive class and an
active class. But on the buttons, they're in the XHTML
without a class, and then there's a CSS "active" class
description with the active image. Why don't we have
an inactive CSS class with these buttons, too?

A: Good question. With the tabs, there were two
distinct states: active (in the forefront) and inactive (in
the background). The buttons we have, though, really
have a normal state, where they sit flat, and an active
state, where the button is highlighted. So it seemed
more accurate to have a button (with no class), and then
assign that button the "active" class when it's rolled over.
Uniformity is a good thing, though, so you could probably
use inactive and active classes if you felt strongly about it.

We need a function to show an active button and hide a button, too

Before we change any of schedule.js, let's add two functions we know we'll need. First, we need a `buttonOver()` function to show the active image for a button. That's just a matter of changing a CSS class:

```
function buttonOver() {
    this.className = "active";
}
```

> When the mouse is over a button, make it active.

We can do just the opposite for when a user's mouse rolls out of the button's area. We just need to change back to the default state, which is no CSS class:

```
function buttonOut() {
    this.className = "";
}
```

> When the mouse rolls out of a button, go back to the default state.

When you initialize the page, you need to assign the new event handlers

Now we need to assign the new functions to the right events. `buttonOver()` should get assigned to a button's onmouseover event, and `buttonOut()` gets assigned to a button's onmouseout event.

We can also update the code to use the new `<a>` elements that represent buttons instead of the older `<img>` elements.

```
function initPage() {
    // code to deal with tabs

    var buttons =
        document.getElementById("navigation").getElementsByTagName("a");
    for (var i=0; i<buttons.length; i++) {
        var currentBtn = buttons[i];
        currentBtn.onmouseover = showHint;
        currentBtn.onmouseout = hideHint;
        currentBtn.onclick = showTab;
        currentBtn.onmouseover = buttonOver;
        currentBtn.onmouseout = buttonOut;
    }
}
```

> We've changed the array that was called images to be called buttons.

> In our updated XHTML, we need all the `<a>` elements nested in the navigation `<div>`.

> Here are our new event handlers.

In JavaScript, an element is represented by an object. That object has a property for each event that can occur on the element that it represents.

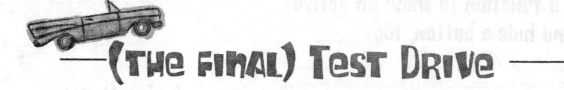

(The Final) Test Drive

Everything should work! Make all the changes from the last few pages to your XHTML, CSS, and JavaScript, and let's impress Marcy with her stunning new interactive class schedule page.

Roll over a button, and you should get the active version with a new image.

Not so fast... have you tried out the page? The images change, but what happened to all those helpful hints when you mouse over the buttons? They're gone!

What happened to the hints that were attached to the button's onmouseover and onmouseout events?

What would YOU do to make sure that Marcy's customers get cool interactive buttons AND helpful hints?

When you've got an idea, turn over to Chapter 4, and let's see how to take your event handling skills to the next level (literally).

4 multiple event handlers

Two's company

I was lost before you came along. I mean, I'm great at onclick, but without a little validation from you, I just wouldn't be that sure of myself.

A single event handler isn't always enough.

Sometimes you've got more than one event handler that needs to be called by an event. Maybe you've got some event-specific actions, as well as some generic code, and stuffing everything into a single event handler function won't cut it. Or maybe you're just trying to build **clean, reusable code**, and you've got **two bits of functionality** triggered by the **same event**. Fortunately, we can use some **DOM Level 2** methods to assign multiple handler functions to a **single event**.

An event can have only one event handler attached to it (or so it seems)

Marcy's page has a problem. We've assigned two event handlers to the `onmouseover` property of her image buttons:

```
function initPage() {
  // code to deal with tabs

  var buttons =
    document.getElementById("navigation").getElementsByTagName("a");
  for (var i=0; i<buttons.length; i++) {
    var currentBtn = buttons[i];
    currentBtn.onmouseover = showHint;
    currentBtn.onmouseout = hideHint;
    currentBtn.onclick = showTab;
    currentBtn.onmouseover = buttonOver;
    currentBtn.onmouseout = buttonOut;
  }
}
```

This is the same event: onmouseover for currentBtn. But we're assigning both the showHint() handler...

...and the buttonOver() handler.

Only the **LAST** event handler assigned gets run

When you assign two event handlers to the same event, only the last event handler that's assigned gets run. So on Marcy's page, mousing over a button triggers `onmouseover`. Then, that event runs the last handler assigned to it: `buttonOver()`.

The image is changing when you roll over a button, so buttonOver() is getting called.

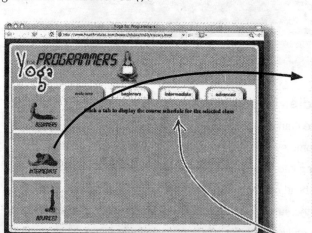

But there's no hint anymore. showHint() is not getting run.

Event handlers are just properties

When you assign an event handler to an event on an XHTML element,
the handler becomes a property of the element, just like the id or title
properties of an <a> element:

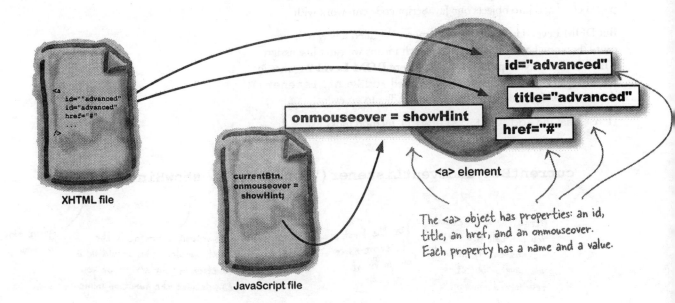

The <a> object has properties: an id,
title, an href, and an onmouseover.
Each property has a name and a value.

A property can have only <u>ONE</u> value

If you assign a value to a property, that property has that single value. So
what happens when you assign another value to that property? The property
then has the *new* value, and *the old value is gone*:

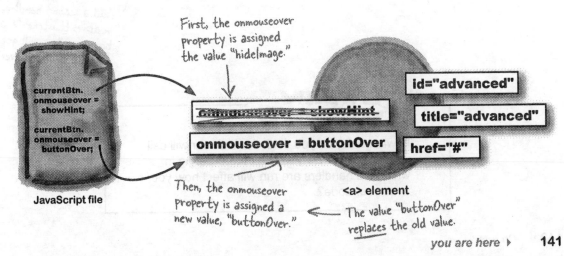

Assign multiple event handlers with addEventListener()

So far, we've been adding event handlers to elements by setting the event property directly. That's called the **DOM Level 0** model. DOM stands for the **Document Object Model**, and it's how elements on a web page get turned into objects our JavaScript code can work with.

But DOM Level 0 isn't cutting it anymore. We need a way to assign more than one handler to an event, which means we can't just assign a handler to an event property. That's where **DOM Level 2** comes in. DOM Level 2 gives us a new method, called addEventListener(), that lets us assign more than one event handler to an event.

Here's what the addEventListener() method looks like:

```
currentBtn.addEventListener("mouseover", showHint, false);
```

Here's the new method. You can call this method on any element you have an object representation for.

For the first argument, use the event name without the "on" in front.

The second argument is the event handler. This should be a function in your script, or you can declare the function inline.

Ignore this for now.

```
currentBtn.addEventListener("mouseover", buttonOver, false);
```

Add a second handler, using addEventListener(), and both handlers will get called for the specified event.

BRAIN POWER

In what order do you think the browser will call your handlers? Do you think the ordering in which the handlers are run will affect how you write your code?

there are no
Dumb Questions

Q: **DOM? What's that?**

A: DOM stands for the Document Object Model. It's a specification that defines how the parts of a web page, like elements and attributes, can be represented as objects that your code can work with.

Q: **And what does Level 0 mean?**

A: Level 0 was actually an interpretation of the DOM published *before* the DOM was formalized. So it works with the DOM but isn't really part of it.

For your purposes, though, DOM Level 0 is what your browser uses to come up with basic objects and properties for each element in a web page. When you assign a handler to an element's `onmouseover` property, you're using DOM Level 0.

Q: **What about DOM Level 1? Do I need to worry about that?**

A: Not right now. DOM Level 1 has to do with how you move around in a document. So DOM Level 1 lets you find the parent of an element, or its second child. We'll look at DOM navigation quite a bit in Chapter 6.

Right now, though, you don't really need to worry too much about what level of the DOM you're using, except to make sure your browser supports that level. All major browsers support DOM Level 0 and Level 1, which is why you can assign event handlers programmatically using event properties like `onclick` and `onmouseover`.

Q: **And addEventListener() is part of DOM Level 2?**

A: Exactly. DOM Level 2 added a lot of specifics about how events should work and dealt with some XML issues that aren't a problem for us right now.

Q: **So I can use addEventListener() to add multiple events, and it will work with all the browsers?**

A: As long as they support DOM Level 2. But there's one major browser that doesn't support DOM Level 2... we'll look at that in just a minute.

Q: **Couldn't I just assign an array to an event property, and give the property multiple values that way?**

A: That's a good idea, but it's the browser that connects events to event handlers. If you assigned an array of handler names to an event property, the web browser wouldn't know what to do with that array.

That's why DOM Level 2 was put into place: it provides a standard way for browsers to deal with multiple events. Ideally, specifications standardize a process and remove any possible guesswork.

Q: **Why are the event property names different than the names you pass to addEventListener()?**

A: That's another great question. That's just the way the authors of the DOM decided to handle event names. So if you're assigning an event property, use `onclick` or `onmouseover`. With `addEventListener()`, use `click` and `mouseover`.

Q: **What's that last parameter you're sending to addEventListener()? And why are you setting it to false?**

A: That last parameter indicates whether you want event bubbling (`false`) or capturing (`true`). We'll talk more about capturing and bubbling in a bit, so don't worry about this too much. For now, always pass false to `addEventListener()`, which indicates you want event bubbling.

You can assign as many handlers as you want to an event using addEventListener().

addEventListener() works in any web browser that supports DOM Level 2.

Your objects can have multiple event handlers assigned to a single event in DOM Level 2

The most important thing that DOM Level 2 added to events is the ability for an event to have more than one handler registered. You've already seen how `addEventListener()` adds a handler to an event:

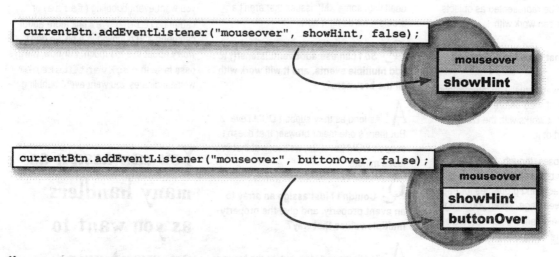

```
currentBtn.addEventListener("mouseover", showHint, false);
```

> mouseover
> **showHint**

```
currentBtn.addEventListener("mouseover", buttonOver, false);
```

> mouseover
> **showHint**
> **buttonOver**

The browser runs every handler for an event when that event is triggered

When an event is triggered by a mouse movement, the browser looks up the right event. Then, the browser runs every event handler function registered to that event:

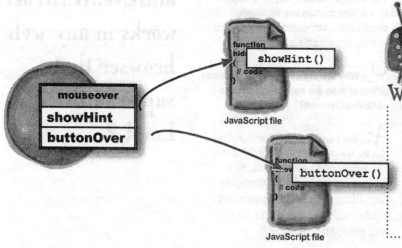

> mouseover
> **showHint**
> **buttonOver**

function
hid
showHint()
// code

JavaScript file

function
ov
buttonOver()
// code

JavaScript file

Watch it!

Event listeners aren't called in any particular order.

You might think that the browser calls the event handlers in the order they're added, but that's not guaranteed. Make sure that your handlers don't depend on the order in which they're called.

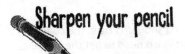

Sharpen your pencil

It's time to make some improvements to Marcy's yoga page. Below is the current code for initPage(). Your job is to cross out anything that shouldn't be in the code, and make any additions you think you need to get the image button mouse events to work.

schedule.js

```
function initPage() {

  var tabs =
    document.getElementById("tabs").getElementsByTagName("a");

  for (var i=0; i<tabs.length; i++) {

    var currentTab = tabs[i];

    currentTab.onmouseover = showHint;

    currentTab.onmouseout = hideHint;

    currentTab.onclick = showTab;

  }


  var buttons =
    document.getElementById("navigation").getElementsByTagName("a");

  for (var i=0; i<buttons.length; i++) {

    var currentBtn = buttons[i];

    currentBtn.onmouseover = showHint;

    currentBtn.onmouseout = hideHint;

    currentBtn.onclick = showTab;

    currentBtn.onmouseover = buttonOver;

    currentBtn.onmouseout = buttonOut;

  }

}
```

Sharpen your pencil
Solution

Your job was to cross out anything that shouldn't be in the code, and make any additions you thought you'd need to get the image button mouse events to work

```javascript
function initPage() {

  var tabs =

    document.getElementById("tabs").getElementsByTagName("a");

  for (var i=0; i<tabs.length; i++) {

    var currentTab = tabs[i];

    currentTab.onmouseover = showHint;

    currentTab.onmouseout = hideHint;

    currentTab.onclick = showTab;

  }


  var buttons =

    document.getElementById("navigation").getElementsByTagName("a");

  for (var i=0; i<buttons.length; i++) {

    var currentBtn = buttons[i];

    currentBtn.onmouseover = showHint;
    currentBtn.addEventListener("mouseover", showHint, false);
    currentBtn.onmouseout = hideHint;
    currentBtn.addEventListener("mouseout", hideHint, false);
    currentBtn.onclick = showTab;

    currentBtn.onmouseover = buttonOver;
    currentBtn.addEventListener("mouseover", buttonOver, false);
    currentBtn.onmouseout = buttonOut;
    currentBtn.addEventListener("mouseout", buttonOut, false);
  }

}
```

schedule.js

You could have changed these to addEventListener(), but there's really no reason to. They work fine as they are.

Remember, the event names are the same, but without the "on" before the name.

Both the mouseover and mouseout events need two handlers each.

Use false for each call right now... we'll talk more about bubbling and capturing later.

Test Drive

Change your copy of schedule.js, and fire up your web browser.
Try out the image buttons that now use addEventListener().
Does everything work?

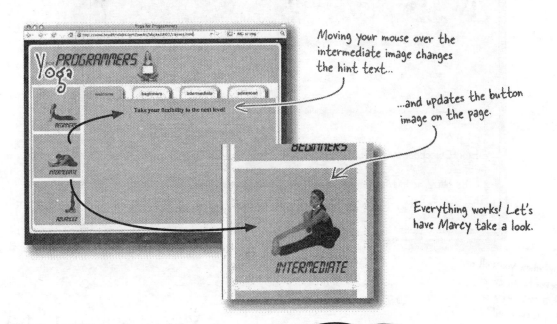

Moving your mouse over the intermediate image changes the hint text...

...and updates the button image on the page.

Everything works! Let's have Marcy take a look.

> Everything works? Are you kidding? Now the hints don't show up, **and** the images don't change. What's up with that?

What's going on with Marcy's browser?

What do you think is going wrong for Marcy? Why isn't the yoga app working?

....

....

....

....

Hint: Try different browsers out

What's going on with Internet Explorer?

The yoga page works great on Firefox, Safari, and a lot of other browsers... but something's definitely wrong on Internet Explorer:

IE shows a little triangular icon in the bottom status bar. Double-click that triangle to see this error message.

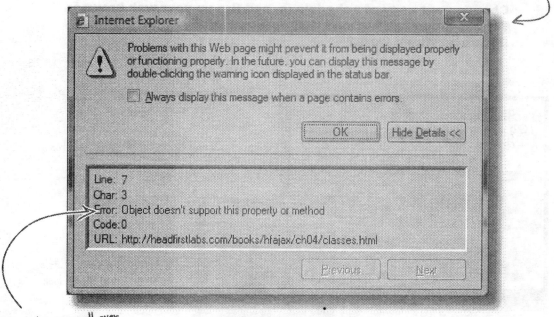

There's a problem when you roll over the images. IE reports an error... something about a property or method not being supported?

You can't control what browsers your users are working with.

It's your job to build cross-browser applications... and always test your code in **LOTS** of browsers.

Internet Explorer uses a totally different event model

Remember that addEventListener() only works on browsers that support DOM Level 2? Well, Internet Explorer isn't one of those browsers. IE has its own event model and doesn't support addEventListener(). That's why Marcy got an error trying the yoga page out on IE.

Fortunately, IE provides a method that does the same thing as addEventListener(). It's called attachEvent():

currentBtn.attachEvent("onmouseover", showHint);

This is the method that adds the event handler in Internet Explorer.

This time you keep the "on" at the beginning of the event name...

You still give the function the name of the handler to run when the event occurs.

That mysterious "false" disappears in attachEvent().

attachEvent() and addEventListener() are <u>functionally</u> <u>equivalent</u>

Even though the syntax is different, these functions do **exactly the same thing**. So you just need to use the right one for your users' browsers.

currentBtn.attachEvent("onmouseover", showHint);

Use attachEvent() for Internet Explorer browsers.

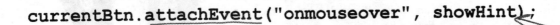

currentBtn.addEventListener("mouseover", showHint, false);

These are all DOM Level 2 browsers.

Use addEventListener() for Firefox...

...Opera...

...as well as Safari and most other modern browsers.

> Okay, I'm sorry, but that's totally stupid. What were the IE people thinking? Two functions that do the same thing?

The browser wars are just part of web development.

Like it or not, not all browsers are the same. Besides, when Microsoft came up with their own event model, it wasn't that obvious that the DOM Level 2 would take off like it did.

And no matter how it all happened, you can't write off people who use IE... or those who don't.

there are no
Dumb Questions

Q: So this is all about which browser is better?

A: No, it's just that not all browsers were developed the same way. It wasn't so long ago that the DOM wasn't a sure thing, and Microsoft just decided to go in another direction. IE isn't better or worse than other browsers; it's just different.

Q: Yeah, but everyone knows IE's a pain. I mean, come on...

A: It's true that lots of web developers think that IE is hard to deal with. That's just because it uses some different syntax. But look at things the other way: if you've been writing code on IE all your life, then it's really Firefox, Safari and Opera that are a pain.

Either way, you've got to write web apps that work on all major browsers, or you're going to miss out on a ton of users.

Q: Why does attachEvent() add the "on" back to the event name?

A: That's just the way IE decided to implement that method.

Q: What about that last argument to addEventListener()? Where did it go on attachEvent()?

A: You may remember that the last argument to addEventListener() indicated whether you wanted event bubbling (false) or event capturing (true). IE only supports event bubbling, so that argument isn't needed.

We'll come back to capturing and bubbling once we've got Marcy's app working on *all* major browsers.

Q: So which one should I use? addEventListener() or attachEvent()?

A: Good question. If you think about it and look back at the createRequest() function, you probably already know the answer...

In IE, event names have "on" in front, for example, "onclick" and "onmouseover."

In Firefox, Safari, and Opera, event names **DON'T** have "on" in front: "click" and "mouseover."

Utility Function Magnets

Just like with createRequest(), we need our event handling to work on
multiple browsers. Your job is to use the magnets below to build a utility
function for adding event handlers to events.

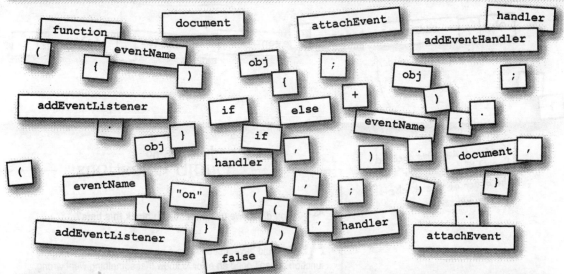

Hint: The expression (`document.someFunction`) returns true if a browser supports
running `someFunction()`, and returns false if that function isn't supported.

Utility Function Magnets Solutions

Your job was to figure out a way to get our event handling to run on
multiple browsers. You should have built a utility function for adding
event handlers to events.

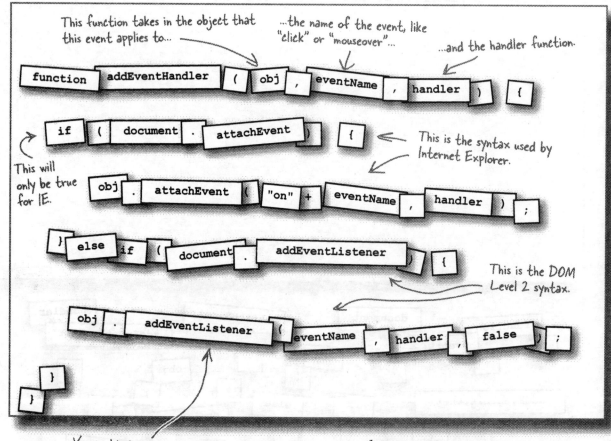

This function takes in the object that this event applies to...

...the name of the event, like "click" or "mouseover"...

...and the handler function.

```
function addEventHandler ( obj , eventName , handler ) {
    if ( document . attachEvent ) {
```

This will only be true for IE.

This is the syntax used by Internet Explorer.

```
        obj . attachEvent ( "on" + eventName , handler ) ;
    } else if ( document . addEventListener ) {
```

This is the DOM Level 2 syntax.

```
        obj . addEventListener ( eventName , handler , false ) ;
    }
}
```

You could also have checked for addEventListener first... the order of the if/else-if doesn't matter.

there are no Dumb Questions

Q: Why didn't we use a try...catch block this time?

A: We could have, but unlike `createRequest()`, this
function doesn't need an error to know that something went wrong.
Using `document.attachEvent` and `document.
addEventListener` works just as well. Besides, the `if...else
if` block is a lot easier to read.

Wouldn't it be dreamy if I never had to worry about adding multiple event handlers again? If only I could take my addEventHandler() utility function with me all the time... I guess it's just a fantasy.

addEventHandler() works for <u>ALL</u> apps, not just Marcy's yoga page

So where should you put your code for `addEventHandler()`?
We'll use it in Marcy's yoga page, but it's really a utility function. It will
work for all our apps and in any browser. So go ahead and add your
new code to `utils.js`, so we can reuse it in later web apps we build.

```
function createRequest() {
  try {
    request = new XMLHttpRequest();
  } catch (tryMS) {
    try {
      request = new ActiveXObject("Msxml2.XMLHTTP");
    } catch (otherMS) {
      try {
        request = new ActiveXObject("Microsoft.XMLHTTP");
      } catch (failed) {
        request = null;
      }
    }
  }
  return request;
}
```

utils.js

> *Just like createRequest(),
> addEventHandler() is
> useful in all our apps.*

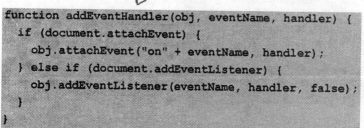

```
function addEventHandler(obj, eventName, handler) {
  if (document.attachEvent) {
    obj.attachEvent("on" + eventName, handler);
  } else if (document.addEventListener) {
    obj.addEventListener(eventName, handler, false);
  }
}
```

Anytime you build cross-browser utility functions, store those methods in scripts that you can easily reuse in your other web applications.

Let's update initPage() to use our new utility function

Now we need to change initPage(), in schedule.js, to use addEventHandler() instead of addEventListener(). Go ahead and make the following changes to your copy of schedule.js:

schedule.js

```
function initPage() {
  var tabs =
    document.getElementById("tabs").getElementsByTagName("a");
  for (var i=0; i<tabs.length; i++) {
    var currentTab = tabs[i];
    currentTab.onmouseover = showHint;
    currentTab.onmouseout = hideHint;
    currentTab.onclick = showTab;
  }


  var buttons =
    document.getElementById("navigation").getElementsByTagName("a");
  for (var i=0; i<buttons.length; i++) {
    var currentBtn = buttons[i];
    addEventHandler(currentBtn, "mouseover", showHint);
    currentBtn.addEventListener("mouseover", showHint, false);
    addEventHandler(currentBtn, "mouseout", hideHint);
    currentBtn.addEventListener("mouseout", hideHint, false);
    currentBtn.onclick = showTab;
    addEventHandler(currentBtn, "mouseover", buttonOver);
    currentBtn.addEventListener("mouseover", buttonOver, false);
    addEventHandler(currentBtn, "mouseout", buttonOut);
    currentBtn.addEventListener("mouseout", buttonOut, false);
  }
}
```

addEventHandler() has to take in the button since it's not a method on that button itself.

Remove all the addEventListener() calls, as they only work on DOM Level 2 browsers.

Test Drive

You should have addEventHandler() in utils.js and an updated version of initPage() in schedule.js. Once you've made those changes, try out the yoga page in Internet Explorer <u>and</u> a DOM Level 2 browser, like Firefox or Safari.

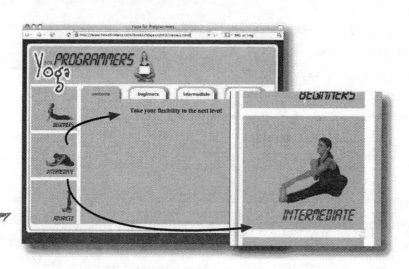

Everything works great in DOM Level 2 browsers. That means our addEventHandler() utility function does the right thing for those browsers.

Uh oh... more trouble with IE.

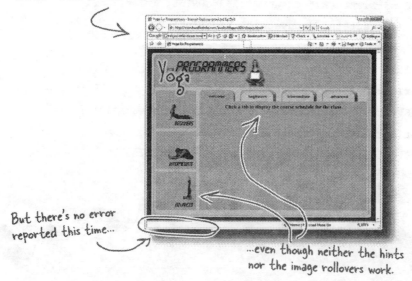

But there's no error reported this time...

...even though neither the hints nor the image rollovers work.

Use an alert() to troubleshoot

Without any error messages, it's hard to know exactly what's going on with Internet Explorer. Try putting in a few `alert()` statements in the event handlers, though, and you'll see they're getting called correctly.

```
function buttonOver() {
    alert("buttonOver() called.");
    this.className = "active";
}


function buttonOut() {
    alert("buttonOut() called.");
    this.className = "";
}
```

So what else could be going wrong?

The event handlers are getting called, so that means that `addEventHandler()` is working like it should. And we've already seen that the code in the handlers worked before we added the rollovers. So what else could be the problem?

```
function buttonOver() {
    this.className = "active";
}

function buttonOut() {
    this.className = "";
}
```

We know these class names are right... so what else could be going wrong?

What do you think the problem could be?
Can you figure out why the code
isn't working like it should?

> We know the CSS works, and there's hardly anything else in those showHint() and hideHint() functions. So it's got to be the **this** reference that's a problem, right?

"this" refers to the owner of the executing function.

The this keyword in JavaScript always refers to the owner of the function that's executing. So if the method bark() was called by an object called Dog, then this in bark() would refer to the Dog object.

When you assign an event handler using DOM Level 0, the element with the event is the owner. So if you did tab.onclick = showTab;, then in showTab(), this would refer to the tab element. That's why showHint() and hideHint() worked great in the last chapter.

"owner" and "caller" aren't the same. In a web environment, the browser calls all the functions, but objects representing elements on the page are the owners of those functions.

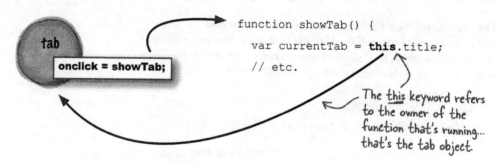

```
function showTab() {
    var currentTab = this.title;
    // etc.
```

tab

onclick = showTab;

The this keyword refers to the owner of the function that's running... that's the tab object.

In DOM Level 2, an event is still the owner of its handlers

When you're using DOM Level 2 browsers like Firefox, Safari, or Opera, the event handling framework sets the owner of a handler to the object that handler is responding to an event on. So you get the same behavior as with DOM Level 1. That's why our handlers still work with DOM Level 2 browsers.

But what about IE?

Event handlers in IE are owned by IE's event framework, <u>NOT</u> the active page object

You already know that IE doesn't implement DOM Level 2. IE has its own event handling framework. So in IE, ***the event framework owns the handler functions***, not the object on the XHTML page that was activated with a click or mouse over. In other words, this in showTab() refers to the IE event framework, *not* to a tab element on Marcy's yoga web page.

Framework just means a set of objects or code that performs some task, like handling events on a web page.

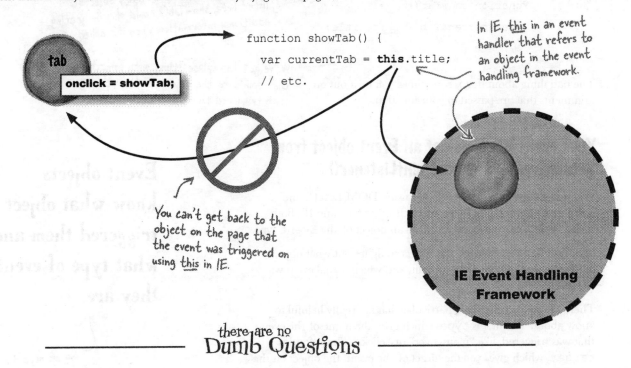

```
function showTab() {
    var currentTab = this.title;
    // etc.
```

tab

onclick = showTab;

In IE, <u>this</u> in an event handler that refers to an object in the event handling framework.

You can't get back to the object on the page that the event was triggered on using <u>this</u> in IE.

IE Event Handling Framework

there are no Dumb Questions

Q: What object does *this* refer to in the IE framework, then?

A: this *always* refers to the owner of the function that's currently running. So in an event handler under IE's event framework, this points at one of the framework's objects.

It really doesn't matter what that object is because it's not all that useful. What we need is a way to get information about the element that the event occurred on.

Q: But if this is how IE handles events, how did our code work back in Chapter 3 on Internet Explorer?

A: Our code worked in IE because we were just using DOM Level 0 syntax. Anytime you assign a handler to a property, like currentBtn.onmouseover = showTab, that's DOM Level 0.

But our code now is using addEventListener() and attachEvent(). That's *not* DOM Level 0, and now this doesn't mean the same thing as it did in that earlier code.

Q: Ok, great. So the page still doesn't work in Internet Explorer. What now?

A: Well, take a moment to think about what exactly you need. It's not so much the this keyword that's important, but the information that keyword let us access.

What exactly do we need to know about in our event handler functions?

attachEvent() and addEventListener() supply another argument to our handlers

One of the cooler things about JavaScript is that you don't need to list all the arguments that your functions take when you declare that function. So even if your function declaration is showTab(), you can pass arguments to showTab() when you call it.

```
function showTab() {

    var currentTab = this.title;

    // etc.
```

Even though there aren't any objects listed here, showTab() could still be getting additional information when it's called.

We've got to replace "this" with something that points to the object on the web page that triggered this event.

The bad thing about that is sometimes you miss out on arguments that are passed to your function.

Your event handlers get an Event object from attachEvent() and addEventListener()

When you register an event handler using DOM Level 2 and addEventListener(), or attachEvent() and IE, both frameworks pass your event handlers an object of the Event type.

Your handlers can then use this object to figure out what object on a page was activated by an event, and which actual event was triggered.

There are two properties in particular that are really helpful to know about. The first is type, which gives the name of the event that was triggered, like "mouseover" or "click." The second is target, which gives you the target of the event: the object on the page that was activated.

Event objects know what object triggered them and what type of event they are.

So we need to get access to the Event object in our handler functions.

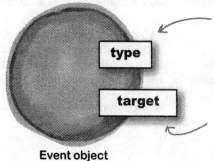

type

This is the name of the event that occurred. It's the same string that you passed to addEventListener(), like "mouseover" or "onload."

target

This is the object the event occurred on, like a tab or an image on a web page.

Event object

The target of an Event object is equivalent to what you get from the "this" keyword in DOM Level 2 browsers.

We need to name the Event argument, so our handlers can work with it

You don't have to list all the arguments a JavaScript function gets. But if you want to actually use those arguments in the function, you **do** need to list the arguments. First, we need to get access to the Event object in our handlers, so we can figure out what object on a page triggered a call to our handler. Then, we need to list the argument for that Event object:

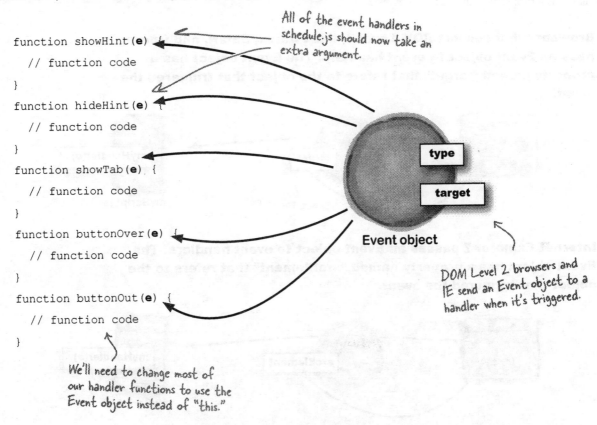

All of the event handlers in schedule.js should now take an extra argument.

```
function showHint(e) {
    // function code
}
function hideHint(e) {
    // function code
}
function showTab(e) {
    // function code
}
function buttonOver(e) {
    // function code
}
function buttonOut(e) {
    // function code
}
```

Event object

type

target

DOM Level 2 browsers and IE send an Event object to a handler when it's triggered.

We'll need to change most of our handler functions to use the Event object instead of "this."

 **BRAIN POWER**

With DOM Level 2 browsers, you can use either this or the Event object passed into an event handler to find out what element was activated. Do you think one approach is better than the other? Why?

You say target tomato, I say srcElement tomato...

The good news is that both IE and DOM Level 2 browsers make the object that triggered an event available. The bad news is that DOM Level 2 and IE use different versions of the Event object, each with different properties.

In some cases, the Event object properties refer to the same thing, but the property *names* are different. And to make matters worse, modern versions of IE pass in an Event object, but earlier versions of IE make the Event object available as a property of the window object.

Browsers that support DOM Level 2, like Firefox, Safari, and Opera, pass an Event object to event handlers. The Event object has a property named "target" that refers to the object that triggered the event.

target points back at the object that was activated.

myScript.js

Internet Explorer 7 passes an Event object to event handlers. The Event object has a property named "srcElement" that refers to the object that triggered the event.

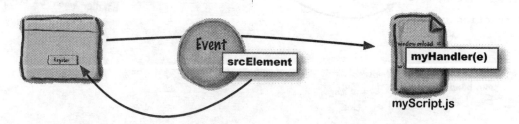

myScript.js

Earlier versions of Internet Explorer provide the object that triggered an event in a property named "srcElement," available on the window object.

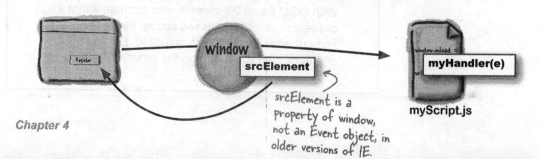

srcElement is a property of window, not an Event object, in older versions of IE.

myScript.js

WHO DOES WHAT?

So you think you really know your browsers? Here's a quiz to help you check your knowledge out for real. For each property, method, or behavior on the left, check off all the boxes for the browsers that support that thing. Good luck!

	Firefox	IE 7	Safari	Opera	IE 5
addEventListener()	☐	☐	☐	☐	☐
srcElement	☐	☐	☐	☐	☐
DOM Level 2	☐	☐	☐	☐	☐
target	☐	☐	☐	☐	☐
addEventHandler()	☐	☐	☐	☐	☐
var currentTab = this.title;	☐	☐	☐	☐	☐
DOM Level 0	☐	☐	☐	☐	☐
window.srcElement	☐	☐	☐	☐	☐
attachEvent()	☐	☐	☐	☐	☐

WHO DOES WHAT?

So you think you really know your browsers? Here's a quiz to help you check your knowledge out for real. For each property, method, or behavior on the left, you were to check off all the boxes for the browsers that support that thing.

This is a DOM Level 2 function. No IE.

	Firefox	IE 7	Safari	Opera	IE 5
addEventListener()	✓	☐	✓	✓	☐
srcElement	☐	✓	☐	☐	✓
DOM Level 2	✓	☐	✓	✓	☐
target	✓	☐	✓	✓	☐
addEventHandler()	✓	✓	✓	✓	✓
var currentTab = this.title;	✓	?	✓	✓	?
DOM Level 0	✓	✓	✓	✓	✓
window.srcElement	☐	☐	☐	☐	✓
attachEvent()	☐	✓	☐	☐	✓

srcElement — All versions of IE have this property, but on different objects.

target — Only DOM Level 2 browsers support target

addEventHandler() — This is our utility function, so it works on all browsers.

var currentTab = this.title; — this is tricky. It works in all browsers with DOM Level 0 events, but not in IE if attachEvent() is used.

attachEvent() — Old versions of IE expose srcElement as a property of the window object

Q: So "this" always refers to the function that called my function?

A: No, `this` refers to the *owner* of the function. Sometimes that's another bit of code, but it also might be an object, like a tab on a form that got clicked.

Q: But that's not true in Internet Explorer, right?

A: `this` still refers to the owner of a function in IE. The difference is that when you use `attachEvent()`, the owner of your function is an object in IE's event handling framework and not an object on your web page.

The DOM provides an object-based model of your web page that your code can work with.

getElementById(), the document object, and the onclick property are all aspects of using the DOM in your code.

Q: So we shouldn't ever use "this" in Internet Explorer?

A: Actually, `this` is still a very useful part of JavaScript, whether you're using IE or a DOM Level 2 browser. But if you're writing an event handler function, you're probably better off avoiding `this`. If you're writing an event handler that's going to be called using the IE event handling framework, via `attachEvent()`, then you've *got* to avoid using `this`.

Q: I'm still a little fuzzy on all this DOM stuff. Can you explain that again?

A: DOM, or the Document Object Model, is how a browser represents your page as objects. JavaScript uses the DOM to work with a web page. So every time you change an element's property or get an element with `getElementById()`, you're using the DOM. That's all you really need to know right now, but we're going to dig into the DOM a lot more in just a few chapters.

Q: As long as I use addEventHandler(), I don't have to worry about all this DOM stuff, though, right?

A: Well, you don't have to worry about whether you should use `attachEvent()` or `addEventListener()`. But as you'll see in Chapter 6, there's still a lot of DOM work you'll end up doing.

`addEventHandler()` takes care of registering an event handler to an event in a browser-neutral way. In other words, `addEventHandler()` works with all modern browsers.

Q: And that's why it's in utils.js, right? Because it's a utility function?

A: Right. `addEventHandler()` works for all browsers and many different kinds of applications, not just Marcy's yoga page. So it's best put into a reusable script, like `utils.js`.

Q: But even if we use addEventHandler(), we've still got these issues with target and srcElement, right?

A: Right. IE 7 passes off to event handlers an `Event` object with a `srcElement` property that points at the object that triggered the event. Older versions of IE make that same object available through the `window.srcElement` property. DOM Level 2 browsers provide an `Event` object with a property called `target` pointing to the object that triggered an event.

Q: I've heard that object called an "activated object" before. Is that the same thing?

A: Yes. An **activated object** just means an object that represents an element on a web page that an event occurred on. So if an image is clicked, the JavaScript object that represents that image is the activated object.

Q: Since addEventHandler() took care of adding events on all browsers, why don't we just build another utility function to deal with all this target/srcElement stuff?

A: Now *that* is a great idea!

So how do we actually GET the object that triggered the event?

The best way to deal with differences in how IE and DOM Level 2 browsers handle events is another utility function. Our handler functions are now getting `Event` objects, but what we really need is the **activated object**: the object representation of the element on the page that the event occurred on.

So let's build a utility function to take the event argument we get from those browsers, and figure out and return the activated object:

```
function getActivatedObject(e) {

    var obj;

    if (!e) {

        // early version of IE

        obj = window.event.srcElement;

    } else if (e.srcElement) {

        // IE 7 or later

        obj = e.srcElement;

    } else {

        // DOM Level 2 browser

        obj = e.target;

    }

    return obj;

}
```

Our handlers get an Event object, so let's pass that object to this utility function.

Early versions of IE actually don't send an object...

...which tells us to check the srcElement property of the window object

IE 7 has a srcElement property, which is what we want on that browser.

DOM Level 2 browsers provide the activated object in the target property of the passed-in event

This function goes in utils.js along with createRequest() and addEventHandler().

```
function
createReq
...
)
```
utils.js

Exercise

You need to update Marcy's code again. In all of the event handlers, you need to use getActivatedObject() to get the activated object. You'll also need to change the rest of those methods to use the object returned from that function instead of this. There are a few other changes you should already have made, too. Check off each task once you're finished.

Update utils.js

Add the addEventHandler() and getActivatedObject() functions to the file.

☐ addEventHandler()   ☐ getActivatedObject()

Use addEventHandler() instead of addEventListener()

Use the generic addEventHandler() to abstract out DOM Level 2 and IE
event handling differences.

☐ Update initPage() to only use addEventHandler()

Use getObject() instead of this

Update all your event handler functions to use getActivatedObject()
instead of the this keyword. You'll need to make other changes to get those
functions working as well.

☐ showHint()   ☐ hideHint()

☐ buttonOver()   ☐ buttonOut()

☐ showTab()

When you think you're done, try things out for yourself. Then, turn the page to
see how we updated the code in schedule.js and utils.js.

Exercise Solution

Your job was to complete the changes to schedule.js so that all the event handlers would take an Event argument, and use the getObject() utility function from utils.js to figure out the activated object. You should have also removed all references to this in your event handler functions.

```javascript
window.onload = initPage;
var welcomePaneShowing = true;

function initPage() {
  var tabs =
    document.getElementById("tabs").getElementsByTagName("a");
  for (var i=0; i<tabs.length; i++) {
    var currentTab = tabs[i];
    currentTab.onmouseover = showHint;
    currentTab.onmouseout = hideHint;
    currentTab.onclick = showTab;
  }

  var buttons =
    document.getElementById("navigation").getElementsByTagName("a");
  for (var i=0; i<buttons.length; i++) {
    var currentBtn = buttons[i];
    addEventHandler(currentBtn, "mouseover", showHint);
    addEventHandler(currentBtn, "mouseout", hideHint);
    currentBtn.onclick = showTab;
    addEventHandler(currentBtn, "mouseover", buttonOver);
    addEventHandler(currentBtn, "mouseout", buttonOut);
  }
}

function showHint(e) {
  if (!welcomePaneShowing) {
    return;
  }
  var me = getActivatedObject(e);
  switch (me.title) {
    case "beginners":
      var hintText = "Just getting started? Come join us!";
      break;
    case "intermediate":
      var hintText = "Take your flexibility to the next level!";
      break;
    case "advanced":
      var hintText = "Perfectly join your body and mind " +
                     "with these intensive workouts.";
      break;
    default:
```

Since these events have just a single handler, DOM Level 0 is fine.

You probably did this step earlier. All the multiple event handling situations should now be setup with addEventHandler().

Make sure you add the extra argument to all your event handler functions, so you can work with the object sent to those handlers.

```
            var hintText = "Click a tab to display the course " +
                           "schedule for the class";
    }
    var contentPane = document.getElementById("content");
    contentPane.innerHTML = "<h3>" + hintText + "</h3>";
}

function hideHint(e) {
    if (welcomePaneShowing) {
        var contentPane = document.getElementById("content");
        contentPane.innerHTML =
            "<h3>Click a tab to display the course schedule for the class</h3>";
    }
}

function showTab(e) {
    var selectedTab = this.title;
    var me = getActivatedObject(e);
    var selectedTab = me.title;
    if (selectedTab == "welcome") {
        welcomePaneShowing = true;
        document.getElementById("content").innerHTML =
            "<h3>Click a tab to display the course schedule for the class</h3>";
    } else {
        welcomePaneShowing = false;
    }

    // everything else is the same...
}

function buttonOver(e) {
    var me = getObject(e);
    me.classNameActivated = "active";
    this.className = "active";
}
function buttonOut(e) {
    var me = getActivatedObject(e);
    me.className = "";
    this.className = "";
}
```

schedule.js

> It's common to call the object returned from getObject() "me."

> The "me" variable stands in for "this." The code stays almost exactly the same.

Test Drive

It's been a long journey, but you're finally ready to test out Marcy's yoga page one more time. See if everything works in both IE browsers <u>AND</u> DOM Level 2 browsers.

Firefox still works great with the new changes.

Yes! IE is working now, using its own event handling.

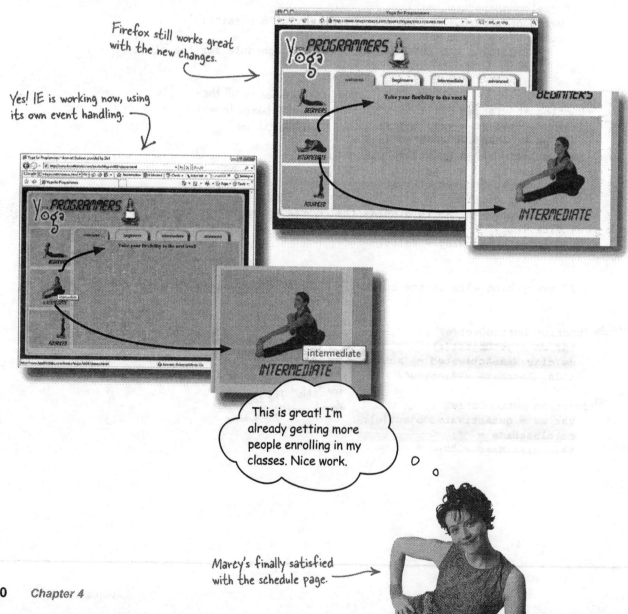

This is great! I'm already getting more people enrolling in my classes. Nice work.

Marcy's finally satisfied with the schedule page.

EventAcrostic

Take some time to sit back and give your right brain something to do. Answer the questions in the top, then use the letters to fill in the secret message where the numbers match.

This model uses object.event = handler syntax

$\overline{\ \ }_1 \ \overline{\ \ }_2 \ \overline{\ \ }_3 \ \overline{\ \ }_4 \ \overline{\ \ }_5 \ \overline{\ \ }_6 \ \overline{\ \ }_7 \ \overline{\ \ }_8 \ \overline{\ \ }_9$

Use this function to register an event in DOM Level 2

$\overline{\ \ }_{10} \ \overline{\ \ }_{11} \ \overline{\ \ }_{12} \ \overline{\ \ }_{13} \ \overline{\ \ }_{14} \ \overline{\ \ }_{15} \ \overline{\ \ }_{16} \ \overline{\ \ }_{17} \ \overline{\ \ }_{18} \ \overline{\ \ }_{19} \ \overline{\ \ }_{20} \ \overline{\ \ }_{21} \ \overline{\ \ }_{22} \ \overline{\ \ }_{23} \ \overline{\ \ }_{24} \ \overline{\ \ }_{25}$

This is what Marcy teaches

$\overline{\ \ }_{26} \ \overline{\ \ }_{27} \ \overline{\ \ }_{28} \ \overline{\ \ }_{29}$

Use this function to register an event in Internet Explorer

$\overline{\ \ }_{30} \ \overline{\ \ }_{31} \ \overline{\ \ }_{32} \ \overline{\ \ }_{33} \ \overline{\ \ }_{34} \ \overline{\ \ }_{35} \ \overline{\ \ }_{36} \ \overline{\ \ }_{37} \ \overline{\ \ }_{38} \ \overline{\ \ }_{39} \ \overline{\ \ }_{40}$

This is the object that triggered the event

$\overline{\ \ }_{41} \ \overline{\ \ }_{42} \ \overline{\ \ }_{43} \ \overline{\ \ }_{44} \ \overline{\ \ }_{45} \ \overline{\ \ }_{46}$

This event happens when the user presses a key

$\overline{\ \ }_{47} \ \overline{\ \ }_{48} \ \overline{\ \ }_{49} \ \overline{\ \ }_{50} \ \overline{\ \ }_{51} \ \overline{\ \ }_{52} \ \overline{\ \ }_{53} \ \overline{\ \ }_{54} \ \overline{\ \ }_{55}$

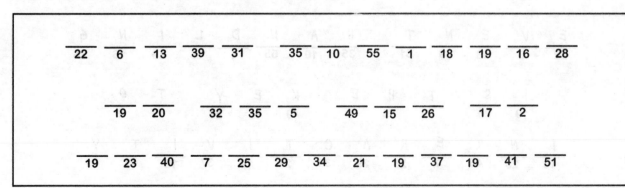

EventAcrostic

Did you figure out the secret message? Do you agree with it?

This model uses object.event = handler syntax

D	O	M		L	E	V	E	L		O
1	2	3		4	5	6	7	8		9

Use this function to register an event in DOM Level 2

A	D	D	E	V	E	N	T	L	I	S	T	E	N	E	R
10	11	12	13	14	15	16	17	18	19	20	21	22	23	24	25

This is what Marcy teaches

Y	O	G	A
26	27	28	29

Use this function to register an event in Internet Explorer

A	T	T	A	C	H	E	V	E	N	T
30	31	32	33	34	35	36	37	38	39	40

This is the object that triggered the event

T	A	R	G	E	T
41	42	43	44	45	46

This event happens when the user presses a key

O	N	K	E	Y	D	O	W	N
47	48	49	50	51	52	53	54	55

E	V	E	N	T		H	A	N	D	L	I	N	G
22	6	13	39	31		35	10	55	1	18	19	16	28

I	S		T	H	E		K	E	Y		T	O
19	20		32	35	5		49	15	26		17	2

I	N	T	E	R	A	C	T	I	V	I	T	Y
19	23	40	7	25	29	34	21	19	37	19	41	51

5 asynchronous applications

It's like renewing your driver's license

Just be patient, dear, your time will come.

Well I'm not going to sit around waiting any longer.

Are you tired of waiting around? Do you hate long delays? You can do something about it with asynchrony!

You've already built a couple of pages that made asynchronous requests to the server to avoid making the user sit around waiting for a page refresh. In this chapter, we'll dive even deeper into the details of building asynchronous applications.

You'll find out what **asynchronous really means**, learn how to use **multiple asynchronous requests**, and even build a **monitor function** to keep all that asynchrony from confusing you and your users.

What does asynchronous <u>really</u> mean?

An **asynchronous request** means that you don't have to **wait around** while a web server is responding to that request. That means you're not stuck: you can go on doing what you want, and have the server let you know when it's finished with your request. Let's take a view of this from 10,000 feet by first looking at what a synchronous request is, and then comparing it to an asynchronous request:

A synchronous request for cola

An asynchronous request for cola

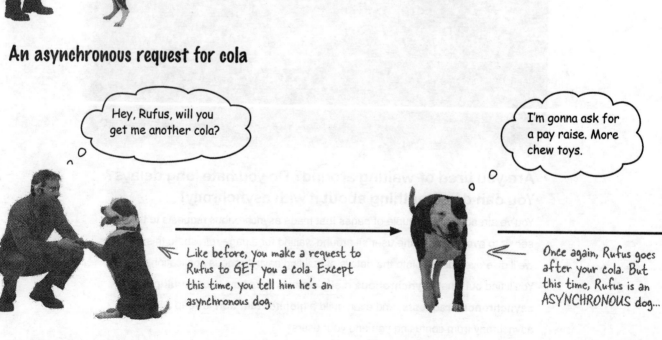

You've been building asynchronous apps all along

Take a look back at the app you built for Mike's Movies in Chapter 2. When a user types in their username and leaves that field, that value gets sent to the server right away for validation. But the user can fill out the rest of the form while that validation is happening. That's because we made the request to the server **asynchronous**.

checkUsername() gets called when a user leaves the username field.

```javascript
function checkUsername() {
  document.getElementById("username").className = "thinking";
  request = createRequest();
  if (request == null)
    alert("Unable to create request");
  else {
    var theName = document.getElementById("username").value;
    var username = escape(theName);
    var url= "checkName.php?username=" + username;
    request.onreadystatechange = showUsernameStatus;
    request.open("GET", url, true);
    request.send(null);
  }
}
```

Remember this last argument to request.open()? It says, "Make this an asynchronous request. Don't make the user wait on the server's response."

Here's where we send a request to the server.

Validate Username

The server sends back response data, like a readyState, status code, and eventually the response itself.

response data

```javascript
function showUsernameStatus() {
  if (request.readyState == 4) {
    if (request.status == 200) {
      if (request.responseText == "okay") {
        document.getElementById("username").className = "approved";
        document.getElementById("register").disabled = false;
      } else {
        document.getElementById("username").className = "denied";
        document.getElementById("username").focus();
        document.getElementById("username").select();
        document.getElementById("register").disabled = true;
      }
    }
  }
}
```

This callback runs every time the server responds with new data.

All of the server processing, AND the callback, happens while the user is still filling out the form... no waiting around.

But sometimes you barely even notice...

When you built Mike's Movies, you probably barely noticed the asynchrony. Requests to and from a server—especially when you're developing, and there's not a lot of network traffic—hardly take any time at all.

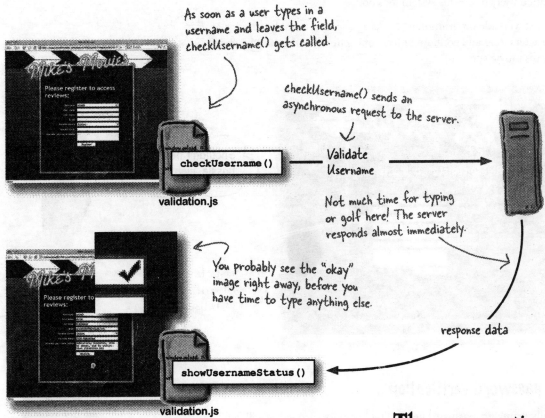

As soon as a user types in a username and leaves the field, checkUsername() gets called.

checkUsername() sends an asynchronous request to the server.

checkUsername()

validation.js

Validate Username

Not much time for typing or golf here! The server responds almost immediately.

You probably see the "okay" image right away, before you have time to type anything else.

response data

showUsernameStatus()

validation.js

But the response time on a live site is almost always going to be *slower*. There are more people competing for server resources, and user machines and connections may not be as powerful and fast as your development machine. And that doesn't even take into account how long it takes a server to respond. If the server's querying a huge database, or has to do lots of server-side processing, that slows the request and response cycle down, too.

The response time on a live site will almost always be slower than on a test site.

The only way to know for sure is to TEST your app on the live site.

Speaking of more server-side processing...

Mike loves the page you built him and has some more ideas. His site's become popular, but some folks have been posting fake reviews under other peoples' usernames. Mike needs you to add a password field to the registration form, verify the username *and* password asynchronously, and keep unwanted users out of his system for good.

Mike's got a server-side program that checks a password to make sure it's at least 6 characters long and contains at least one letter. That should be good enough for his movie site.

> Shouldn't be a big hassle, right?

Mike wants to add password verification to the registration page.

Oh, and password verification...

Mike actually wants *two* password fields. The first password value will get sent to the server for validation. The second field is for password re-entry. The value in both password fields have to match. We'll handle that at the client's browser.

And... how about some eye candy, too?

Mike's not happy with how long it takes to get a user processed when the user clicks the Register button. Since we can't let users in until they are registered, Mike's got an idea: while the form is being submitted and processed, he wants images from his collection of movies and posters to scroll by and whet the user's appetite for reviews on those items.

The very-demanding owner of Mike's Movies... Mike.

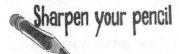

Sharpen your pencil

There's a lot to do on Mike's site. Below, we've given you a screenshot of what Mike's final app should look like. It's up to you to make notes about the interactions that need to happen to add all the behavior Mike's asking for.

What should be happening between the page and your JavaScript, and your JavaScript and the server?

There are two new password fields. We'll need to add those to Mike's XHTML.

Mike also lays out his password requirements in red text. That's just more XHTML.

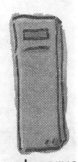

web server

Mike wants images of his reviewed movies at the bottom of the page.

Don't forget about the server-side requirements! You'll need two different server-side processes for this version of Mike's app. Label the arrows below to indicate what you're sending to the server, and what you think it should send back in response.

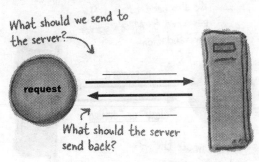

What should we send to the server?

What should the server send back?

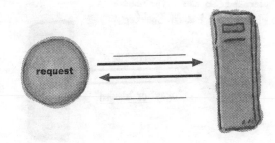

Sharpen your pencil Solution

There's a lot to do on Mike's site. Your job was to figure out the interactions that have to occur to get all this behavior working like it should.

We want to keep everything we've already got, so entering a username still triggers validation.

When the user enters a password, we need to call a JavaScript function...

...that sends a request to the server for password validation.

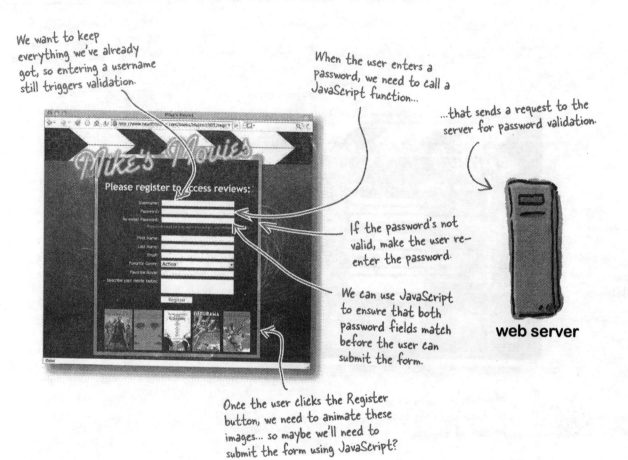

web server

If the password's not valid, make the user re-enter the password.

We can use JavaScript to ensure that both password fields match before the user can submit the form.

Once the user clicks the Register button, we need to animate these images... so maybe we'll need to submit the form using JavaScript?

Were you able to figure out what our JavaScript needed to send to Mike's server, and what the server-side programs should send back?

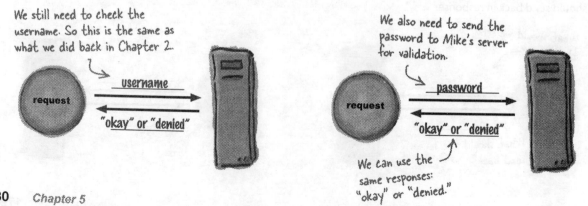

We still need to check the username. So this is the same as what we did back in Chapter 2.

We also need to send the password to Mike's server for validation.

request → **username**
← **"okay" or "denied"**

request → **password**
← **"okay" or "denied"**

We can use the same responses: "okay" or "denied."

(More) Asynchrony in 3 easy steps

We need to finish up Mike's web page, and then add all the extra interactions that he wants. Then, we've got to figure out a way to submit his form and animate those images at the bottom.

Here's how we're going to take on the improved version of Mike's Movies in this chapter:

1   Update the XHTML page
We need to add two more password fields: one for entering a password, and one for verifying that password. We'll also need a section for putting in those movie images.

2   Validate the user's passwords
Then, we need to handle the user's password. We've got to build a handler function that takes a password, sends it to the server, and sets up a callback that checks to see if the password was valid. Then we can use the same icons we used on the username field to let the user know if their password is valid.

Somewhere in here we should make sure both password fields match, too.

3   Submit the form
Finally, we've got to build code to submit the form, and animate the images along the bottom. We can attach that code to the Register button's `click` event instead of letting the form submit through a normal XHTML Submit button.

We need code to submit the form since we've got to animate the images at the same time.

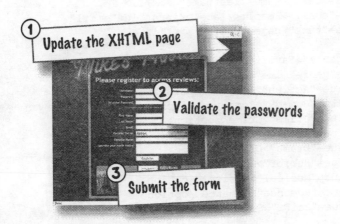

1 Update the XHTML page

Please register to access reviews:

2 Validate the passwords

3 Submit the form

We need two password fields and a ⟨div⟩ for the cover images

We've got to add a couple of password fields to the form, and then we also need a <div> at the bottom to hold all those cover images. Here are the changes you should make to your copy of registration.html:

```
<html xmlns="http://www.w3.org/1999/xhtml">
<head>
  <title>Mike's Movies</title>
  <link rel="stylesheet" href="css/movies.css" />
  <script src="scripts/utils.js" type="text/javascript"></script>
  <script src="scripts/validation.js" type="text/javascript"></script>
</head>
<body>
<div id="wrapper">
  <h1>Please register to access reviews:</h1>
  <form action="register.php" method="POST">
    <ul>
      <li><label for="username">Username:</label><input id="username"
                type="text" name="username" /></li>
      <li><label for="password1">Password:</label><input id="password1"
                type="password" name="password1" /></li>
      <li><label for="password2">Re-enter Password:</label><input id="password2"
                type="password" name="password2" /></li>
      <li class="tip">Passwords must be 6 or more characters and
                contain a number.</li>
      <li><label for="firstname">First Name:</label><input id="firstname"
                type="text" name="firstname" /></li>
      <li><label for="lastname">Last Name:</label><input id="lastname"
                type="text" name="lastname" /></li>
      <li><label for="email">Email:</label><input id="email"
                type="text" name="email" /></li>
      <li>
        <label for="genre">Favorite Genre:</label>
        <select name="genre" id="genre">
          <option value="Action">Action</option>
          <option value="Comedy">Comedy</option>
          <option value="Crime">Crime</option>
          <option value="Documentary">Documentary</option>
          <option value="Drama">Drama</option>
          <option value="Horror">Horror</option>
          <option value="Musical">Musical</option>
          <option value="Romance">Romance</option>
          <option value="SciFi">Sci-Fi/Fantasy</option>
```

We're using the same scripts as before. We can just add new code to validation.js.

We need two fields: one for the initial password, and one to verify the password.

Make the type of these "password" so nobody can see what users are typing.

This label lays out Mike's password requirements, and the CSS styles it to be red.

```
          <option value="Suspense">Suspense</option>
          <option value="Western">Western</option>
        </select>
      </li>
      <li><label for="favorite">Favorite Movie:</label><input id="favorite"
              type="text" name="favorite" /></li>
      <li><label for="tastes">Describe your movie tastes:</label><textarea
              name="tastes" cols="60" rows="2" id="tastes"></textarea></li>
      <li><label for="register"></label><input id="register"
              type="submit" value="Register" name="register" /></li>
    </ul>
  </form>
```

This is pretty straightforward. We add a <div> with an id...

...and then a bunch of movie covers that Mike said he's got reviews for.

```
<div id="coverBar">
  <img src="images/coverMatrix.jpg" width="82" height="115"
       style="left: 0px;" />
  <img src="images/coverDeadRingers.jpg" width="82" height="115"
       style="left: 88px;" />
  <img src="images/coverDrStrangelove.jpg" width="82" height="115"
       style="left: 176px;" />
  <img src="images/coverFuturama.jpg" width="82" height="115"
       style="left: 264px;" />
  <img src="images/coverHolyGrail.jpg" width="82" height="115"
       style="left: 356px;" />
  <img src="images/coverRaisingArizona.jpg" width="82" height="115"
       style="left: 444px;" />
  <img src="images/coverRobotChicken.jpg" width="82" height="115"
       style="left: 532px;" />
</div>
```

```
</div>
</body>
</html>
```

Download the CSS and graphics from Head First Labs.

Go to the Head First Labs site and download the examples for Chapter 5. You'll find the cover graphics, as well as a version of `registration.html` that matches this XHTML, and a new version of `movies.css` to go with the new XHTML.

there are no Dumb Questions

Q: Why are you using style attributes on those cover images? Isn't mixing style into the XHTML a really bad idea?

A: It is. But the only other option is to have a different class for each image in that `<div>`. It's good to try and separate content from presentation, but if it makes your XHTML and CSS a real mess, then you sometimes have to break a rule to make your XHTML and CSS manageable. Who wants to keep up with 10 or 15 different CSS classes, one for each movie image?

Test Drive

Check out Mike's Movies... with password and images.

Once you've made all the changes to registration.html, or downloaded the examples, open up the page in your web browser. Make sure that all the cover images show up, and that there are two password fields. You should also check that the username field still sends a request to the server for validation, and that the Register button is disabled when the page first loads.

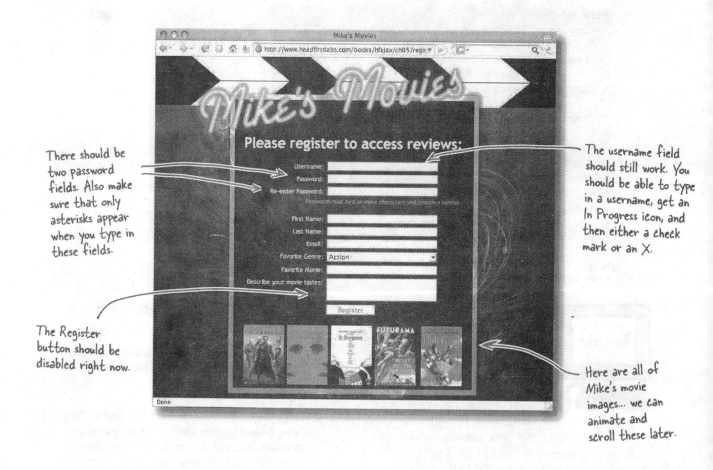

There should be two password fields. Also make sure that only asterisks appear when you type in these fields.

The username field should still work. You should be able to type in a username, get an In Progress icon, and then either a check mark or an X.

The Register button should be disabled right now.

Here are all of Mike's movie images... we can animate and scroll these later.

With the XHTML done, we can move on to validating passwords.

Procedure Magnets

By now, you should be pretty comfortable figuring out how to tie an event on a page to a request for a server-side program to process some data. Put the magnets under the right task. Order doesn't matter in most cases, so just match the magnet to what that magnet helps you accomplish.

To handle an event:

To send a request object to the server:

Register each handler function to the correct event(s).

Create a callback function that will be called when the server responds to the request

Obtain an instance of a request object

Trigger the event registration function before the user can work with the web page.

Send the request object

Configure the request object

Create a function to register handlers to events.

Write event handlers for each event you want to perform behavior on.

Procedure Magnet Solution

Your job was to build a process for connecting an
event on a web page to a server-side program.

To handle an event:

Here's where your event-specific behavior occurs. Nothing works without event handlers.

> Write event handlers for each event you want to perform behavior on.

We've been calling this initPage().

> Create a function to register handlers to events.

> Register each handler function to the correct event(s).

> Trigger the event registration function before the user can work with the web page.

You can create these in any order. You just have to have all four things in place before your code will work.

The statement "window.onload = initPage()" makes sure event handlers are set up before users can work with a page.

Obtain a reference to an object, and then either assign the handler to its event property or use addEventHandler() to register the handler to an event on that object.

To send a request object to the server:

createRequest() in utils.js handles this task.

> Obtain an instance of a request object

> Configure the request object

> Send the request object

> Create a callback function that will be called when the server responds to the request

These have to happen in this specific order.

You need to give the request a URL to send information to, and a callback for the browser to call when the server responds.

You use request.send() for this.

This should take the server's response and do something with that response.

If you need new behavior, you probably need a new event handler function

We've got to validate a password once a user enters something in the password form fields. So we need a new event handler to validate passwords. We also need to register an `onblur` event handler for the right password field.

`validation.js` already sets up event handlers in `initPage()`, so we just need to add a new event handler assignment:

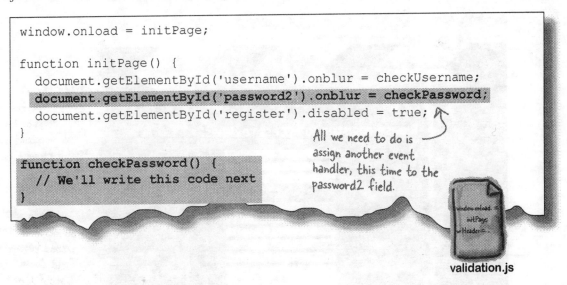

```
window.onload = initPage;

function initPage() {
   document.getElementById('username').onblur = checkUsername;
   document.getElementById('password2').onblur = checkPassword;
   document.getElementById('register').disabled = true;
}

function checkPassword() {
   // We'll write this code next
}
```

All we need to do is assign another event handler, this time to the password2 field.

validation.js

there are no
Dumb Questions

Q: Why didn't you use addEventHandler() to register the checkPassword() handler?

A: Because we're only assigning one handler to the password2 field. If we needed multiple handlers for that field, then you would need DOM Level 2 or IE's `attachEvent()`. In those cases, you'd want to use `addEventHandler()`. But since this is a single handler on an event, we can stick with DOM Level 0.

Sharpen your pencil

Why do you think checkPassword() is registered to the password2 field, and not the password1 field?

....
....
....
....

Sharpen your pencil
Solution

Why do you think checkPassword() is registered to the password2 field, and not the password1 field?

We need to check the passwords against each other before sending them to the server for validation. So we can't do anything until the user's entered a password for both password fields.

Your answer doesn't have to be exactly the same, but it should be pretty close.

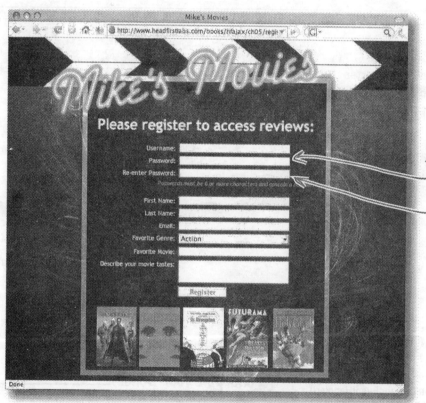

When there's a value for the first password field, we could send a request to the server...

...but then what do we do if the second password field doesn't match? Our request would be meaningless.

We really need to check and see if both fields match *first*, and *then* send the password to the server for validation.

Exercise

It's time to write some code. Using what you've already figured out, plus the hints below, you should be able to write the code for the checkPassword() event handler and the showPasswordStatus() callback. Take your time... you can do it.

A callback runs when the server returns a response to your request. An event handler runs when a certain event on your page occurs.

HintS:

● There's a CSS class called "thinking" that you can set either password field to in order to get an "in progress" icon. The "approved" class shows a check mark, and the "denied" class shows an X.

● The program on the server that validates passwords is at the URL "checkPass.php". The program takes a password and returns "okay" if the password is valid, and "denied" if it's not. The parameter name to the program should be "password."

Write the code for checkPassword()
and a callback called
showPasswordStatus() here:

EXERCISE SOLUTION

Your job was to write the code for the checkPassword() event handler and the showPasswordStatus() callback. See how close your solution is to ours.

```
function checkPassword() {

  var password1 = document.getElementById("password1");

  var password2 = document.getElementById("password2");

  password1.className = "thinking";

  // First compare the two passwords

  if ((password1.value == "") || (password1.value != password2.value)) {

    password1.className = "denied";

    return;

  }


  // Passwords match, so send request to server

  var request = createRequest();

  if (request == null) {

    alert("Unable to create request");

  } else {

    var password = escape(password1.value);

    var url = "checkPass.php?password=" + password;

    request.onreadystatechange = showPasswordStatus;

    request.open("GET", url, true);

    request.send(null);

  }

}
```

Since we'll use these field elements a lot, it makes sense to put them both into variables.

As soon as we start, we need to show the "in progress" icon.

First, make sure the password1 field isn't empty.

Then, we need to compare the values of the two fields.

If the non-empty passwords don't match, show an error and stop processing.

This is pretty standard. Get a request object, and make sure it's good to use.

We can use either password field's value... we know they're the same now.

Set the callback.

We're making this an asynchronous request. That will be really important later...

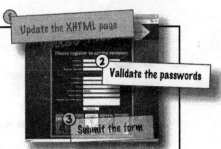

Update the XHTML page

② Validate the passwords

③ Submit the form

Make sure this function name
exactly matches the value of the
onreadystatechange property of
the request object.

```
function showPasswordStatus() {
    if (request.readyState == 4) {
        if (request.status == 200) {
            var password1 = document.getElementById("password1");
            if (request.responseText == "okay") {
                password1.className = "approved";
                document.getElementById("register").disabled = false;
            } else {
                password1.className = "denied";
                password1.focus();
                password1.select();
                document.getElementById("register").disabled = true;
            }
        }
    }
}
```

If we get a response of "okay",
show the check mark icon for the
password1 field.

If the password's not valid,
change the CSS class...

Remember to
enable the
Register button!

...move to the password1 field...

...and highlight the password1 field.

Since the password isn't valid,
we can't let the user register,
so disable that button.

there are no
Dumb Questions

Q: **Should we be sending a password as part of a GET request? Is that safe?**

A: Great question! We'll talk a lot more about GET, and how secure it is, in Chapter 12. For now, just focus on the details of asynchrony, and we'll look at securing Mike's users' passwords a bit better later on.

Q: **I tried this out, and I think there are some problems...**

A: Really? What were they? What do you think caused them? Try out our code, and see what you get. Are there things you would change or improve? Try entering in just a username, or just valid passwords. What do you see happening?

Test Drive

How does Mike's page look and behave?

Make the changes to `validation.js` that we did, or use your own version (as long as it does the same basic things). Then, try the page out. What's happening? Do you think our code works, or are there problems?

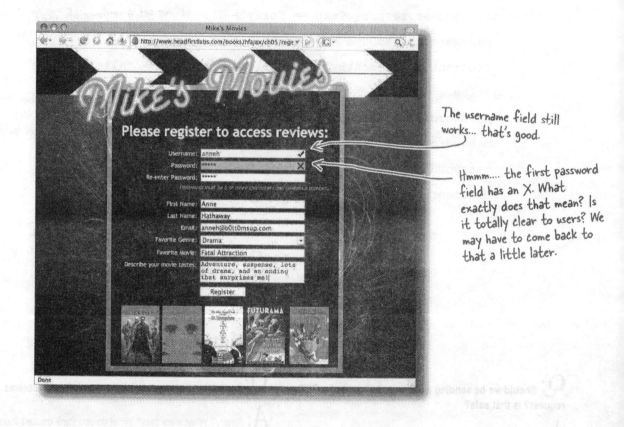

The username field still works... that's good.

Hmmm.... the first password field has an X. What exactly does that mean? Is it totally clear to users? We may have to come back to that a little later.

really fast

BE the USER

Your job is to play like you're one of Mike's potential customers... and a fast-typing one, at that. Try and figure out what happens when someone types in a username, and then quickly moves to typing a password in both of the password fields.

Type in a username...

...and then quickly type in your password, once...

...and then again.

Finally, tab out of the second password field to trigger the checkPassword() event handler.

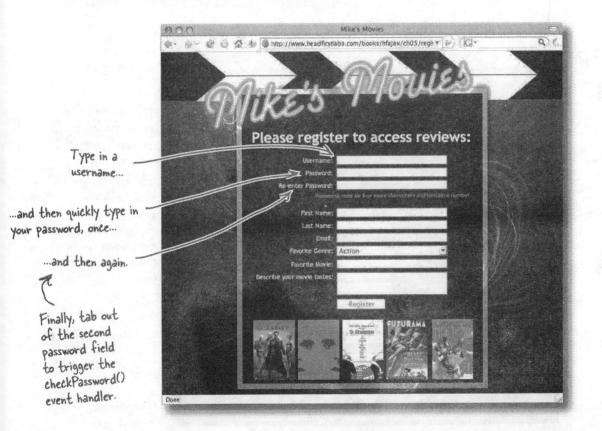

Does anything strange happen? What's going on? What do you think might be causing the problem?

really fast

BE the USER Solution

Your job was to play like you're one of
Mike's potential customers... and a fast-
typing one, at that. Try and figure out
what happens when someone
types in a username, and
then quickly moves to
typing a password in both of
the password fields.

Your instructions

The results

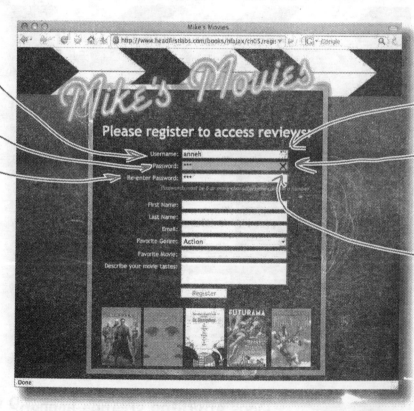

Type in a
username...

...and then quickly type in
your password, once...

...and then again.

Finally, tab out
of the second
password field
to trigger the
checkPassword()
event handler.

The username field
shows the "In
Progress" icon. So far,
so good.

Once both
passwords are
in, the password
field moves to "In
Progress." That's
good, too.

The password
status changes to
okay or denied, so
that's okay, but...

The username
request never
returns! The field
still shows the "In
Progress" icon.

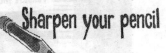

Sharpen your pencil

It's time to figure out what's going on with our asynchronous requests. Below is the request variable named "request", as well as the server. Your job is to draw and label the interactions that are going on between the checkUsername(), showUsernameStatus(), checkPassword(), and showPasswordStatus() functions.

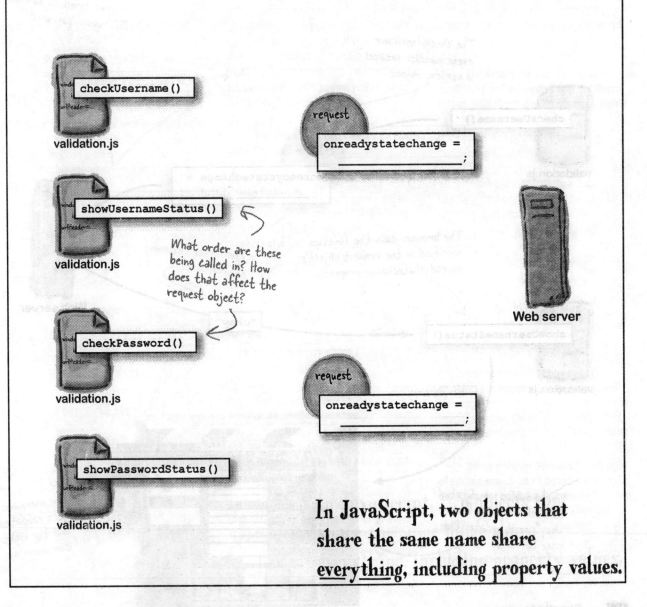

checkUsername()

validation.js

request

onreadystatechange =
_____ ;

showUsernameStatus()

validation.js

What order are these being called in? How does that affect the request object?

Web server

checkPassword()

validation.js

request

onreadystatechange =
_____ ;

showPasswordStatus()

validation.js

In JavaScript, two objects that share the same name share everything, including property values.

With **ONE** request object, you can safely send and receive **ONE** asynchronous request

Both checkUsername() and checkPassword() use the same request object. Because both use the variable name request, it's just a single object being used by both. Take a close look at what happens when you're just making a single request, and there's no password validation involved:

Remember, all these problems came up when we tried to validate users' passwords.

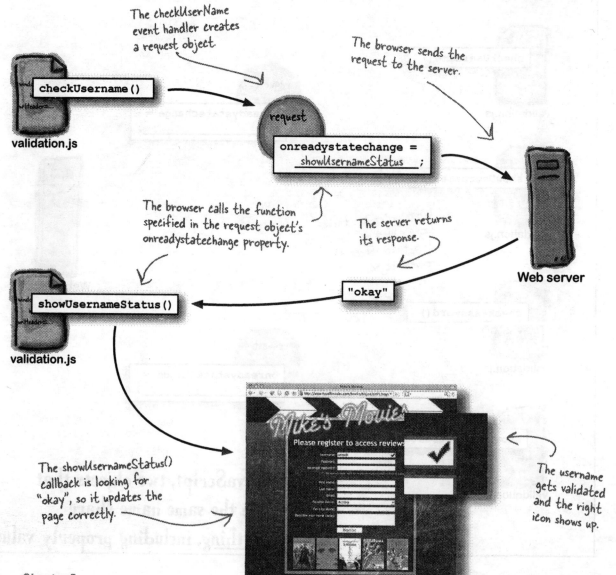

The checkUserName event handler creates a request object.

checkUsername()

validation.js

The browser sends the request to the server.

request

onreadystatechange = showUsernameStatus ;

The browser calls the function specified in the request object's onreadystatechange property.

The server returns its response.

Web server

showUsernameStatus()

validation.js

"okay"

The showUsernameStatus() callback is looking for "okay", so it updates the page correctly.

The username gets validated and the right icon shows up.

Asynchronous requests don't wait on anything... including themselves!

But what happens when there are two requests sharing the same request object? That object can only store one callback function to deal with server responses. That means that you could have two totally different server responses being handled by the *same* callback... and that might not be the *right* callback.

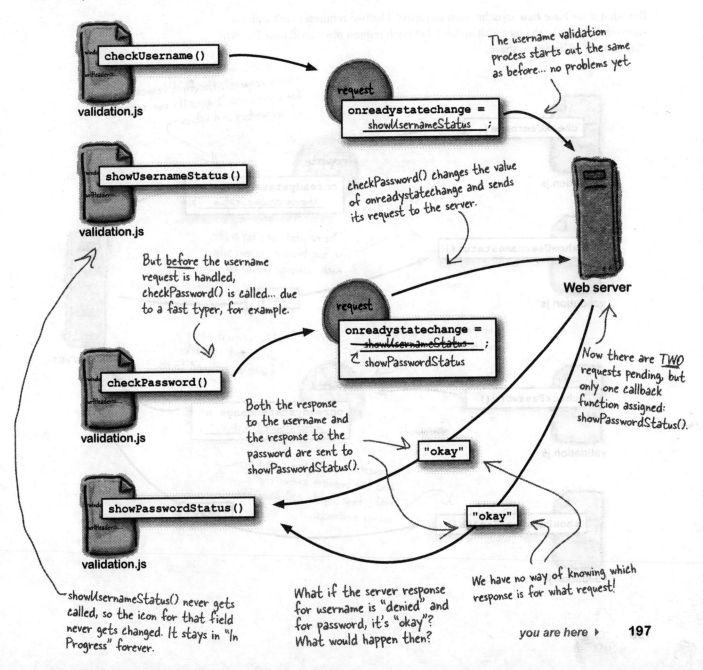

checkUsername()

validation.js

showUsernameStatus()

validation.js

But *before* the username request is handled, checkPassword() is called... due to a fast typer, for example.

checkPassword()

validation.js

showPasswordStatus()

validation.js

request

onreadystatechange = showUsernameStatus ;

The username validation process starts out the same as before... no problems yet

checkPassword() changes the value of onreadystatechange and sends its request to the server.

request

onreadystatechange = ~~showUsernameStatus~~ ; showPasswordStatus

Web server

Now there are TWO requests pending, but only one callback function assigned: showPasswordStatus().

Both the response to the username and the response to the password are sent to showPasswordStatus().

"okay"

"okay"

We have no way of knowing which response is for what request!

showUsernameStatus() never gets called, so the icon for that field never gets changed. It stays in "In Progress" forever.

What if the server response for username is "denied" and for password, it's "okay"? What would happen then?

If you're making <u>TWO</u> separate requests, use <u>TWO</u> separate request objects

The problem is that we're using a single request object to make two aynchronous requests. And what does asynchrony mean? That those requests won't wait on a browser or server to get moving. So we end up overwriting one request's data with data from another request.

But what if we have *two* asynchronous requests? The two requests won't wait on each other, or make the user wait around, but each request object will have its own data instead of having to share.

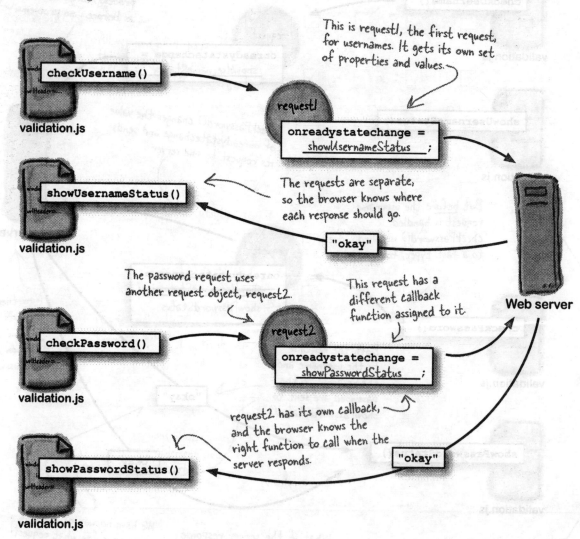

checkUsername()

validation.js

This is request1, the first request, for usernames. It gets its own set of properties and values.

request1

onreadystatechange = showUsernameStatus ;

showUsernameStatus()

validation.js

The requests are separate, so the browser knows where each response should go.

"okay"

Web server

The password request uses another request object, request2.

This request has a different callback function assigned to it

checkPassword()

validation.js

request2

onreadystatechange = showPasswordStatus ;

request2 has its own callback, and the browser knows the right function to call when the server responds.

"okay"

showPasswordStatus()

validation.js

Exercise

You should be ready to update your code to use two request objects. You'll have to change code in validation.js in several different places. See if you can find them all. For username-related requests, use the variable name usernameRequest. For password-related requests, use passwordRequest. When you think you've got them all, turn the page.

there are no Dumb Questions

Q: What does any of this have to do with asynchrony?

A: Well, think about this: what if the request to validate usernames was *not* asynchronous? Then there'd be no way that the password request could get sent before the username request completed. So this problem wouldn't exist in a synchronous environment.

Q: Wouldn't it be easier to just make the username request synchronous?

A: It would be easier, but would that be the best application? Then users would have to wait for their username to get processed. Then, and only then, could they move on to the password field. Sometimes the easiest technical solution is actually the worst usability solution.

Q: Why do the two request variables share property values? Isn't each declared locally within separate functions?

A: It looks that way, but request is actually first defined in the createRequest() function. Not only that, but request is defined in createRequest() *without* the var keyword. Any variable declared in JavaScript inside a function, but without the var keyword, becomes a global variable.

Q: So why not just use the var keyword in createRequest() to fix all of this? Wouldn't that make request local?

A: Good question, but that would cause a different set of problems. If request is local, then how would a callback function get access to the request object? The callbacks need request to be global, so they can access the variable and its property values.

Q: So how does assigning request to two other variable names help?

A: In JavaScript, assignment is handled by *copying*, and not by *reference*. So when you assign one variable to another value, the new variable gets a copy of the assigned variable. Consider this code:

```
var a = 1;
var b = a;
b = 2;
alert("a = " + a);
alert("b = " + b);
```

You might expect both values to be 2, right? But they're not. When JavaScript interprets var b = a;, it creates a new variable named b, and puts a copy of a into that variable. So no matter what you do to b, it won't change a.

In the case of the request object, if you create two variables and assign request to both, you'll get two *copies* of the original request object. That's two independent request objects that won't affect each other. That's just what we want.

Q: Wow, this is kind of hairy. I'm still confused... what should I do?

A: You may want to pick up a good JavaScript book, like *Head First JavaScript* or *JavaScript: The Definitive Guide*, for more on variable scope and assignment in JavaScript. Or you may want to just follow along, and pick up what you're a little unsure about as you go.

> **JavaScript considers any variable outside a function, or a variable declared without the var keyword, to be <u>GLOBAL</u>. That variable can be accessed by any function, anywhere.**

Exercise Solution

Change all the variable names in checkUserName(), showUsernameStatus(), checkPassword() and showPasswordStatus() fuctions in the registration.js file.

```
function checkUsername() {
    document.getElementById("username").className = "thinking";
    var usernameRequest = createRequest();
    if (usernameRequest == null)
        alert("Unable to create request");
    else {
        var theName = document.getElementById("username").value;
        var username = escape(theName);
        var url= "checkName.php?username=" + username;
        usernameRequest.onreadystatechange = showUsernameStatus;
        usernameRequest.open("GET", url, true);
        usernameRequest.send(null);
    }
}

function showUsernameStatus() {
    if (usernameRequest.readyState == 4) {
        if (usernameRequest.status == 200) {
            if (usernameRequest.responseText == "okay") {
                document.getElementById("username").className = "approved";
                document.getElementById("register").disabled = false;
            } else {
                document.getElementById("username").className = "denied";
                document.getElementById("username").focus();
                document.getElementById("username").select();
                document.getElementById("register").disabled = true;
            }
        }
    }
}

function checkPassword() {
    var password1 = document.getElementById("password1");
    var password2 = document.getElementById("password2");
    password1.className = "thinking";
```

It's very important to remove this var... we need usernameRequest to be global, so the callback can reference this variable.

We're using usernameRequest for the request object related to username checks.

Set properties and send the request just like you did before.

Here's why you needed usernameRequest to be global: this callback also has to access the same object.

```
// First compare the two passwords
if ((password1.value == "") || (password1.value != password2.value)) {
  password1.className = "denied";
  return;
}

// Passwords match, so send request to server
var passwordRequest = createRequest();
if (passwordRequest == null) {
  alert("Unable to create request");
} else {
  var password = escape(password1.value);
  var url = "checkPass.php?password=" + password;
  passwordRequest.onreadystatechange = showPasswordStatus;
  passwordRequest.open("GET", url, true);
  passwordRequest.send(null);
  }
}
function showPasswordStatus() {
  if (passwordRequest.readyState == 4) {
    if (passwordRequest.status == 200) {
      var password1 = document.getElementById("password1");
      if (passwordRequest.responseText == "okay") {
       password1.className = "approved";
       document.getElementById("register").disabled = false;
      } else {
       password1.className = "denied";
       password1.focus();
       password1.select();
       document.getElementById("register").disabled = true;
      }
    }
  }
}
```

Just like with the other request variable, do <u>not</u> use the var keyword.

passwordRequest is used for all password-related requests.

Now this code has no chance of overwriting properties of the username request object

There's still a problem with the registration page. Can you figure out what it is?

> Once I enter a valid username, I can click Register... even if the password's rejected.

Validation requires both VERIFICATION and RESTRICTION.

Verification is making sure that a certain piece of data is okay for your system to accept. **Restriction** is not allowing a user to do something until that verification is complete. Good validation combines both of these components.

When we wrote the first version of Mike's page, we disabled the Register button in the `initPage()` function, and re-enabled it once the server validated the user's username. So we *verified* the username and *restricted* the Register button.

But now there's another level of validation: we have to make sure the user's password is okay. Something's going wrong, though... even if a password is rejected, the Register button is getting enabled, and users can click the button.

Validation requires verification AND restriction.

In asynchronous applications, it's not enough to just verify data entered by the user. While that verification is occurring, you have to restrict the user from doing things that depend upon verification.

there are no Dumb Questions

Q: How is enabling the Register button part of restriction? That doesn't make sense...

A: Restriction is the process of not letting a user do something until verification is complete. So part of the restriction process is enabling a button or activating a form. In fact, the end of every restriction process is the *lifting* of that restriction.

Right now, we disable the Register button in initPage()...

The movie page works correctly at the beginning. When the page loads, the Register button is disabled:

```
function initPage() {
    document.getElementById("username").onblur = checkUsername;
    document.getElementById("password2").onblur = checkPassword;
    document.getElementById("register").disabled = true;
}
```

This button is disabled... we (correctly) make sure users can't do anything until they've got a valid username and password.

Register

...and enable the button in the callback functions

We enabled the Register button in the two callback functions, showUsernameStatus() and showPasswordStatus(). But we're still getting incorrect actions on the form.

showUsernameStatus()

```
if (usernameRequest.responseText == "okay") {
    document.getElementById("username").className = "approved";
    document.getElementById("register").disabled = false;
} else {
    // code to reject username and keep Register disabled
}
```

showPasswordStatus()

```
if (passwordRequest.responseText == "okay") {
    password1.className = "approved";
    document.getElementById("register").disabled = false;
} else {
    // code to reject username and keep Register disabled
}
```

Both of these callbacks enable the Register button only when their verification successfully completes.

But the Register button is still getting enabled when the username is valid, and the password isn't. What gives?

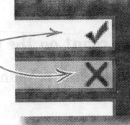

Asynchrony means you can't count on the <u>ORDERING</u> of your requests and responses

When you send asynchronous requests, you can't be sure of the order that the server will respond to those requests. Suppose that a request to verify a username is sent to the server. Then, another request is sent, this time to verify a password. Which one will return first? ***There's no way of knowing!***

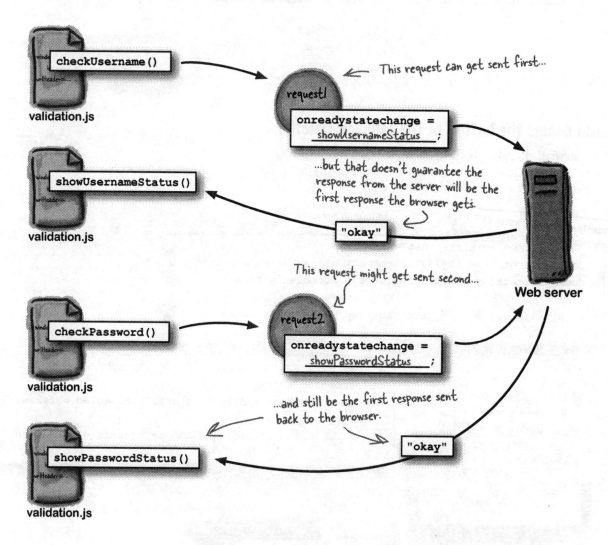

Never count on the <u>ORDER</u> or <u>SEQUENCE</u> of requests and responses in asynchronous applications.

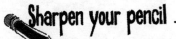

Sharpen your pencil

Can you figure out at least one sequence of requests and responses that would result in the Register button being enabled when either the username or the password is invalid? Draw or list the steps that would have to occur for that to happen.

Sharpen your pencil
Solution

Here are two different sequences where the Register button ended up enabled when it shouldn't be. Did you come up with one of these? Or something similar?

The Register button always starts out disabled.

① **The user enters a valid username.**

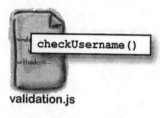

validation.js

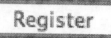

② **The user enters two passwords that don't match.**

validation.js

If the two passwords don't match, there's no request to the server... so there's an almost instant denied result.

Web server

③ **The password field shows the "denied" X mark.**

The server returns its response after the passwords have already been denied.

④ **The username callback gets an "okay" response and sets the username field to show the "approved" check mark... and enables the Register button.**

The end result is a valid username, invalid password, and enabled Register button.

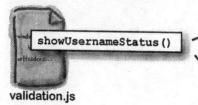

validation.js

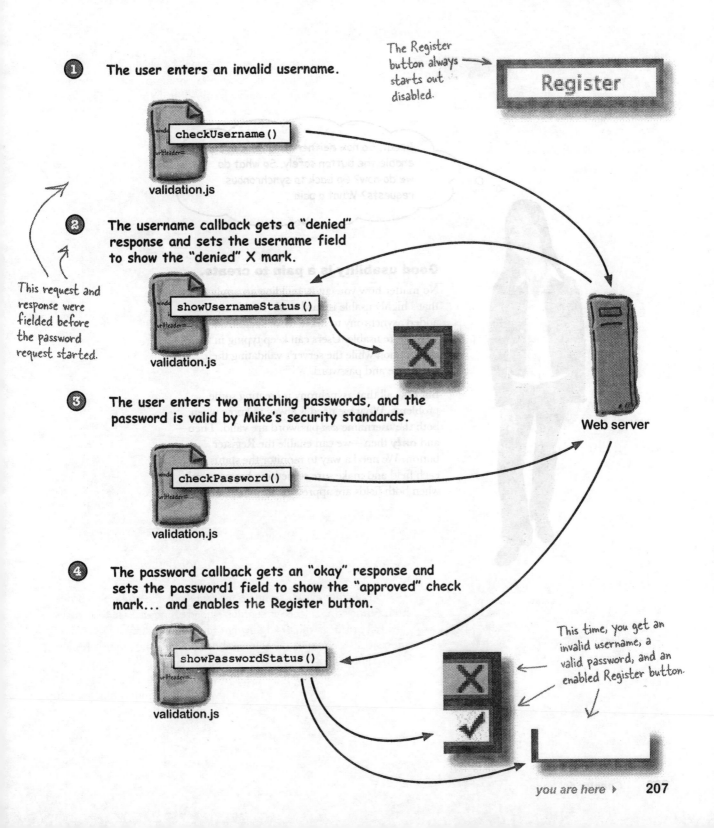

The Register button always starts out disabled.

1 The user enters an invalid username.

`checkUsername()`

validation.js

2 The username callback gets a "denied" response and sets the username field to show the "denied" X mark.

This request and response were fielded before the password request started.

`showUsernameStatus()`

validation.js

3 The user enters two matching passwords, and the password is valid by Mike's security standards.

`checkPassword()`

validation.js

Web server

4 The password callback gets an "okay" response and sets the password1 field to show the "approved" check mark... and enables the Register button.

`showPasswordStatus()`

validation.js

This time, you get an invalid username, a valid password, and an enabled Register button.

> Great. So now **neither** function can enable the button safely. So what do we do now? Go back to synchronous requests? What a pain...

Good usability is a pain to create.

No matter how you cut it, building an application that's highly usable is hard work. In this case, we added asynchrony to make Mike's registration page more usable. Users can keep typing in their information while the server's validating their username and password.

But now all that asynchrony is creating some problems. What we need is a way to know when both the username *and* password are valid. Then—and *only* then—we can enable the Register button. We need a way to monitor the status of each field and make sure something happens only when both fields are approved.

A monitor function MONITORS your application... from OUTSIDE the action

We need a monitor function. That's a function that monitors certain variables or parts of an application, and then takes action based on the things it's monitoring.

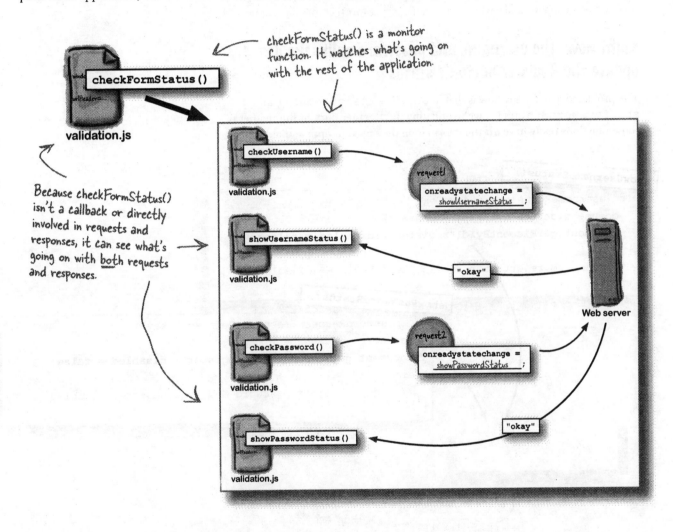

checkFormStatus() is a monitor function. It watches what's going on with the rest of the application.

checkFormStatus()

validation.js

Because checkFormStatus() isn't a callback or directly involved in requests and responses, it can see what's going on with both requests and responses.

checkUsername()

validation.js

request1

onreadystatechange = showUsernameStatus ;

showUsernameStatus()

validation.js

"okay"

Web server

checkPassword()

validation.js

request2

onreadystatechange = showPasswordStatus ;

showPasswordStatus()

validation.js

"okay"

Exercise

Can you figure out what a checkFormStatus() monitor function should do? You'll also need to call that function. Where in your code should that happen? If you're not sure, think about it for a while... and then turn the page for a few helpful hints.

You call a monitor function when action MIGHT need to be taken

Monitor functions are usually used to update a part of an application or page that depends on several variables. So you call the monitor when you think it **might** be time to update a page... like when a username or password comes back approved.

Right now, the username and password callbacks directly update the Register button's status

The problem we're having now is that in showUsernameStatus() and showPasswordStatus(), we're updating the Register button. But neither of those functions really have **all** the information they need to update that button.

showUsernameStatus()

```
if (usernameRequest.responseText == "okay") {
   document.getElementById("username").className = "approved";
   document.getElementById("register").disabled = false;
} else {
   // code to reject username and keep Register disabled
}
```

showPasswordStatus()

```
if (passwordRequest.responseText == "okay") {
   password1.className = "approved";
   document.getElementById("register").disabled = false;
} else {
   // code to reject password and keep Register disabled
}
```

This enabling is being done with incomplete information! The username callback doesn't check to see if the password is valid, and the password callback doesn't check to see if the username is valid. The result: the button gets enabled when it shouldn't be.

Let's have the callbacks run the monitor function...

So instead of directly changing the button status, we can change our callback
functions to run the monitor function. That way, it's not up to either callback to
figure out what status the Register button should be in.

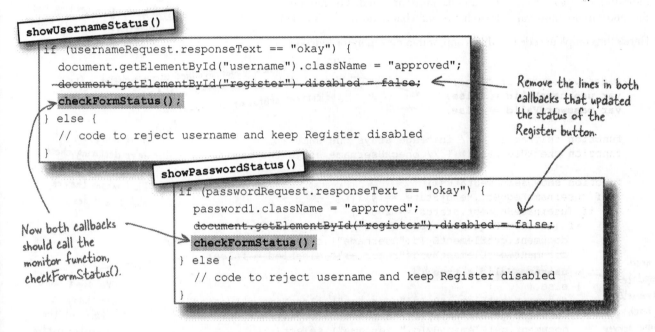

`showUsernameStatus()`

```
if (usernameRequest.responseText == "okay") {
    document.getElementById("username").className = "approved";
    document.getElementById("register").disabled = false;
    checkFormStatus();
} else {
    // code to reject username and keep Register disabled
}
```

Remove the lines in both
callbacks that updated
the status of the
Register button.

`showPasswordStatus()`

```
if (passwordRequest.responseText == "okay") {
    password1.className = "approved";
    document.getElementById("register").disabled = false;
    checkFormStatus();
} else {
    // code to reject username and keep Register disabled
}
```

Now both callbacks
should call the
monitor function,
checkFormStatus().

...and let the monitor function update the Register button

Since the monitor function is separate from either the username or
password checks, it can get all the information it needs. The monitor
function can check the username and password fields, and make the
right decision about what status the Register button should be set to.

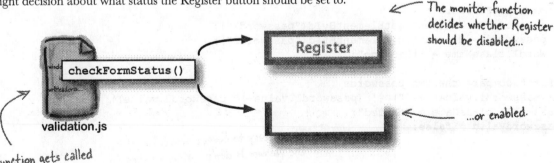

`checkFormStatus()`

validation.js

This function gets called
every time a username or
password is accepted.

The monitor function
decides whether Register
should be disabled...

Register

...or enabled.

Status variables let monitors know what's going on

We're ready to write a monitor function to set the status of the Register button's `disabled` property, and now both callbacks call that monitor. All that's left is to have those callbacks set some status variables, indicating whether the username and password are valid. The monitor function can use those variables to figure out what to do when it's called.

Believe it or not, we're *still* working on getting the password functionality right.

Here's the complete code for Mike's app, with a new monitor function:

```
window.onload = initPage;
var usernameValid = false;
var passwordValid = false;
```

We need two new global variables. usernameValid is the current status of the username, and passwordValid is the the current status of the password.

We're using var, but we're declaring these outside of any function. That means they're global variables.

```
function initPage() { // initPage stays the same }
function checkUsername() { // checkUsername stays the same }

function showUsernameStatus() {
  if (usernameRequest.readyState == 4) {
    if (usernameRequest.status == 200) {
      if (usernameRequest.responseText == "okay") {
        document.getElementById("username").className = "approved";
        document.getElementById("register").disabled = false;
        usernameValid = true;
      } else {
        document.getElementById("username").className = "denied";
        document.getElementById("username").focus();
        document.getElementById("username").select();
        document.getElementById("register").disabled = true;
        usernameValid = false;
      }
      checkFormStatus();
    }
  }
}
```

We need to update usernameValid for both possible server responses.

We don't want to change the status of the Register button in *either* of the if/else branches.

Since we need to call the monitor function in either case, it's easier to leave it outside the if/else statement.

```
function checkPassword() {
  var password1 = document.getElementById("password1");
  var password2 = document.getElementById("password2");
  password1.className = "thinking";

  // First compare the two passwords
  if ((password1.value == "") || (password1.value != password2.value)) {
    password1.className = "denied";
    passwordValid = false;
```

This is easy to forget about, but if the passwords don't match, we need to update the passwordValid status variable.

None of our code should set the status of the Register button except for the monitor.

validation.js

```
    checkFormStatus();
    return;
  }

  // Passwords match, so send request to server
  passwordRequest = createRequest();
  if (passwordRequest == null) {
    alert("Unable to create request");
  } else {
    var password = escape(password1.value);
    var url = "checkPass.php?password=" + password;
    passwordRequest.onreadystatechange = showPasswordStatus;
    passwordRequest.open("GET", url, true);
    passwordRequest.send(null);
  }
}

function showPasswordStatus() {
  if (passwordRequest.readyState == 4) {
    if (passwordRequest.status == 200) {
      var password1 = document.getElementById("password1");
      if (passwordRequest.responseText == "okay") {
        password1.className = "approved";
        document.getElementById("register").disabled = false;
        passwordValid = true;
      } else {
        password1.className = "denied";
        password1.focus();
        password1.select();
        document.getElementById("register").disabled = true;
        passwordValid = false;
      }
      checkFormStatus();
    }
  }
}

function checkFormStatus() {
  if (usernameValid && passwordValid) {
    document.getElementById("register").disabled = false;
  } else {
    document.getElementById("register").disabled = true;
  }
}
```

This is just like the username callback. Update the global status variable for password...

...and then call the monitor function.

All this function has to do is check the two status variables...

...and set the Register button's status accordingly.

Explicitly set the button to disabled, in case there was a valid username or password before, but now there's a change that makes one of those invalid.

Test Drive

Finally! But does it all work?

Make sure your version of validation.js matches the version shown on the last two pages. You should have two new global variables, an updated version of checkPassword(), two updated callback functions, and a new monitor function, checkFormStatus().

Load everything up. Try out the scenarios you worked out for the exercise from page 205. Do they still break the page? If not, you've solved Mike's asynchrony problems!

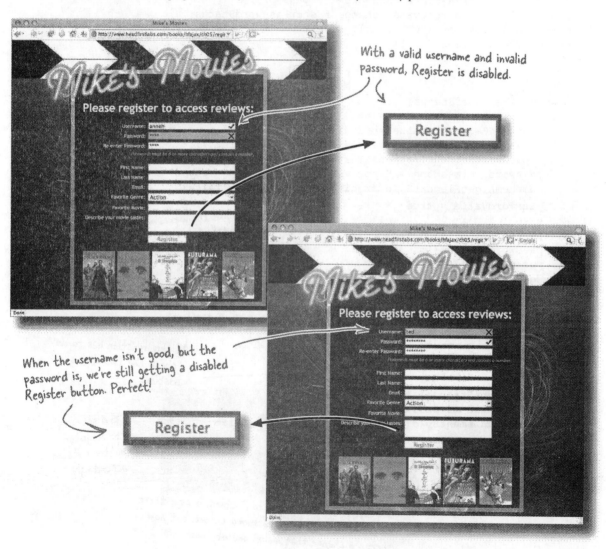

With a valid username and invalid password, Register is disabled.

When the username isn't good, but the password is, we're still getting a disabled Register button. Perfect!

there are no
Dumb Questions

Q: Can you explain what a monitor function is again?

A: Sure. A monitor function is just a function that monitors your application. So for Mike's registration page, the monitor function is monitoring the state of the username and password variables, and it's changing the form to match the current status.

Q: I thought monitor functions usually ran automatically, like at set intervals.

A: Sometimes they do. In systems where you have a lot more threading capability—the ability to run a process in the background—it's common to have a monitor function execute periodically. Then, you don't have to explicitly call the monitor, which is what we do in the username and password callbacks.

Refactoring code is pulling out common parts and putting those parts into a single, easily-maintainable function or method. Refactoring makes code easier to update and maintain.

Q: Why didn't you declare usernameValid and passwordValid in initPage()?

A: You could do that. But if you do declare the variables inside `initPage()`, be sure *not* to use the `var` keyword. `usernameValid` and `passwordValid` need to be global variables.

Variables declared *outside* of any function (with or without `var`) are global. Variables declared *inside* a function, but *without* `var`, are also global. And variables declared *inside* a function, *with* `var`, are local. It's a bit confusing, that's for sure.

In fact, that's why they're left outside of any function: it makes it a little clearer that those two variables are global, and not local to any particular function.

Q: So then why aren't usernameRequest and passwordRequest declared there also?

A: That's actually a good idea, and you might want to make that change. In our code, we left them in `checkUsername()` and `checkPassword()` because that's where those variables were originally created (back when they were both called `request`).

Q: Couldn't I set the status of the username and password1 fields in my monitor function, too?

A: You sure could. In fact, that's probably a good idea. That would mean that there'd be less CSS class-changing happening all over the code. Most of that display logic would be handled by the monitor, which

is already dealing with the display of the Register button.

Anytime you can consolidate (or **refactor**) code without a lot of ill consequences, it's a good idea. Cleaner code is easier to modify and maintain.

Q: Just adding in a password field sure made things complicated. Is that normal?

A: In asynchronous apps, adding an additional asynchronous request is usually pretty tricky. The thing that added a lot of complexity to Mike's app wasn't the additional password *fields*, but the additional *request* we needed to make to deal with those fields.

Q: And this is all just so users can keep typing instead of waiting?

A: It sure is. You'd be surprised at how impatient web users are (or maybe you wouldn't!). Typing in a username, waiting for the username to get validated, typing in a password, and then also waiting for the password to get validated... that's a lot of waiting. It's even worse that after all that waiting, the user still has to fill out the rest of the form.

Saving a couple of seconds here and there really adds up on the Web. In fact, it might be the difference between keeping a customer and losing them.

Q: So what about form submits? There's going to be waiting there, too, right?

A: Now you're getting ahead! But that's exactly what Mike was thinking when he asked for scrolling images...

And now for our last trick...

Mike's got one last request. When users click the Register button, the images along the bottom should begin to scroll while the form is processing. This gives the user something interesting to watch while they're waiting on Mike's registration logic.

And now we know the Register button works right.

Fortunately, this shouldn't be too difficult. Here's what we need to do to put this into action:

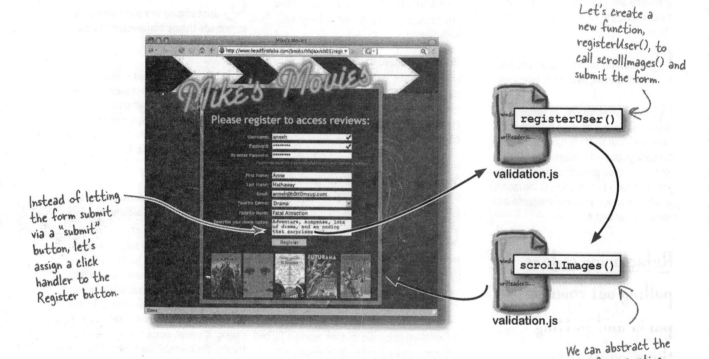

Let's create a new function, registerUser(), to call scrollImages() and submit the form.

registerUser()

validation.js

Instead of letting the form submit via a "submit" button, let's assign a click handler to the Register button.

scrollImages()

validation.js

We can abstract the code for animating the images into another function, scrollImages(), and call that when we need to scroll the images.

Sharpen your pencil

Do you think the request to submit the form to Mike's server should be synchronous or asynchronous?

☐ Synchronous   ☐ Asynchronous

Why? ....
....
....

Does your choice above have any affect on the scrolling of the images along the bottom of the page?
....
....
....
....

The answers to these questions are spread out over the rest of the chapter, so you'll have to keep reading to find out if you got these right.

Synchronous requests block ALL YOUR CODE from doing anything

When you send an entire form off to be processed, you usually want that request to be **synchronous**. That's because you don't want users to change that data while the server is working with it.

But Mike wants scrolling images *while* the user is waiting on the server. That means you need your code to run *while the server is working on a response*. So even though the request would ideally be synchronous, you need it to be an **asynchronous** request to fulfill image-loving Mike's needs.

This isn't a perfect solution, but lots of times you've got to make this sort of choice: satisfying the client's needs even when the result is a little less than ideal. Mike's willing to let users mess around with the form, if they really want to, while their request is being processed. He figures they won't do that, though, **because** of the scrolling images. They'll be too busy thinking about which movie review they want to check out when they're logged in.

First, we no longer need a "submit" button

A "submit" button in XHTML submits a form. And since we no longer need the Register button to submit the form, we can make it a normal button. Then, we can submit the form in our JavaScript.

```
        <li><label for="favorite">Favorite Movie:</label><input id="favorite"
                type="text" name="favorite" /></li>
        <li><label for="tastes">Describe your movie tastes:</label><textarea
                name="tastes" cols="60" rows="2" id="tastes"></textarea></li>
        <li><label for="register"></label><input id="register"
                type="button" value="Register" name="register" /></li>
    </ul>
  </form>

  <!-- Cover images -->
</div>
</body>
</html>
```

We need a regular button now, not a submit button.

The original version of our XHTML was shown way back on page 182.

registration.html

Second, we need to register a new event handler for the button's onclick event

Now we need to attach an event handler to that button. We'll call the function we want to run `registerUser()`, and we can make the assignment in `initPage()`:

```
function initPage() {
  document.getElementById("username").onblur = checkUsername;
  document.getElementById("password2").onblur = checkPassword;
  document.getElementById("register").disabled = true;
  document.getElementById("register").onclick = registerUser;
}
```

Assign the new callback we'll write to the Register button's onclick event.

validation.js

Third, we need to send an <u>ASYNCHRONOUS</u> request to the server

Finally, we need a new event handler function. This function needs to get a new request object, and send it to the server. And this should be an asynchronous request, so we can animate and scroll those images while the user is waiting.

Let's change the text on the button to provide a little information to the user.

This is all new code.

```
function registerUser() {
  document.getElementById("register").value = "Processing...";
  registerRequest = createRequest();
  if (registerRequest == null) {
    alert("Unable to create request.");
  } else {
    var url = "register.php?username=" +
      escape(document.getElementById("username").value) + "&password=" +
      escape(document.getElementById("password1").value) + "&firstname=" +
      escape(document.getElementById("firstname").value) + "&lastname=" +
      escape(document.getElementById("lastname").value) + "&email=" +
      escape(document.getElementById("email").value) + "&genre=" +
      escape(document.getElementById("genre").value) + "&favorite=" +
      escape(document.getElementById("favorite").value) + "&tastes=" +
      escape(document.getElementById("tastes").value);
    registerRequest.onreadystatechange = registrationProcessed;
    registerRequest.open("GET", url, true);
    registerRequest.send(null);
  }
}
```

Create another request object...

...and configure the object's properties.

It's tempting to make this synchronous, but that would block the image scrolling we're going to add in a few pages.

validation.js

> Hang on a sec. We've worked all this time to make the form super-usable, and now we're throwing it all away just so Mike can scroll little movie covers across the screen? You've got to be kidding!

Usability is in the eye of the ~~beholder~~... err... the client.

Sometimes clients do things that don't make sense to you. That's why they're paying the bills, and you're collecting the checks. You can suggest alternatives to your client, but at the end of the day, you're going to be a lot happier if you just build the client what they ask for.

In Mike's case, he wants to entice users with reviews available on his site, so he wants images to scroll while users are waiting on their registration request. That makes his form a little less usable, though. Now, instead of waiting on a response, users can actually type over their entries. That could create some confusion about what information Mike's system actually registered for that user.

Then again, Mike will probably just call you later when he realizes that for himself... and that's not altogether a bad thing, is it?

You can suggest alternative ideas to your clients, but ultimately, you should almost **ALWAYS** build what the client asked for... even if you don't agree with their decisions.

there are no
Dumb Questions

Q: Could I disable all the fields while the images are scrolling?

A: That's a great idea! Why don't you take some time now to do that. Mike will love that he gets scrolling, and you'll still keep the nice usability you've built into the registration page so far. We won't show that code, though, so consider it a little extra-credit project.

Use setInterval() to let <u>JavaScript</u> run your process, instead of your own code

setInterval() is a handy method that lets you pass in a function, and have the JavaScript interpreter run your code over and over, every so often. Since it's the interpreter running your code, the function you send setInterval() will run even while your code is busy doing other things like, say, registering a user.

To use setInterval(), you pass it a function to execute and the interval at which the function should be called, in <u>milliseconds</u>. The method returns a **token**, which you can use to modify or cancel the process.

1 second is 1000 milliseconds.

Here's setInterval() in action.

```
t = setInterval(scrollImages, 50);
```

This is the token that you can use to cancel the interval.

setInterval() is the method itself.

The first argument to setInterval() is the statement to be evaluated. In this case, we want it to call the function called scrollImages. You leave off the parentheses so that JavaScript will actually reference the function, not just run it once.

This tells JavaScript how often to execute the statement. We've chosen 40 milliseconds, which is a good average rate to scroll something.

You can use any valid JavaScript here, including an anonymous function.

there are no Dumb Questions

Q: Is the function you pass to setInterval() a callback?

A: Yes. Every time the interval you set passes, the function you pass in here will be called back by the browser.

Q: So do you write that function just like the callback for a request object?

A: Well, there isn't a request object involved, and so you don't need to check any readyState or status properties. And there's no server response to evaluate. So you just need a JavaScript function that does something every time it's called.

Q: So I can do anything inside a setInterval() callback that I can do in JavaScript?

A: Yes, that's right. There's no limitation on what you can do inside the function.

Q: Why do you use the parentheses when you specify the function?

A: Because you're not setting a property, like you do when you assign an event handler. You're actually passing code to the JavaScript interpreter. The interpreter will then execute that code every time the interval elapses.

Q: How many times does the callback happen?

A: Until you cancel the timer. You can do that with clearInterval().

You can pass any JavaScript function to setInterval(), and have it run automatically at pre-determined intervals.

So this isn't really more asynchronous behavior, is it?

setInterval() is essentially JavaScript's version of multi-threading.

Some programming languages, like C# and JavaScript, allow you to specify that a function be executed on a separate thread. If the computer has more than one CPU, two different threads *might* actually execute simultaneously. On most computers, the operating system executes one thread for a short time, then switches to another thread, then back. It's sort of like driving and talking on a cell phone, without the risk of plowing into the guy in the big SUV to your left.

In our case, the JavaScript interpreter is able to do two things more or less at once: keep executing `scrollImages()` every few seconds, and deal with the asynchronous request from our code to Mike's web server.

Exercise

You're in the home stretch now. There are just a few things left to do to finish up Mike's registration page... and you're going to do them all right now. Here's your list of things to take care of before turning the page:

☐ Add the following Ready-Bake Code for scrolling the cover images to `validation.js`.

```
function scrollImages() {
  var coverBarDiv = document.getElementById("coverBar");          ← Find all
  var images = coverBarDiv.getElementsByTagName("img");              the images.
  for (var i = 0; i < images.length; i++) {
    var left = images[i].style.left.substr(0,        ← For each image, figure
              images[i].style.left.length - 2);         out what its current
    if (left <= -86) {                                   position is using the
      left = 532;                                        "left" attribute of its
    }                                                    style property...
    images[i].style.left = (left - 1) + "px";  ←
  }
}                                        ...and then move the image
                                         just a bit further to the
                                         left (or loop it around).
```

Ready Bake Code

☐ Add a line to the Register button's event handler callback that tells the JavaScript interpreter to run `scrollImages()` every 50 milliseconds.

↖ We don't explain this code because it's standard JavaScript. You can use it safely, though... and dig into Head First JavaScript for more details.

☐ Write a callback function for the asynchronous registration request. When the callback gets a response from the server, it should replace the "wrapper" `<div>`'s content with the server's response. You can assume the server returns an XHTML fragment suitable for display.

☐ Test your code out before turning the page. You can do this!

↖ Make sure you've got the CSS from the Chapter 5 examples. The earlier version of Mike's CSS doesn't have styles for the cover images.

Exercise Solution

Your job was to complete Mike's registration page. Did you figure everything out? Here's how we finished up the page.

```
function registerUser() {
  t = setInterval("scrollImages()", 50);
  document.getElementById("register").value = "Processing...";
  registerRequest = createRequest();
  if (registerRequest == null) {
    alert("Unable to create request.");
  } else {
    var url = "register.php";
    registerRequest.onreadystatechange = registrationProcessed;
    registerRequest.open("GET", url, true);
    registerRequest.send(null);
  }
}


function registrationProcessed() {
  if (registerRequest.readyState == 4) {
    if (registerRequest.status == 200) {
      document.getElementById('wrapper').innerHTML =
        registerRequest.responseText;
    }
  }
}

function scrollImages() {
  var coverBarDiv = document.getElementById("coverBar");
  var images = coverBarDiv.getElementsByTagName('img');
  for (var i = 0; i < images.length; i++) {
    var left = images[i].style.left.substr(0, images[i].style.left.length - 2);
    if (left <= -86) {
      left = 532;
    }
    images[i].style.left = (left - 1) + 'px';
  }
}
```

Here's where we start the animation.

This callback is pretty simple. It gets a response and replaces the content of main <div> on the page with that response.

This is the Ready Bake Code from the last page. It handles scrolling the images.

```
window.onload = 
  initPage;
url.Header = 
```

validation.js

TEST DRIVE

Let's show Mike what we've done.

It's been a long, fast ride since all Mike cared about was validating usernames. We've added a lot... let's show him what we've come up with.

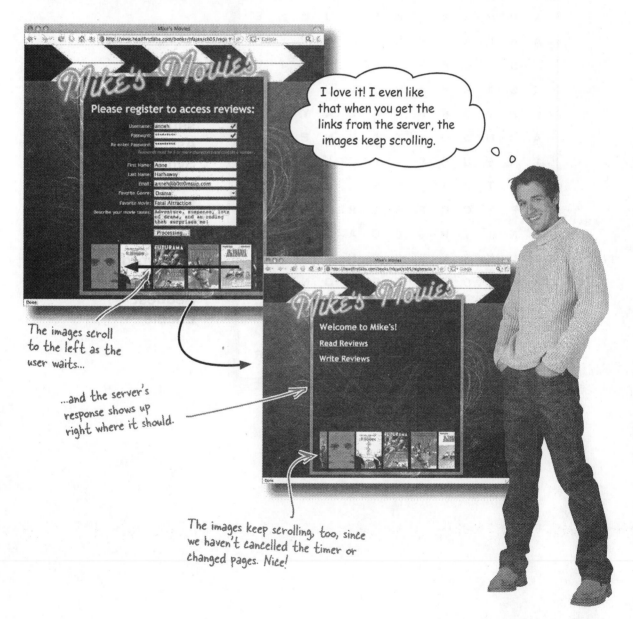

> I love it! I even like that when you get the links from the server, the images keep scrolling.

The images scroll to the left as the user waits...

...and the server's response shows up right where it should.

The images keep scrolling, too, since we haven't cancelled the timer or changed pages. *Nice!*

Word Search

Take some time to sit back and give your right brain something to do. See if you can find the key words below in the letter scramble. Good luck!

```
X  P  R  S  M  O  K  E  J  U  D  H  E
A  A  L  A  V  R  E  T  N  I  T  E  S
A  S  I  O  R  E  M  A  L  T  R  T  V
Q  S  L  X  H  A  N  D  L  E  R  S  L
C  W  Y  O  R  U  H  A  E  A  Y  E  R
A  O  N  N  O  N  T  L  B  N  E  U  A
L  R  E  U  C  S  T  F  C  L  N  Q  S
L  D  T  K  A  H  P  H  N  L  E  E  N
B  E  Y  C  C  E  R  L  R  X  L  R  R
A  N  I  T  H  O  E  O  A  E  D  G  R
C  U  N  B  N  D  Q  B  N  R  A  A  K
K  N  G  O  F  E  U  R  L  O  N  D  A
N  D  U  L  R  I  V  F  R  I  U  D  Y
A  S  E  A  D  I  V  E  A  T  E  S  D
J  E  R  C  I  C  T  H  R  I  Z  A  R
```

Word list:

setInterval
Asynchronous
Synchronous
DIV
Handlers
Callback
Thread
Password
Event
Request
Enable

Fireside Chats

Tonight's talk: **Asynchronous and Synchronous applications go toe-to-toe**

Synchronous:

Hey there, long time, no talk.

I'm a busy guy, you know? And I don't let anything get in the way of paying attention to the user I'm serving.

They'll get their turn, too. Sometimes it's much better to take care of one thing at a time, and then move on to the next job. Slow and steady...

Just because I don't let people interrupt me while I'm working—

One-track mind? I just make sure I finish what I start.

I don't seem to get too many complaints.

Hey, enjoy your 15 minutes of fame, bro. I've seen fads like you come and go a million times.

Asynchronous:

No kidding. Every time I call you, I get a busy signal.

But what about all your *other* users? They're just left waiting around?

You can say *that* again!

Hey, I can listen *and* talk, all at the same time. You're the one with the one-track mind.

Sure, but what if that takes 10 seconds? Or 10 minutes? Or an hour? Do you really think people enjoy that little hourglass whirling around?

Yeah, well, I'd love to sit around like this all day, but my users don't like to wait on me. That's more your department, isn't it?

I bet you thought U2 was a one-hit wonder, too. I'm not going anywhere—except to make the Web a hip place again. See you when I see you...

Word Search Solution

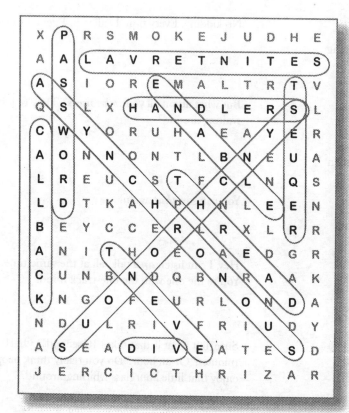

Word list:

setInterval
Asynchronous
Synchronous
DIV
Handlers
Callback
Thread
Password
Event
Request
Enable

6 the document object model

Web Page Forestry

Now, Son, you'll be a man soon, so its time to have a little talk about the birds and the trees.

Did he say **trees**? And here I thought I was gonna learn how to manipulate my web pages like all the other guys.

Wanted: easy-to-update web pages. It's time to take things into your own hands and start writing code that updates your web pages on the fly. Using the **Document Object Model**, your pages can take on new life, responding to users' actions, and you can ditch unnecessary page reloads forever. By the time you've finished this chapter, you'll be able to find, move, and update content virtually anywhere on your web page. So turn the page, and let's take a stroll through the Webville Tree Farm.

You can change the <u>CONTENT</u> of a page...

So far, most of the apps we've built have sent requests, gotten a response, and then used that response to update part of a page's content.

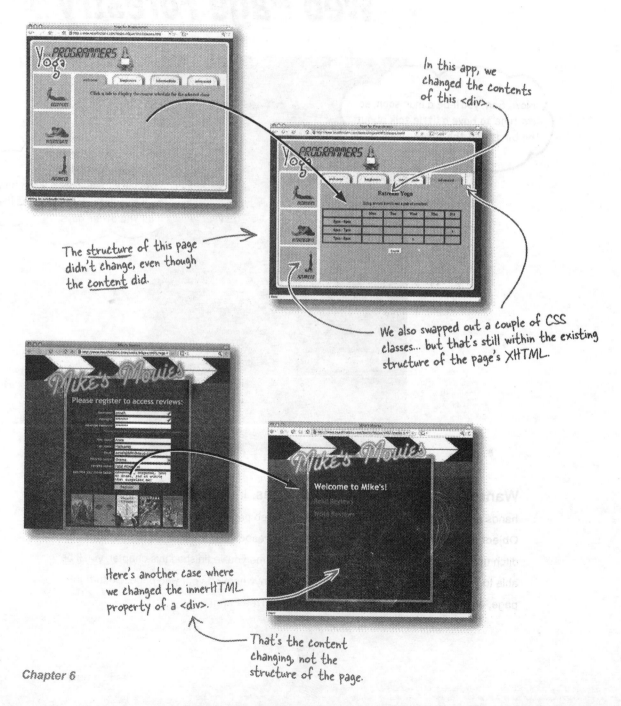

In this app, we changed the contents of this <div>.

The structure of this page didn't change, even though the content did.

We also swapped out a couple of CSS classes... but that's still within the existing structure of the page's XHTML.

Here's another case where we changed the innerHTML property of a <div>.

That's the content changing, not the structure of the page.

...or you can change the <u>STRUCTURE</u> of a page

But what if you need to do more than just change the content of a `<div>` or replace the label on a button? What if an image needs to actually move on a page? How would you accomplish that?

> You can't change the structure of a page, duh! Why would anyone bother writing XHTML in the first place if someone could just move things around?

Your users can't change your XHTML.

The structure of your page is defined in your XHTML, and people viewing your pages definitely can't mess around with that structure. Otherwise, all the work you'd put into your pages would be a total waste of time.

> But what about the **browser**? You'd think it would be okay if the browser moved stuff around... because we can control that with our JavaScript, right?

The browser <u>CAN</u> change your web page's structure

You've already seen that the browser lets you interact with a server-side program, grab elements from a page, and even change properties of those elements. So what about the structure of a page?

Well, the browser can change that, too. In fact, think about it like this: in a lot of ways, the structure of your page is just a property of the page itself. And you already know how to change an object's properties...

Browsers use the <u>Document</u> <u>Object</u> <u>Model</u> to represent your page

Most people call this the <u>DOM</u> for short.

The browser doesn't see your XHTML as a text file with a bunch of letters and angle brackets. It sees your page as a set of objects, using something called the **Document Object Model**, or DOM.

And everything in the DOM begins with the document object. That object represents the very "top level" of your page:

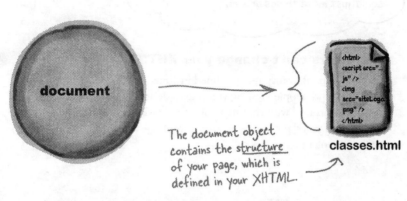

The document object contains the structure of your page, which is defined in your XHTML.

classes.html

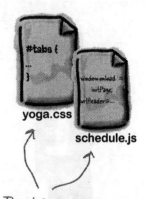

yoga.css

schedule.js

The style and even the code attached to your structure is also represented in the DOM.

The document object is just an <u>OBJECT</u>

You've actually used the DOM, and in particular the document object, several times. Every time you look up an element, you use document:

```
var tabs =
    document.getElementById("tabs").getElementsByTagName("a");
```

The document object

getElementById() is a method of the document object.

In fact, every time you treat an element on a page like an object and set properties of that object, you're working with the DOM. That's because the browser uses the DOM to represent every part of your web page.

```
currentTab.onmouseover = showHint;
currentTab.onmouseout = hideHint;
currentTab.onclick = showTab;
```

It's the DOM that lets browsers work with parts of a page as JavaScript objects with properties.

The document object... Up Close

Everything in the web browser's model of your web page can be accessed using the JavaScript document object. You've already seen the getElementById() and getElementsByTagName() methods, but there's a lot more that you can do with the document object.

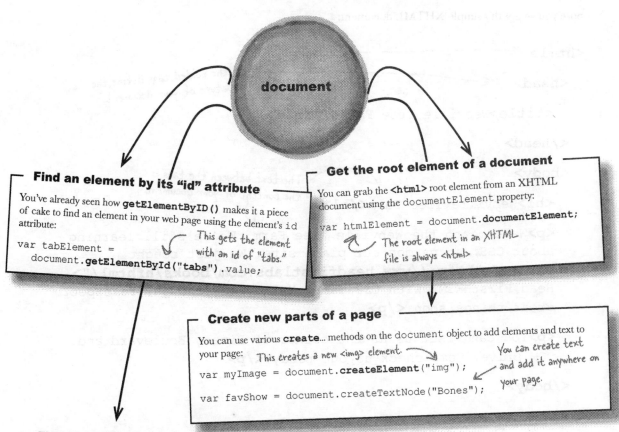

Find an element by its "id" attribute

You've already seen how **getElementByID()** makes it a piece of cake to find an element in your web page using the element's id attribute:

This gets the element with an id of "tabs."

```
var tabElement =
   document.getElementById("tabs").value;
```

Get the root element of a document

You can grab the **<html>** root element from an XHTML document using the documentElement property:

```
var htmlElement = document.documentElement;
```

The root element in an XHTML file is always <html>

Create new parts of a page

You can use various **create...** methods on the document object to add elements and text to your page:

This creates a new <img> element.

You can create text and add it anywhere on your page.

```
var myImage = document.createElement("img");

var favShow = document.createTextNode("Bones");
```

Find nodes by their tag type

If you want all the elements of a certain type, for example, all the images, you can use **getElementsByTagName()**. This returns an array, so you'll need to loop through the array to get a particular element:

This returns all the <div> elements.

```
var allDivs =
   document.getElementsByTagName("div");

var firstPara =
   document.getElementsByTagName("p")[0];
```

Get all the <p> elements...

...and return just the first one in the array.

Here's the XHTML that you write...

When you're creating a web page, you write XHTML to represent the structure and content of your page. Then you give that XHTML to the browser, and the browser figures out how to represent the XHTML on the screen. But if you want to change your web page using JavaScript, you need to know exactly how the **browser** sees your XHTML.

Suppose you've got this simple XHTML document:

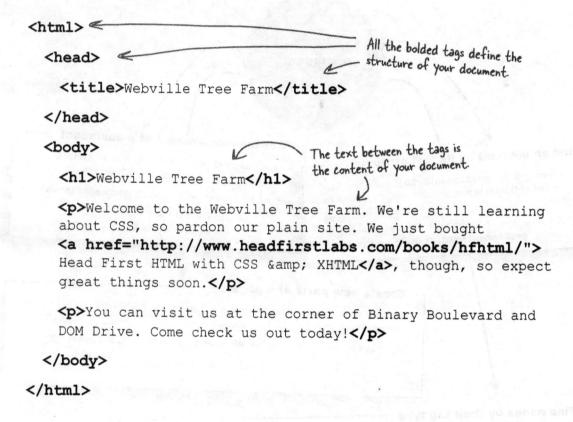

All the bolded tags define the structure of your document.

The text between the tags is the content of your document.

...and here's what your browser sees

The browser has to make some sense of all that markup, and organize it in a way that allows the browser—and your JavaScript code—to work with the page. So the browser turns your XHTML page into a tree of objects:

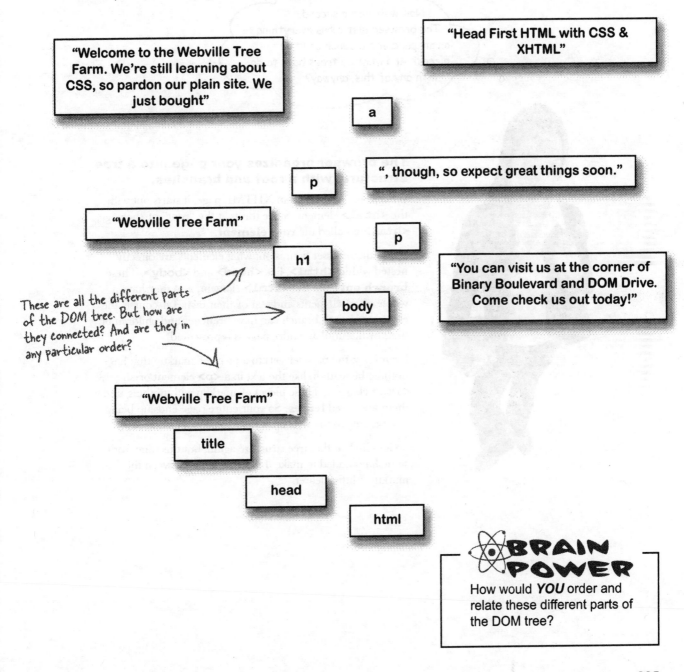

"Welcome to the Webville Tree Farm. We're still learning about CSS, so pardon our plain site. We just bought"

"Head First HTML with CSS & XHTML"

a

", though, so expect great things soon."

p

"Webville Tree Farm"

p

h1

"You can visit us at the corner of Binary Boulevard and DOM Drive. Come check us out today!"

body

These are all the different parts of the DOM tree. But how are they connected? And are they in any particular order?

"Webville Tree Farm"

title

head

html

BRAIN POWER

How would *YOU* order and relate these different parts of the DOM tree?

Now wait just a second. The browser just turns everything on my page into a bunch of little pieces? And what do trees have to do with any of this, anyway?

The browser organizes your page into a tree structure, with a root and branches.

When a browser loads an XHTML page, it starts out with the **\<html\>** element. Since this is at the "root" of the page, **\<html\>** is called the **root element**.

Then, the browser figures out what elements are directly nested within **\<html\>**, like **\<head\>** and **\<body\>**. These **branch out** from the **\<html\>** element, and they have a whole set of elements and text of their own. Of course, the elements in each branch can have branches and children of their own...until an entire page is represented.

Eventually, the browser gets to a piece of markup that has nothing beneath it, like the text in a **\<p\>** element or an **\<img\>** element. These pieces of markup with nothing under them are called **leaves**. So your entire page ends up being one big tree to the web browser.

So let's look at that tree structure again, but this time, with some lines added to make the connections between the markup a little clearer.

Your page is a set of <u>related</u> objects

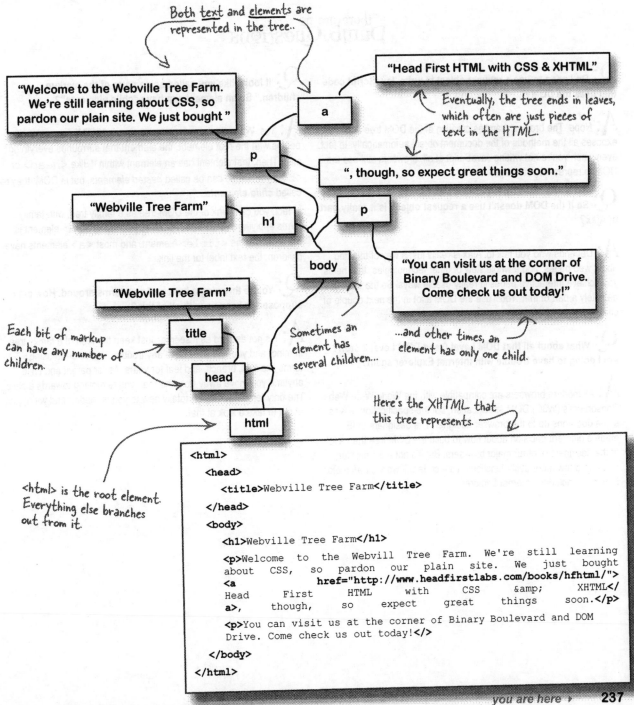

Both <u>text</u> and <u>elements</u> are represented in the tree.

"Head First HTML with CSS & XHTML"

"Welcome to the Webville Tree Farm. We're still learning about CSS, so pardon our plain site. We just bought "

Eventually, the tree ends in leaves, which often are just pieces of text in the HTML.

a

p

", though, so expect great things soon."

"Webville Tree Farm"

h1

p

body

"You can visit us at the corner of Binary Boulevard and DOM Drive. Come check us out today!"

"Webville Tree Farm"

Each bit of markup can have any number of children.

title

Sometimes an element has several children...

...and other times, an element has only one child.

head

html

Here's the XHTML that this tree represents.

<html> is the root element. Everything else branches out from it.

```
<html>
  <head>
    <title>Webville Tree Farm</title>
  </head>
  <body>
    <h1>Webville Tree Farm</h1>
    <p>Welcome to the Webvill Tree Farm. We're still learning
    about CSS, so pardon our plain site. We just bought
    <a href="http://www.headfirstlabs.com/books/hfhtml/">
    Head First HTML with CSS &amp; XHTML</
    a>, though, so expect great things soon.</p>
    <p>You can visit us at the corner of Binary Boulevard and DOM
    Drive. Come check us out today!</>
  </body>
</html>
```

there are no
Dumb Questions

Q: Do I need to use a request object to write JavaScript code that uses the DOM?

A: Nope. The browser handles creation of the DOM tree and exposes all the methods of the document object automatically. In fact, even when you're not writing JavaScript at all, browsers still use the DOM to represent your page.

Q: So if the DOM doesn't use a request object, is it really part of Ajax?

A: Depends who you talk to. Ajax is really just a way of thinking about web pages, and a whole slew of other technologies, that helps you achieve interactive pages in really usable ways. So the DOM is definitely a part of that. You'll use the DOM a lot in the next couple of chapters to build interactive and usable apps.

Q: What about all that DOM Level 0 and DOM Level 2 stuff? Am I going to have trouble with Internet Explorer again?

A: All modern browsers are compatible with the World Wide Web Consortium's (W3C) DOM specification, but the specification leaves some decisions up to the browser designer. The designers of IE made a different decision about how to build the DOM tree than a lot of the designers of other major browsers. But it's not a big problem, and with a few more utility functions, your code will work on *all* major browsers, including Internet Explorer.

Q: It looks like you called some parts of the markup "children." So an element can have "child elements"?

A: Yes. When the browser organizes your XHTML into a tree, it begins with the root element, the element that surrounds everything else. Then, that element has an element within it, like <head> or <body>. Those can be called *nested elements*, but in DOM, they're called **child elements**.

In fact, you can think of the DOM tree as a family tree, with family terms applying everywhere. For example, the <head> element is the parent of the <title> element, and most <a> elements have children: the text label for the link.

Q: You're throwing a bunch of new terms around. How am I supposed to keep up with all of this?

A: It's not as hard as it seems. Just keep the idea of a family tree in mind, and you shouldn't have any trouble. You've been using terms like root, branch, and leaf for years. As for parent and child, anytime you move away from the root, you're moving towards a child. The only term that may be totally new to you is "node," and we're just about to take a look at that...

Exercise

Write Your Own Web Dictionary

What good is looking at a bunch of definitions? This is Head First, and we want your brain working, not just your eyes. Below are several entries from a Web Dictionary, with some of the words in each definition removed. Your job is to complete each entry by filling in the blanks.

node: Any _____ piece of markup, such as an element or text. The <a> element is an _____ node, while the "Head First HTML with CSS & XHTML" text is a _____node.

leaf: A piece of markup that has _____ such as an element with _____text content, like <img>, or textual data. Also known as: **leaf node.**

"Head First HTML with CSS & XHTML"

"Webville Tree Farm"

a

child: Any piece of markup that is _____ by another piece of markup. The text "Head First HTML with CSS & XHTML" is the _____ of the <a> element, and the <p>s in this markup are _____ of the <body> element. Also known as: **child node**

p

h1

p

branch: A branch is a _____ of elements and content. So the "body" branch is all the elements and text _____ the <body> element in the tree.

parent: Any piece of markup that contains _____ . <h1> is the parent of the text "Webville Tree Farm," and <html> is the parent of the _____ element. Also known as: parent element, parent node.

body

html

root element: The element in a _____ that _____all other elements. In XHTML, the root element is always _____ .

no children	child	children	under	contained
other markup	text	collection	single	document
element	contains	<body>	no	<html>

Here are the words you should use to fill in the blanks.

Sharpen your pencil

It's time to load markup trees into your brain. Below is an XHTML document. Your job is to figure out how a web browser organizes this markup into a tree structure. On the right is the tree, ready for you to fill in its branches and the relationships between each piece. To get you started, we've provided spaces for each piece of markup; be sure you've filled each space with an element or text from the XHTML markup before showing off your DOM tree to anyone else!

```
<html>

  <head>

    <title>Binary Tree Selection</title>

  </head>

  <body>

    <p>Below are two binary tree options:</p>

    <div>

    Our <em>depth-first</em> trees are great for folks who
    are far away.

    </div>

    <div>

    Our <em>breadth-first</em> trees are a favorite for
    nearby neighbors.

    </div>

    <p>You can view other products in the

      <a href="menu.html">Main Menu</a>. </p>

  </body>

</html>
```

Go ahead and draw lines in connecting
the different elements and the text.
Make sure you get all those family
relationships right!

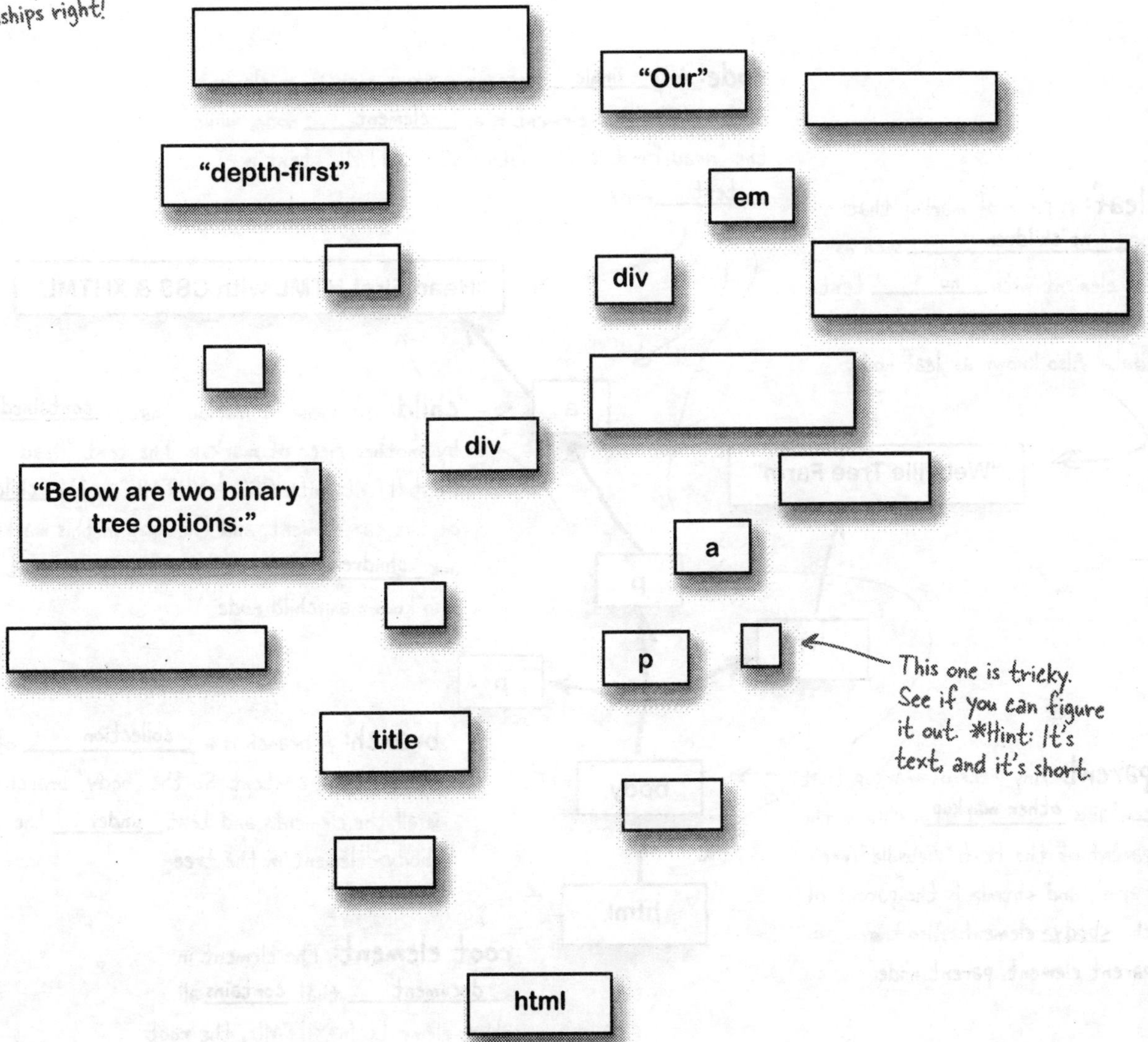

"Our"

"depth-first"

em

div

div

"Below are two binary
tree options:"

a

p

p

This one is tricky.
See if you can figure
it out. *Hint: It's
text, and it's short.

title

html

Answers on page 243.

Exercise Solution

Write Your Own Web Dictionary

Below are several entries from a Web Dictionary, with some of the words in each definition removed. Your job was to complete each entry by filling in the blanks.

node: Any __single__ piece of markup, such as an element or text. The <a> element is an __element__ node, while the "Head First HTML with CSS & XHTML" text is a __text__ node.

leaf: A piece of markup that has __no children__ such as an element with __no__ text content, like <img>, or textual data. Also known as: **leaf node**.

"Head First HTML with CSS & XHTML"

a

"Webville Tree Farm"

p

h1

p

body

html

child: Any piece of markup that is __contained__ by another piece of markup. The text "Head First HTML with CSS & XHTML" is the __child__ of the <a> element, and the <p>s in this markup are __children__ of the <body> element. Also known as: **child node**

parent: Any piece of markup that contains __other markup__. <h1> is the parent of the text "Webville Tree Farm", and <html> is the parent of the __<body>__ element. Also known as: parent element, parent node.

branch: A branch is a __collection__ of elements and content. So the "body" branch is all the elements and text __under__ the <body> element in the tree.

root element: The element in a __document__ that __contains__ all other elements. In XHTML, the root element is always __<html>__.

Sharpen your pencil
Solution

Your job was to build a DOM tree from the XHTML on page 240. You also should have drawn in the connections between the different elements and text. How did you do?

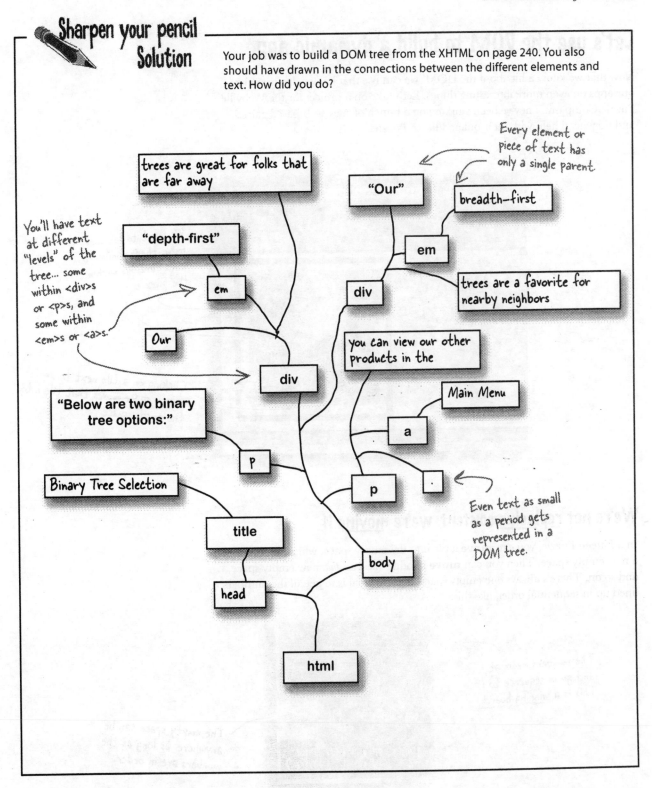

trees are great for folks that are far away

Every element or piece of text has only a single parent.

"Our"

breadth-first

You'll have text at different "levels" of the tree... some within <div>s or <p>s, and some within <em>s or <a>s.

"depth-first"

em

em

Our

div

trees are a favorite for nearby neighbors

div

you can view our other products in the

"Below are two binary tree options:"

Main Menu

a

p

Binary Tree Selection

p

.

title

Even text as small as a period gets represented in a DOM tree.

head

body

html

Let's use the DOM to build a dynamic app

Now that we know a bit about the DOM, we can use that knowledge to make our apps do even more interesting things. Let's take on a project for the Webville Puzzle Company. They've been working on a bunch of new web-based games, and they need help with their online Fifteen Puzzle.

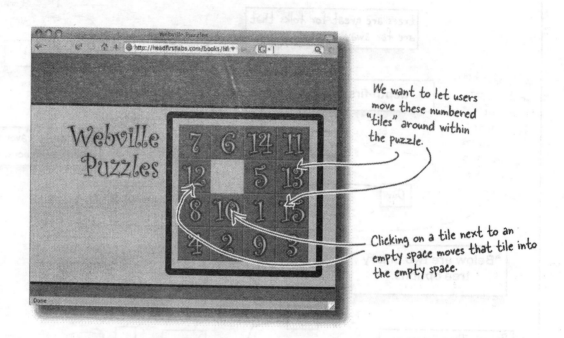

We want to let users move these numbered "tiles" around within the puzzle.

Clicking on a tile next to an empty space moves that tile into the empty space.

We're not <u>replacing</u> content, we're <u>moving</u> it

In a Fifteen Puzzle, you can **move** a tile into the empty space, which then creates a new empty space. Then you can **move** another tile into *that* new empty space, and so on. There's always one empty space, and the goal is to get all the numbers lined up in sequential order, like this:

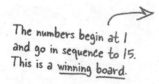

The numbers begin at 1 and go in sequence to 15. This is a <u>winning board</u>.

The empty space can be anywhere, as long as the numbers are in order.

First, you're rambling on about trees. Now, we're playing games. What gives? And what does **any** of this have to do with Ajax?

We need to move those tiles around... and that requires the DOM.

This is a perfect example of needing the DOM. We don't want to just change the content of a table, or replace some text on a button or in a <p>. Instead, we need to move around the images that represent a tile.

Webville Puzzles is using a table with four rows and four columns to represent their board. So we might need to move an image in the third row, fourth column to the empty space in the third row, third column. We can't just change the innerHTML property of a <div> or <td> to get that working.

What we need is a way to actually grab an <img>, and move it within the overall table. And that's where the DOM comes in handy. And, as you'll soon see, this is *exactly* the sort of thing that Ajax apps have to do all the time: dynamically change a page.

All Ajax apps need to respond DYNAMICALLY to users.

The DOM lets you CHANGE a page without reloading that page.

POWER

What specific steps do you think you'll have to take to move an <img> from one cell of a table to a different cell?

You start with XHTML...

To really understand how the DOM helps out, let's take a look at Webville
Puzzles' XHTML, and see what the browser does with that XHTML. Then we
can figure out how to use the DOM to make the page do what **we** want.

```html
<html xmlns="http://www.w3.org/1999/xhtml">
<head>
  <title>Webville Puzzles</title>
  <link rel="stylesheet" href="css/puzzle.css" type="text/css" />
  <script src="scripts/fifteen.js" type="text/javascript"></script>
</head>
<body>
 <div id="puzzle">
 <h1 id="logo">Webville Puzzles</h1>
 <div id="puzzleGrid">
  <table cellspacing="0" cellpadding="0">
    <tr>
     <td id="cell11">
       <img src="images/07.png" alt="7" width="69" height="69" />
     </td>
     <td id="cell12">
       <img src="images/06.png" alt="6" width="69" height="69" />
     </td>
     <td id="cell13">
       <img src="images/14.png" alt="14" width="69" height="69" />
     </td>
     <td id="cell14">
       <img src="images/11.png" alt="11" width="69" height="69" />
     </td>
    </tr>
    <tr>
     <td id="cell21">
       <img src="images/12.png" alt="12" width="69" height="69" />
     </td>
     <td id="cell22">
       <img src="images/empty.png" alt="empty" width="69" height="69" />
     </td>
     <td id="cell23">
       <img src="images/05.png" alt="5" width="69" height="69" />
     </td>
     <td id="cell24">
       <img src="images/13.png" alt="13" width="69" height="69" />
     </td>
    </tr>
    ... etc ...
  </table>
 </div>
 </div>
</body>
</html>
```

There's no JavaScript
yet, but we'll need
some soon. Go ahead
and add a reference to
fifteen.js, which we'll
build throughout this
chapter.

The puzzle is
represented by a
<table> element.

Each table cell is labeled with an id.

Each tile is a
single <img> within
a single table cell.

The empty tile is
also an image.

The XHTML for the puzzle is
in fifteen-puzzle.html. You can
download the source from the
Head First Labs website.

fifteen-puzzle.html

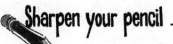

Sharpen your pencil

Go ahead and draw what you think the DOM tree for fifteen-puzzle.html looks like. This time, though, you don't have to put the root element at the base of the tree. You can put it anywhere you want: the top, the bottom, or to one side.

---

there are no Dumb Questions

Q: There isn't any request being made in this puzzle, is there?

A: No, at least not right now. The program is all client-side.

Q: So this isn't Ajax at all, is it?

A: Well, that gets back to the "What is Ajax?" question. If you think Ajax apps are only ones that make requests using `XMLHttpRequest`, then this isn't an Ajax app. But if you think of Ajax apps more as responsive, JavaScript-driven apps that are very usable, then you might decide otherwise.

Either way, this app is really all about controlling the DOM... and that's something that will help your Ajax programming, no matter what you think constitutes an Ajax app.

Sharpen your pencil
Solution

Your job was to draw out a DOM tree for the fifteen-puzzle.html's XHTML structure and content. Here's what we did... we started with the root element on the top-left, and worked our way down. Did you come up with something similar?

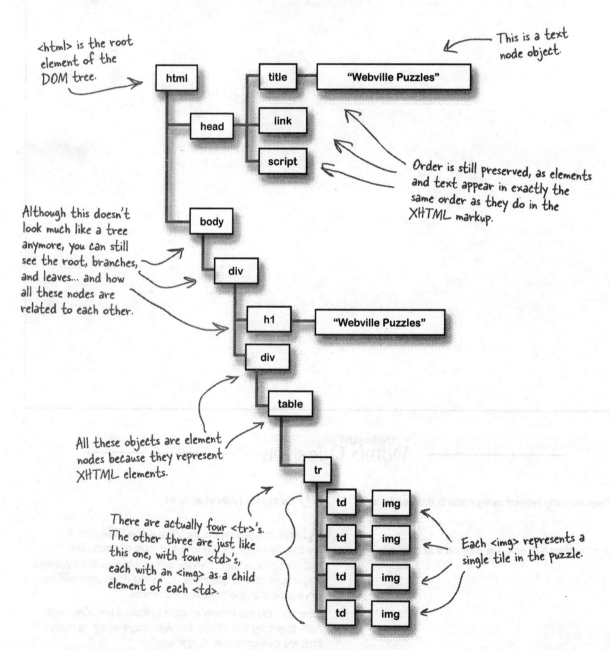

`<html>` is the root element of the DOM tree.

This is a text node object.

Order is still preserved, as elements and text appear in exactly the same order as they do in the XHTML markup.

Although this doesn't look much like a tree anymore, you can still see the root, branches, and leaves... and how all these nodes are related to each other.

All these objects are element nodes because they represent XHTML elements.

There are actually four `<tr>`'s. The other three are just like this one, with four `<td>`'s, each with an `<img>` as a child element of each `<td>`.

Each `<img>` represents a single tile in the puzzle.

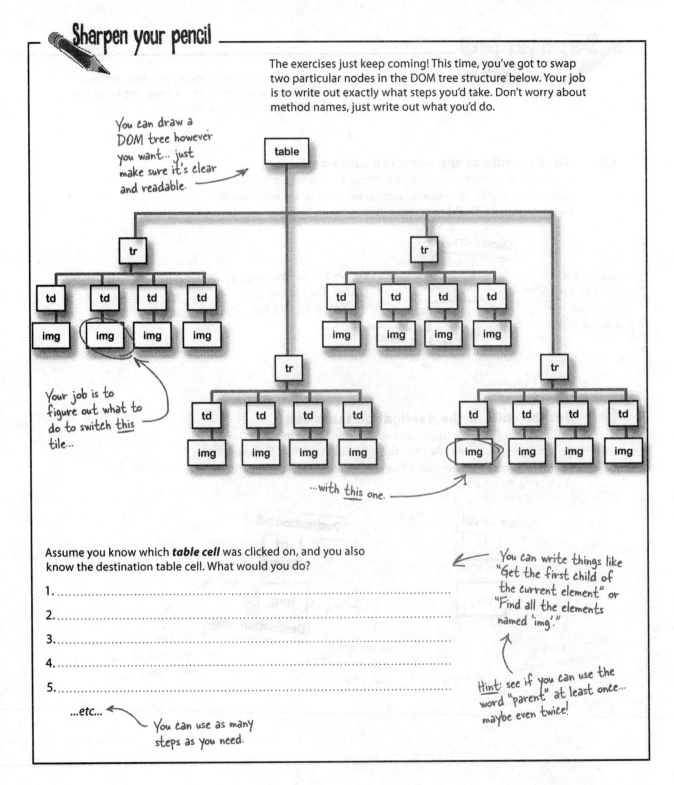

Sharpen your pencil

The exercises just keep coming! This time, you've got to swap two particular nodes in the DOM tree structure below. Your job is to write out exactly what steps you'd take. Don't worry about method names, just write out what you'd do.

You can draw a DOM tree however you want... just make sure it's clear and readable.

Your job is to figure out what to do to switch this tile...

...with this one.

Assume you know which **table cell** was clicked on, and you also know the destination table cell. What would you do?

1. ....

2. ....

3. ....

4. ....

5. ....

...etc...

You can use as many steps as you need.

You can write things like "Get the first child of the current element" or "Find all the elements named 'img'."

Hint: see if you can use the word "parent" at least once... maybe even twice!

Sharpen your pencil
Solution

Your job was to write out exactly what steps you'd take. Assume you know which **table cell** was clicked on, and you also know the destination table cell. What would you do?

① Get the child of the selected table cell

You could use getElementsByTagName(), but we know that the <img> representing the clicked-on tile is the child of the selected cell. So we can use the DOM to get that child element.

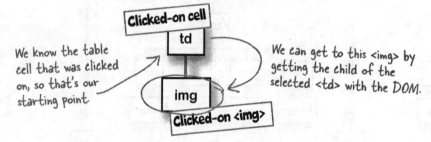

We know the table cell that was clicked on, so that's our starting point

Clicked-on cell

td

img

Clicked-on <img>

We can get to this <img> by getting the child of the selected <td> with the DOM.

② Get the child of the destination table cell

Once we start swapping things around, it's going to be harder to keep the selected <img> separate from the destination <img>. So before we start moving things around, let's get a reference to the <img> in the destination <td>, too.

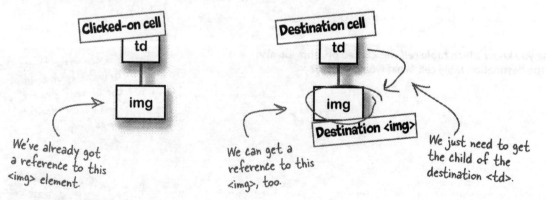

Clicked-on cell

td

img

We've already got a reference to this <img> element.

Destination cell

td

img

Destination <img>

We can get a reference to this <img>, too.

We just need to get the child of the destination <td>.

③ **Add the clicked on <img> as a child of the new <u>destination</u> table cell.**

We need to move the <img> in the selected cell to the destination cell. So we can just add the clicked-on <img> to the destination <td>'s list of children.

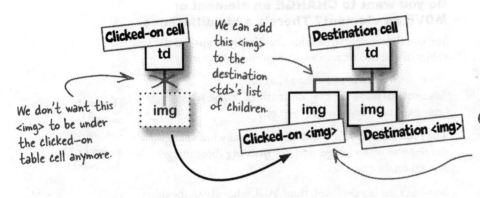

We don't want this <img> to be under the clicked—on table cell anymore.

We can add this <img> to the destination <td>'s list of children.

Once we've added this to the destination <td>, we've moved the <img> to a new location in the DOM tree.

④ **Add the <img> in the destination cell as a child of the <u>originally</u> clicked-on table cell.**

Now for the other part of the swap. We need to move the destination <img> under the <td> that was originally clicked on. Here's why we got the reference to this <img> in step 2: since there are two child <img>'s under the destination <td>, having a reference already makes this easy.

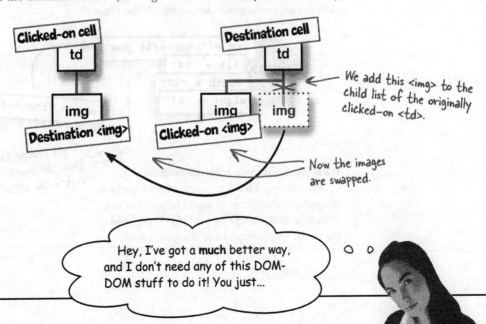

We add this <img> to the child list of the originally clicked—on <td>.

Now the images are swapped.

Hey, I've got a **much** better way, and I don't need any of this DOM-DOM stuff to do it! You just...

...get the src property of the first <img>, and swap it out with the src property of the second <img>. All you need is a temporary string, and you're done. No DOM, no new syntax. Nice, huh?

Do you want to CHANGE an element or MOVE an element? There's a big difference.

You could definitely write code that simply swaps out the values of the two <img>'s src properties, like this:

```
var tmp = selectedImage.src;
selectedImage.src = destinationImage.src;
destinationImage.src = tmp;
```

This code swaps the textual src property of two images.

The problem with this is that you're actually just changing the *properties* of an image, and not ***moving*** those images around on the page.

So what's the big deal with that? Well, what about the other properties of each image? Remember that each <img> had an alt attribute?

```
<img src="images/14.png" alt="14"
     width="69" height="69" />
```

The alt, width, and height are properties of this image, just like its src attribute.

If you change the src attribute, you're only changing a part of the <img>. The rest would stay the same... and then the alt attribute would not match the image!

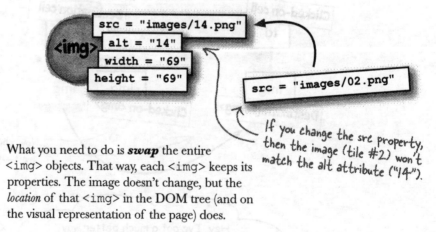

If you change the src property, then the image (tile #2) won't match the alt attribute ("14").

What you need to do is ***swap*** the entire <img> objects. That way, each <img> keeps its properties. The image doesn't change, but the *location* of that <img> in the DOM tree (and on the visual representation of the page) does.

JavaScript & DOM Magnets

You've already figured out what needs to happen to swap two tiles. Now it's time to turn those general steps into actual code. Below is the skeleton for a new function, swapTiles(). But all the pieces of code have fallen to the ground... can you figure out how to complete the function?

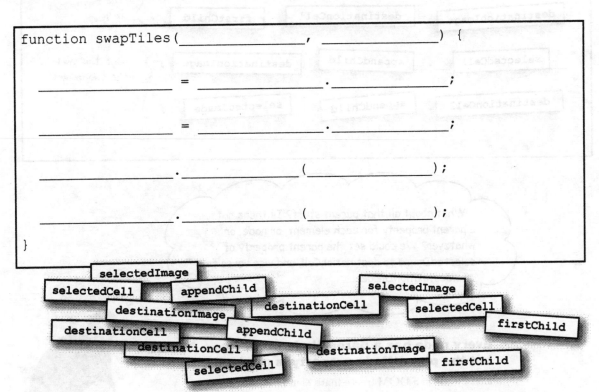

```
function swapTiles(_____, _____) {

    _____ = _____._____;

    _____ = _____._____;


    _____._____(_____);

    _____._____(_____);
}
```

selectedImage

selectedCell   appendChild   selectedImage

destinationImage   destinationCell   selectedCell

destinationCell   appendChild   firstChild

destinationCell   destinationImage   firstChild

selectedCell

JavaScript & DOM Magnet Solutions

It's time to turn those general steps from page 250 into actual code. Below is the skeleton for a new function, swapTiles(). Your job was to put the pieces of code into a working function.

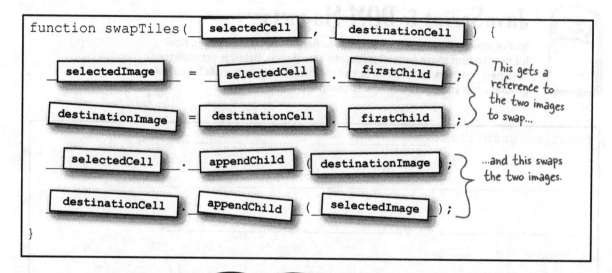

```
function swapTiles( selectedCell , destinationCell ) {

    selectedImage = selectedCell . firstChild ;

    destinationImage = destinationCell . firstChild ;

    selectedCell . appendChild ( destinationImage ) ;

    destinationCell . appendChild ( selectedImage ) ;

}
```

This gets a reference to the two images to swap...

...and this swaps the two images.

> What about all that parent stuff? Is there not a parent property for each element, or node, or whatever? We could set the parent property of selectedImage to destinationCell, and vice versa for the destinationImage.

Every node has a parentNode property... but the parentNode property is <u>read-only</u>.

Every node in a DOM tree—that's elements, text, even attributes—has a property called parentNode. That property gives you the *parent* of the current node. So for example, the parent node of an <img> in a table cell is the enclosing <td>.

But in the DOM, that's a *read-only* property. So you can get the parent of a node, but you can't set the parent. Instead, you have to use a method like appendChild().

appendChild() <u>adds</u> a new child to a node

appendChild() is a method used to add a new child node to an element. So if you run destinationCell.appendChild(selectedImage), you're adding the selectedImage node to the children that destinationCell already has:

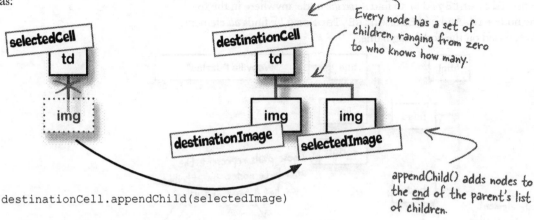

Every node has a set of children, ranging from zero to who knows how many.

destinationCell.appendChild(selectedImage)

appendChild() adds nodes to the <u>end</u> of the parent's list of children.

A new child gets a new parent... <u>automatically</u>

When you assign a node a new child, that new child's parentNode property is *automatically updated*. So even though you can't change the parentNode property directly, you can move a node, and let the DOM and your browser handle changing the property for you.

there are no
Dumb Questions

Q: So I can use all the DOM methods from my JavaScript automatically?

A: That's mostly right. There are a few exceptions that we'll look at soon, but for the most part, the DOM is yours to use from any JavaScript code you're writing.

Q: And a DOM tree is made up of nodes, like elements and text, right?

A: Right, but don't forget about attributes, too. A node is pretty much anything that can appear on a page, but the most common nodes are elements, attributes, and text.

Q: And a node has a parent and children?

A: All nodes have parents, but not all nodes have children. Text and attribute nodes have no children, and an empty element with no content has no children.

Q: What's the parent of the root element?

A: The document object. That's why you can use the document object to find anything in your web page.

Q: Are there other methods to add child nodes like appendChild()?

A: There sure are. We'll be looking at lots of those in the next chapter.

Q: Why is this better than changing out the src property of an <img>?

A: Because you don't want to *modify* the image displayed; you want to *move* that image to a new cell. If you wanted an image to stay the same, with its alt tag and height and title, you'd change the src property. But we want to move the image, so we use the DOM.

You can locate elements by <u>name</u> or by <u>id</u>

If you think about your page as a collection of nodes in a DOM tree, methods like getElementById() and getElementsByTagName() make a lot more sense.

You use getElementById() to find a *specific* node anywhere in the tree, using the node's id. And getElementsByTagName() finds *all* elements in the tree, based on the node's tag name.

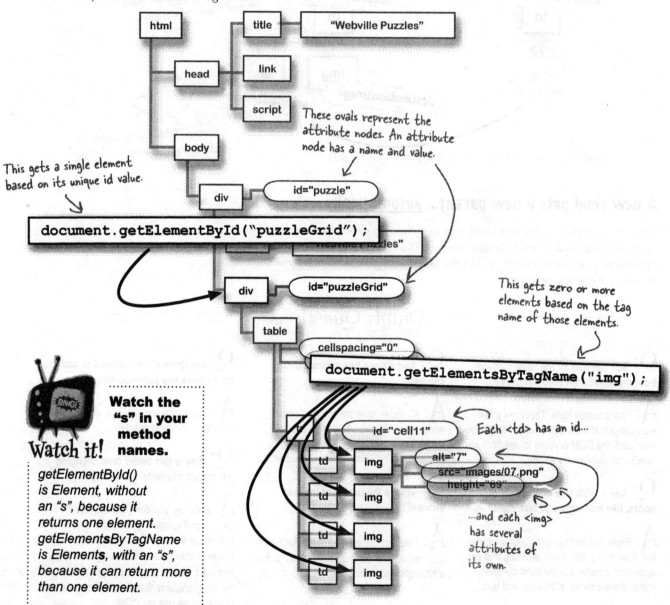

These ovals represent the attribute nodes. An attribute node has a name and value.

This gets a single element based on its unique id value.

`document.getElementById("puzzleGrid");`

This gets zero or more elements based on the tag name of those elements.

`document.getElementsByTagName("img");`

Each <td> has an id...

...and each <img> has several attributes of its own.

Watch the "s" in your method names.

Watch it!

getElementById() is Element, without an "s", because it returns one element. getElementsByTagName is Elements, with an "s", because it can return more than one element.

Exercise

Go ahead and write the code for an initPage() function. You need to make sure that every time a table cell is clicked on, an event handler called tileClick() gets run. We'll write the code for tileClick() later, but you may want to build a test version with an alert() statement to make sure your code works before turning the page.

→ **Answers on the next page.**

Sharpen your pencil

Here are a few questions to get your left brain into gear. Answer each before turning the page... and once you're done, you might want to double-check your code for initPage() above, too.

1. Should the event handler for moving a tile be on the table cell or the image within that cell?

☐ table cell (`<td>`)   ☐ image (`<img>`)

2. Why did you make the choice you did? ....
....

3. How can we figure out if an empty tile was clicked on? ....
....

4. How can we figure out the destination cell for a tile? ....
....

→ **Answers on page 261.**

Exercise Solution

Your job was to write an initPage() function that set up the event handlers for the Fifteen Puzzle. What did you come up with? Here's what we did:

← Remember to assign the initPage() function to the window.onload event.

```
window.onload = initPage;

function initPage() {
  var table = document.getElementById("puzzleGrid");
  var cells = table.getElementsByTagName("td");
  for (var i=0; i<cells.length; i++) {
    var cell = cells[i];
    cell.onclick = tileClick;
  }
}

function tileClick() {
  alert("You clicked me!");
}
```

First, we locate the <div> with the table and cells we want to attach handlers to.

We want every <td> in that table.

For each cell...

...assign tileClick() to the onclick event.

We built a simple event handler to test things out.

Test Drive

Add initPage(), tileClick(), and swapTiles() to a script called fifteen.js. Be sure you reference the file in your XHTML, and try out the Fifteen Puzzle with the event handlers on each table cell.

Click a cell...

...and you should get an alert box.

Table Cells Exposed

This week's interview:
Interview with a new parent

Head First: So I hear you're a new parent, <td>?

<td>: That's right. I've got a sweet little <img> to call my own.

Head First: So is this your first child?

<td>: Well, it depends on who you ask. Some browsers say that <img> is my first child, but others think I've got a lot of empty children floating around.

Head First: Empty children?

<td>: Yup. You know, empty spaces, carriage returns. It's nothing to worry about.

Head First: Nothing to worry about? That sounds pretty serious... you might have more children, and that's no big deal?

<td>: Relax, it's all in how you handle it. Most people just skip over all those nothings to get to my flashy little <img>.

Head First: This is all pretty confusing. Do you think our audience really understands what you're talking about?

<td>: If they don't know, I'll bet they will soon. Just wait and see.

Head First: Well... hmmm... I guess... I guess that's all for now. Hopefully we'll make some sense of all this, and get back to you soon, faithful listeners.

---

there are no Dumb Questions

Q: **Why do you have the puzzleGrid id on a <div>, and not on the <table> itself?**

A: DOM Level 2 browsers and Internet Explorer handle tables, and CSS styles applied to those tables, pretty differently. The easiest way to get a page with a table looking similar on IE and Firefox, Safari, etc., is to style a <div> surrounding a <table>, instead of the <table> itself.

Since it's easiest to style an element with an id, we put the puzzleGrid id on the <div> we wanted to style: the one surrounding the <table> cell.

Q: **So that's why you used getElementById() to find that <div>, and not the actual <table>?**

A: Right. We could have put an id on the <table>, too, but it's not really necessary. The only thing in the puzzleGrid <div> is the table we want, along with all those clickable cells. So it was easier to just find the <div>, and then find all the <td>'s within that.

BRAIN POWER

What do you think <td> is talking about in the interview above? Are there any functions we've written or will write that might need to worry about those "nothing" children that <td> mentioned?

Can I move the clicked tile?

Now that the basic structure is in place, it's time to get the puzzle working. Since a tile can only be moved to the empty square, the first thing we need to figure out is, "Where's the empty square?"

For any clicked-on tile, there are six different possibilities for where the empty tile is. Suppose the user clicked the "10" tile on the board below:

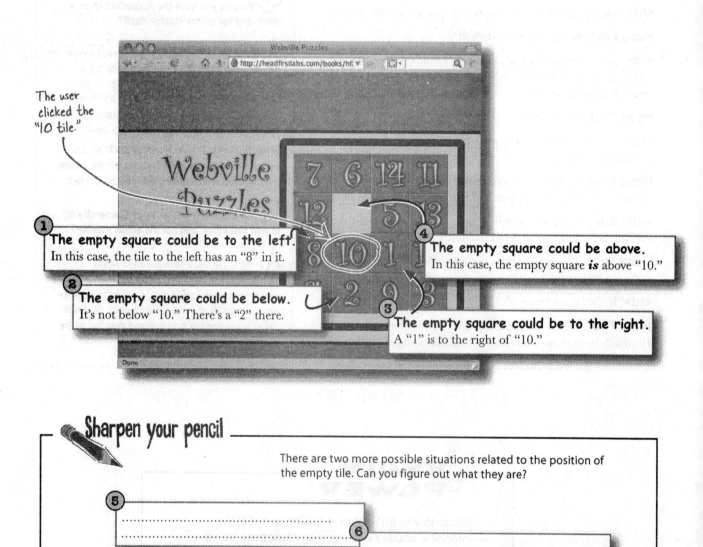

The user clicked the "10 tile."

① **The empty square could be to the left.**
In this case, the tile to the left has an "8" in it.

④ **The empty square could be above.**
In this case, the empty square *is* above "10."

② **The empty square could be below.**
It's not below "10." There's a "2" there.

③ **The empty square could be to the right.**
A "1" is to the right of "10."

✎ Sharpen your pencil

There are two more possible situations related to the position of the empty tile. Can you figure out what they are?

⑤ ....
....

⑥ ....
....

→ Answers on page 265.

Sharpen your pencil
Solution

Here are a few questions to get your left brain into gear. Answer each before turning the page... and once you're done, you might want to double-check your code for initPage() above, too.

1. Should the event handler for moving a tile be on the table cell or the image within that cell?

☐ table cell (<td>)   ☐ image (<img>)

2. Why did you make the choice you did?

3. How can we figure out if an empty tile was clicked on?

4. How can we figure out the destination cell for a tile?

> Well, first of all, I think we should put the event handler on the table cell, not on the image itself.

Joe: Why? The user's clicking on "7," not the second tile on the third row.

Frank: Well, they're clicking on the table cell that image is in, too.

Jill: So suppose we put the handler on the image. And then when a user clicks on the image...

Joe: ...we swap that image out with the empty square...

Jill: Right. But the handler's attached to the *image*, not the table cell.

Frank: Oh. I see.

Joe: What? I don't get it.

Frank: The event handler would move with the image. So every time an image gets moved, the event handler moves with it.

Joe: So?

Frank: Well, we're going to use the DOM to figure out where the empty square is in relation to the clicked-on image, right?

Joe: I guess so. What's that got to do with the handler on the image?

Frank: If the handler's on the image, we'll constantly have to be getting the image's parent. If the handler's on the cell, we can avoid that extra step. We can just check the cells around the clicked-on cell.

Jill: Exactly! We don't need to move to the image's parent cell in our handler.

Joe: So all this is to avoid one line of code? Just asking the image for its parent?

Jill: One line of code *for every click*. That could be hundreds of clicks... or even thousands! Have you ever worked one of those puzzles? It takes some time, you know.

Joe: Wow. I'm not even that clear on how we'd find the empty square in the first place...

You can move around a DOM tree using FAMILY relationships

Suppose you wanted to find out the parent of an `<img>` or get a reference to the next `<td>` in a table. A DOM tree is all connected, and you can use the family-type properties of the DOM to move around in the tree.

`parentNode` moves up the tree, `childNodes` gives you an element's children, and you can move between nodes with `nextSibling` and `previousSibling`. You can also get an element's `firstChild` and `lastChild`. Take a look:

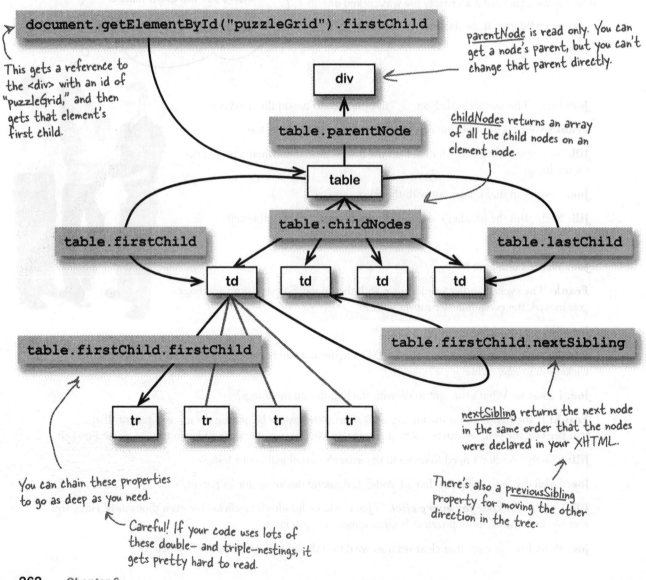

`document.getElementById("puzzleGrid").firstChild`

This gets a reference to the `<div>` with an id of "puzzleGrid," and then gets that element's first child.

parentNode is read only. You can get a node's parent, but you can't change that parent directly.

`table.parentNode`

childNodes returns an array of all the child nodes on an element node.

`table.childNodes`

`table.firstChild`

`table.lastChild`

`table.firstChild.firstChild`

`table.firstChild.nextSibling`

nextSibling returns the next node in the same order that the nodes were declared in your XHTML.

You can chain these properties to go as deep as you need.

There's also a previousSibling property for moving the other direction in the tree.

Careful! If your code uses lots of these double- and triple-nestings, it gets pretty hard to read.

Sharpen your pencil

Below is a DOM tree and some JavaScript statements. In the JavaScript, each letter is a variable that represents the matching node in the DOM tree. Can you figure out which node each statement refers to?

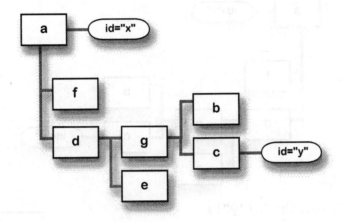

document.getElementById("y"); _____

g.parent; _____

document.getElementById("y").nextSibling; _____

a.firstChild; _____

c.parent.parent; _____

d.firstChild.lastChild; _____ ,

c.previousSibling; _____

Sharpen your pencil
Solution

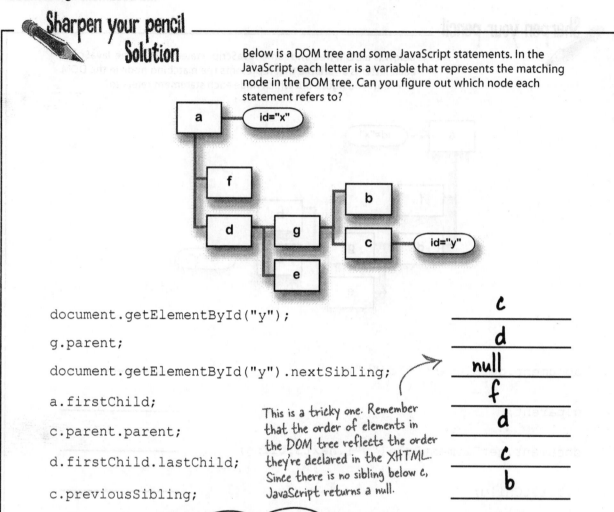

Below is a DOM tree and some JavaScript statements. In the JavaScript, each letter is a variable that represents the matching node in the DOM tree. Can you figure out which node each statement refers to?

```
document.getElementById("y");                          c

g.parent;                                              d

document.getElementById("y").nextSibling;             null

a.firstChild;                                          f

c.parent.parent;                                       d

d.firstChild.lastChild;                               c

c.previousSibling;                                    b
```

This is a tricky one. Remember that the order of elements in the DOM tree reflects the order they're declared in the XHTML. Since there is no sibling below c, JavaScript returns a null.

Those are awful names for elements. Why in the world would you name your nodes with just letters?

Use descriptive names for your elements and your id attributes.

When you're writing XHTML, the element names are already pretty clear. Nobody's confused about what `<div>` or `<img>` means. But you should still use descriptive ids like "background" or "puzzleGrid." You never know when those ids will show up in your code, and make your code easier to understand... or harder.

The clearer your element names and ids, the clearer your code will be to you and other programmers.

Sharpen your pencil
Solution

There were two more possibilities for where an empty tile could be on a puzzle grid. Did you figure out what they were?

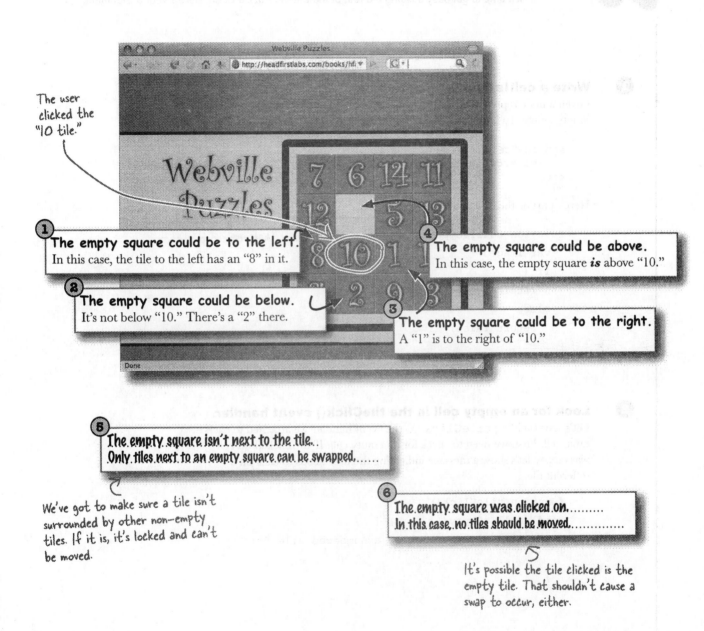

The user clicked the "10 tile."

(1) The empty square could be to the left.
In this case, the tile to the left has an "8" in it.

(2) The empty square could be below.
It's not below "10." There's a "2" there.

(4) The empty square could be above.
In this case, the empty square *is* above "10."

(3) The empty square could be to the right.
A "1" is to the right of "10."

(5) The empty square isn't next to the tile.
Only tiles next to an empty square can be swapped.

We've got to make sure a tile isn't surrounded by other non-empty tiles. If it is, it's locked and can't be moved.

(6) The empty square was clicked on.
In this case, no tiles should be moved.

It's possible the tile clicked is the empty tile. That shouldn't cause a swap to occur, either.

Long Exercise

It's time to get busy building the rest of the Fifteen Puzzle Code. Here's your assignment:

1 **Write a cellIsEmpty() function.**
Given a node representing a `<td>`, figure out if the image in that cell is the empty image. To help you out, here's the XHTML for the empty cell:

```
<td id="cell22">
  <img src="images/empty.png" alt="empty" width="69" height="69" />
</td>
```

Here's part of the function to get you started:

```
function cellIsEmpty(cell) {
    var image = .....................................
    if (.........................................)
      return true;
    else
      return false;
}
```

cell is a node in the browser's DOM tree that represents a `<td>`.

2 **Look for an empty cell in the tileClick() event handler.**
Let's start building `tileClick()`, the event handler we attached to each table cell. First, we need to check for an empty cell. If the clicked-on cell was empty, let's show a message indicating the user needs to click on a different tile.

```
function tileClick() {
    if (cellIsEmpty(..........)) {
      alert("Please click on a numbered tile.");
      .....................................
    }
}
```

❸ Figure out what row and column was clicked.

Here's the XHTML for a couple of cells in the puzzle:

```
<td id="cell13">
 <img src="images/14.png" alt="14" width="69" height="69" />
</td>
<td id="cell14">
 <img src="images/11.png" alt="11" width="69" height="69" />
</td>
</tr>
<tr>
<td id="cell21">
 <img src="images/12.png" alt="12" width="69" height="69" />
</td>
... etc ...
```

Given this (and the rest of the XHTML, on page 246), can you figure out
how to get the row and column of the clicked on tile?

```
var currentRow = this.................................;
var currentCol = this.................................;
```

*Hint: you'll need to use
JavaScript's charAt(int position)
function at least once.*

*For the string "cows
gone wild," charAt(2)
returns "w."*

❹ Finish up the tileClick() event handler.

Once we've made sure that the empty tile wasn't clicked, and gotten the
current row and column, you have everything you need. Your job is to
handle the 5 remaining possible situations for where the empty square is,
and then if possible, swap the selected tile with the empty square.

To get you started, here's the code to check above the selected tile:

*Only check
above if we're
not on row 1.*

*The id of the cell
above is "cell," and
then (currentRow –1),
and then the current
column number.*

*Number converts text
into a numeric format.*

*JavaScript automatically
turns these numbers into
strings when they're added
together with another string.*

```
// Check above
if (currentRow > 1) {
  var testRow = Number(currentRow) - 1;
  var testCellId = "cell" + testRow + currentCol;
  var testCell = document.getElementById(testCellId);
  if (cellIsEmpty(testCell)) {
    swapTiles(this, testCell);
    return;
  }
}
```

*Get the test cell
based on its id...*

*...see if it's the empty
square...*

*...and then swap out the current
cell and the empty square.*

If we swapped tiles, we're done!

The rest of tileClick() is up to you. Refer back to the different
possibilities you have to handle from page 265, and good luck!

LONG EXERCISE SOLUTION

Your job was to build the cellIsEmpty() function, and then complete the clickTile() event handler. Did you figure everything out? Here's what we did:

```
function cellIsEmpty(cell) {
  var image = ....cell.firstChild;.....
  if (......image.alt == "empty"......)
    return true;
  else
    return false;
}
```

The first child of each table cell is its <img>.

The empty image has an alt tag of "empty."

td	img	alt="empty"
		src="images/empty.png"
		height="69"

```
function tileClick() {
  if (cellIsEmpty( this )) {
    alert("Please click on a numbered tile.");
    ....return;....
  }
```

"this" in tileClick() is the activated object. That's the clicked-on tile.

← Be sure to return if the empty tile was clicked on.

```
  var currentRow = this........id.... ...charAt(4)... ;
  var currentCol = this.........id....... ....charAt(5)... ;
```

| td | id="cell21" |

The id of each table cell gives the row, and then the column.

```
  // Check above
  if (currentRow > 1) {
    var testRow = Number(currentRow) - 1;
    var testCellId = "cell" + testRow + currentCol;
    var testCell = document.getElementById(testCellId);
    if (cellIsEmpty(testCell)) {
      swapTiles(this, testCell);
      return;
    }
```

```
  }

  // Check below
  if (currentRow < 4) {
    var testRow = Number(currentRow) + 1;
    var testCellId = "cell" + testRow + currentCol;
    var testCell = document.getElementById(testCellId);
    if (cellIsEmpty(testCell)) {
      swapTiles(this, testCell);
      return;
    }
  }
  // Check to the left
  if (currentCol > 1) {
    var testCol = Number(currentCol) - 1;
    var testCellId = "cell" + currentRow + testCol;
    var testCell = document.getElementById(testCellId);
    if (cellIsEmpty(testCell)) {
      swapTiles(this, testCell);
      return;
    }
  }
  // Check to the right
  if (currentCol < 4) {
    var testCol = Number(currentCol) + 1;
    var testCellId = "cell" + currentRow + testCol;
    var testCell = document.getElementById(testCellId);
    if (cellIsEmpty(testCell)) {
      swapTiles(this, testCell);
      return;
    }
  }

  // The clicked-on cell is locked
  alert("Please click a tile next to an empty cell.");
}
```

Make sure that we're not on the bottom row.

Get the cell one row down, in the same column.

If the target cell is empty, do a swap.

Now we're looking side-to-side. Make sure we're not in the leftmost column.

Find the cell one column over, in the same row.

See if that cell is empty. If so, swap and return.

Each of these cases—below, left, and right—follow the same pattern.

If we got here, the clicked-on tile isn't empty, and it's not next to an empty square.

Let's give the user some feedback, so they know what to do.

Q: Wow, that was a lot of code. Am I supposed to understand all that?

A: It is a lot of code, but if you walk through things step by step, it should all make sense to you. There's not a lot of new stuff in there, but there's definitely more DOM and positioning than you've done up to this point.

Q: And all of this is DOM code?

A: Well, there's really no such thing as DOM code. It's all JavaScript, and lots of it does use the DOM.

Q: So which parts use the DOM?

A: Anytime you use a property that moves around the tree, you're using the DOM in some form. So `firstChild` and `previousSibling` are DOM properties. But code that uses `getElementById()` is also using the DOM because that's a property on the `document` object. `document` is the top-level object of a browser's DOM tree.

The DOM is great for code that involves positioning and moving nodes around on a page.

Q: Is it safe to assume the id of a table cell has the row and column in it?

A: If you have control of the XHTML, like we do, it's safe. Since the Webville Puzzles company set up their XHTML so that table cells had those handy ids, we were able to figure out a cell's position by its id. If you had a different setup, you might need to figure out the cell's position relative to other cells and rows.

Q: We could do that with the DOM, too, right?

A: You bet. You'd probably be using some sort of counter, as well as `previousSibling` to figure out how many `<td>`'s over you are. And you'd need `parentNode` and similar properties to see which row you were on.

Q: So this DOM stuff can get pretty complex, can't it?

A: It can, very fast. Although lots of times, you'll only need to get as complex as we had to for the Fifteen Puzzle. In fact, with just the properties you've already learned, you're halfway to being a DOM master!

Q: Halfway? What's the other half?

A: So far, we've only moved around nodes in the DOM. In the next chapter, we'll look at creating new nodes and adding those to the tree on the fly.

Q: Back to that code... so the firstChild of a table cell is always the image in that cell?

A: That's the way `cellIsEmpty()` is written right now, yes. Can you think of a case where an image would *not* be the first child of a table cell?

Q: If an image isn't the first child of a table cell, that screws things up, doesn't it?

A: It sure does.

Q: Well, didn't we do the same thing in swapTiles(), back on page 254? We assume the image is the firstChild there, too, right?

A: Exactly right. So would that assumption ever be false?

Q: Who's asking the questions here, anyway?

A: Maybe we should actually test out the fifteen puzzle, and see what happens.

TEST DRIVE

Open your copy of fifteen.js, and add the code for cellIsEmpty() and tileClick(). Make sure you've got initPage() and swapTiles() working, too. Load things up. Does the puzzle work?

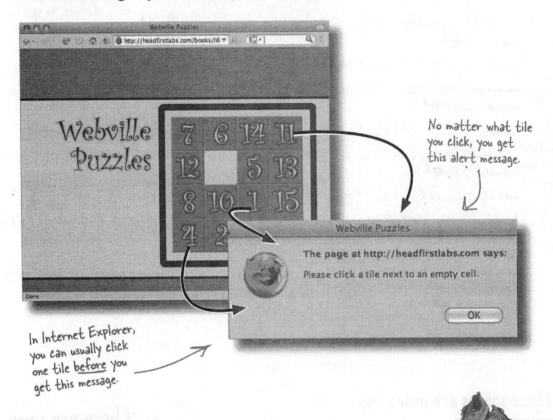

No matter what tile you click, you get this alert message.

In Internet Explorer, you can usually click one tile *before* you get this message.

Here's the XHTML for each table cell in the fifteen puzzle web page:

```
<td id="cell22">
  <img src=" mages/empty.png" alt="empty" width="69" height="69" />
</td>
```

Is there any difference between that XHTML and this fragment:

```
<td id="cell22"><img src="images/empty.png" alt="empty" width="69" height="69" /></td>
```

Take a close look at swapTiles() and cellIsEmpty(). Do you see a problem related to the difference in the two XHTML fragments shown above?

Exercise

A DOM tree has nodes for <u>EVERYTHING</u> in your web page

Most XHTML pages don't have every element, from the opening `<html>` to the closing `</html>` crammed onto one line. That would be a real pain to read. Instead, your page is full of spaces, tabs, and returns (sometimes called "end-of-lines"):

```
<table cellspacing="0" cellpadding="0">↵
␣<tr>↵
␣␣<td id="cell11">↵
␣␣␣<img src="images/07.png" alt="7" width="69" height="69" />↵
␣␣</td>↵
␣␣<td id="cell12">↵
␣␣␣<img src="images/06.png" alt="6" width="69" height="69" />↵
␣␣</td>↵
␣␣<td id="cell13">↵
␣␣␣<img src="images/14.png" alt="14" width="69" height="69" />↵
␣␣</td>↵
␣␣<td id="cell14">↵
␣␣␣<img src="images/11.png" alt="11" width="69" height="69" />↵
␣␣</td>↵
␣</tr>↵
   ... etc ...
</table>↵
```

You've got returns, or end-of-lines, to split up the page and make it easier to read.

You also have spaces or tabs for indentation.

Those spaces are nodes, too

Even though those spaces are invisible to you, the browser tries to figure out what to do with them. Usually they get represented by text nodes in your DOM tree. So a `<table>` node might have lots of text nodes full of spaces in addition to all the `<tr>` children you'd expect.

The bad news is that not all browsers do things the same way. So sometimes you get empty text nodes, and sometimes you don't. It's up to you to account for these text nodes, but you can't assume they'll always be there. Sounds a bit confusing, doesn't it?

There are some inconsistencies in how browsers treat whitespace. Never assume a browser will always ignore, or always represent, whitespace.

One browser might create a DOM tree for your page that looks like this:

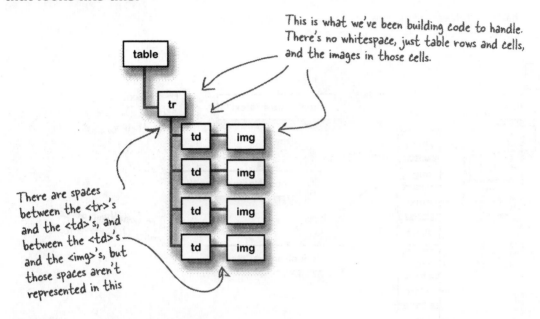

This is what we've been building code to handle. There's no whitespace, just table rows and cells, and the images in those cells.

There are spaces between the <tr>'s and the <td>'s, and between the <td>'s and the <img>'s, but those spaces aren't represented in this

Another browser might create a different DOM tree for the same XHTML:

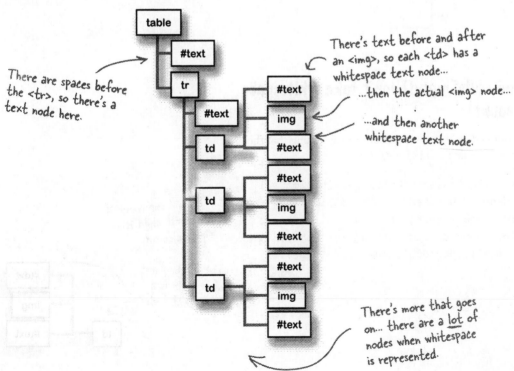

There are spaces before the <tr>, so there's a text node here.

There's text before and after an <img>, so each <td> has a whitespace text node...

...then the actual <img> node...

...and then another whitespace text node.

There's more that goes on... there are a *lot* of nodes when whitespace is represented.

The nodeName of a text node is "#text"

A text node always has a `nodeName` property with a value of "#text." So you can find out if a node is a text node by checking its `nodeName`:

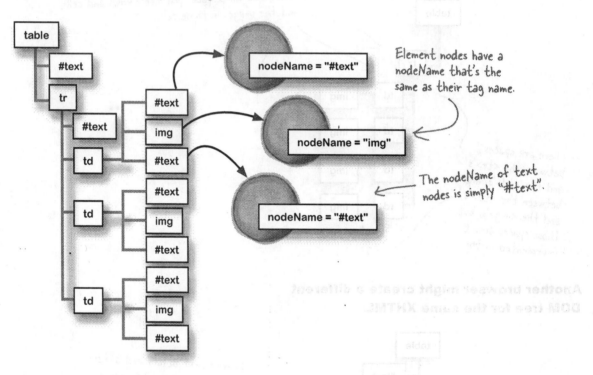

Element nodes have a nodeName that's the same as their tag name.

The nodeName of text nodes is simply "#text".

swapTiles() and cellIsEmpty() don't take whitespace nodes into account

The problem with our code is that our functions are assuming that the `<img>` in a table cell is the first child of a `<td>`:

```
function swapTiles(selectedCell, destinationCell) {
  selectedImage = selectedCell.firstChild;
  destinationImage = destinationCell.firstChild;
  selectedCell.appendChild(destinationImage);
  destinationCell.appendChild(selectedImage);
}
```

This will only work if the first child is an `<img>` element.

But what if the first child of a `<td>` is a whitespace text node?

Sharpen your pencil

We've got to deal with browsers that are creating whitespace nodes in their DOM trees. See if you can fill in the blanks to fix up the swapTiles() and cellIsEmpty() functions below:

```
function swapTiles(selectedCell, destinationCell) {
  selectedImage = selectedCell.firstChild;
  while (selectedImage._____ == _____) {
    selectedImage = selectedImage._____;
  }
  destinationImage = destinationCell.firstChild;
  while (destinationImage._____ == _____) {
    destinationImage = destinationImage._____;
  }
  selectedCell.appendChild(destinationImage);
  destinationCell.appendChild(selectedImage);
}


function cellIsEmpty(cell) {
  var image = cell.firstChild;
  while (image._____ == _____) {
    image = image._____;
  }
  if (image.alt == "empty")
    return true;
  else
    return false;
}
```

there are no Dumb Questions

Q: If the nodeName of a text node is always "#text", how can I get the text in that node?

A: Text nodes store the text they represent in a property called nodeValue. So the nodeValue for a whitespace node would be "" (an empty value), or possibly " " (two spaces).

Q: Shouldn't we be checking to see if text nodes have a nodeValue of whitespace, then?

A: In the table cells in the fifteen puzzle, there's no need to check the nodeValue. Since we only care about <img> nodes, we don't care about anything else. So we can skip over any node that's a text node.

Sharpen your pencil
Solution

Were you able to figure out how to skip over the whitespace text nodes in cellIsEmpty() and swapTiles()?

```
function swapTiles(selectedCell, destinationCell) {
  selectedImage = selectedCell.firstChild;
  while (selectedImage. nodeName == "#text" ) {
    selectedImage = selectedImage. nextSibling ;
  }
  destinationImage = destinationCell.firstChild;
  while (destinationImage. nodeName == "#text" ) {
    destinationImage = destinationImage. nextSibling ;
  }
  selectedCell.appendChild(destinationImage);
  destinationCell.appendChild(selectedImage);
}


function cellIsEmpty(cell) {
  var image = cell.firstChild;
  while (image. nodeName == "#text" ) {
    image = image. nextSibling ;
  }
  if (image.alt == "empty")
    return true;
  else
    return false;
}
```

We can find out if we've got a text node by comparing the nodeName to "#text".

If we've got a text node, move to the next sibling and try again.

Make sure you've got open-quote, then the # symbol, then text, then close quote.

All three of these cases use the same basic pattern: as long as the current node is text, go to the next node.

Check for a text node, and use DOM methods to move to the next node if we've got text

Test Drive

Update your versions of swapTiles() and cellIsEmpty(). Try the puzzle again... you should be able to move tiles around without a problem.

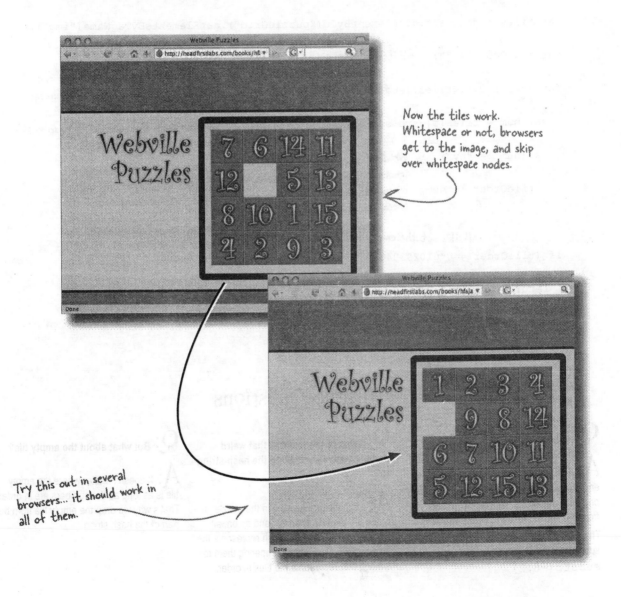

Now the tiles work. Whitespace or not, browsers get to the image, and skip over whitespace nodes.

Try this out in several browsers... it should work in all of them.

Did I win? Did I win?

All that's left is to figure out when a player's won. Then, every time two tiles are swapped, we can check this function to see if the board is in order. If it is, the player's solved the puzzle.

Here's a `puzzleIsComplete()` function that uses the names of each image to see if all the tiles are in order:

```
function puzzleIsComplete() {

    var tiles = document.getElementById("puzzleGrid").getElementsByTagName("img");

    var tileOrder = "";

    for (var i=0; i<tiles.length; i++) {

        var num = tiles[i].src.substr(-6,2);

        if (num != "ty")

            tileOrder += num;

    }

    if (tileOrder == "010203040506070809101112131415")

        return true;

    return false;

}
```

First, we get all the <img> tags in the grid.

We iterate over each tile image.

If you go back 6 characters from the end of the src of the image, you'll be at the image name: 02.png or empty.png.

We want just the numeric part, so that's 2 from −6 characters back.

We don't care about the empty image... we ignore it. Since the two characters returned by substr() for the empty image are "ty", check for that and ignore it.

If it's not the empty image, add the number (as a string) to our hash string.

If the numbers are in order, the puzzle's complete.

there are no Dumb Questions

Q: substr(-6, 2)? I don't get it.

A: A negative number means start at the end of the string, and count back. Since "02.png" is 6 characters, we want to go back from the *end* of the string by 6 characters.

Then, we want 2 characters of that substring, so we get "02" or "15." So you use `substr(-6,2)`.

Q: What in the world is that weird number you're comparing the hash string to?

A: It's just every number in the puzzle, in order: 01, then 02, then 03, and so on, all the way to 15. Since the hash represents the orders of the tiles, we're comparing them to a string that represents the tiles in order.

Q: But what about the empty tile?

A: It doesn't matter where the empty tile is as long as the numbers are in order. That's why we drop the empty tile from being part of the hash string.

But seriously... did I win?

There's even a special class that Webville Puzzles put in their CSS for showing a winning animation. The class is called "win," and when the puzzle is solved, you can set the `<div>` with an id of "puzzleGrid" to use this class and display the animation.

That means we just need to check if the puzzle is solved every time we swap tiles.

```
function swapTiles(selectedCell, destinationCell) {
  selectedImage = selectedCell.firstChild;
  while (selectedImage.nodeName == "#text") {
    selectedImage = selectedImage.nextSibling;
  }
  destinationImage = destinationCell.firstChild;
  while (destinationImage.nodeName == "#text") {
    destinationImage = destinationImage.nextSibling;
  }

  selectedCell.appendChild(destinationImage);
  destinationCell.appendChild(selectedImage);

  if (puzzleIsComplete()) {
    document.getElementById("puzzleGrid").className = "win";
  }
}
```

Every time we swap tiles, we need to see if the new arrangement makes the puzzle complete.

If the puzzle's solved, change the CSS class for the puzzleGrid `<div>`.

Test Drive

You need to add the puzzleIsComplete() function to your JavaScript, and update swapTiles(). Then, try everything out. But you've got to solve the puzzle to see the winning animation...

...good luck!

Half the code we used was just ordinary JavaScript. I don't think this DOM stuff is really all that hard... and we didn't even need to use it very much, anyway.

The DOM is just a tool, and you won't use it all the time... or sometimes, all that much.

You'll rarely write an application that is mostly DOM-related code. But when you're writing your JavaScript, and you really need that *next* table cell, or the containing element of an image, then the DOM is the perfect tool.

And, even more importantly, without the DOM, there's really no way to get around a page, especially if every element on your page doesn't have an `id` attribute. The DOM is just one more tool you can use to take control of your web pages.

In the next chapter, you're going to see how the DOM lets you do more than just move things around... it lets you create elements and text on the fly, and put them anywhere on the page you want.

The DOM is a great tool for getting around within a web page.

It also makes it easy to find elements that DON'T have an id attribute.

DOMAcrostic

Take some time to sit back and give your right brain something to do. Answer the questions up top, and then use the answer letters to fill in the secret message.

This method returns a specific element based on its ID

1	2	3	4	5	6	7	8	9	10	12	13	14	15

This property returns all the children of an element

16	17	18	19	20	21	22	23	24	25

The browser translates this into an element tree

26	27	28	29	30	31

This element property represents the element's container

32	33	34	35	36	37

This is what the browser creates for you

38	39	40		41	42	43	44

This element gives you access to the whole tree

45	46	47	48	49	50	51	52

49	27	25	41	35	28		52	17	8		45	22	7		33	51	20

13	39	48		26	33	25	10	2	34

13	46	30	34		32	27	1	43

DOMAcrostic

Your job was to answer the questions up top, and then use the answer letters to fill in the secret message.

This method returns a specific element based on its ID

G	E	T	E	L	E	M	E	N	T	B	Y	I	D
1	2	3	4	5	6	7	8	9	10	12	13	14	15

This property returns all the children of an element

C	H	I	L	D	N	O	D	E	S
16	17	18	19	20	21	22	23	24	25

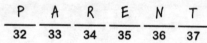 *This property is an array of nodes.*

The browser translates this into an element tree

M	A	R	K	U	P
26	27	28	29	30	31

A node that has children "contains" those children.

This element property represents the element's container

P	A	R	E	N	T
32	33	34	35	36	37

This is what the browser creates for you

D	O	M		T	R	E	E
38	39	40		41	42	43	44

This element gives you access to the whole tree

D	O	C	U	M	E	N	T
45	46	47	48	49	50	51	52

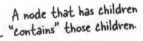 *The document object contains everything else in the DOM tree.*

M	A	S	T	E	R		T	H	E		D	O	M		A	N	D
49	27	25	41	35	28		52	17	8		45	22	7		33	51	20

Y	O	U		M	A	S	T	E	R
13	39	48		26	33	25	10	2	34

Y	O	U	R		P	A	G	E
13	46	30	34		32	27	1	43

7 manipulating the DOM

My wish is your command

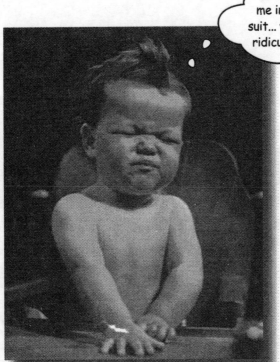

You will *not* put me in that ridiculous sailor suit... you will *not* put me in that ridiculous sailor suit...

DOM

Sometimes you just need a little ~~mind~~ control.

It's great to know that web browsers turn your XHTML into DOM trees. And you can do a lot by moving around within those trees. But real power is **taking control of a DOM tree** and making the tree look like *you* want it to. Sometimes what you really need is to **add a new element** and some text, or to **remove an element**, like an <img>, from a page altogether. You can do all of that and more with the DOM, and along the way, **banish that troublesome innerHTML property** altogether. The result? Code that can do more to a page, *without* having to mix presentation and structure in with your JavaScript.

Webville Puzzles... the franchise

All the cool kids have been playing the Fifteen Puzzle you developed for Webville Puzzles. The company's been making so much on subscription fees that they want a new puzzle... and they've come to you to build the interactivity.

This time, the company wants something a little more educational: **Woggle**, an online word generation game. They've already built the XHTML, and even know exactly how they want the puzzle to work.

Here's the initial Woggle page:

The game starts out by creating a 4-by-4 grid of letters. The letters should be random each time.

Players can click letters to "build" words in this word pane.

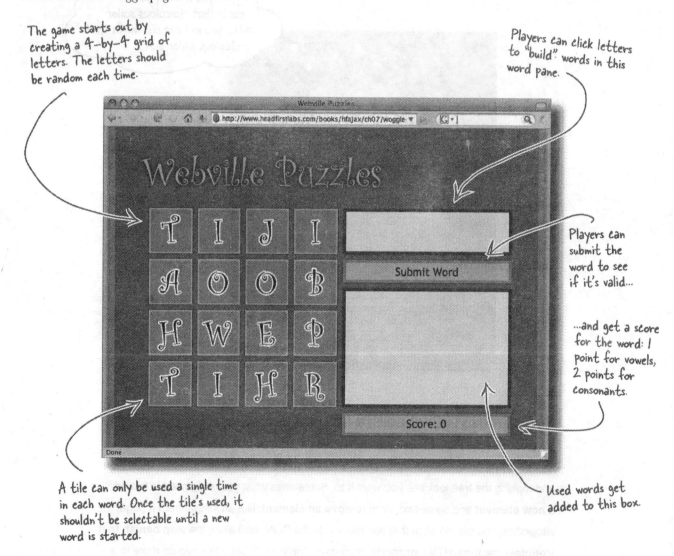

Players can submit the word to see if it's valid...

...and get a score for the word: 1 point for vowels, 2 points for consonants.

A tile can only be used a single time in each word. Once the tile's used, it shouldn't be selectable until a new word is started.

Used words get added to this box.

Exercise

There's a lot to build to get Woggle working, and of course the company wants their new app working immediately. Before you dig into the XHTML and CSS, think about what tasks are involved, and what JavaScript each one will need. Try and list each basic task for which you'll need to write code, and then make notes about what tools and techniques you might use for that task.

Task 1: ....

    Notes: ....

....

....

....

Task 2: ....

    Notes: ....

....

....

....

Task 3: ....

    Notes: ....

....

....

....

Task 4: ....

    Notes: ....

....

....

....

Task 5: ....

    Notes: ....

....

....

....

Your job was to figure out the basic tasks we'd need to take care of to get Woggle working. Here's what we came up with. You might have some differences in your details, but make sure you got these same core ideas down in some form or fashion.

Task 1: Set up the game board with random tiles

Notes: We need a way to come up with a random set of letters. Then we've got to display the right image for each letter on the 4x4 game board. This probably should all be done in an initPage() type of function.

As usual, we'll need an initPage() to set up event handlers and the basic page.

Each board should be different.

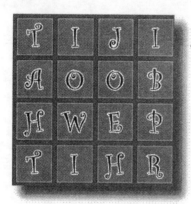

We can name these images something related to the letter they represent... so when we know what letter we want, we can display the right image.

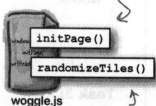

woggle.js

Let's build a function, randomizeTiles(), to handle creating the tile grid.

Task 2: Clicking on a tile adds the letter to the current word.

Notes: We need an event handler on each tile. The handler should figure out what letter was clicked, and add it to the "current word" box over on the right. Then the tile that was clicked should be disabled in the grid.

Clicking a letter does two things:

1. The letter gets added to the "current word" box.

2. The letter is disabled in the grid.

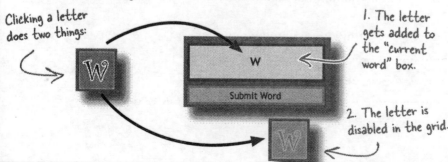

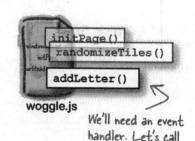

woggle.js

We'll need an event handler. Let's call it addLetter().

Task 3: Users can submit words to the server.

Notes: When a user clicks "Submit Word," the current word is sent to the server-side program. We'll also need to register a callback to deal with the server's response.

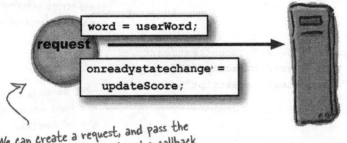

word = userWord;

request

onreadystatechange = updateScore;

We can create a request, and pass the server the current word and a callback to run when the server responds.

initPage()
randomizeTiles()
addLetter()
submitWord()

woggle.js

submitWord() can set up and send a server-side program request.

Task 4: Update the score using the server's response.

Notes: When the server responds, we've got to update the score, and add a valid word to the "used words" box. We've also got to remove the word from the "current word" box and enable the tiles again.

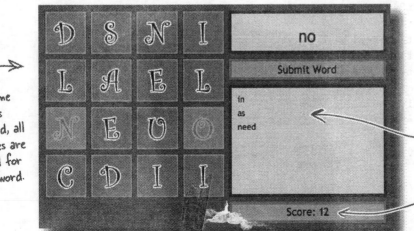

Each time a word's accepted, all the tiles are enabled for a new word.

initPage()
randomizeTiles()
addLetter()
submitWord()
updateScore()

woggle.js

One more function... our callback.

no

Submit Word

in
as
need

Valid words get added to this box...

Score: 12

...and the score gets updated with each valid word.

Woggle doesn't use table cells for the tiles

Now that we've got a plan, let's look at the XHTML for the Woggle game. The designers at Woggle have heard some bad things about tables, so the page is structured a bit differently. Each tile is represented by an <a> element this time, instead of being in a table cell. Better for them, but that might mean a little more work for us.

Here's what the XHTML looks like:

```
<html>
<head>
 <title>Webville Puzzles</title>
 <link rel="stylesheet" href="css/puzzle.css" type="text/css" />
 <script src="scripts/utils.js" type="text/javascript"></script>
 <script src="scripts/woggle.js" type="text/javascript"></script>
 </head>
<body>
 <div id="background">
  <h1 id="logotype">Webville Puzzles</h1>
  <div id="letterbox">
   <a href="#" class="tile t11"></a>
   <a href="#" class="tile t12"></a>
   <a href="#" class="tile t13"></a>
   <a href="#" class="tile t14"></a>
   <a href="#" class="tile t21"></a>
   <a href="#" class="tile t22"></a>
   <a href="#" class="tile t23"></a>
   <a href="#" class="tile t24"></a>
   <a href="#" class="tile t31"></a>
   <a href="#" class="tile t32"></a>
   <a href="#" class="tile t33"></a>
   <a href="#" class="tile t34"></a>
   <a href="#" class="tile t41"></a>
   <a href="#" class="tile t42"></a>
   <a href="#" class="tile t43"></a>
   <a href="#" class="tile t44"></a>
  </div>
  <div id="currentWord"></div>
  <div id="submit"><a href="#">Submit Word</a></div>
  <div id="wordListBg">
   <div id="wordList"></div>
  </div>
  <div id="score">Score: 0</div>
 </div>
</body>
</html>
```

You should go ahead and add these script references. We'll use utils.js for creating a request object...

...and woggle.js is the script we'll build for our puzzle-specific functions.

Each set of 4 <a>'s represents one row in the puzzle grid.

Here's where the current word will go...

...and the "Submit Word" button will go here.

There's a place for words already used...

...and finally, the score.

woggle-puzzle.html

The tiles in the XHTML are CSS-positioned

Instead of putting the tiles inside of a table, each <a> element that represents a tile is given a general class ("tile") and then a specific class, indicating where on the board it is (for example, "t21"):

<a href="#" class="tile t21"></a>

"tile" is a general CSS class that applies to all tiles in the grid.

This is for the specific tile. 2 is the row, and 1 is the column. So this is the first column in the second row.

The CSS then uses both the general "tile" class and the specific tile class ("t21", "t42", etc.) to style and position the tiles.

This CSS class applies to all tiles, so each element with a "tile" class gets these properties.

```
/* tile defaults */
#letterbox a.tile {
    background: url('../images/tiles.png') 120px 80px no-repeat;
    height: 80px;
    position: absolute;
    width: 80px;
}

/* tile positioning */
#letterbox a.t11 { top: 3px; left: 3px; }
#letterbox a.t12 { top: 3px; left: 93px; }
#letterbox a.t13 { top: 3px; left: 183px; }
#letterbox a.t14 { top: 3px; left: 273px; }
... etc ...
```

There's an entry in the CSS for each tile... 16 in all.

This CSS sets the position for each individual <a> that represents a tile.

```
#letterbox
{
}
a.tile {
}
```
puzzle.css

Download the XHTML and CSS for Woggle.

Visit **www.headfirstlabs.com**, and find the **chapter07** folder. You'll see the XHTML and CSS for Woggle. You should add the <script> tags to woggle-puzzle.html, and get ready to dig into some code.

Run it!

Q: CSS-positioned? I'm not sure I know what that means.

A: CSS-positioned just means that instead of relying on the structure of your XHTML to position something on a page, CSS is used instead. So if you want to CSS-position an `<a>` element, you give that element a class or id, and then in your CSS, set its `left`, `right`, `top`, and/or `bottom` properties, or use the `position` and `float` CSS attributes.

Q: Is that better than using tables?

A: A lot of people think so, especially web designers. By using CSS, you're relying on your CSS to handle presentation and positioning, rather than the way cells in a table line up. That's a more flexible approach to getting your page to look like you want.

Q: So which should I use? Tables or CSS-positioning?

A: Well, you really can't go wrong with CSS-positioning, because it's the easiest approach to getting things to look the same across browsers.

But more importantly, you should be able to write code that works with tables *or* CSS positioning. You can't always control the pages you write code for, so you need to be able to work with lots of different structures and types of pages.

Q: I don't understand how the CSS positioning actually worked, though. Can you explain that again?

A: Sure. Each tile is represented by an `<a>` in the XHTML. And each `<a>` has a `class` attribute, and actually has two classes: the general class, "tile," and a specific class representing that tile, like "t32." So the class for the tile on the third row, second column would be "tile t32."

Then, in the CSS, there are *two* selectors applied to each tile: the general rule, "tile," and the specific selector for a tile, like "t32." So you have selectors like `a.tile`, and `a.t32`. Both of those selectors get applied to a tile with a class of "tile t32."

The general rule handles common properties for all tiles, like height and width and look. The specific selector handles that tile's position on the page.

Q: Why are `<a>`'s used for the tiles? They're not links, right?

A: No, not really. That's just what Webville Puzzles used (maybe they've been checking out the tabs on Marcy's yoga site). It really doesn't matter what you use, as long as there's one element per tile, and you can position that element in the CSS.

There are a few considerations that using an `<a>` brings up for our event handlers, though, and we'll look at those a bit later.

Q: I don't see a button for "Submit Word." There's just a `<div>`. What gives?

A: You don't have to have an actual form button to make something *look* like a button. In this case, the Webville Puzzle designers are using a `<div>` with a background image that looks like a button for the "Submit Word" button. As long as we attach an event handler to that `<div>` to capture clicks, we can treat it like a button in our code, too.

> You should be able to write code to work with **ALL TYPES** of pages... even if the structure of those pages isn't how **YOU** would have done things.

BRAIN POWER

An event handler attached to an `<a>` element usually returns either true or false. What do you think the browser uses that return value for?

Here are the tasks from page 286. First, we need to set up the board.

"We don't want TOTALLY random letters..."

The guys in the puzzle labs at Webville Puzzles just called. They've decided they don't want totally random letters for the board after all. Instead, they want letters to appear according to a letter frequency chart they're faxing over... that way, common letters like "e" and "t" show up in the grid a lot more often than uncommon ones like "z" and "w."

Here's what the guys faxed over to you.

Letter	# of times appears out of 100
a	8
b	1
c	3
d	3
e	12
f	2
g	2
h	6
i	7
j	1
k	1
l	4
m	2
n	6
o	8
p	2
q	6
r	6
s	8
t	3
u	2
v	2
w	1
x	1
y	2
z	1

Given 100 random letters from actual English words, "e" appears about 12 times.

Thanks, Webville Puzzles

Sharpen your pencil

Let's get started. First, you need to build an initPage() and randomizeTiles() function. Here's what you know:

1. There's a class for each lettered tile in puzzle. css. The class for tile "a," for example, is called "la" (the letter "l" for letter, plus the letter the tile represents).

2. Webville Puzzles has faxed you a letter frequency table. There are 100 entries, with each letter represented the number of times out of 100 it typically appears. You need to represent that table as an array in your JavaScript. There should be 100 entries, where each entry is a single letter.

3. Randomly choosing a letter from the frequency table is like choosing a letter based on the frequency in which it appears in a word.

4. Math.floor(Math.random()*2000) will return a random number between 0 and 1999.

5. You'll need to use getElementById() and getElementsByTagName() each *at least* once.

Try to complete both initPage() and randomizeTiles() *before* you turn the page. Good luck!

Sharpen your pencil
Solution

Your job was to use the information on page 291 to write code for initPage() and randomizeTiles(). You also may have come up with some other JavaScript outside of those functions... how did you do?

Did you remember this line? We've got to call initPage() to get anything working.

```
window.onload = initPage;
```

We made this a global variable. Any function in our JavaScript can use this table now.

```
var frequencyTable = new Array(
  "a", "a", "a", "a", "a", "a", "a", "a", "b", "c", "c", "c", "d", "d", "d",
  "e", "e", "e", "e", "e", "e", "e", "e", "e", "e", "e", "e", "f", "f", "g",
  "g", "h", "h", "h", "h", "h", "h", "i", "i", "i", "i", "i", "i", "i", "j",
  "k", "l", "l", "l", "l", "m", "m", "n", "n", "n", "n", "n", "n", "o", "o",
  "o", "o", "o", "o", "o", "o", "p", "p", "q", "q", "q", "q", "q", "q", "r",
  "r", "r", "r", "r", "r", "s", "s", "s", "s", "s", "s", "s", "s", "t", "t",
  "t", "u", "u", "v", "v", "w", "x", "y", "z");
```

Here's how we represented the letter frequency table. Each letter appears in the array the number of times out of 100 it shows up in the frequency table Webville Puzzles faxed us.

Put this JavaScript into a new file, woggle.js.

woggle.js

All initPage() does right now is call randomizeTiles() to set up the puzzle grid.

```
function initPage() {
  randomizeTiles();
}

function randomizeTiles() {

  var tiles = document.getElementById("letterbox").getElementsByTagName("a");

  for (i = 0; i < tiles.length; i++) {

    var index = Math.floor(Math.random() * 100);

    var letter = frequencyTable[index];

    tiles[i].className = tiles[i].className + ' l' + letter;
  }
}
```

First, we grab all the <a> elements in the letterbox <div>.

For each tile, we get a random index between 0 and 99...

...and choose a letter from the letter frequency table.

Next, we change the class name of the tile. To do this, keep the existing class name...

We separate each class name with a space.

...and then add "l" plus the letter chosen, like "la" for letter a, or "lw" for letter w.

Our presentation is <u>ALL</u> in our CSS

By using class names instead of directly inserting `<img>`'s into the XHTML, we've kept our JavaScript behavior totally separate from the presentation, content, and structure of the page. So suppose that for the tile in the second row, first column, the random index returned by `Math.floor(Math.random() * 100)` was 4.

Array indices are zero-based, so index "4" points to the 5th item (a, a, a, a, a).

5th item

The fifth entry in frequencyTable is "a", so that tile should be an "a." But instead of having our code insert the "a" image directly, and deal with image URLs, it just adds to the class of that tile:

```
<a href="#" class="tile t21 la"></a>
```

This part was already in the page's XHTML for the tile.

This part gets added by randomizeTiles().

Now we use the CSS to say how that letter is displayed:

```
/* tile letters */
#letterbox a.la { background-position: 0px 0px; }
#letterbox a.lb { background-position: -80px 0px; }
#letterbox a.lc { background-position: -160px 0px; }
#letterbox a.ld { background-position: -240px 0px; }
#letterbox a.le { background-position: -320px 0px; }
... etc ...
```

puzzle.css

Now the designers have options

Since all the presentation is in the CSS, the designers of the page can do whatever they want to show the tiles. They might use a different background image for each letter. In the case of Woggle, though, the designers have used a single image for all tiles, `tiles.png`. `tiles.png`, It actually has every lettered tile in it, each in just the right size. That image is set as the background image in the selector for the `a.tile` class.

This is how we handled the "In Progress" and "Denied" image back in Chapter 5.

You can check out the CSS selector for a.tile back on page 289.

Then, in each letter-specific class, like `a.la` or `a.lw`, they've adjusted the position of the image so the right portion of that single image displays. Depending on the position, you get a different letter. And the designers can change the CSS anytime they want a new look... ***all without touching your code***.

Test Drive

Try out your early version of Woggle.

Download the samples files, and make sure you've added a reference to
`woggle.js` in your version of `woggle-puzzle.html`. Then, load
the Woggle main page in your browser... and load it again... and again...

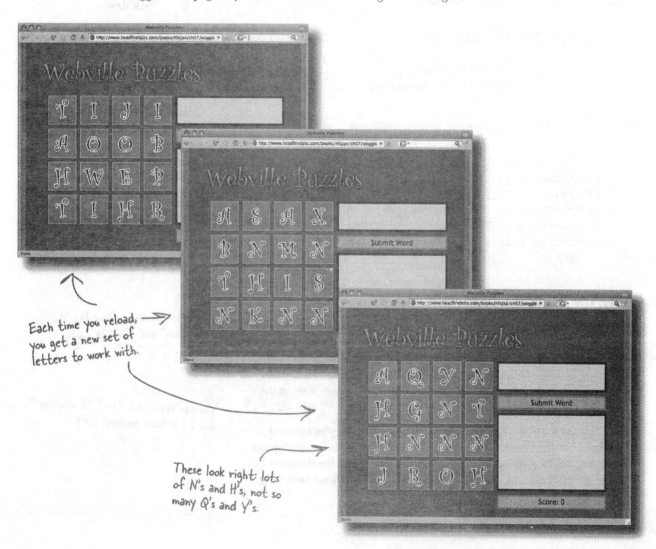

Each time you reload, you get a new set of letters to work with.

These look right: lots of N's and H's, not so many Q's and Y's.

We need a new event handler for handling tile clicks

Next up, we need to assign an event handler to the tiles on the grid. The handler needs to do several things:

① Figure out which letter was clicked.

All our handler will know about is the <a> element on the page that was clicked. From that, we've got to figure out which letter is shown on the tile that the clicked-upon <a> represents.

② Add a letter to the current word box.

Once we know what letter was selected, we've got to add that letter to the current word box in the "currentWord" <div>.

③ Disable the clicked-on letter.

We've also got to keep the tile that was clicked from being clicked again. So we need to disable the letter. There's a CSS class for that, called "disabled," that works with the "tile," "t23," and "lw" classes already on each title.

This class handles formatting for all tiles.

This class represents the position of the tile.

This class represents the letter that's shown.

Sharpen your pencil

There are actually a couple of things missing from the list above... can you figure out what they are?

....
....
....
....
....

Start building the event handler for each tile click

The best way to write a big chunk of code is to take things one
step at a time. First, let's build a skeleton for our handler. That's
just a function block with a name, so we can hook everything up
and test out code as we go.

Add this function to woggle.js:

We'll fill in each piece of
this function as we go.

```
function addLetter() {
    // Figure out which letter was clicked

    // Add a letter to the current word box

    // Disable the clicked-on letter
}
```

function initPage (
...
)

woggle.js

**The best way
to write a large
piece of code is
to take things one
step at a time.**

We can assign an event handler in our randomizeTiles() function

Now let's go ahead and hook up our handler to each tile. We're
already iterating over all the tiles in randomizeTiles(), so
that seems like a good place to assign our event handler:

```
function randomizeTiles() {
    var tiles = document.getElementById("letterbox")
                        .getElementsByTagName("a");
    for (i = 0; i < tiles.length; i++) {
        var index = Math.floor(Math.random() * 100);
        var letter = frequencyTable[index];
        tiles[i].className = tiles[i].className +
                                ' l' + letter;
        tiles[i].onclick = addLetter;
    }
}
```

Now we can start testing our event
handler as we write it.

function initPage (
...
)

woggle.js

**Get each piece
of code working
BEFORE moving
on to the next
piece of code.**

Property values are just strings in JavaScript

So far, we've mostly used the `className` property of an object to change a CSS class. For Woggle, we actually added classes to that property... but what if we want to read that value? Suppose the second tile on the third row represents the letter "b." That tile would have a `className` value that looks like this:

```
<a href="#" class="tile t32 lb"></a>
```

Third row
Second column
Letter "b"

So we've got a `className` property that has the letter of the tile that's represented... how can we get to that letter? Fortunately, JavaScript has a lot of useful string-handling utility functions:

substring

substring(startIndex, endIndex) returns a string from startIndex to endIndex, based on an existing string value.

foo has the value "foo."

```
var foo = "foolish".substring(0,3);
var is = "foolish".substring(4,6);
```

is has the value "is."

split

split(splitChar) splits a string into pieces separated by splitChar. The pieces are returned in an array. *This will output "Succeed,Commit,Decide."*

```
var pieces = "Decide,Commit,Succeed".split(",");
alert(pieces[2] + "," + pieces[1] + "," + pieces[0]);
```

Sharpen your pencil

What code would you write to get the letter represented by the clicked-on tile?

....
....
....
....

Sharpen your pencil
Solution

What code would you write to get the letter represented by the clicked-on tile?

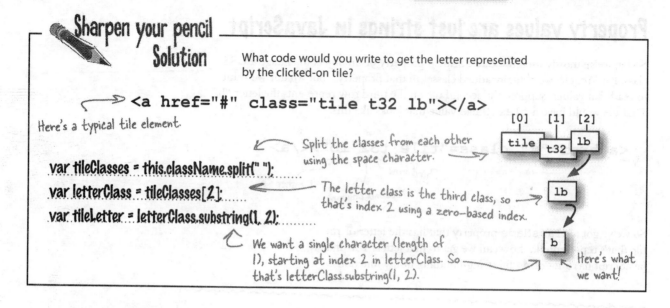

```
<a href="#" class="tile t32 lb"></a>
```

Here's a typical tile element.

Split the classes from each other using the space character.

[0]   [1]   [2]

tile   t32   lb

```
var tileClasses = this.className.split(" ");
```

```
var letterClass = tileClasses[2];
```

The letter class is the third class, so that's index 2 using a zero-based index.

lb

```
var tileLetter = letterClass.substring(1, 2);
```

We want a single character (length of 1), starting at index 2 in letterClass. So that's letterClass.substring(1, 2).

b

Here's what we want!

TEST DRIVE

Test out your letter recognition.

Add the code above to your `addLetter()` function, and also add an `alert()` statement to display the value of `tileLetter` at the end of the function. Then reload Woggle and see if everything's working...

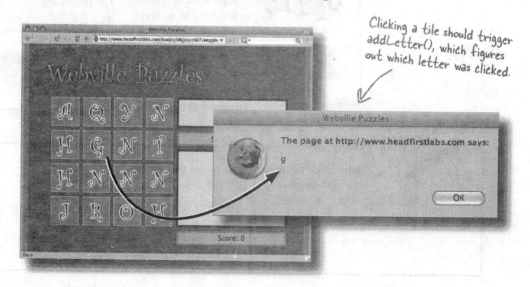

Clicking a tile should trigger addLetter(), which figures out which letter was clicked.

Exercise

Now you've got to take the clicked-on letter, and add it into the currentWord <div>. How would you do that? Oh, and by the way... ***you can't use the innerHTML property on this one!***

You keep saying innerHTML is bad. What's so wrong with it? It sure seems to be pretty handy...

innerHTML forces you to mix XHTML syntax into your script... and offers you no protection from silly typos, either.

Anytime you set the innerHTML property on an element, you're directly inputting XHTML into a page. For example, in Marcy's yoga page, here's where we inserted XHTML directly into a <div> with JavaScript:

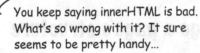

```
contentPane.innerHTML = "<h3>" + hintText + "</h3>";
```

But that <h3> is ***XHTML***. Anytime you directly type XHTML into your code, you're introducing all sorts of potential for typos and little mistakes (like forgetting a closing tag for a <p>). In addition to that, different browsers sometimes treat innerHTML in different ways.

If at all possible, you should never change content or presentation directly from your code. Instead, rely on CSS classes to change presentation, and ... what can you use from your code to change structure *without* introducing typos or misplaced end tags? Figure out the answer to that, and you're well on your way to a solution for the exercise above.

We need to add content AND structure to the "currentWord" <div>

When a player clicks on a letter, that letter should be added to the current word. Right now, we've got a <div> with an id of "currentWord," but nothing in that <div>:

```
<div id="currentWord"></div>
```

So what do we need? Well, we've got to insert text in that <div>, but text doesn't usually go directly inside a <div>. Text belongs in a textual element, like a <p>. So what we really want is something more like this:

```
<div id="currentWord">
  <p>Current Word</p>
</div>
```

Use the DOM to change a page's structure

You already know that using code like this isn't that great of an idea:

```
var currentWordDiv = getElementById("currentWord");
currentWordDiv.innerHTML = "<p>" + tileLetter + "</p>";
```

Besides this being a hotbed for typos, what do you do afterward to get the existing current word and append to it?

But there's a way to work with the structure of a page without using `innerHTML`: the DOM. You've already used the DOM to get around on a page, but you can use the DOM to **change** a page, too.

From the browser's point of view, here's the part of the DOM tree representing the currentWord <div>:

The DOM sees the <div> as an element node named div with an id attribute having a value of "currentWord."

We need to create something that looks more like this:

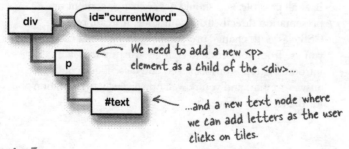

We need to add a new <p> element as a child of the <div>...

...and a new text node where we can add letters as the user clicks on tiles.

Use createElement() to create a DOM element

Remember the document object? We're going to use it again. You can call `document.createElement()` to create a new element. Just give the `createElement()` method the name of the element to create, like "p" or "img":

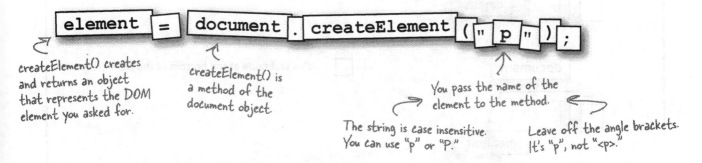

createElement() creates and returns an object that represents the DOM element you asked for.

createElement() is a method of the document object.

You pass the name of the element to the method.

The string is case insensitive. You can use "p" or "P."

Leave off the angle brackets. It's "p", not "<p>."

Sharpen your pencil

The createElement() method is part of the document element, which contains everything else in the browser's DOM tree. Where do you think the new element is added in the DOM tree?

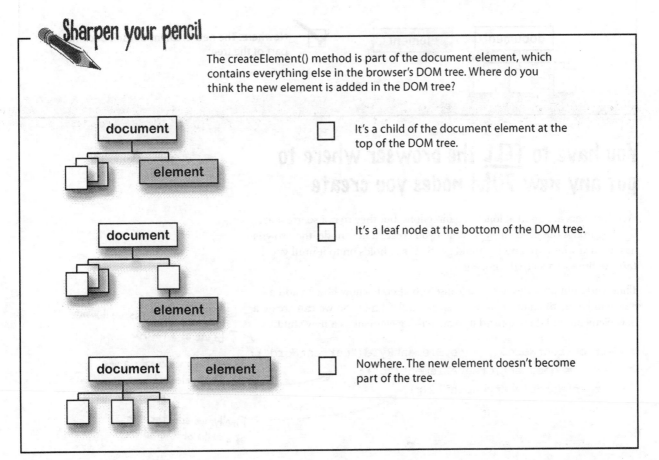

☐ It's a child of the document element at the top of the DOM tree.

☐ It's a leaf node at the bottom of the DOM tree.

☐ Nowhere. The new element doesn't become part of the tree.

Sharpen your pencil
Solution

The createElement() method is part of the document element, which contains everything else in the browser's DOM tree. Where do you think the new element is added in the DOM tree?

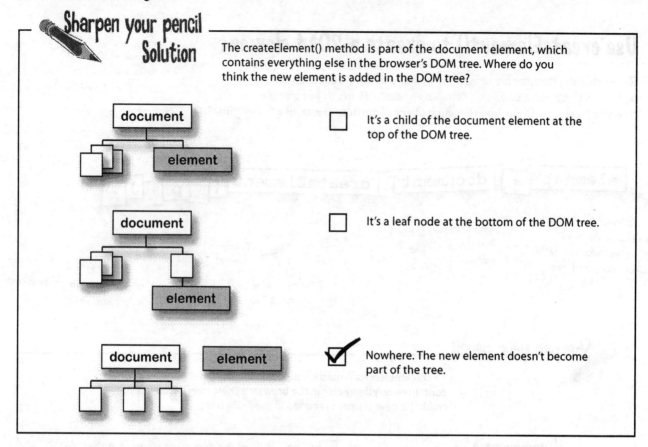

It's a child of the document element at the top of the DOM tree.

It's a leaf node at the bottom of the DOM tree.

☑ Nowhere. The new element doesn't become part of the tree.

You have to TELL the browser where to put any new DOM nodes you create

Web browsers are good at following directions, but they're not so great at figuring things out on their own. When you create a new node, the browser has no idea where that node should go. So it just holds on to it until you **tell** the browser where the node goes.

That works out pretty well, too, because you already know how to add a new child node to an element: with appendChild(). So we can create a new element, and then append it to an existing element as a new child:

```
var currentWordDiv = getElementById("currentWord");
var p = document.createElement("p");
currentWordDiv.appendChild(p);
```

This gets the <div> we'll want to use as a parent.

Then we create a new <p> element.

Finally, we add the <p> as a child of the <div>.

So can we do the same thing with a text node? Just create a new node, set the text, and add it to the <p> element?

You can create elements, text, attributes, and a lot more.

The document object has all sorts of helpful create methods. You can createElement(), createTextNode(), createAttribute(), and a lot more.

Each method returns a new node, and you can insert that node anywhere into your DOM tree you want. Just remember, until you insert the node into the DOM tree, it won't appear on your page.

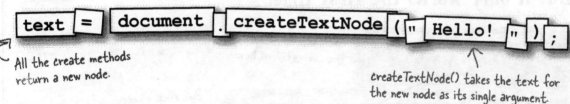

All the create methods return a new node.

createTextNode() takes the text for the new node as its single argument.

```
att = document.createAttribute("id", "tile21");
```

An attribute node belongs on an element... that's up to you to take care of, though.

createAttribute() takes an attribute name and value as arguments.

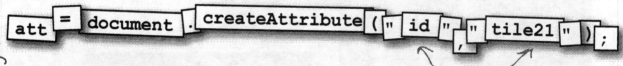

Exercise

See if you can complete the code for adding a letter to the currentWord <div>. Add your code into the addLetter() event handler, and try things out. Does everything work like you expected?

Exercise Solution

Your job was to finish up adding letters to the currentWord <div>. Were you able to finish the code up? Were there any problems?

```
function addLetter() {
  var tileClasses = this.className.split(" ");
  var letterClass = tileClasses[2];
  var tileLetter = letterClass.substring(1,2);          Get the right <div>...

  var currentWordDiv = document.getElementById("currentWord");    ...create and add
  var p = document.createElement("p");                           a <p>...
  currentWordDiv.appendChild(p);
  var letterText = document.createTextNode(tileLetter);    ...and then create
  p.appendChild(letterText);                               and add the letter
}                                                          to that <p>.
```

function initPage {
...
}

woggle.js

But it only works the first time!

Click a letter, and it appears in the currentWord box.

But click a <u>second</u> letter, and nothing shows up. What gives?

DOM Magnets

Let's try and figure out what's going on with Woggle and our addLetter() event handler. Use the DOM magnets below to build the DOM tree under the currentWord <div> for:

...the first time addLetter() is called:	**...the second time addLetter() is called:**	**...the third time addLetter() is called:**

| div | id="currentWord" | div | id="currentWord" | div | id="currentWord" |

You can use each of these magnets as many times as you'd like.

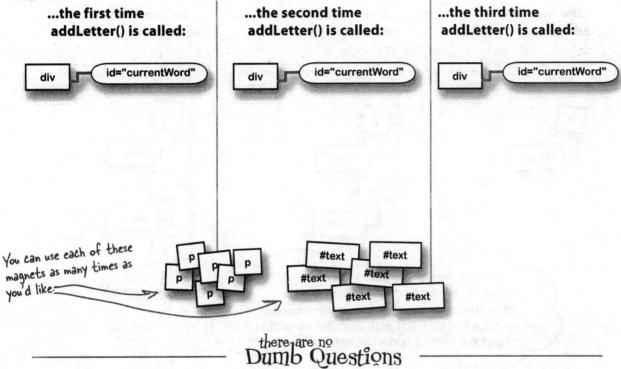

there are no
Dumb Questions

Q: When I call appendChild(), where exactly is the node I pass into that method added?

A: appendChild() adds a node as the *last* child of the parent element.

Q: What if I don't want the new node to be the last child?

A: You can use the insertBefore() method. You pass insertBefore() *two* nodes: the node to add, and an existing node that the new node should *precede*.

Q: Didn't we use appendChild() to move elements in the last chapter?

A: We sure did. Whatever node is passed to appendChild(), or insertBefore(), is added as a new child node to the parent you call appendChild() on. The browser moves the node if it's already in the DOM tree, or adds the node into the DOM tree if it's not part of the tree already.

Q: What happens when you append or insert a node that already has children of its own?

A: The browser inserts the element you insert *and all of its children* into the DOM tree. So when you move a node, you're moving that node and everything underneath that node in the DOM tree.

Q: Can you just remove a node from a DOM tree?

A: Yes, you can use the removeNode() methods to remove a node completely from a DOM tree.

DOM Magnet Solutions

Let's try and figure out what's going on with Woggle and our addLetter() event handler. Use the DOM magnets below to build the DOM tree under the currentWord <div> for:

**...the first time
addLetter() is called:**

**...the second time
addLetter() is called:**

**...the third time
addLetter() is called:**

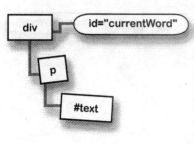

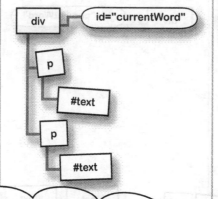

> So that's the problem, right? We're not adding to that first text node each time addLetter() gets called. We're actually adding a new <p> and a new text node each time. But we need to change the existing text node, right?

Some nodes have a nodeName, others have a nodeValue, and still others have both.

The first time addLetter() gets called, we create a new text node. But on future calls, we need addLetter() to change the text in that node. We can do that using the text node's nodeValue property.

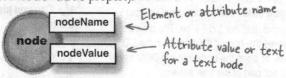

Element or attribute name

Attribute value or text for a text node

Every DOM node has a nodeName and nodeValue property.

Every DOM node has two basic properties: nodeName and nodeValue. For an element, the nodeName is the name of the element. For an attribute, nodeName is the attribute name, and nodeValue is the attribute value. And for a text node, the nodeValue is the text in the node.

The nodeName and nodeValue properties tell you about nodes

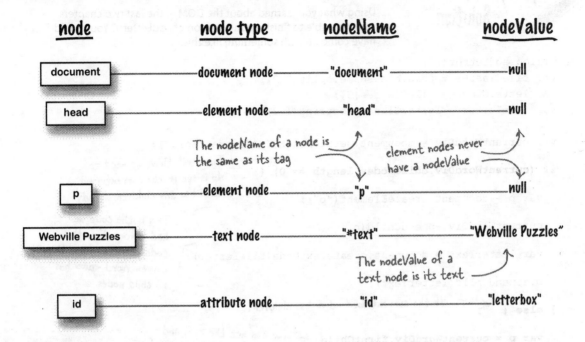

node	node type	nodeName	nodeValue
document	document node	"document"	null
head	element node	"head"	null
p	element node	"p"	null
Webville Puzzles	text node	"#text"	"Webville Puzzles"
id	attribute node	"id"	"letterbox"

The nodeName of a node is the same as its tag

element nodes never have a nodeValue

The nodeValue of a text node is its text

Sharpen your pencil

You're ready to finish up the section of addLetter() that gets a letter from a clicked-on tile, and adds the clicked-on letter to the currentWord <div>. See if you can write the rest of the function now... and don't forget to test things out!

Write your version of addLetter() here.

Hint: node.childNodes returns an array of a node's children, and node.childNodes.length tells you how many children a node has.

Sharpen your pencil Solution

Using what you learned about the DOM in the last two chapters, were you able to finish up this section of addLetter()? You should have come up with something like this:

```
function addLetter() {
    var tileClasses = this.className.split(" ");
    var letterClass = tileClasses[2];
    var tileLetter = letterClass.substring(1,2);

    var currentWordDiv = document.getElementById("currentWord");

    if (currentWordDiv.childNodes.length == 0) {

        var p = document.createElement("p");

        currentWordDiv.appendChild(p);

        var letterText = document.createTextNode(tileLetter);

        p.appendChild(letterText);

    } else {

        var p = currentWordDiv.firstChild;

        var letterText = p.firstChild;

        letterText.nodeValue += tileLetter;

    }
}
```

The first thing we need to do is see if the currentWord <div> has any children already.

This is the code we had before. Now this code only runs when the currentWord <div> has no child nodes.

If the currentWord <div> has children...

...we can get the <p>, and then the text node child of that <p>...

...and add the new letter to the text node.

there are no Dumb Questions

Q: What is that childNodes property again?

A: `childNodes` is a property available on every node. It returns an array of all of a node's children, or `null` if there aren't any children for that node. And since it's an array, it has a `length` property that tells you how many nodes are in the array.

Q: Can't I just keep up with whether or not addLetter() has been called, and use that as my conditional?

A: No, that won't always work. It's true that the first time `addLetter()` is called, you need to create a `<p>` and text node. But if the player submits a word, and the board is reset, `addLetter()` would again need to create a new `<p>` and text node. So just checking to see how many times `addLetter()` has run won't be enough.

Q: I wrote my code a different way. Is that okay?

A: Sure. There are usually at least two or three different ways to solve a problem. But you need to be sure that your code always works... and that it's not creating DOM nodes unless it needs to. If both of those things are true, then feel free to use your own version of `addLetter()`.

Hey, what about text nodes full of whitespace, like we ran into last chapter. Isn't it bad to use currentWordDiv.firstChild and p.firstChild like that? Couldn't those first nodes be whitespace nodes?

When you control the DOM structure, nothing happens that you don't specify.

When the browser creates a DOM tree based on an XHTML text file, *the browser is in control*. It's doing what it thinks is best to represent that XHTML - and sometimes, that means interpreting line endings or extra tabs and spaces as text nodes filled with whitespace.

But when you're making changes to a DOM tree, *you're* the one in control. The browser won't insert anything unless you tell it to. So when you're working with the DOM nodes you inserted into the currentWord <div>, you don't have to worry about extra whitespace text nodes. Instead, you can go right to the first child of the <div>, and know that it's a <p>.

Test Drive

Test out your new-and-improved event handler.

See how addLetter() works now. Each time you click a tile, it should add another letter to the current word box. Does it work?

There are a few things we still need to do related to clicking on tiles, though... can you figure out what they are?

We need to disable each tile. That means changing the tile's CSS class...

Once a player's clicked on a tile, they can't re-click on that tile. So we need to disable each tile once it's been clicked.

Clicking on a tile should change the look of that tile.

This is presentation, so you probably already know what to do, don't you? In `addLetter()`, we need to add another CSS class to the clicked-on tile. There's a class in `puzzle.css` called "disabled" that's perfect for the job.

Add this line to the end of `addLetter()`:

```
function addLetter() {
   // existing code

   this.className += " disabled";
}
```

We need to add this class to the existing tile classes, not just replace those classes.

Make sure there's a space to separate the CSS classes from each other.

Now, once `addLetter()` runs, the clicked-on tile fades, and then looks like it can't be clicked anymore.

...AND turning OFF the addLetter() event handler

As long as there have been games, there have been gamers looking for an edge. With Woggle, even though we can disable the **look** of a tile, that doesn't mean clicking on the tile doesn't do anything. Clicking on a tile— even if it's got the `disabled` class—will still trigger the `addLetter()` event handler. That means a letter can be clicked on an infinite number of times... unless you put a stop to it!

So we need to take another step at the end of `addLetter()`. We need to remove the `addLetter()` event handler for the clicked-on tile.

```
function addLetter() {
   // existing code

   this.className += " disabled";
   this.onclick = "";
}
```

Set onclick to an empty string. That removes the addLetter() event handler.

TEST DRIVE

We've handled tile clicks... completely!

Have you made all the additions you need to addLetter()? Once you
have, fire up Woggle, and build some words.

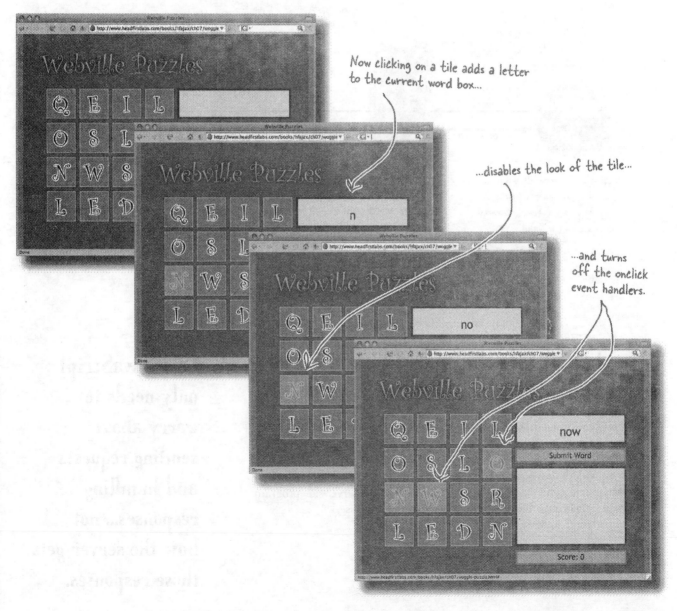

Now clicking on a tile adds a letter
to the current word box...

...disables the look of the tile...

...and turns
off the onclick
event handlers.

Submitting a word is just (another) request

`addLetter()` was all about using the DOM, and submitting a word to the server is all about request objects. Woggle's already got a program on their server that takes in a word and returns a score for that word... or a -1 if the word isn't a real English word.

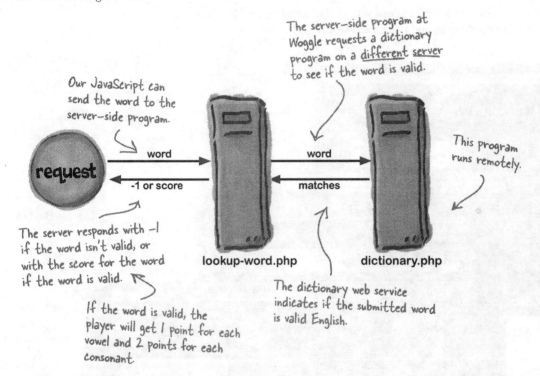

The server-side program at Woggle requests a dictionary program on a *different* server to see if the word is valid.

Our JavaScript can send the word to the server-side program.

This program runs remotely.

word → → word →
← **-1 or score** ← ← **matches** ←

request

lookup-word.php   **dictionary.php**

The server responds with -1 if the word isn't valid, or with the score for the word if the word is valid.

The dictionary web service indicates if the submitted word is valid English.

If the word is valid, the player will get 1 point for each vowel and 2 points for each consonant.

Our JavaScript doesn't care how the server figures out its response to our request

With Woggle, it really doesn't matter that the server-side program we're calling makes *another* request to *another* program. In fact, it wouldn't matter even if `lookup-word.php` called a PHP program, then made a SOAP request to a Java web service, and then sent a message to a cell phone using an SMS gateway. All that *does* matter is that we send the server-side program the right information, and it returns to us the right response.

Your JavaScript only needs to worry about sending requests and handling responses... not how the server gets those responses.

Sharpen your pencil

You've built and sent a lot of request objects by now. Using what you've learned, can you write the submitWord() function?

→ Answers on page 316.

Wait a second... before you start waving around all your fancy asynchronous request objects again, why should we be making an asynchronous request here? Shouldn't players have to **wait** for the server to check their word and return a score?

Not every request should be an <u>ASYNCHRONOUS</u> request.

In all the earlier chapters, we made asynchronous requests, so users weren't stuck waiting on a password to get checked or a page to get loaded. But in Woggle, we really want users to wait on the server before doing anything else. So when a word is sent to the server for scoring, we need to use a *synchronous* request.

BRAIN BARBELL

There are some other advantages to using a synchronous request for submitting a word to the server in Woggle. Can you think of any?

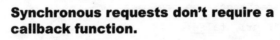

So if we're using a synchronous request, do we need a callback function? If the program waits on the server, why not just write the code to handle the server's response right in our submitWord() function?

Synchronous requests don't require a callback function.

When a request is asynchronous, the browser keeps running your code. So after it runs `request.send(null)`, the browser goes to the next line of your sending function. That's usually the end of the function because we want users to be able to keep working with a web page. Then, when the server responds, a callback gets run that can update the page or respond to what the server said.

But with a *synchronous* request, the browser ***waits on the server***. No more code is run until the server comes back with a response. So in that case, we really don't *need* a callback. We can just continue on with the sending function, and ***know that the request object will have the server's response data in it!***

Sharpen your pencil

REVISITED

Go back to the code you wrote on page 313, and make a few changes. First, make sure your request is synchronous, and not asynchronous. Then, remove a reference to a callback; we don't need one! Finally, at the end of the function, display the response from the server using an alert box.

Sharpen your pencil Solution

Your job was to build the submitWord() function... and to make sure it works synchronously. What did you come up with?

```
function submitWord() {
  var request = createRequest();
  if (request == null) {
    alert ("Unable to create request object.");
    return;
  }
  var currentWordDiv = document.getElementById("currentWord");
  var userWord = currentWordDiv.firstChild.firstChild.nodeValue;
  var url = "lookup-word.php?word=" + escape(userWord);
  request.onreadystatechange = updateScore;
  request.open("GET", url, false);
  request.send(null);

  alert("Your score is: " + request.responseText);
}
```

This is pretty standard stuff. Make sure you've got utils.js referenced in your XHTML page.

First we get the <div> with the current word...

...and then we want the first child (the <p>), followed by the first child of that (the text node), and then the node value of that

We send the request like always, but we use "false," making this a _synchronous_ request

We're sending a synchronous request, so there's no need for a callback function this time.

The code won't get here until the server responds, so it's safe to use the responseText property.

.... there are no
Dumb Questions
....

Q: I got a little lost on that currentWordDiv.firstChild.firstChild. nodeValue bit. Can you explain that?

A: Sure. You can break that statement down into parts. So first, there's currentWordDiv.firstChild. That's the first child of the <div>, which is a <p>. Then, we get the firstChild of that, which is a text node. And finally, we get the nodeValue of _that_, which is the text in the node—the word the user entered.

Q: Wow, that's confusing. Do I have to write my code that way?

A: You don't have to, but it's actually a bit faster than breaking things into lots of individual lines. Since this entire statement is parsed at one time, and there's only one variable created, JavaScript will execute this line a bit faster than if you'd broken it into several pieces.

Q: Didn't you forget to check the readyState and status codes of the request object?

A: When you're making a synchronous request, there's no need to check the readyState of the request object. The browser won't start running your code again until the server's finished with its response, so the readyState would _always_ be 4 by the time your code could check it.

You could check the status to make sure your request got handled without an error. But since you'll be able to tell that from the actual response, it's often easier to just go right to the responseText. Remember, we're not making an asynchronous request. With a synchronous request, there's no need to check readyState and status in your callback.

Usability check: WHEN can submitWord() get called?

Did you try and test out your new `submitWord()` function? If you did, you probably realized that the function isn't connected to anything. Right now, the "Submit Word" button doesn't do anything. In fact, "Submit Word" is an `<a>` element, and not a button at all!

```
<div id="submit"><a href="#">Submit Word</a></div>
```

This `<div>` and `<a>` are then styled to look like a button on the page. We had a similar situation with the tiles, though, so this shouldn't be a problem. We can assign an event handler to the onclick event of the `<a>` representing the "Submit Word" button:

```
var submitDiv = document.getElementById("submit");
var a = submitDiv.firstChild;
while (a.nodeName == "#text") { a = a.nextSibling; }
a.onclick = submitWord;
```

← Get the right <div>.

← Get the first child of the <div>.

Since the browser created this part of the DOM, we should make sure we don't have a whitespace text node.

Assign the event handler.

All of this new code...

...goes right here.

You can't submit a word if there's no word to submit

So where do you think this code goes? In `initPage()`? But that doesn't make sense... in `initPage()`, there aren't any letters in the current word box, so players shouldn't be able to submit anything.

The first time there's a word to submit is the first time there's a letter in the current word box. That's also the first time that a tile is clicked, which turns out to be the first time `addLetter()` is called for a new word.

Fortunately, we've already got a special case: the first time `addLetter()` is called for a new word, we're creating the `<p>` and text node underneath the currentWord `<div>`. So we just need to add the code above to that part of the `addLetter()` event handler:

```
if (currentWordDiv.childNodes.length == 0) {
    // existing code to add a new <p> and text node
    // existing code to add in first letter of new word
    // code to enable Submit Word button
} else {  // ... etc ...
```

Test Drive

Get your word score. Go on, get it!

Have you made all the additions you need to `addLetter()`? Once you
have, fire up Woggle, and build some words.

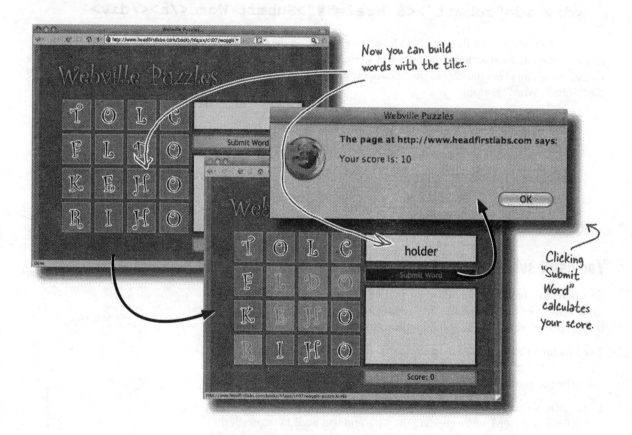

Now you can build
words with the tiles.

Clicking
"Submit
Word"
calculates
your score.

Even though clicking "Submit Word" doesn't call
submitWord() until at least one letter's entered, "Submit Word"
still looks like a button. Can you write code to let users know
what they should do if they click "Submit Word" too early?

Match the DOM properties and methods on the left to the tasks you'd use those properties and methods to accomplish on the right.

nodeValue

Well, this isn't a DOM method, but you never know when you'll need it parseInt

removeChild

previousSibling

childNodes

replaceNode

You want the table cell just to the left of the table cell you're in.

You want all the <p>'s within a particular <div>.

You want to get rid of all the <br> elements on a page.

You want to exchange an <img> element with some descriptive text.

You want to print out a name, which is in the <div> with an id of "name."

You need to add the numeric values of two form fields.

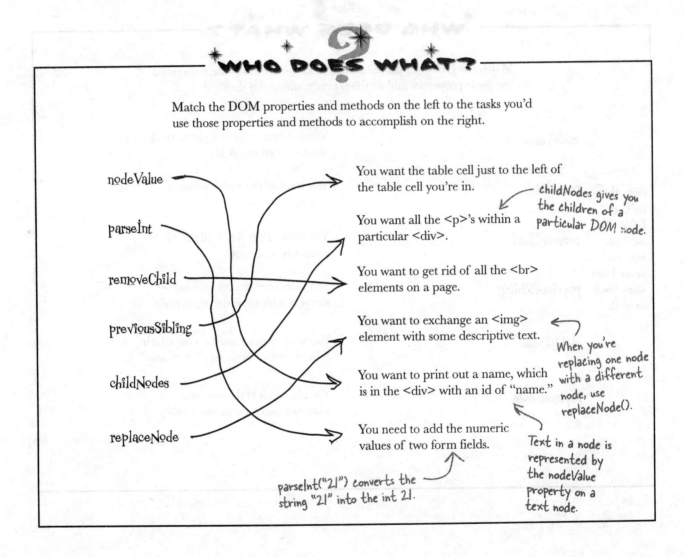

WHO DOES WHAT?

Match the DOM properties and methods on the left to the tasks you'd
use those properties and methods to accomplish on the right.

nodeValue

parseInt

removeChild

previousSibling

childNodes

replaceNode

You want the table cell just to the left of
the table cell you're in.

You want all the <p>'s within a
particular <div>.

You want to get rid of all the
elements on a page.

You want to exchange an <img>
element with some descriptive text.

You want to print out a name, which
is in the <div> with an id of "name."

You need to add the numeric
values of two form fields.

childNodes gives you the children of a particular DOM node.

When you're replacing one node with a different node, use replaceNode().

Text in a node is represented by the nodeValue property on a text node.

parseInt("21") converts the string "21" into the int 21.

Long Exercise

It's time to put everything you've learned so far to use: DOM manipulation, creating DOM nodes, JavaScript string functions, handling the request from a server... this exercise has it all. Follow the directions below, and tick off the boxes as you complete each step.

☐ If the server rejects the submitted word, let the player know with a message that reads, "You have entered an invalid word. Try again!"

☐ If the server accepts the submitted word, add the accepted word to the box of accepted words just below the "Submit Word" button.

☐ Get the current score, and add the score that the server returns for the just-accepted word. Using this new score, update the "Score: 0" text on the screen.

☐ Whether the server accepts or rejects the word, remove the current word from the current word box.

☐ Enable all the tiles on the playing board, and reset the "Submit Word" button to its original state.

☐ Below is the DOM tree for the sections of the page you're working with, as the browser initially creates the tree. Draw what the DOM tree will look like after your code has run for two accepted words (the specific two words don't matter, as long as the server accepted both of them).

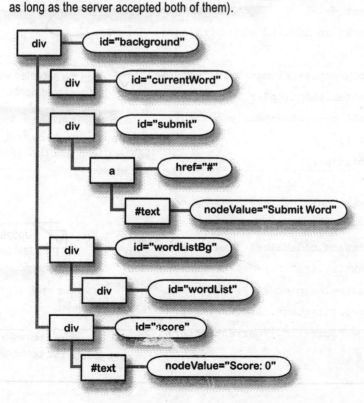

Long Exercise
Solution

Below is the completed version of submitWord(). Now it not only submits a word, but updates the score on the page. How close if your solution to ours?

```
function submitWord() {
  var request = createRequest();
  if (request == null) {
    alert ("Unable to create request object.");
    return;
  }
  var currentWordDiv = document.getElementById("currentWord");
  var userWord = currentWordDiv.firstChild.firstChild.nodeValue;
  var url = "lookup-word.php?word=" + escape(userWord);
  request.open("GET", url, false);
  request.send(null);
```

The server returns –1 if the
submitted word is invalid.

✓ If the server rejects the submitted word, let the player know.

```
  if (request.responseText == -1) {
    alert("You have entered an invalid word. Try again!");
  } else {
    var wordListDiv = document.getElementById("wordList");
    var p = document.createElement("p");
    var newWord = document.createTextNode(userWord);
    p.appendChild(newWord);
    wordListDiv.appendChild(p);
```

✓ Add the accepted word to the box of accepted words.

This creates a new <p>, a new text node
with the user's word, and then adds both to
the wordList <div>.

```
    var scoreDiv = document.getElementById("score");
    var scoreNode = scoreDiv.firstChild;
    var scoreText = scoreNode.nodeValue;
    var pieces = scoreText.split(" ");
    var currentScore = parseInt(pieces[1]);
    currentScore += parseInt(request.responseText);
    scoreNode.nodeValue = "Score: " + currentScore;
  }
}
```

You can split "Score: 0" into
two parts using split(" ").

✓ Update the "Score: 0"
text on the screen.

We want the second part, and
we want it as an int.

Add the server's response, and
then update the text node.

```
var currentWordP = currentWordDiv.firstChild;
currentWordDiv.removeChild(currentWordP);
enableAllTiles();
var submitDiv = document.getElementById("submit");
var a = submitDiv.firstChild;
while (a.nodeName == "#text") {
  a = a.nextSibling;
}
a.onclick = function() {
  alert("Please click tiles to add letters and create a word.");
};
}

function enableAllTiles() {
  tiles = document.getElementById("letterbox").getElementsByTagName("a");
  for (i=0; i<tiles.length; i++) {
    var tileClasses = tiles[i].className.split(" ");
    if (tileClasses.length == 4) {
      var newClass =
        tileClasses[0] + " " + tileClasses[1] + " " + tileClasses[2];
      tiles[i].className = newClass;
      tiles[i].onclick = addLetter;
    }
  }
}
```

> Remove the current word from the word box.

> Enable all the tiles.

Remember to reset the "Submit Word" button to an alert() function for the event handler.

We built a utility function for enabling all the tiles.

A tile that has 4 classes has the "disabled" class at the end.

We use the first three existing classes, but drop the fourth.

Remember to reset the event handler to addLetter.

Solution continues on the next page.

LONG EXERCISE
SOLUTION (CONTINUED)

☑ Below is the DOM tree for the sections of the page you're working with, as the browser initially creates the tree. Draw what the DOM tree will look like after your code has run for two accepted words (the specific two words don't matter, as long as the server accepted both of them).

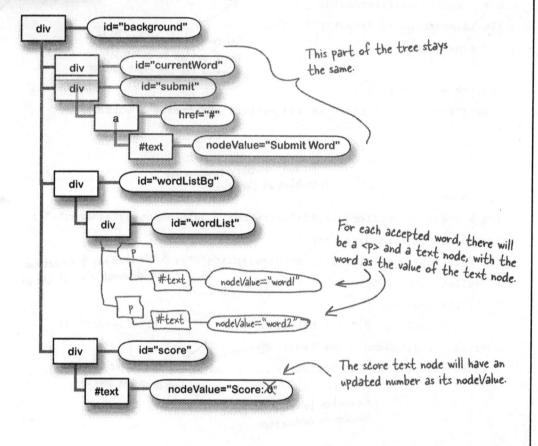

This part of the tree stays the same.

For each accepted word, there will be a <p> and a text node, with the word as the value of the text node.

The score text node will have an updated number as its nodeValue.

Test Drive

Anyone for Woggle?

Do you have everything working? Try out Woggle... it's all working just the way we imagined way back on page 286.

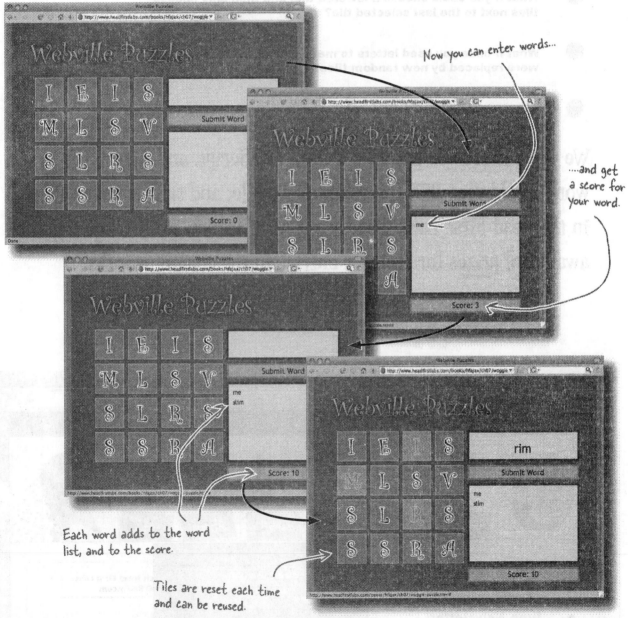

Now you can enter words...

...and get a score for your word.

Each word adds to the word list, and to the score.

Tiles are reset each time and can be reused.

But there's still more to do!

- **What if there was a timer that gave you 60 seconds to enter as many words as you could think of?**

- **What if you could choose a lettered tile, and then only choose tiles next to the last selected tile?**

- **What if once you used letters to make a valid word, those tiles were replaced by new random tiles?**

- **And besides all that, how do YOU think Woggle could be improved?**

We want to see you put your DOM, JavaScript, and Ajax skills to work. Build your BEST version of Woggle, and submit your URL in the Head First Labs "Head First Ajax" forum. We'll be giving away cool prizes for the best entries in the coming months.

Click here to go to the forums and tell us how to access your version of Woggle.

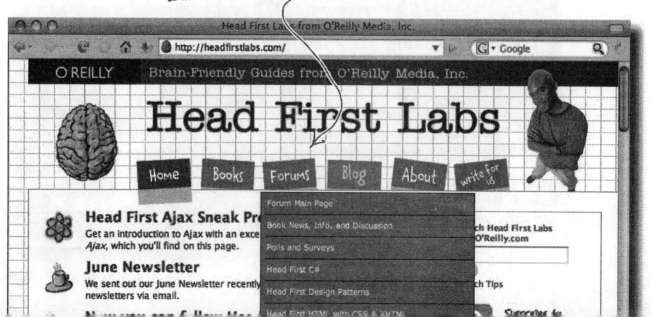

DOMAcrostic

Take some time to sit back and give your right brain something to do. Answer the questions in the top, then use the letters to fill in the secret message.

This method creates an element of the specified type:

___ ___ ___ ___ ___ ___ ___ ___ ___ ___ ___ ___ ___
1 2 3 4 5 6 7 8 9 10 12 13 14

This is the name of the game we built in this chapter:

___ ___ ___ ___ ___ ___
15 16 17 18 19 20

This method adds an element to the DOM tree:

___ ___ ___ ___ ___ ___ ___ ___ ___ ___ ___
21 22 23 24 25 26 27 28 29 30 31

A DOM tree is a just collection of these:

___ ___ ___ ___ ___ ___ ___
32 33 34 35 36 37 38

This method substitutes one node for another:

___ ___ ___ ___ ___ ___ ___ ___ ___ ___ ___ ___
39 40 41 42 43 44 45 46 47 48 49 50

This method removes a node from the DOM tree:

___ ___ ___ ___ ___ ___ ___ ___ ___ ___ ___
51 52 53 54 55 56 57 58 59 60 61

___ ___ ___ ___ ___ ___ ___ ___ ___ ___
37 58 3   33 39 16 15 38 45 51

___ ___ ___ ___ ___ ___ ___ ___ ___ ___ ___ ___ ___
5 2 21 25 38 8 43 14 45 38 26 32 10

___ ___ ___ ___ ___ ___ ___ ___ ___ ___ ___ ___ ___ ___ ___
13 16 50 52 38 59 13 37 16 54 33 34 9 57 5 38

*manipulating **the dom***

you are here ▶   **327**

DOMAcrostic

Take some time to sit back and give your right brain something to do. Answer the questions in the top, then use the letters to fill in the secret message.

This method creates an element of the specified type:

C	R	E	A	T	E	E	L	E	M	E	N	T
1	2	3	4	5	6	7	8	9	10	12	13	14

This is the name of the game we built in this chapter:

W	O	G	G	L	E
15	16	17	18	19	20

This method adds an element to the DOM tree:

A	P	P	E	N	D	C	H	I	L	D
21	22	23	24	25	26	27	28	29	30	31

A DOM tree is a just collection of these:

O	B	J	E	C	T	S
32	33	34	35	36	37	38

This method substitutes one node for another:

R	E	P	L	A	C	E	C	H	I	L	D
39	40	41	42	43	44	45	46	47	48	49	50

This method removes a node from the DOM tree:

R	E	M	O	V	E	C	H	I	L	D
51	52	53	54	55	56	57	58	59	60	61

T	H	E		B	R	O	W	S	E	R
37	58	3		33	39	16	15	38	45	51

T	R	A	N	S	L	A	T	E	S		D	O	M
5	2	21	25	38	8	43	14	45	38		26	32	10

N	O	D	E	S		I	N	T	O		O	B	J	E	C	T	S
13	16	50	52	38		59	13	37	16		54	33	34	9	57	5	38

8 frameworks and toolkits

Trust No One

Mr. Smith may think I'm just following his instructions, but wait until he sees this memo about Christmas bonuses going up 20%. That'll teach him to give me a lousy kitchen apron for Secretary's Day!

So what's the *real* story behind all those Ajax frameworks?

If you've been in Webville awhile, you've probably run across at least one JavaScript or Ajax framework. Some frameworks give you **convenience methods for working with the DOM**. Others make **validation** and **sending requests** simple. Still others come with libraries of pre-packaged JavaScript **screen effects**. But which one should you use? And how do you know what's really going on inside that framework? It's time to do more than use other people's code... it's time to *take control of your applications*.

> Finally! This is where you show me jQuery and mooTools and Prototype, and all those other cool Ajax frameworks, right? And I can quit writing all these stupid request.send() and request.onreadystatechange calls?

There are a **LOT** of options for frameworks that let you work with Ajax in different (and sometimes easier) ways.

If you Google the Internet for "JavaScript framework" or "Ajax library," you'll get a whole slew of links to different toolkits. And each framework's a bit different. Some are great for providing slick screen effects, like drag-and-drop, fades, and transitions. Others are good at sending and receiving Ajax requests in just a line or two of code.

In fact, you've been using a framework of sorts every time you reference a function from `utils.js`. All that script does is provide common functionality in a reusable package. Of course, most frameworks have a lot more functionality, but the principle is still the same.

So which framework should you use? Even more importantly... should you use one at all?

Sharpen your pencil

Deciding to use a JavaScript framework for writing your code is a big deal. Below, write down three reasons that you think it would be a good idea to use a framework... and three reasons you think it might ***not*** be a good idea.

Reasons to use a framework

1. ....
....
....

2. ....
....
....

3. ....
....
....

Reasons NOT to use a framework

1. ....
....
....

2. ....
....
....

3. ....
....
....

there are no Dumb Questions

Q: I don't even know what a framework is. How am I supposed to answer these questions?

A: A framework is just a JavaScript file—or set of files—that has functions, objects, and methods that you can use in your code. Think of a framework like a bigger, more complete version of the `utils.js` file we've been using.

Q: But I've never used one before!

A: That's okay. Just think about reasons you might like to try out a framework, and what advantages that framework might have over doing things the way you've been doing them so far. Then, think about what you like about how you've been writing code so far... those are reasons you might not use a framework.

Q: Is there a difference between a framework and a toolkit?

A: Not really. Framework and toolkit are used pretty interchangeably in the JavaScript world. Some people will tell you a framework is a structure for how you write all your code, while a toolkit is a collection of utility functions. But that's a distinction that not every framework or toolkit makes, so it's not worth getting hung up on.

Fireside Chats

Tonight's talk: **Ajax Framework and Do-It-Myself JavaScript go head-to-head on utility functions, toolkits, and the pros and cons of do-it-yourself thinking.**

Ajax Framework:

Wow, I thought you guys were never going to have me on. What is this, like page 332 or something, and I'm just now making an appearance?

Do-It-Myself JavaScript:

Hey, we figured you'd show up when you were needed. And lookie here, seven chapters down, and you're just now getting involved.

Oh boy. Here we go... you're one of these JavaScript purists, aren't you? No frameworks, no utility functions, just hard work and thousands of lines of code in a single `.js` file, am I right?

Not at all. In fact, I'm a big fan of abstracting common code into utility methods, not writing duplicate code, and even having different `.js` files for different sets of functionality.

So what's your problem with me? I'd think a guy like you would love me. I take all those routine, boring, annoying tasks and wrap them up into user-friendly function and method calls.

Well, that's just it. You wrap them up... you don't abstract them into a different file. You actually hide those details away.

And? What's the problem with that? I don't even see the difference... wrapping? abstracting?

Hey, you can always look at my code. Just open another script, and you know exactly what's going on. No mystery, no "magic function." That's me, alright.

You're kidding, right? I'm just JavaScript, too. You can open me up anytime you want. So how is my JavaScript `.js` file any different than yours?

Ajax Framework:

Oh, all the time. What's your point, Mr. Heavy-Handed?

I've got options, man. Tons of options. Sometimes almost a hundred for certain methods. Beat that!

Uhhh... gee, lemme think... well, how about when you don't know how to do what you need to do yourself? Ever tried to code drag-and-drop? Or move around within an image, zooming in and zooming out? You want to build all that yourself?

Hey, we're not talking about atomic fusion here. Sometimes you just need to get some little visual effect done... or an Ajax request sent. That's no time to be digging around on the Internet for some code a junior high dropout posted to his blog three years ago.

Yeah, and he's also driving a '76 Pinto 'cause no one will **hire** him. Because he's so **slow** at writing basic code!

Do-It-Myself JavaScript:

Have you ever looked at yourself? Maybe in a mirror, or in the reflection from one of those bright shiny widgets you're so proud of?

You're impossible to figure out! There's like a thousand lines of code to wade through. What if I want to do something just a bit *differently* than you're set up for? What then?

Why in the world would I want to? Who wants to figure out what the eighth parameter to a method is? Since when is that helpful?

If that's what it takes to actually understand what's going on, you bet I do!

I'll bet that kid knows what he's **doing**, though!

Whatever.

Sharpen your pencil
Solution

Your job was to think of some good reasons to use a framework, and some not-so-good reasons that come with using a framework. What did you write down?

Reasons to use a framework

1. You don't have to write code for functions that someone else has already figured out. You can just use the existing code in frameworks.

2. Frameworks have functions you might not have time to write yourself but would use if those functions were available. So you get more functionality.

3. The code in frameworks is tested more because more people are using the framework. So there's less chance of bugs, and less need for testing.

4. Frameworks usually take care of cross-browser issues for you, so you don't have to worry about IE, or Firefox, or Opera.

Reasons NOT to use a framework

1. You don't really know what the framework's doing. It might be doing things well... or it might be doing them more inefficiently than you would.

2. The framework might not have all the options you want or need. So you might end up changing your code to accommodate the framework.

3. Sometimes a framework hides important concepts that would be helpful to know. So you might not learn as much using a framework.

We only asked for three, but we couldn't resist adding this one. It's a BIG reason for using frameworks.

BRAIN POWER

Are there certain categories of functionality that you think would be better suited for a framework? What about things you *don't* want a framework doing for you?

So what frameworks <u>ARE</u> there?

There are several popular frameworks out there... and most of them do a few different things. Here's the ones that most people are buzzing about:

Prototype (http://www.prototypejs.org)

Prototype is a workhorse library. It provides lots of low-level JavaScript utilities, including support for Ajax.

jQuery is one of the most popular toolkits for JavaScript programming, including Ajax requests.

jQuery (http://www.jquery.com)

script.aculo.us is an add-on to Prototype, and is aimed at providing screen effects in JavaScript.

mooTools (http://mootools.net)

mooTools is newer, but very full-featured. You get screen effects and Ajax request utilities.

script.aculo.us (http://script.aculo.us)

How often do these things change? Are frameworks releasing new versions very often? Is that something we should be worried about?

Frameworks usually change <u>FASTER</u> than the underlying JavaScript syntax does.

Frameworks are controlled by the people who write them, and so a framework might release a new version every few months... or in early stages, every few weeks! In fact, a framework might lose popularity and totally disappear over the course of six or seven months.

But the core JavaScript syntax and objects, like XMLHttpRequest and the DOM, are controlled by big, slow-moving standards groups. So that sort of syntax won't change very often. At the most, you'll see something change every few ***years***.

Every framework uses a different syntax to do things

Each framework uses a different syntax to get things done. For example, here's how you'd make a request and specify what to do with the server's response in Prototype:

> The first part of both bits of code gets a value from the page.

```
function checkUsername() {

  var usernameObj = $("username");

  usernameObj.className = "thinking";

  var username = escape(usernameObj.value);

  new Ajax.Request("checkName.php", {

    method:"get",

    parameters: "username=" + username,

    onSuccess: function(transport){

      if (transport.responseText == "okay") {

        $("username").className = "approved";

        $("register").disabled = false;

      } else {

        var usernameObj = $("username");

        usernameObj.className = "denied";

        usernameObj.focus();

        usernameObj.select();

        $("register").disabled = true;

      }

    },

    onFailure: function() { alert("Error in validation."); }

  });

}
```

> This gets the element with an id of "username."

> This is the Ajax object for making requests in Prototype.

> transport is the Prototype "stand-in" for the request object.

> The onSuccess function runs when the server responds normally.

> The onFailure function runs if there's a problem with the request or response.

> Then a request is made. This is a lot shorter in Prototype.

> You usually give Prototype the callback inline... but it's the same basic code, just a little different syntax.

> We haven't been providing an error message if the status code isn't 200, or if other problems occur. Prototype handles this nicely, though.

The syntax may change... but the JavaScript is still the same

At a glance, that Prototype code looks pretty different from anything you've written before. But take a look at the equivalent JavaScript from an early version of Mike's Movies registration page:

This code looks a lot different at first... but it turns out to be very similar to the code you write to use a toolkit.

```javascript
function checkUsername() {
  document.getElementById("username").className = "thinking";
  request = createRequest();
  if (request == null)
    alert("Unable to create request");
  else {
    var theName = document.getElementById("username").value;
    var username = escape(theName);
    var url= "checkName.php?username=" + username;
    request.onreadystatechange = showUsernameStatus;
    request.open("GET", url, true);
    request.send(null);
  }
}

function showUsernameStatus() {
  if (request.readyState == 4) {
    if (request.status == 200) {
      if (request.responseText == "okay") {
        document.getElementById("username").className = "approved";
        document.getElementById("register").disabled = false;
      } else {
        document.getElementById("username").className = "denied";
        document.getElementById("username").focus();
        document.getElementById("username").select();
        document.getElementById("register").disabled = true;
      }
    }
  }
}
```

> But that's just the same code we've been writing... it looks a little different, but it's the same stuff! I don't want to learn **another** new set of syntax.

JavaScript and Ajax frameworks are just new and different ways to do what you've <u>already</u> <u>been</u> doing.

When you boil it all down to code, an asynchronous request is an asynchronous request is an asynchronous request. In other words, under the hood, your JavaScript code still has to create a request object, set up code to run based on what the server returns, and then send that request. No matter how the syntax changes, the basic process stays the same.

Using a framework might make parts of setting up and sending that request easier, but a framework won't fundamentally change what you've been doing. And yes, you'll definitely need to learn some new syntax to use any framework effectively.

> But I'll bet there are some pretty big advantages, too, right? Like cool visual effects, and maybe some more robust error handling?

Frameworks offer a lot of nice features "for free."

Most frameworks come with a lot of convenience methods and cool visual effects. And the syntax isn't really that hard to pick up if you're already familiar with basic JavaScript and Ajax concepts and principles.

And one of the best features of frameworks is that a lot of them handle situations where users don't have JavaScript enabled in their browsers.

there are no Dumb Questions

Q: You didn't mention my favorite framework, [insert your framework name here]. What's up with that?

A: Well, there are a lot of frameworks out there, and more are showing up every day. The frameworks on page 335 are some of the most popular right now, but your framework might show up on that list in a few months.

In any case, the main thing is that a framework doesn't provide fundamentally different functionality than the code you've been writing. It just makes that functionality more convenient, or it takes less time to write, or it adds visuals... you get the idea.

Q: Do all frameworks make working with elements on a page so easy?

A: If you use a framework, you probably won't be writing a lot of DOM methods, like `getElementById()` or `getElementsByTagName()`. Since those are such common operations, most frameworks provide syntax to make that easier, like `$("username")` to get an element with an id of "username."

Q: So what's the framework using to get the element, then?

A: The same DOM methods you'd use without the framework. `$("username")` just gets turned into a call to `document.getElementById("username")`. Additionally, the returned object has its normal DOM methods available, as well as additional methods the framework might provide.

Q: So frameworks are a good thing, right?

A: Well, some people use frameworks because they don't want to take the time to learn the underlying concepts. That's *not* a good thing because those folks don't really know what's going on in their code.

If *you* use a framework, though, you *do* know the concepts and code underneath. That means you'll probably be more effective as a programmer, and be able to hunt down problems a little more effectively, too.

Q: So a framework just does what we've already been doing ourselves?

A: Well, frameworks often do a little *more* than we've been doing. They typically provide more options, and they also tend to have a more robust error handling setup than just showing an `alert()` box. But they're still making requests and handling responses and grabbing elements on a page using the DOM, just like the code you've been writing.

Q: So we shouldn't use frameworks since we already know how to write all that request and response and DOM code, right?

A: Well, frameworks do offer a lot of convenience functions, and those screen effects are pretty cool...

Q: So then we *should* use frameworks?

A: We didn't say that either. There's a certain amount of control you lose with a framework because it might not do just what you want it to in a certain situation. Sometimes it's best to take complete control, and just write the code you need without putting a framework in the mix.

Q: So which is it? Use a framework, or don't use one?

A: That's the question, isn't it? Turn the page, and let's try and figure that out.

Frameworks can't solve your programming problems for you.

It's up to YOU to UNDERSTAND your code, whether or not you use a framework to make that code easier to write.

To framework or not to framework?

There are a lot of good reasons to use a framework... and plenty of reasons to not use one. Some people go back and forth between projects where they use a framework and projects where they don't. It really depends on the situation and your personal preferences.

My users want high-end visuals, and script.aculo. us gives me that. I can do tons of cool screen effects with that toolkit.

I spend all my time dealing with accessibility... I use a framework because it's more convenient, and it saves me time to focus on how my site works for the disabled.

Accessibility-minded web designer

Hobbyist programmer, running a popular gaming web site

I'm just learning JavaScript, so I stick with pure request object calls... I'm learning a lot more that way, and that's what I want.

Maintains her own blog, tinkering with JavaScript programming

I use a toolkit to handle errors, deal with weird mobile browsers, and let my team focus on functionality, not the browser wars.

Business developer building a micro site for mobile devices

We have lots of weird requests that interact with our server programs and the data... I avoid toolkits because I want complete control of how my requests are configured and sent.

Database engineer at a media company

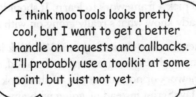

I think mooTools looks pretty cool, but I want to get a better handle on requests and callbacks. I'll probably use a toolkit at some point, but just not yet.

Junior software developer

The choice is up to you...

Is it important for you to really control every aspect of your code? Do you go crazy wondering how efficient every function you use in your JavaScript really is? Can you not stand the thought of missing out on learning some new tool, trick, or technique? If this is you, you may just end up frustrated and annoyed by frameworks. Stick with writing your own requests, callbacks, and utility functions, building an ever-growing library of code in `utils. js`, and not having to update to a new version of a framework every few months.

Don't care so much about every internal line of code? If you're a productivity nut, and want great apps with a minimal amount of time spent dealing with errors, weird browser inconsistencies, and oddities of the DOM, frameworks might be just for you. Say goodbye to `request.send(null)` forever, and pick a framework to learn. It shouldn't take you long... you already know what's really going on with asynchronous requests.

Either way, the choice is yours. We think it's pretty important to know what's going on under the hood, whether you use a framework or not, so the rest of this book will stick with plain old JavaScript instead of going with any particular framework. But everything you'll learn still is useful, even if you later use a framework to hide away the details of what's going on.

More Than Words Can Say

> Oh, Bob... I love it when you describe yourself with angle brackets, and tell me all about your attributes. You're just so darn... extensible!

How will you describe yourself in 10 years? How about 20?

Sometimes you need **data that can change with your needs**... or the needs of your customers. Data you're using now might need to change in a few hours, or a few days, or a few months. With XML, the *extensible markup language*, your data can **describe itself**. That means your scripts won't be filled with ifs, elses, and switches. Instead, you can use the descriptions that XML provides about itself to figure out how to **use** the data the XML contains. The result: **more flexibility** and **easier data handling**.

As a special bonus, we're bringing back the DOM in this chapter... keep an eye out!

this is a new chapter   **343**

Classic rock gets a 21st century makeover

Rob's Rock and Roll Memorabilia has hit the big time. Since going online with the site you built for Rob, he's selling collectible gear to rich customers around the world.

In fact, Rob's gotten lots of good feedback on the site, and he's making some improvements. He wants to include a price for each item, in addition to the description, and he also wants to be able to include a list of related URLs so customers can find out more about each item.

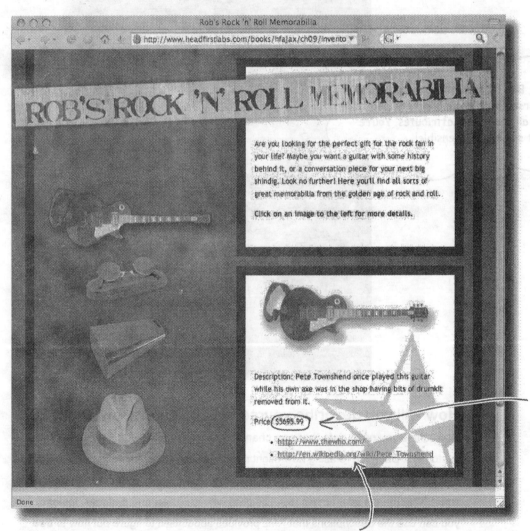

Rob wants to add a price for each item.

Each item will have one or more URLs to find out more about the item.

Server Response Magnets

Below are diagrams of the interactions between several of the apps you've built and programs on the server that those apps use. Can you place the right server response magnets on each diagram?

If you don't remember, flip back to these earlier chapters, or check your own code.

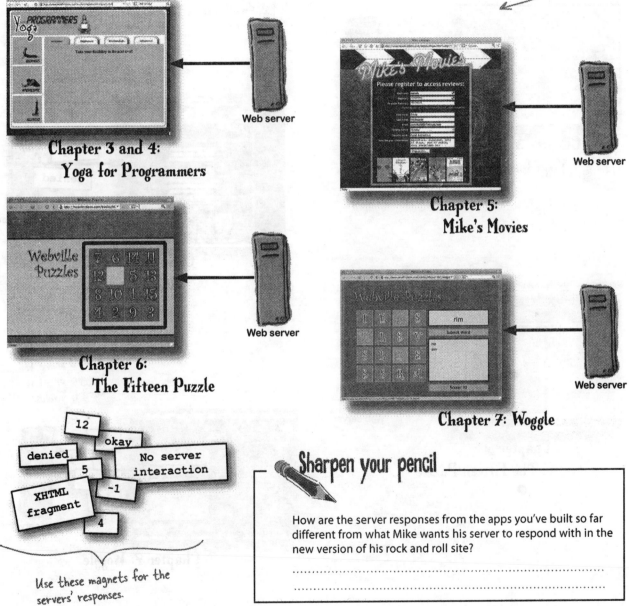

Web server

Chapter 3 and 4:
Yoga for Programmers

Web server

Chapter 5:
Mike's Movies

Web server

Chapter 6:
The Fifteen Puzzle

Web server

Chapter 7: Woggle

| 12 |
| okay |
| denied |
| No server interaction |
| 5 |
| -1 |
| XHTML fragment |
| 4 |

Use these magnets for the servers' responses.

Sharpen your pencil

How are the server responses from the apps you've built so far different from what Mike wants his server to respond with in the new version of his rock and roll site?

....
....

Server Response Magnet **Solutions**

Below are diagrams of the interactions between several of the apps you've built and programs on the server that those apps use. Can you place the right server response magnets on each diagram?

The Yoga app requested XHTML page fragments from the server, but didn't call any server-side programs

XHTML fragment

Web server

Chapter 3 and 4: Yoga for Programmers

Mike's server-side script returns "okay" or "denied" for a username and password.

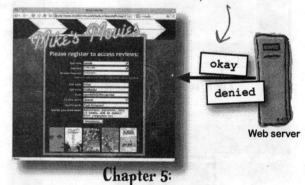

okay

denied

Web server

Chapter 5: Mike's Movies

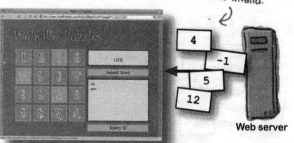

No server interaction

Web server

Chapter 6: The Fifteen Puzzle

Using the DOM for the Fifteen Puzzle didn't involve a server-side program.

The server returns a word score for Woggle, or -1 if the word is invalid.

4

-1

5

12

Web server

Chapter 7: Woggle

How are the server responses from the apps you've built so far different from what Mike wants his server to respond with in the new version of his rock and roll site?

All the servers so far sent out a single response... Mike's server is going to send back more than one piece of data.

How should a server send a MULTI-valued response?

So far, all the server-side programs we've worked with have sent back a single piece of data, like −1 or "okay." But now Mike wants to send back several pieces of data at one time:

1 A string description of the selected item.

2 A numeric price for the item, like 299.95.

3 A list of URLs with related information about the item.

> I tell you what... this is pretty big business these days. If you can figure out how to help me, I'll give you an all-original '59 Les Paul electric guitar, okay?

What would you do?

There are lots of ways to handle getting more than one value back from the server, and this time, the choice is up to you. What do you think?

I'm going with XML. It's flexible, it's industry standard, and I even think there's a responseXML property on the request object we've been using.

CSV, baby... comma-separated values. They're easy, pure text, and a piece of cake to produce. Hello, Les Paul.

You guys are making this way too hard. The server can format its response as XHTML, and we can stick with the innerHTML property.

Frank

Jim

Joe

Sharpen your pencil

Time to place your bets. We're going to follow Frank, Jim, and Joe and see which one comes up with the best solution. Who do you think will solve Rob's site problems and win the Les Paul?

☐ **XML is the best choice.** Frank's gonna win.

☐ **CSV is simple and functional.** Go, Jim!

☐ **innerHTML: it ain't broke.** Joe's got it in the bag.

Sharpen your pencil

You're not done sharpening that pencil just yet. Suppose you had the following information for an item:

Item ID: itemCowbell
Description: Remember the famous "more cowbell" skit from Saturday Night Live? Well this is the actual cowbell.
Price: 299.99
URLs: http://www.nbc.com/Saturday_Night_Live/
http://en.wikipedia.org/wiki/More_cowbell

How would a server represent this information...

1   ...as XML?

In this space, write what you think the XML for this item would look like.

2   ...as CSV (comma-separated values)?

What would the CSV look like from the server?

3   ...as an XHTML fragment?

What about XHTML, suitable for innerHTML?

Sharpen your pencil
Solution

You're not done sharpening that pencil just yet. Suppose you had the following information for an item:

Item ID: itemCowbell
Description: Remember the famous "more cowbell" skit from Saturday Night Live? Well this is the actual cowbell.
Price: 299.99
URLs: http://www.nbc.com/Saturday_Night_Live/
http://en.wikipedia.org/wiki/More_cowbell

How would a server represent this information...

1 **...as XML?**

All XML documents begin like this.

```
<?xml version="1.0"?>
<item id="itemCowbell">
  <description>Remember the famous "more cowbell" skit from
    Saturday Night Live? Well this is the actual cowbell.</description>
  <price>299.99</price>
  <resources>
    <url>http://www.nbc.com/Saturday_Night_Live/</url>
    <url>http://en.wikipedia.org/wiki/More_cowbell</url>
  </resources>
</item>
```

We used an attribute for the item ID.

The description and price are in XML elements.

We grouped the URLs with a resources element, and then put each URL in a url element.

* These solutions are just ONE way to represent the item data as XML, CSV, and XHTML. You might have come up with something a little different. As long as you got the right <u>values</u> in the right <u>format</u>, you're all set.

② **...as CSV (comma-separated values)?**

```
itemCowbell,Remember the famous 'more cowbell' skit from
    Saturday Night Live? Well this is the actual cowbell, 299.99,
    http://www.nbc.com/Saturday_Night_Live,
    http://en.wikipedia.org/wiki/More_cowbell
```

Each item in a CSV string is separated by a comma.

③ **...as an XHTML fragment?**

```
<p>Description: Remember the famous 'more cowbell" skit from
    Saturday Night Live? Well this is the actual cowbell.</p>
<p>Price: $299.99</p>
<ul>
  <li><a href="http://www.nbc.com/Saturday_Night_Live/">
          http://www.nbc.com/Saturday_Night_Live/</a></li>
  <li><a href="http://en.wikipedia.org/wiki/More_cowbell">
          http://en.wikipedia.org/wiki/More_cowbell</a></li>
</ul>
```

This is the XHTML exactly as it needs to be inserted into the rock and roll page. CSS styles it, and the data from the server is wrapped up in XHTML tags.

So here's what we need to get going on the server... *this* XHTML, with *these* values here... and here...

Jill, a server-side expert, is helping out the team.

Joe, still working on innerHTML and an XHTML server response.

Jill: I don't know, Joe. That's a lot of formatting for the server-side guys to keep up with.

Joe: But they've got all the data about the item, right?

Jill: Well, sure... but server-side programmers don't really like to mess around with XHTML. That's the whole reason a lot of these folks move over to the server-side in the first place... no XHTML.

Joe: But the CSS doesn't change that much, so the XHTML won't change that often.

Jill: Oh, the XHTML will change sometimes?

Joe: Well, sure, maybe... but not very often. Only if we need to add a tag, or maybe an ID for CSS...

Jill: Oh, no. You're not going to be able to get server-side guys to write XHTML, and then change it all the time on top of that.

Joe: Hmmm. This is sounding harder than I thought. I thought innerHTML was going to be really simple...

innerHTML is only simple for the <u>CLIENT</u> side of a web app

From a client-side point of view, innerHTML is pretty simple to use.
You just get an XHTML response from the server, and drop it into a
web page with an element's innerHTML property.

```
function displayDetails() {
  if (request.readyState == 4) {
    if (request.status == 200) {
      detailDiv = document.getElementById("description");
      detailDiv.innerHTML = request.responseText;
    }
  }
}
```

The problem is that the server has to do a *lot* of extra work. Not only
does the server have to get the right information for your app's request,
it has to format that response in a way that's specific to your application.
In fact, that format is specific to *one individual page on your site!*

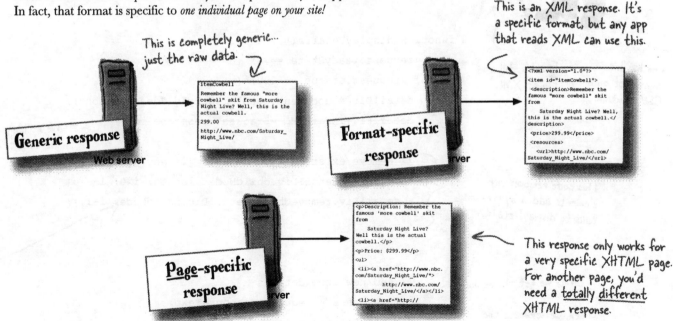

This is completely generic...
just the raw data.

Generic response
Web server

This is an XML response. It's
a specific format, but any app
that reads XML can use this.

Format-specific response

Page-specific response

This response only works for
a very specific XHTML page.
For another page, you'd
need a <u>totally</u> different
XHTML response.

If you were a server-side developer... which would <u>YOU</u> prefer?

Look, this CSV thing is gonna get me that Les Paul, and quick. I just called the server-side guys; they said sending a response as CSV was no problem.

Frank: I'm not sure, Jim. Something's bugging me about this CSV thing.

Jim: What, just because I'm already almost done?

Frank: No, seriously. It just seems so ... I don't know. Inflexible?

Jim: What do you mean? Here, look at my code to take the server's response in my callback, and update the item detail for the page. It's a little long, but it's all pretty basic stuff:

Jim has his sights set on a CSV solution.

Frank's still a fan of XML.

```
function displayDetails() {
  if (request.readyState == 4) {
    if (request.status == 200) {
      detailDiv = document.getElementById("description");
      detailDiv.innerHTML = request.responseText;
```
← We no longer use innerHTML.

This code removes any elements added by previous calls to displayDetails().

```
      // Remove existing item details (if any)
      for (var i=detailDiv.childNodes.length; i>0; i--) {
        detailDiv.removeChild(detailDiv.childNodes[i-1]);
      }
```

First, we get the response.

Then, we separate the values using the commas.

```
      // Add new item details
      var response = request.responseText;
      var itemDetails = response.split(",");
```

(continued on the next page)

```
var descriptionP = document.createElement("p");
descriptionP.appendChild(
  document.createTextNode("Description: " +
    itemDetails[1]));
detailDiv.appendChild(descriptionP);
var priceP = document.createElement("p");
priceP.appendChild(
  document.createTextNode("Price: $" + itemDetails[2]));
detailDiv.appendChild(priceP);
var list = document.createElement("ul");
for (var i=3; i<itemDetails.length; i++) {
  var li = document.createElement("li");
  var a = document.createElement("a");
  a.setAttribute("href", itemDetails[i]);
  a.appendChild(document.createTextNode(itemDetails[i]));
  li.appendChild(a);
  list.appendChild(li);
}
detailDiv.appendChild(list);
  }
 }
}
```

This creates a new <p> with the description of the item in it.

Next, we add another <p> with the price.

Let's display the URLs as list items in an unordered list.

Each URL goes into an <a>, which is added as the content of an <li>...

...and then the <li> gets added to a <ul>...

...which finally ends up under the details <div>.

All of this code goes into thumbnails.js, replacing the old version of displayDetails().

thumbnails.js

BRAIN BARBELL

Why do you think the loop deleting any pre-existing elements from the details <div> counts down, instead of counting up?

If you're stumped, try reversing the loop and see what happens. Can you figure out what's going on?

Test Drive

Try out CSV for yourself.

Download the examples for Chapter 9 from the Head First Labs website. Open
`thumbnails.js`, and make two changes:

1 Update `displayDetails()` to match page 354.

2 In `getDetails()`, change the URL of the server-side
script to `getDetailsCSV.php`.

The downloads for Chapter 9 include a server-side script that returns CSV instead of plain text.

Now try out the site. Does everything work?

This looks right... there's a description, price, and list of URLs.

there are no Dumb Questions

Q: What is CSV again?

A: CSV stands for comma-separated values. It just means that several values are put together into a single string, with commas separating each individual value.

Q: I've also heard about TSV. Is that similar?

A: TSV refers to *tab*-separated values. The idea is the same, but tabs are used instead of commas. In fact, you can use anything you want to separate the values: a pipe symbol (|), an asterisk (*), or anything else that's a fairly uncommon character.

Q: Why do you need to use an uncommon character to separate values?

A: If you use something common, like a period or letter, that same character might show up in your data. Then, your JavaScript might split the data incorrectly, giving you problems when you display or interpret that data.

In fact, CSV is a bit dangerous because an item description might have a comma in it. In that case, you'd end up splitting the description on the comma, and having all sorts of problems.

Q: So is that why we shouldn't use CSV?

A: Good question. Frank, Jim, and Joe are still debating the merits of CSV, but you could always swap out those commas for something else, and change your client code to split on that new character instead of commas. As for whether or not you should use CSV, you may want to keep reading...

Q: What is setAttribute()? I've never seen that before.

A: `setAttribute()` creates a new attribute on an element. The method takes two arguments: the name of the attribute and its value. If there's no attribute with the supplied name, a new attribute is created. If there's already an attribute with the supplied name, that attribute's value is replaced with the one you supplied to `setAttribute()`.

Q: What about childNodes? What's that?

A: `childNodes` is a property on every DOM node. The property returns an array of all the child nodes for that node. So you can get an element's children, for example, and iterate over them or delete them.

Q: So why *did* you iterate backwards over the childNodes array?

A: That's a tricky one. Here's a hint to get you thinking in the right direction: when you call `removeChild()`, the node you supply to that method is removed from its parent immediately.

That also means that all references to that now-removed node—say in an array full of an element's child nodes—have to be updated. Without a child to point to, all the child nodes that come after the removed node have to be moved up in the array.

So if you iterated over an array like `childNodes` from front to back, removing nodes as you went, what would happen?

What do you think Frank meant on the last page about CSV being inflexible? Are there problems with the server's response being in CSV that adding new types of items might cause?

Listen, can I get an item's details in XML from the server? I'm already behind, but I still think there's a problem with that CSV solution. I want to get my XML-based version of the app working ASAP.

Jill: Sure, XML is easy. The server-side guys shouldn't have any problem with that at all. It's certainly a lot better than XHTML...

Frank: Yeah, I heard Joe was working on that. The server guys couldn't get him an XHTML response?

Jill: Well, they could've, but nobody wanted to. XHTML is a mess to work with on the server, and it changes all the time.

Frank: You know XHTML is just a flavor of XML, right?

Jill: Sure, but lots of people and apps can use XML. Dealing with a certain `<div>` with this id, or only using `<p>`'s and not `<br />`'s... that's pretty fragile.

Frank: No kidding. Well, I've got to rewrite my callback, but let me know when the XML response is ready, okay?

Frank's asked Jill for some advice from a server–side perspective.

XML is pervasive in the programming world. If you respond in XML, LOTS of different applications can work with that XML response.

there are no
Dumb Questions

Q: What do you mean, "XHTML is just a flavor of XML"?

A: A flavor of XML is like a specific implementation of XML, with certain elements and attributes defined. So XHTML uses elements like `html` and `p` and `div`, and then those elements are used along with attributes and text values. You can't make up new elements, but instead you just use the ones already defined.

With XML, you can define flavors like this—sometimes called *XML vocabularies*—and extend XML for whatever your needs are. That's why XML is so flexible: it can change to match the data it represents.

You use the DOM to work with XML, just like you did with XHTML

Since XHTML is really a particular implementation of XML, it makes sense that you can use the DOM to work with XML, too. In fact, the DOM is really designed to work with XML from the ground up.

Even better, the request object you've been using to talk to the server has a property that returns a DOM tree version of the server's response. That property is called `responseXML`, and you use it like this:

```
var responseDoc = request.responseXML;
```

responseXML holds a DOM tree version of the server's response.

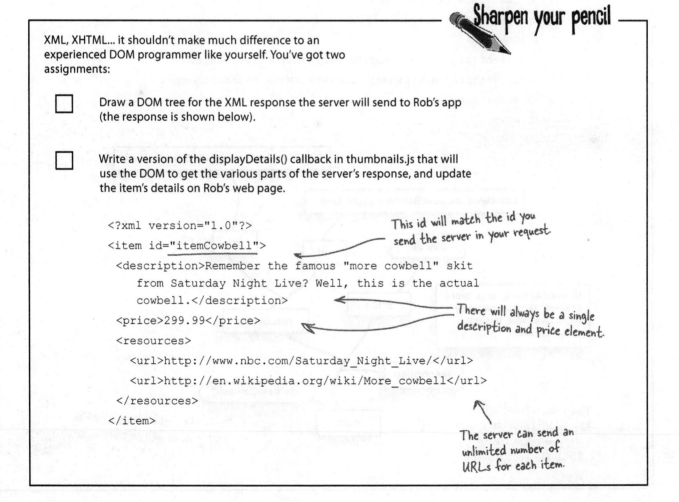

Sharpen your pencil

XML, XHTML... it shouldn't make much difference to an experienced DOM programmer like yourself. You've got two assignments:

☐ Draw a DOM tree for the XML response the server will send to Rob's app (the response is shown below).

☐ Write a version of the displayDetails() callback in thumbnails.js that will use the DOM to get the various parts of the server's response, and update the item's details on Rob's web page.

```
<?xml version="1.0"?>
<item id="itemCowbell">
  <description>Remember the famous "more cowbell" skit
    from Saturday Night Live? Well, this is the actual
    cowbell.</description>
  <price>299.99</price>
  <resources>
    <url>http://www.nbc.com/Saturday_Night_Live/</url>
    <url>http://en.wikipedia.org/wiki/More_cowbell</url>
  </resources>
</item>
```

This id will match the id you send the server in your request.

There will always be a single description and price element.

The server can send an unlimited number of URLs for each item.

Sharpen your pencil
Solution

XML, XHTML... it shouldn't make much difference to an experienced DOM programmer like yourself. You had two different assignments:

☐ Draw a DOM tree for the XML response the server will send to Rob's app (the response is shown below).

```xml
<?xml version="1.0"?>
<item id="itemCowbell">
  <description>Remember the famous "more cowbell" skit
      from Saturday Night Live? Well, this is the actual
      cowbell.</description>
<price>299.99</price>
<resources>
  <url>http://www.nbc.com/Saturday_Night_Live/</url>
  <url>http://en.wikipedia.org/wiki/More_cowbell</url>
</resources>
</item>
```

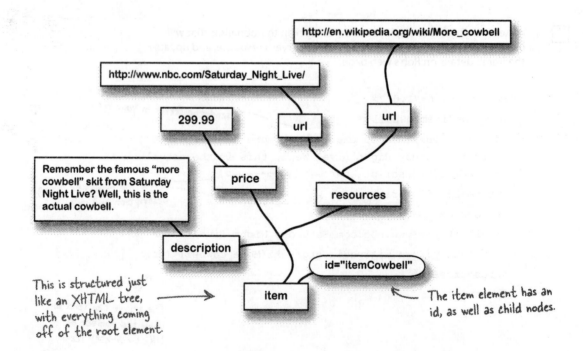

This is structured just like an XHTML tree, with everything coming off of the root element.

The item element has an id, as well as child nodes.

Write a version of the displayDetails() callback in thumbnails.js that will use the DOM to get the various parts of the server's response, and update the item's details on Rob's web page.

Most of the code that works on the page itself is identical to the CSV version on page 354.

```javascript
function displayDetails() {
  if (request.readyState == 4) {
    if (request.status == 200) {
      var detailDiv = document.getElementById("description");

      // Remove existing item details (if any)
      for (var i=detailDiv.childNodes.length; i>0; i--) {
        detailDiv.removeChild(detailDiv.childNodes[i-1]);
      }

      // Add new item details
      var responseDoc = request.responseXML;
      var description = responseDoc.getElementsByTagName("description")[0];
      var descriptionText = description.firstChild.nodeValue;
      var descriptionP = document.createElement("p");
      descriptionP.appendChild(
        document.createTextNode("Description: " + descriptionText));
      detailDiv.appendChild(descriptionP);
      var price = responseDoc.getElementsByTagName("price")[0];
      var priceText = price.firstChild.nodeValue;
      var priceP = document.createElement("p");
      priceP.appendChild(
        document.createTextNode("Price: $" + priceText));
      detailDiv.appendChild(priceP);
      var list = document.createElement("ul");
      var urlElements = responseDoc.getElementsByTagName("url");
      for (var i=0; i<urlElements.length; i++) {
        var url = urlElements[i].firstChild.nodeValue;
        var li = document.createElement("li");
        var a = document.createElement("a");
        a.setAttribute("href", url);
        a.appendChild(document.createTextNode(url));
        li.appendChild(a);
        list.appendChild(li);
      }
      detailDiv.appendChild(list);
    }
  }
}
```

The big difference is in how we handle the response from the server.

First, we get the response in the form of an XML DOM tree.

We can get the <description> element, and then get its first child: a text node. From there, we just get the text node's value.

Getting the price is the same pattern: grab the element, get its text, and get that text node's value.

We can get all the <url> elements and loop through each one.

Test Drive

And now for an XML solution...

Open thumbnails.js, and make two more changes:

1 Update displayDetails() to match the XML version of the callback shown on page 361.

2 In getDetails(), change the URL of the server-side script to getDetailsXML.php.

How does the XML version of Rob's online shop look?

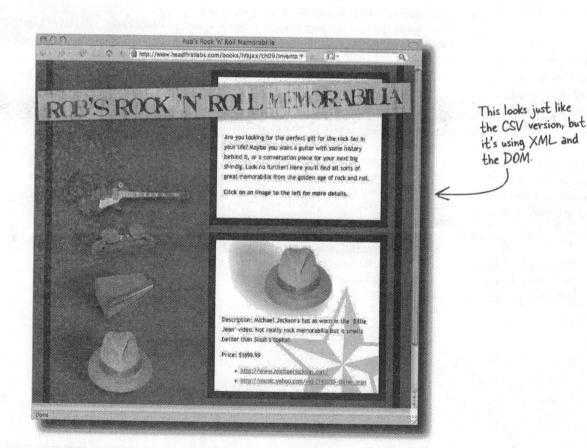

This looks just like the CSV version, but it's using XML and the DOM.

> Hey guys... these are looking great. That CSV deal was quick! But I've got one more change before I declare a winner... customers want more details specific to each item. So for rock memorabilia, I might have an artist name and band name, and for instruments I might have a manufacturer and year. No big deal, right?

Rob wants data that changes depending on the request.

If you ask the server for details about a guitar, you'll get a manufacturer and year. Clothing? A manufacturer, sure, but also a size. And for bands, you'll get a band name, and possibly the name of the individual in the band that the item belonged to or is associated with.

How would *you* handle a changing response from the server? And who's better equipped to handle this new requirement? Frank, with his XML, or Jim, with his CSV?

You may not have known...

```
html
 ├─ head
 │   └─ title
 │       └─ "Binary Tree Selection"
 │   └─ body
 │       └─ p
 │           └─ p
 │               └─ "Below are our fine binary tree options:"
 │               └─ div
 │                   └─ "Our"
 │                   └─ em
 │                       └─ "depth-first"
 │                       └─ " trees are great for folks that are far away."
 │           └─ a
 │               └─ "Main Menu"
 │               └─ "You can view other products in the "
 │               └─ div
 │                   └─ "trees are a favorite for nearby neighbors."
 │                   └─ em
 │                       └─ "Our "
 │                       └─ "breadth-first"
 │           └─ "."
```

≠ ...that just as the browser sees your HTML as a DOM tree, web browsers automatically convert any XML they have to deal with into DOM trees.

≠ ...that you can work with more than one DOM tree in the same JavaScript function. For example, you can read an XML DOM tree and update an HTML DOM tree, all at the same time.

≠ ...that HTML elements and XML elements are both just element nodes in the DOM. There's no difference between an XML type and an HTML type, at least when it comes to the DOM.

≠ ...that the responseXML property always returns a DOM document object, even if that object is a single element, or just a single text node.

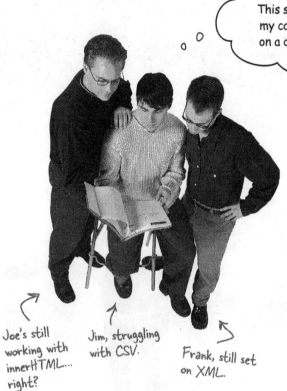

This sucks! I'm going to have to rewrite my callback now. I built everything based on a description, price, and list of URLs.

Joe's still working with innerHTML... right?

Jim, struggling with CSV.

Frank, still set on XML.

You can't always know in advance what the data structure you get from the server will look like.

And even if you do, that format might change... at anytime.

Frank: Yeah, I've got a lot of changes to make, too. But I was thinking... Jim, how are you going to handle a changing response with your CSV?

Jim: Well, I was thinking about that...

Joe: Hey, guys, I had an idea. You know I've been doing some research—

Jim: So I think what I can do is assume that every other value is a category, like "Description" or "Price." And the values after each category are the actual category values, like the textual description, or 399.99, or whatever.

Frank: Hmmm. Sounds a little hairy.

Jim: It's not too bad. Except for cases where there's more than one value, like for those URLs? Then I think I have to check for maybe a special character before each category to indicate that it's a multi-value category.

Joe: Listen, guys, I wanted to show you—

Frank: Wow, Jim, that's nasty. Sounds like this latest change from Rob is really going to be a pain.

Jim: Yeah, it kinda is. But what else can I do?

Wouldn't it be dreamy if there was actually a data format that described itself? It could tell me what every bit of data was used for. But I suppose it's just a fantasy...

XML is <u>self-describing</u>

The thing that's cool about XML is that you can create your own vocabulary. XHTML is an XML vocabulary that's specific to displaying things on the web. But suppose we needed a vocabulary for describing items, like at Rob's online store.

But the format can't be locked into elements like `<price>` or `<resources>` because we want each item to define its own categories. We might use something like this:

```
<?xml version="1.0"?>
<item id="item ID">
   <category>
     <name>Label for this category</name>
     <value>The value to display for this category</value>
   </category>
   <category>
     <name>Name of the next category</name>
     <value>Next value</value>
   </category>
   <category type="list">
     <name>Name of multi-valued category</name>
     <value>First value for this category</value>
     <value>Second value for this category</value>
   </category>
   ...
</item>
```

The `<category>` element contains the label and value for each bit of information we need to display.

Every category has a `<name>` and a `<value>`. They contain the actual data we'll display.

We can have multi-valued categories, and even indicate that with an attribute on the `<category>` element.

`<item>` is the root element. It's the container for all the `<category>` elements, just like the `<html>` element in an XHTML file.

The XML can contain as many `<category>` elements as necessary. We don't need to know how many there are or what they are in advance.

Sharpen your pencil

Here's some more data from Rob's inventory database:

Item ID: itemGuitar
Manufacturer: Gibson
Model: Les Paul Standard
Description: Pete Townshend once played this guitar while his own axe was in the shop having bits of drumkit removed from it.
Price: 5695.99
URLs: http://www.thewho.com/
http://en.wikipedia.org/wiki/Pete_Townshend

How would you represent this item's details using the XML format from the last page?

Write your XML in right here. ➞

Sharpen your pencil
Solution

Here's some more data from Rob's inventory database:

Item ID: itemGuitar
Manufacturer: Gibson
Model: Les Paul Standard
Description: Pete Townshend once played this guitar while his own axe was in the shop having bits of drumkit removed from it.
Price: 5695.99
URLs: http://www.thewho.com/
http://en.wikipedia.org/wiki/Pete_Townshend

Your job was to represent this in XML using the vocabulary from page 366.

```xml
<?xml version="1.0"?>
<item id="itemGuitar">
   <category>
     <name>Manufacturer</name>
     <value>Gibson</value>
   </category>
   <category>
     <name>Model</name>
     <value>Les Paul Standard</value>
   </category>
   <category>
     <name>Description</name>
     <value>Pete Townshend once played this guitar while his own axe
            was in the shop having bits of drumkit removed from it.</value>
   </category>
   <category>
     <name>Price</name>
     <value>5695.99</value>
   </category>
   <category type="list">
     <name>URLs</name>
     <value>http://www.thewho.com/</value>
     <value>http://en.wikipedia.org/wiki/Pete_Townshend</value>
   </category>
</item>
```

Most of this is just "fill in the blanks." You drop in the name of a category and its value, and you're all set.

The URLs are a list, so we have to set the category type to "list"

Exercise

It's time for the big finish (at least for now). Your job is to take what you've learned about the DOM, server-side responses in XML, and the format from the last few pages, and put it all together. Here's what you've got to do:

☐ Change your request URL to use getDetailsXML-updated.php. That script is in with the other downloads for this chapter from Head First Labs.

☐ Rewrite the displayDetails() callback to work with the XML vocabulary we've been looking at. Remember, you may get more—or less—categories for different items. And you've got to handle those list categories, too.

☐ Test everything out! Once you've got everything working, turn the page to claim your Les Paul (at least, that's what we hope)!

there are no Dumb Questions

Q: So the big deal about XML is that it describes itself? That can't be useful all that often...

A: Actually, self-describing data is useful in a number of situations, just like here, with Rob's online store. It's pretty convenient to be able to define elements and structure that's suited to your business.
Even better, XML is a standard, so tons of people know how to work with it. That means your vocabulary is usable by lots of programmers, in client-side and server-side programs.

Q: Wouldn't it be easier to just make up our own data format?

A: It might seem that way at first, but proprietary data formats—ones that you make up for your own use—can really cause a lot of problems. If you don't document them, people may forget how they work. And if anything changes, you need to make sure everything is up-to-date: the client, the server, the database, the documentation... that can be a real headache.

Q: Okay, I get why we should use XML, but doesn't it become a "proprietary data format" when we start declaring element names?

A: No, not at all. That's the beauty of XML: it's flexible. The server and the client need to be looking for the same element names, but you can often work that out at run-time. That's what's meant by *self-describing*: XML describes itself with its element names and structure.

Exercise Solution

It's time for the big finish (at least for now). Your job was to take what you've learned about the DOM, server-side responses in XML, and the format from the last few pages, and complete an updated version of the displayDetails() callback.

```
function displayDetails() {
  if (request.readyState == 4) {
    if (request.status == 200) {
      var detailDiv = document.getElementById("description");

      // Remove existing item details (if any)
      for (var i=detailDiv.childNodes.length; i>0; i--) {
        detailDiv.removeChild(detailDiv.childNodes[i-1]);
      }
```

This is the same as before. We start by getting rid of any existing content.

```
      // Add new item details
      var responseDoc = request.responseXML;
      var categories = responseDoc.getElementsByTagName("category");
      for (var i=0; i<categories.length; i++) {
        var category = categories[i];
        var nameElement = category.getElementsByTagName("name")[0];
        var categoryName = nameElement.firstChild.nodeValue;
        var categoryType = category.getAttribute("type");
        if ((categoryType == null) || (categoryType != "list")) {
          var valueElement = category.getElementsByTagName("value")[0];
          var categoryValue = valueElement.firstChild.nodeValue;
          var p = document.createElement("p");
          var text = document.createTextNode(
            categoryName + ": " + categoryValue);
```

First up, we get the categories...

...and then get the name and type of each category.

We can check the type to see if it's a list. If not...

...get the value, create a <p>, and add text with the category name and value.

This gets categories with no type attribute, or a type with a value other than "list."

```
                    p.appendChild(text);
                    detailDiv.appendChild(p);
```

This block handles lists of values. →

```
                } else {
                    var p = document.createElement("p");
                    p.appendChild(document.createTextNode(categoryName));
                    var list = document.createElement("ul");
```

First, we get all the values. →

```
                    var values = category.getElementsByTagName("value");
                    for (var j=0; j<values.length; j++) {
                        var li = document.createElement("li");
```

For each value, we → add an <li> to an unordered list (<ul>).

```
                        li.appendChild(
                            document.createTextNode(values[j].firstChild.nodeValue));
                        list.appendChild(li);
                    }
                    detailDiv.appendChild(p);
                    detailDiv.appendChild(list);
```

← Add both the list heading and the list itself to the <div>.

```
                }
            }
```

> Check it out... this is even better than my old version! I can handle anything now, including those multi-valued categories. Hey, how's your CSV coming along?

> <mumble, mumble>

← Things don't look like they're going so well for Jim and his CSV solution.

TEST DRIVE

Test out the new, improved, more flexible version of Rob's page.

Once you've got all your code updated, let's take it for a spin, and show Rob what we've come up with. Here's what the page looks like now:

Be sure to change the URL in your getDetails() request function, too.

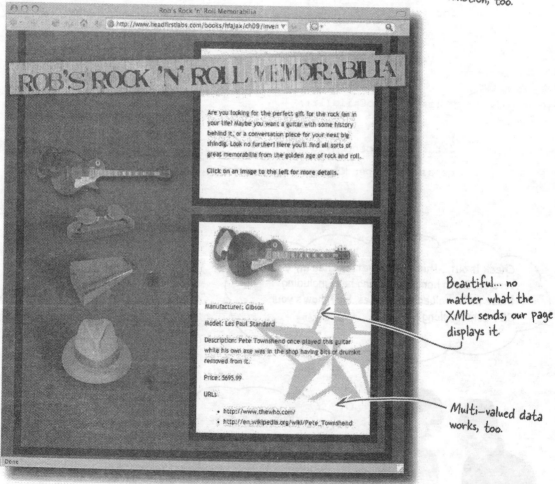

Beautiful... no matter what the XML sends, our page displays it

Multi-valued data works, too.

WHICH DATA FORMAT?

Welcome to this week's edition of "Which Data Format?" You've got to decide which data format is best for the 5 examples below. Be careful: some are requests, while others are responses. Good luck!

Text or XML

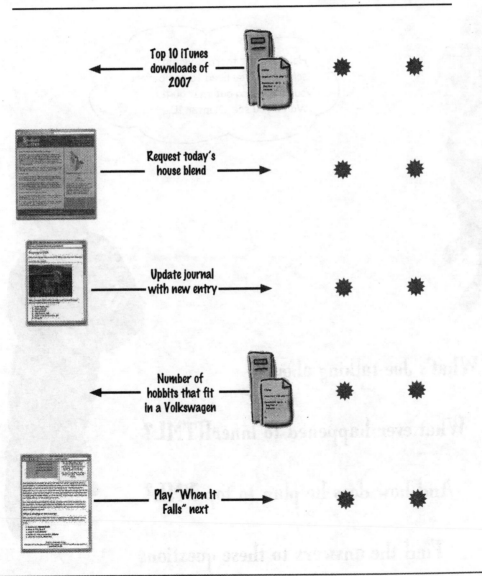

Top 10 iTunes downloads of 2007

Request today's house blend

Update journal with new entry

Number of hobbits that fit in a Volkswagen

Play "When It Falls" next

Answers on Page 377.

This looks fantastic, and I don't have time to wait on anyone else. Frank, I love the XML approach. So the Les Paul guitar goes to—

Hold it right there. I've got something you need to see before you go handing out that guitar. Wait'll you see Chapter 10...

Rob's thrilled with the XML solution.

What's Joe talking about?

What ever happened to innerHTML?

And how does he plan to top XML?

Find the answers to these questions and more... all in Chapter 10.

It's Joe, recovered from his failures with innerHTML.

XMLAcrostic

Take some time to sit back and give your right brain something
to do. Answer the questions in the top, then use the letters to fill
in the secret message.

Our original version put pre-formatted XHTML in this property:

___ ___ ___ ___ ___ ___ ___ ___ ___
1   2   3   4   5   6   7   8   9

We addded a <br> element to the detailDiv to do this:

___ ___ ___ ___ ___ ___
10 12 13 14 15 16

This property of the request object contains text returned by the server:

___ ___ ___ ___ ___ ___ ___ ___ ___ ___ ___ ___
17 18 19 20 21 22 23 24 25 26 27 28

The response to our request is generated here:

___ ___ ___ ___ ___ ___   ___ ___ ___ ___
29 30 31 32 33 34   35 36 37 38

The browser puts the XML DOM into a property of this object:

___ ___ ___ ___ ___ ___ ___
39 40 41 42 43 44 45

This was our client in this chapter:

___ ___ ___
46 47 48

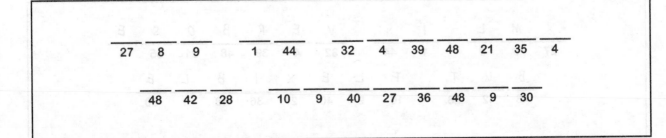

___ ___ ___   ___ ___   ___ ___ ___ ___ ___ ___ ___
27 8 9   1 44   32 4 39 48 21 35 4

___ ___ ___   ___ ___ ___ ___ ___ ___ ___ ___
48 42 28   10 9 40 27 36 48 9 30

XMLAcrostic

Take some time to sit back and give your right brain something to do. Answer the questions in the top, then use the letters to fill in the secret message.

Our original version put pre-formatted XHTML in this property:

I	N	N	E	R	H	T	M	L
1	2	3	4	5	6	7	8	9

We addded a <br> element to the detailDiv to do this:

F	O	R	M	A	T
10	12	13	14	15	16

This property of the request object contains text returned by the server:

R	E	S	P	O	N	S	E	T	E	X	T
17	18	19	20	21	22	23	24	25	26	27	28

The response to our request is generated here:

S	E	R	V	E	R	-	S	I	D	E
29	30	31	32	33	34		35	36	37	38

The browser puts the XML DOM into a property of this object:

R	E	Q	U	E	S	T
39	40	41	42	43	44	45

This was our client in this chapter:

R	O	B
46	47	48

X	M	L		I	S		V	E	R	B	O	S	E
27	8	9		1	44		32	4	39	48	21	35	4

	B	U	T		F	L	E	X	I	B	L	E
	48	42	28		10	9	40	27	36	48	9	30

WHICH DATA FORMAT?

Welcome to this week's edition of "Which Data Format?" You've got to decide which data format is best for the 5 examples below. Be careful: some are requests, while others are responses. Good luck!

Text or XML

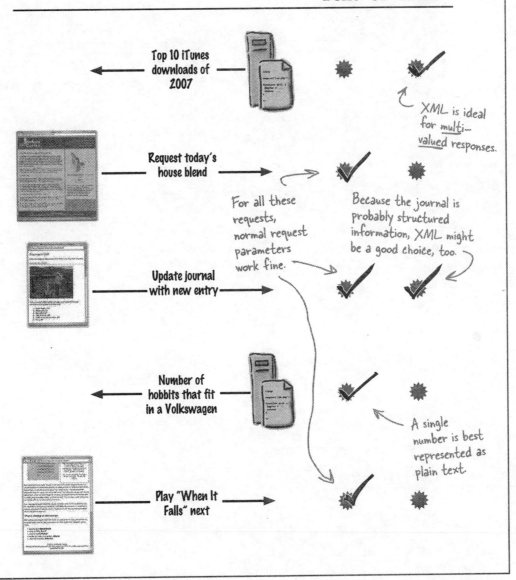

Top 10 iTunes downloads of 2007

XML is ideal for multi-valued responses.

Request today's house blend

For all these requests, normal request parameters work fine.

Because the journal is probably structured information, XML might be a good choice, too.

Update journal with new entry

Number of hobbits that fit in a Volkswagen

A single number is best represented as plain text.

Play "When It Falls" next

10 json

SON of JavaScript

He appears to be perfectly standard, sir. Everything's in the right place, and he's already representing you well to everyone else. So what should we be calling him? Most of the nurses love JSON... what do you think?

JavaScript, objects, and notation, oh my!

If you ever need to represent objects in your JavaScript, then you're going to love JSON, **JavaScript Standard Object Notation**. With JSON, you can **represent complex objects and mappings** with text and a few curly braces. Even better, you can **send and receive JSON** from other languages, like PHP, C#, Python, and Ruby. But how does JSON stack up as a data format? Turn the page and see...

Joe, buddy, I don't know what you think you've got, but my XML solution is perfect. Do you see this thing running? It's flawless!

Frank, of XML fame in Chapter 9.

Jim

Joe, with some new, amazing idea.

Joe: I think we might have different definitions of flawless, man. *Two* DOM trees to work with, and dealing with whitespace in the server's response?

Jim: That's a good point, Frank. Did you even check for whitespace nodes?

Frank: No, but that's easy enough to add in—

Joe: And your code will get even more convoluted.

Frank: Hey, at least my code works. And that CSV stuff was a total bust.

Jim: It worked great! At least... well, it worked pretty well until we had data where the structure changed depending on the item.

Joe: So you've got broken CSV, or convoluted XML. What a choice! Good thing there's *another* option.

Jim: What? What did you find?

Frank: This better not be another innerHTML fiasco...

Joe: I found JSON!

Jim and Frank: JSON? What the heck is that?

Joe: JSON is JavaScript Standard Object Notation. It's a way to represent a JavaScript object in plain text. So the server can send us JSON—which is just text, no XML or DOM issues to deal with—and our JavaScript can work with that response as an object.

Jim: What's the big deal about that?

Frank: Hmm. Well, if Joe's really onto something—

Joe: I am!

Frank: —then you wouldn't need all this DOM stuff, or even `split()` and other text manipulation code. You could just say, for example, `var description = itemDetails.description`. That *would* be pretty cool.

Joe: Look, here's how it works...

JSON can be text <u>AND</u> an object

With CSV, comma-separated values, the CSV data was pure text. The server sent over the text, and our JavaScript had to use string manipulation routines like, `split()`, to turn the string into individual pieces of data.

CSV

```
itemDetails = response.split(",");
```

Web server

With XML, the server sent text over, too, but that text was self-describing. So we could get a DOM representation of the text using the request object's `responseXML` property. But then we had to use all those DOM methods to work with the object, instead of actual property names like `description` or `urls`.

XML

```
responseDoc = request.responseXML;
```

Web server

But suppose we had a way to get text from the server, and then treat that text as a JavaScript object. Instead of using string manipulation or DOM methods, we'd just use code like `item.description` or `itemDetails.urls`. In other words, we'd have a format that was represented as text for easy network transmission, but an object when we needed to work with the data.

JSON

```
description = item.description;
```

Web server

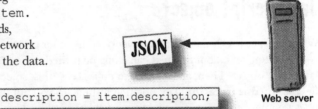

Sharpen your pencil

Suppose you had an item's ID, description, price, and a list of URLs for that item. What do you think an object representing that information might look like? Draw a circle for the object below, and then add in whatever fields you think the object might have.

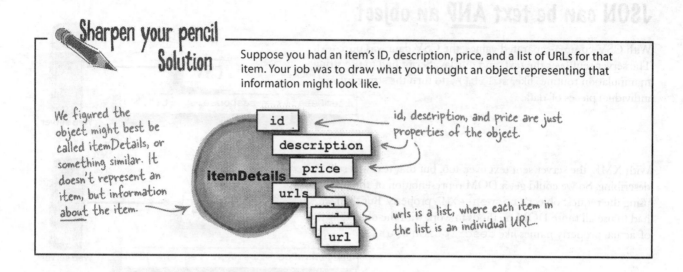

Sharpen your pencil Solution

Suppose you had an item's ID, description, price, and a list of URLs for that item. Your job was to draw what you thought an object representing that information might look like.

We figured the object might best be called itemDetails, or something similar. It doesn't represent an item, but information about the item.

itemDetails

id

description

price

urls

url
url
url

id, description, and price are just properties of the object.

urls is a list, where each item in the list is an individual URL.

JSON data can be treated as a JavaScript object

Don't worry... we're going to talk about how to get the JSON data from the server in a minute.

When you get JSON data from a server or some other source, you're getting text... but that text can easily be turned into a JavaScript object. Then, all you need to do is access that object's fields using **dot notation**. Dot notation just means you put the object name, and then a dot, and then a field name, like this:

```
var weakness = superman.weakness;
```

For instance, suppose you had an object like the one shown in the solution above. How do you think you'd access the value of the description field?

....

If you're looking at your answer, and thinking it's too simple, then you've probably got things just right. Working with JavaScript objects is about as easy as it gets.

I told you, guys, JSON rocks!

So how do we get JSON data from the server's response?

When a server sends its response as JSON data, that data comes across the network as text. So you can get that data using the `responseText` property of your request object:

```
var jsonData = request.responseText;
```

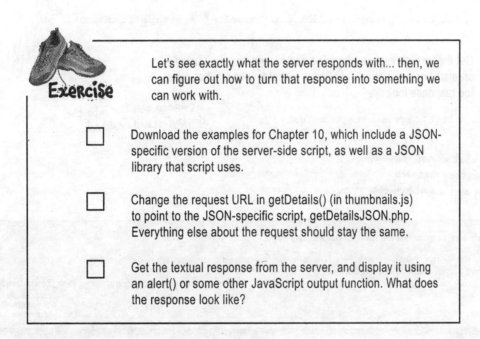

Let's see exactly what the server responds with... then, we can figure out how to turn that response into something we can work with.

☐ Download the examples for Chapter 10, which include a JSON-specific version of the server-side script, as well as a JSON library that script uses.

☐ Change the request URL in getDetails() (in thumbnails.js) to point to the JSON-specific script, getDetailsJSON.php. Everything else about the request should stay the same.

☐ Get the textual response from the server, and display it using an alert() or some other JavaScript output function. What does the response look like?

What did the server respond with? Does it look like a JavaScript object?

Exercise Solution

☐ Download the examples for Chapter 10, which include a JSON-specific version of the server-side script, as well as a JSON library that script uses.

☐ Change the request URL in getDetails() (in thumbnails.js) to point to the JSON-specific script, getDetailsJSON.php. Everything else about the request should stay the same.

This is the line we used from getDetails() that requests a response from the JSON server-side script.

```
var url= "getDetailsJSON.php?ImageID=" + escape(itemName);
```

☐ Get the textual response from the server, and display it using an alert() or some other JavaScript output function. What does the response look like?

We added this line into the displayDetails() callback.

```
alert(request.responseText);
```

Here's what we got reloading the inventory page, and clicking on the guitar image.

The page at http://www.headfirstlabs.com says:

{"id":"itemGuitar","description":"Pete Townshend once played this guitar while his own axe was in the shop having bits of drumkit removed from it.","price":5695.99,"urls":["http:\/\/www.thewho.com\/","http:\/\/en.wikipedia.org\/wiki\/Pete_Townshend"]}

OK

What the heck is this? And what do we <u>DO</u> with it?

JavaScript can <u>evaluate</u> textual data

JavaScript is pretty good at turning text into objects, functions, and lots of other things. You can give JavaScript some text, and it's smart enough to figure out what that text represents.

For example, remember how we've been assigning event handlers?

It looks like we're assigning a textual description of a function to the image's onclick event.

```
image.onclick = function () {
    var detailURL = 'images/' + this.title + '-detail.jpg';
    document.getElementById("itemDetail").src = detailURL;
    getDetails(this.title);
}
```

JavaScript takes this textual function, and creates an actual function in memory. So when an image is clicked, the function code sitting in memory is executed. That all happens behind the scenes, though, and isn't something you need to worry about.

But what about when you have text, and you need to TELL JavaScript to turn it into something more than text?

```
{"id":"itemGuitar",
  "description":"Pete Townshend once played this guitar ...",
  "price":5695.99,
  "urls":["http://www.thewho.com/",
          "http://en.wikipedia.org/wiki/Pete_Townshend"]}
```

This response from the server looks like it's a bunch of property names and values... but how can we tell JavaScript to turn this into something we can use?

Use eval() to manually evaluate text

The `eval()` function tells JavaScript to actually evaluate text. So if you passed the text describing a statement to `eval()`, JavaScript would actually run that statement, and give you the result:

```
alert(eval("2 + 2"));
```

4

JavaScript evaluates the text "2 + 2"...

...and turns it into the statement 2 + 2...

...and evaluates th t expression, returning the result

Evaluating JSON data returns an object representation of that data

So how does this apply to JSON data? Well, when you run `eval()` on text that describes a set of property names and values, then JavaScript returns an object representation of those properties and values. Suppose you ran `eval()` on this text:

```
{"id":"itemGuitar",
  "description":"Pete Townshend once played this guitar ...",
  "price":5695.99,
  "urls":["http://www.thewho.com/",
          "http://en.wikipedia.org/wiki/Pete_Townshend"]}
```

JavaScript figures, "Hey, this looks like an object." So it turns this data into an actual object, and returns that object:

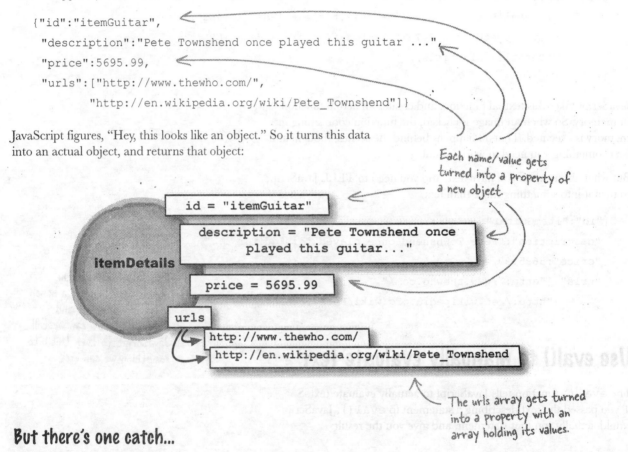

Each name/value gets turned into a property of a new object

itemDetails

```
id = "itemGuitar"
```
```
description = "Pete Townshend once
              played this guitar..."
```
```
price = 5695.99
```
```
urls
```
```
http://www.thewho.com/
http://en.wikipedia.org/wiki/Pete_Townshend
```

The urls array gets turned into a property with an array holding its values.

But there's one catch...

It looks like the object JavaScript creates from a JSON response is perfect for Rob's rock inventory page. There's just one thing to watch out for. You need to make sure that the overall JSON response string is seen as a single object. So when you call `eval()`, wrap the whole response in parentheses, like this:

```
eval(   '('  +  JSON data string  +  ')'  );
```

This last parentheses closes the eval() statement.

Enclosing the entire text in parentheses says to JavaScript: "Treat this all as ONE THING."

there are no
Dumb Questions

Q: Do I need any special libraries to read JSON data?

A: No. `eval()` is built into JavaScript, and it's all you need to turn JSON data into a JavaScript object.

Q: Why should I mess with eval()? Couldn't I just parse the raw text from the server?

A: You could, but why bother? `eval()` turns all that text into a very simple object, and you can avoid counting characters and messing with `split()`.

Q: eval() just stands for evaluate, right?

A: Right. `eval()` *evaluates* a string.

Q: So eval() runs a piece of text?

A: Well, not always. `eval()` takes a string, and turns it into an expression. Then, the result of that expression is returned. So for a string like "2 + 2", the expression would be 2 + 2, and the result of that expression is 4. So 4 is returned from
`eval("2 + 2");`
But take a string like '{"id":"itemGuitar","price":5695.99}.' Turning that into an expression and executing the expression results in a new object, not a specific "answer." So sometimes `eval()` doesn't really run text as much as it *evaluates* (or *interprets*) text.

Q: What are those curly braces around everything in the server's response?

A: JSON data is enclosed within curly braces: { and }. It's sort of like how an array is enclosed within [and]. It's just a way of telling JavaScript, "Hey, I'm about to describe an object."

Q: And each name/value pair in the text becomes a property of the object and a value for that property?

A: Right. The text "id":"itemGuitar" in an object description tells JavaScript that there's an **id** property, and the value of that property should be "itemGuitar."

Q: What about the urls property? That looks sort of weird.

A: urls is an array. So the property name is "urls," and the value is an array, indicated by those opening and closing square brackets ([and]).

Exercise

You've got a script that returns JSON data, and now you know how to convert that response into an object. All that's left to do is use that object in your callback. Open up thumbnails.js, and see if you can rewrite displayDetails() to convert the JSON data from the server into an object, and then use that object to update Rob's inventory page.

Exercise Solution

You've got a script that returns JSON data, and now you know how to convert that response into an object. Your job was to use that object in your callback. How did you do?

```javascript
function displayDetails() {
  if (request.readyState == 4) {
    if (request.status == 200) {
      var detailDiv = document.getElementById("description");

      var itemDetails = eval('(' + request.responseText + ')');

      // Remove existing item details (if any)
      var children = detailDiv.childNodes;
      for (var i=children.length; i>0; i--) {
        detailDiv.removeChild(children[i-1]);
      }

      // Add new item details
      var descriptionP = document.createElement("p");
      descriptionP.appendChild(
        document.createTextNode("Description: " + itemDetails.description));
      detailDiv.appendChild(descriptionP);
      var priceP = document.createElement("p");
      priceP.appendChild(
        document.createTextNode("Price: $" + itemDetails.price));
      detailDiv.appendChild(priceP);
      var list = document.createElement("ul");
      for (var i=0; i<itemDetails.urls.length; i++) {
        var url = itemDetails.urls[i];
        var li = document.createElement("li");
        var a = document.createElement("a");
        a.setAttribute("href", url);
        a.appendChild(document.createTextNode(url));
        li.appendChild(a);
        list.appendChild(li);
      }
      detailDiv.appendChild(list);
    }
  }
}
```

Here's where we ask JavaScript to convert the server's response into an object.

Remember these extra parentheses!

There's no need for using DOM to get values from the server with JSON.

Most of this code to update the display of the page itself is identical to the XML version from Chapter 9.

Getting the details about each item is really simple now.

This code is a bit shorter than the XML version, and only uses one DOM. Do you think this version is better or worse than the XML version?

Q: This is all just about a data format, right?

A: That's right. Any time you send information between your web page and a server, you're going to need some way to format that information. So far, we've used plain text to send requests, and text and XML to retrieve responses. JSON is just one more way to send data back and forth.

Q: If we've already got XML and text as options, why do we need JSON?

A: Since JSON is JavaScript, it's often a lot easier for both JavaScript programmers and browsers to work with. Also, because JSON creates a standard JavaScript object, it winds up looking more like a "business object" that combines data and functionality, instead of an untyped XML DOM tree. You can create similar objects from an XML response, but it requires a lot of additional work, with schemas and databinding tools.

Q: So JSON does things XML can't do?

A: It's not so much that it does more; JSON actually does *fewer* things than XML. But what JSON does, it does simply and elegantly, without a lot of the overhead that XML requires to do all the bazillion things a more fully-featured markup language was designed to handle.

Q: Can we go back to syntax? I'm still a little fuzzy on the textual representation of an item. Can you explain how that's working again?

A: The curly braces, { and }, define an object, which is an unordered set of name/value pairs. Square brackets, [and], indicate an *ordered* array. In your code, you reference elements inside curly braces by their name, but the ones inside square brackets are referenced by number. Here's a closer look:

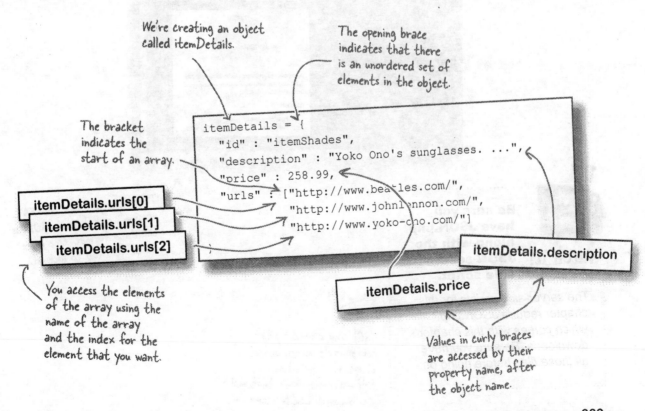

We're creating an object called itemDetails.

The opening brace indicates that there is an unordered set of elements in the object.

The bracket indicates the start of an array.

```
itemDetails = {
  "id" : "itemShades",
  "description" : "Yoko Ono's sunglasses. ...",
  "price" : 258.99,
  "urls" : ["http://www.beatles.com/",
            "http://www.johnlennon.com/",
            "http://www.yoko-ono.com/"]
}
```

itemDetails.urls[0]
itemDetails.urls[1]
itemDetails.urls[2]

You access the elements of the array using the name of the array and the index for the element that you want.

itemDetails.description

itemDetails.price

Values in curly braces are accessed by their property name, after the object name.

Test Drive

But does JSON actually impress Rob?

The code looks a bit simpler, and there's one less DOM to work with. But does the JSON version of Rob's inventory page actually work? Change your callback to match the version on page 388, update your request URL to getDetailsJSON.php, and try out the new version of the inventory page.

> This looks just like the XML version... but it uses JSON as the data format. One more choice for Rob to look at...

Watch it!

Be sure you have JSON.php along with the JSON server-side script.

The server-side scripts for this chapter require JSON.php, which comes with this chapter's downloads. Be sure you have all those files before going on.

> JSON.php is used by the server-side script in this chapter. It handles some PHP-specific issues that make dealing with JSON easier on the server.

Look, Joe's using the old specs for the site. Rob wants to send dynamic data, like group names and artists and hat sizes.

Frank: You're right! His JSON code doesn't really help much in that case. His code depends on knowing the names of the object's properties.

Jim: Exactly. And there's no way it works with dynamic item descriptions, where the property names change.

Frank: Hmmm. You know, I was able to solve that problem with XML. I wonder if Joe—

Jim: No way, man. You've always read the name of properties from your element's tag names. His code has the property names as part of the code... they're not even parameters to search methods like `getElementsByTagName()`.

Frank: You're right. I'll bet this will hang him up pretty good.

Frank, who thought he had the Les Paul guitar in the bag.

Jim just doesn't want to see Joe win.

I'm not done yet. There's got to be a way to handle dynamic properties...

What would a JavaScript object that had to change based on the specifics of an item look like?

JavaScript objects are <u>ALREADY</u> dynamic... because they're not <u>COMPILED</u> objects

In compiled languages, you define your objects in a source file, like a `.java` or `.cpp` file. Then, you compile those files into bytecode. So once your program's running, you're stuck with the definitions that are compiled into bytecode. In other words, a `Car` object can't suddenly have a new `manufacturer` property without recompilation. That lets everyone who's using the `Car` object know what to expect.

.cpp is for C++ code.

JavaScript, however, *isn't* compiled; it's ***interpreted***. Things can change at any time. Not only that, but the objects the server sends are created at runtime, using `eval()`. So whatever's sent to our JavaScript, that's what we get in the `itemDetails` object.

eval() doesn't need to know what kind of object it's creating ahead of time. It just evaluates the text you give it.

```
var itemDetails = eval('(' + request.responseText + ')');
```

This version of itemDetails has two new properties: manufacturer and model.

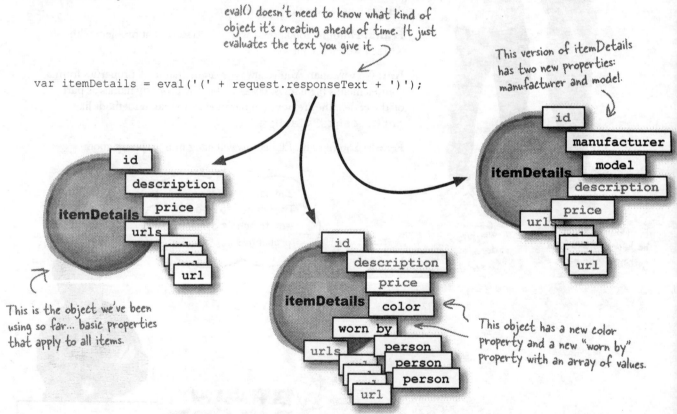

This is the object we've been using so far... basic properties that apply to all items.

This object has a new color property and a new "worn by" property with an array of values.

We don't need to change our object at all! We just need to know how to figure out what's <u>IN</u> the object.

You can access an object's members... and then get an object's values with those members

JavaScript will tell you what properties an object has. You just have to ask it, using the `for/in` syntax. Suppose you've got an object called `itemDetails`, and you want to know what properties `itemDetails` has. You'd use this code to get those properties:

```
for (var property in hero) {
  alert("Found a property named: " + property);
}
```

Pretty simple, right? So the variable `property` would have values like `id`, `description`, `price`, and `urls`.

But we don't want just the property names; we also want the *values* for each property. That's okay, though, because JavaScript lets you access an object's properties as if the object were an array. But instead of supplying an array index, like `itemDetails[0]`, you supply a property name, like `itemDetails["price"]`.

In other words, the value returned for `itemDetails["price"]` for an object is the value of the property named `price` in that object.

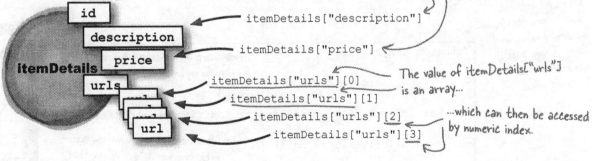

These lines of code return the values of the matching properties in the itemDetails object

```
itemDetails["id"]
itemDetails["description"]
itemDetails["price"]
itemDetails["urls"][0]
itemDetails["urls"][1]
itemDetails["urls"][2]
itemDetails["urls"][3]
```

The value of itemDetails["urls"] is an array... ...which can then be accessed by numeric index.

Exercise

You know what to do. Update your version of the inventory page to work with dynamic data from the server. You never know what you'll get... just that the server will return an object in JSON format with properties and values for those properties. Good luck!

> Hold on there. I got the single-valued properties working, but how am I supposed to deal with arrays? How do I know if a property value, like urls, holds an array?

JavaScript does __NOT__ give you a built-in way to see if a value is an array.

Dealing with dynamic data is tricky business. For instance, when you write in your code `itemDetails.urls`, you know that the value for that property will be an array. But what about `itemDetails[propertyName]`? Is the value for that property an array or a single value, like a string?

Unfortunately, JavaScript doesn't give you a simple way to check and see if a value is an array. You can use the `typeof` operator, but even for arrays, `typeof` returns "object," and not "array" like you might expect.

To help you out, here's a little Ready Bake Code that will tell you if a value is an array or not. Add this function to the end of `thumbnails.js`, and then see if you can finish up your exercise from the last page.

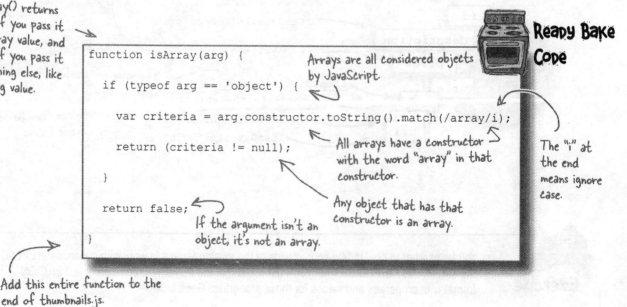

isArray() returns true if you pass it an array value, and false if you pass it something else, like a string value.

Ready Bake Code

```
function isArray(arg) {

    if (typeof arg == 'object') {

        var criteria = arg.constructor.toString().match(/array/i);

        return (criteria != null);

    }

    return false;

}
```

Arrays are all considered objects by JavaScript.

All arrays have a constructor with the word "array" in that constructor.

Any object that has that constructor is an array.

The "i" at the end means ignore case.

If the argument isn't an object, it's not an array.

Add this entire function to the end of thumbnails.js.

You know what to do. Update your version of the inventory page to work with dynamic data from the server. You never know what you'll get... just that the server will return an object in JSON format with properties and values for those properties. How did you do?

```javascript
function displayDetails() {
  if (request.readyState == 4) {
    if (request.status == 200) {
      var detailDiv = document.getElementById("description");

      var itemDetails = eval('(' + request.responseText + ')');
      // Remove existing item details (if any)
      var children = detailDiv.childNodes;
      for (var i=children.length; i>0; i--) {
        detailDiv.removeChild(children[i-1]);
      }

      // Add new item details
      for (var property in itemDetails) {
        var propertyValue = itemDetails[property];
        if (!isArray(propertyValue)) {
          var p = document.createElement("p");
          p.appendChild(
              document.createTextNode(property + ": " + propertyValue));
          detailDiv.appendChild(p);
        } else {
          var p = document.createElement("p");
          p.appendChild(document.createTextNode(property + ":"));
          var list = document.createElement("ul");
          for (var i=0; i<propertyValue.length; i++) {
            var li = document.createElement("li");
            li.appendChild(document.createTextNode(propertyValue[i]));
            list.appendChild(li);
          }
          detailDiv.appendChild(p);
          detailDiv.appendChild(list);
        }
      }
    }
  }
}
```

Nothing's changed in this section... this just clears out existing content.

We can cycle through each property of the returned object.

Start by getting the property's value and seeing if that value is an array.

Remember to add isArray() to your code, or this JavaScript won't work.

Single-valued properties are easy. We just need a <p> and some text.

For multi-valued properties, we have to iterate through the array of property values.

For each value in the array, create a new <li> and add the value to it.

Test Drive

JSON testing, part deux

Now our code handles dynamic objects, values that might be strings *or* arrays, and should run like a dream. Let's see the new-and-improved JSON page...

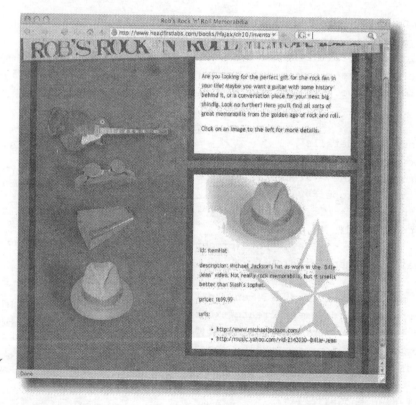

Everything works... do you think Rob will be impressed?

⚛ BRAIN POWER

Do you think isArray() belongs in thumbnails.js or utils.js? Put the function where you think it really belongs, and make any needed changes to the rest of your code now.

I love this JSON stuff... my engineers tell me you've got the simplest and cleanest code of all the solutions so far. But there are some problems. What's that "id: itemHat" thing? And why are the labels all lowercase?

Good property names aren't usually good label names, too.

Take a close look at the property names for an item's description:

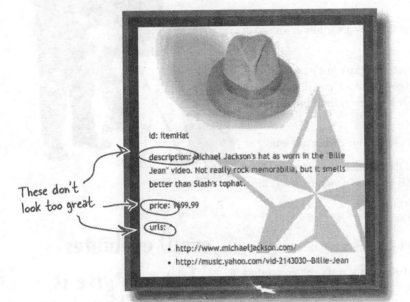

id: itemHat

description: Michael Jackson's hat as worn in the "Billie Jean" video. Not really rock memorabilia, but it smells better than Slash's tophat.

price: ?699.99

urls:

- http://www.michaeljackson.com/
- http://music.yahoo.com/vid-2143030--Billie-Jean

These don't look too great

We've been printing out the property name and then the value for that property. But those property names look more like code than "human speak."

Not only that, but the ID of each item is showing, too. That could wind up being a real security bug down the line.

What would YOU do to fix these problems?

Those aren't the only problems. eval()s not safe to use like that... do you realize you're evaluating text from another source?

Joe: Well, yeah, that's kind of the point.

Frank: Do you really think that's a good idea? Just running code that someone else gave you?

Joe: I'm not running it, I'm evaluating it. Haven't you been paying attention?

Jim: Someone's getting cranky that their JSON solution isn't so easy...

Frank: Whether JSON's easy or not, you can't just evaluate that code blindly. What if it's malicious code, like a script that hacks the user's browser or something? Or it redirects their browser to a porn site?

Joe: Are you kidding me? It's Rob's server, for crying out loud!

Frank: What if it's not correct JSON? What if there's an error? Evaluating code with an error in it is going to generate errors for the users?

Jim: Sounds pretty dismal, Joe...

Joe: You're both just annoyed that I was gonna win that guitar.

Frank: Hey, safety first, man. I'm telling you, you can't go around using `eval()` on code that you don't have any control over.

Joe: Great. *Now* what am I gonna do?

BRAIN BARBELL

Ajax request objects can only make requests to programs on the same server that the JavaScript creating the request was served from. Does that reduce, increase, or change the dangers of using eval() on a server's response text?

eval() evaluates what you give it, **WITHOUT** regard for the results of that evaluation.

You **ONLY** have direct control of eval() code.

You need to **PARSE** the server's response, not just **EVALUATE** it

Calling eval() initiates a simple process: take a bit of text, and evaluate that text. What we need is an additional step. Suppose we could take a bit of text, and make sure it's actually JSON-formatted data. **Then**, we could reasonably assume it's safe to evaluate that data, and turn it into a JavaScript object.

That extra step—parsing the data and making sure the data is JSON—protects us from two important potential problems:

1 We'll know that the data is safe to evaluate, and not a malicious script or program. ← *JavaScript code, or other scripts, won't pass a simple, "Is this JSON?" test.*

2 We can be sure that not only is the data JSON, but it's *correctly formatted* JSON and won't cause our users any errors. ← *A parser can catch errors and report them, instead of just giving up and creating an error.*

Fortunately for Joe (and us!), the JSON website at http://www.json.org provides a JSON parser that does all of these things, and more. You can download a script from json.org called json2.js, and then use this command to parse JSON-formatted data:

```
var itemDetails = JSON. parse( request.responseText );
```

You still need to assign the result of calling the parse() function to a variable.

This JSON object is created when json2.js is first loaded by the web browser.

parse() takes in a string and returns an object if the string is valid JSON-formatted data.

We can pass the server's response directly to JSON.parse().

Run it!

> ### Change your code to use JSON.parse().
> The examples for Chapter 10 already include json2.js in the scripts/ directory. Add a reference to this new script in inventory.html, and update your version of thumbnails.js to use JSON.parse() instead of eval().

Put the reference to json2.js before the reference to thumbnails.js since the thumbnails script uses the json2 script.

There's still lots to do. Can <u>YOU</u> help Joe out?

● **How could you avoid showing the ID of an item when a user clicks on that item?**

● **What about those labels? Can you figure out a way to show better, more- readable labels?**

● **What about those URLs? Can you figure out a way to format URLs as links (using <a> elements) so they're clickable?**

● **And besides all that, how do <u>YOU</u> think Rob's inventory page could be improved?**

● **Don't forget to use a JSON parser, instead of eval()!**

Can you make Rob's inventory page even cooler using JSON? Build your best version of Rob's page, and submit your URL in the Head First Labs "Head First Ajax" forum. We'll be giving away cool prizes for the best entries in the coming months.

Visit us here, tell us about your entry, and give us a URL to check out what you've done (and how).

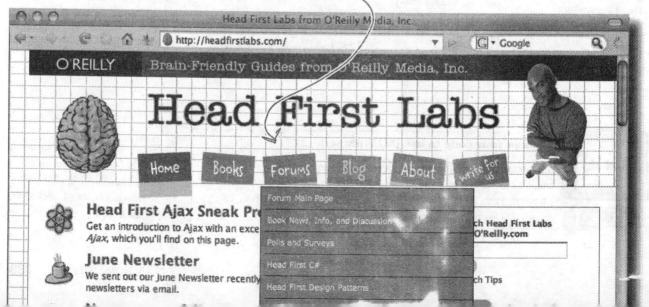

there are no
Dumb Questions

Q: So I shouldn't ever use eval()?

A: `eval()` is an important part of JavaScript. If you need to pass textual data to another function for evaluation, or even between scripts, `eval()` is really helpful.

However, `eval()` can be a problem when you're evaluating data that you can't control, like from someone else's program or server. In those cases, you won't know ahead of time exactly what you're evaluating. So in situations where you're not in control of all the data, stick to a parser or some other approach *other than* `eval()`.

Q: But a JSON parser keeps my code safe, right?

A: A JSON parser keeps your code safer than `eval()`, but that doesn't mean you can completely relax. When you're writing web code, security is *always* an issue. In the case of JSON data, `JSON.parse()` will ensure you've got valid JSON data, but you still don't know what that data actually *is*. So you may still need additional checks before using the data in the rest of your scripts.

Q: We didn't do any checks like that for Rob's page. Should we?

A: That's a good question. When you're reworking the app to help out Joe, think about the data you're getting. Could it be used maliciously? Do you think you need additional security checks?

Q: What about that json2.js script? Can I trust and rely on that code?

A: Now you're thinking like a web programmer! Anytime you use code from another source, like from `http://www.json.org`, you should thoroughly test out the code. We've done that testing here at Head First Labs, and `json2.js` is safe to use.

Q: Is it free, too? Do I have to pay anyone anything to use json2.js?

A: `json2.js` is free and open source. You can actually read through the source code at `http://www.json.org/json2.js`, and see what it does for yourself.

Q: So what about XML versus JSON? Which is better? And who won the guitar?

A: That's another good question. You've seen a lot of JSON and XML code now... which do you like best?

Security is ALWAYS a concern when you're programming for the web.

Always thoroughly test any code that you don't have complete control over.

So which is the better data format?

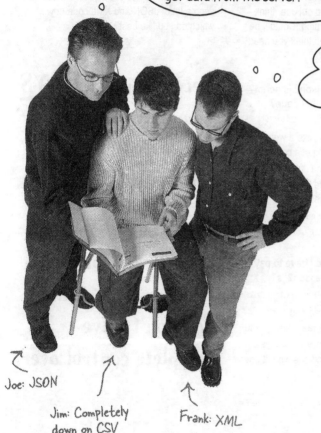

Well, it seems pretty obvious...JSON is current, it's JavaScript-friendly, and I don't need to do any weird DOM navigation to get data from the server.

Obvious to whom? I still think XML is the clear winner. It's a standard, and I don't have to download any libraries to get things working. Besides, we already know the DOM. How great is that?

Joe: JSON

Jim: Completely down on CSV

Frank: XML

Joe: I know about lots of things I don't like. Brussel sprouts, Melrose Place, velcro shoes... just because I know about something, doesn't mean I like it!

Frank: I just don't see what you really gain by using JSON. Maybe it's a little easier for *you* to use, but it's a pretty big pain when you get to dynamic data.

Jim: I don't know, Frank... I got really confused dealing with 2 DOMs at once.

Frank: But XML is self-describing! We didn't have any of those property-names-as-labels issues with XML.

Joe: I still think JSON lets me think in JavaScript, not some other language.

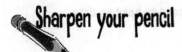

Sharpen your pencil

What do YOU think? Below are two columns: one for XML, and one for JSON. Under each heading, write why you think that format is better. See if you can come up with **at least** 5 good arguments for XML, and 5 more for JSON.

XML

JSON

Fireside Chats

Tonight's talk: **XML and JSON go head-to-head on data formats and standardization**

XML:

(glares at JSON)

JSON:

Your time has finally come, XML. Tonight, the world is gonna see that you've lost a step, especially when it comes to JavaScript and asynchronous applications.

I've heard that one before... but here I am, still the reigning data format in the world.

You're only at the top because people think that there's nothing else available. I know lots of people that can't stand you, XML... you're big and bloated, and a real pain to work with.

I'm big because I can handle anything: product memorabilia, HTML, purchase orders... you throw it at me, I'll take care of it. No problem. You think a little pipsqueak can handle all those different types of data? I don't think so.

Maybe not, but I'm fast... a lot faster than you, most of the time.

I'm plenty fast, especially if you use my attributes. And I'm versatile... I can do all sorts of things, like represent a math equation or a book.

Yeah, well, most of my users aren't too interested in sending math equations across the network. Besides, all those angle brackets? Ugh... anyone that knows arrays can start working with me without having to learn all that weird XML syntax.

But can someone transform you into something else? Like with XSLT? Or what about web services... you're gonna tell me you can handle web services?

XML:

Uh, yeah. Hello? We've got a whole group of DOM experts out there these days, writing killer user interfaces. Did you see that Fifteen Puzzle? That was pretty cool, and it was only about 100 lines of code. Anyone that knows the DOM is ready to use XML, *today*!

What are all the servers going to think about this? You know, PHP and ASP.Net and Java... I don't see them lining up to throw their support to you and your "lightweight data format" spiel.

Libraries? If they've got to use a library, why not use a standard like the Document Object Model?

But here I am, being used right now, because I'm *already* a standard. At the end of the day, you're just one more proprietary data format. Maybe you've got a few more fans than comma-separated values, but I'll put an end to that.

JSON:

Wow, you've really been a bit overused, haven't you... you're missing the point, Bracket-Head. I don't care about all those things. I just care about getting information from a web page to a server and back, without a bunch of extra work... like having to crawl up and down a DOM tree. Know anyone who thinks *that's* fun?

Look, all developers really need is a lightweight data format that's easy to work with in JavaScript. And that's me, Big Boy, not you.

Well, I guess that's true... but there are libraries that those guys can use to work with me.

I'm already standard in PHP 5. And who knows who's going to adopt me next?

Oh really? Let's see about that...

Sharpen your pencil
Solution

What do YOU think? Below are two columns: one for XML, and one for JSON. Under each heading, write why you think that format is better. See if you can come up with **at least** 5 good arguments for XML, and 5 more for JSON.

XML   **JSON**

ANSWERS OBSCURED INTENTIONALLY

These are <u>YOUR</u> answers. It's up to you to decide between JSON and XML, based on the factors that are important to you.

Hop online and continue the XML vs. JSON discussion at the Head First Ajax forum on http://www.headfirstlabs.com.

11 forms and validation

Say what you meant to say

Everyone makes mistakes from time to time.

Give a human being a chance to talk (or type) for a few minutes, and they'll probably make at least one or two **mistakes**. So how do your web apps **respond to those mistakes**? You've got to **validate** your users' input and react when that input has problems. But who does what? What should your web page do? What should your JavaScript do? And what's the role of the server in **validation** and **data integrity**? Turn the page to answer all of these questions, and a lot more...

Marcy's Yoga for Programmers... a booming new enterprise

With her hip new site and super-fast response times, Marcy's Yoga for Programmers site has exploded. She's got some of Silicon Valley's highest-end clientele signing up daily. She's even added online enrollment, so once a potential client finds the perfect class, they can sign up right away:

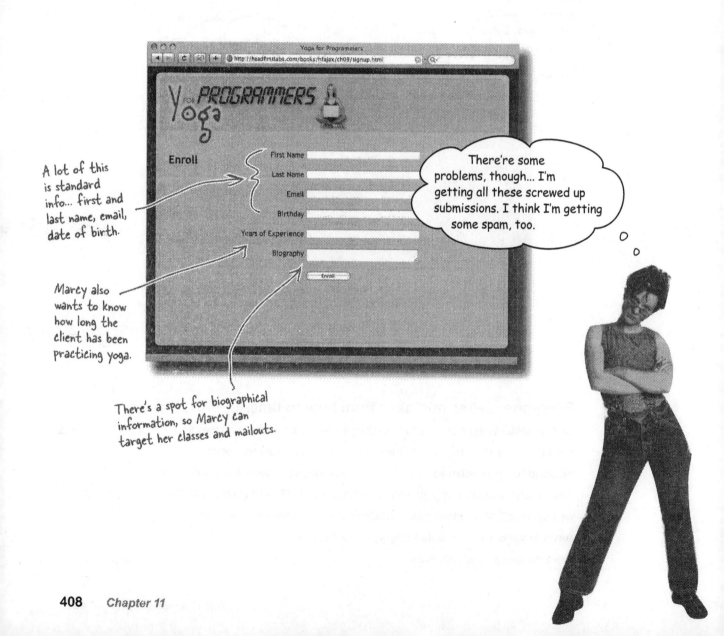

A lot of this is standard info... first and last name, email, date of birth.

Marcy also wants to know how long the client has been practicing yoga.

There's a spot for biographical information, so Marcy can target her classes and mailouts.

There're some problems, though... I'm getting all these screwed up submissions. I think I'm getting some spam, too.

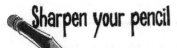

Sharpen your pencil

Below are a few entries from Marcy's ever-growing customer database. There are some big problems... can you figure out what they are?

firstname	lastname	email	bday	yrs	bio
Susan	Smith	ss@myjob.com	1 January	0	I'm a systems analyst
Bob	Brown		August 300	5	
Susan	Smith	ss@myjob.com	1 January	0	I'm a systems analyst
F0b#2938					View my porn for free!!!! 192.72.90.234
Jones	Jane	www.myjob.com			
Gerry	MacGregor	mac@myjob	March 23, 1972	99	
Mary		mw@myjob. com			I've been doing yoga for 12 years
Bill	Bainfield	bb@myjob.com	5-27-69		

1. ....

2. ....

3. ....

4. ....

5. ....

6. Gerry MacGregor isn't old enough to have been practicing yoga for 99 years. ....

7. ....

8. ....

9. ....

10. ....

How many problems can you spot with this data?

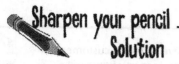

Sharpen your pencil
Solution

Below are a few entries from Marcy's ever-growing customer database. How many problems were you able to spot?

firstname	lastname	email	bday	yrs	bio
Susan	Smith	ss@myjob.com	1 January	0	I'm a systems analyst
Bob	Brown		August 300	5	
Susan	Smith	ss@myjob.com	1 January	0	I'm a systems analyst
F0b#2938					View my porn for free!!!! 192.72.90.234
Jones	Jane	www.myjob.com			
Gerry	MacGregor	mac@myjob	March 23, 1972	99	
Mary		mw@myjob.com			I've been doing yoga for 12 years
Bill	Bainfield	bb@myjob.com	5-27-69		

1. Susan Smith is registered twice.
2. Bob Brown didn't give his email address.
3. The F0b#2938 entry is spam, not a real client.
4. Jane Jones entered in a website URL, not an email address.
5. Gerry MacGregor's email isn't valid... he probably left off .com or .org.
6. Gerry MacGregor couldn't have been practicing yoga for 99 years.
7. Mary didn't enter in a last name.
8. Everyone's using a different format for their birthday.
9. There's information missing for Jane Jones, Bob Brown, and Bill Bainfield.
10. ....

← Did you come up with any other problems?

Sharpen your pencil

Based on the data that Marcy's trying to gather, what sorts of things would you do to ensure she isn't having the sorts of problems you saw on the last couple of pages?

For each field below, write down what you think you need to check.

First name

....

....

....

Last name

....

....

....

E-Mail

....

....

....

Birthday

....

....

....

Years of Yoga

....

....

....

Biography

....

....

....

Sharpen your pencil
Solution

Based on the data that Marcy's trying to gather, what sorts of things would you do to ensure she isn't having the sorts of problems you saw on the last couple of pages?

Do we allow initials? That might mean we can allow periods. ←

First name This should be a required field.
Names should only have letters.

What about spaces? Those might be okay, too... ←

Last name This should be a required field.
Names should only have letters.

E-Mail This should be a required field.
We also need to make sure it's formatted like an e-mail.

Birthday This should be a required field.
This should be some sort of consistent format, like
MM-DD-YY, or something similar.

Years of Yoga This should be a required field.
This should be a number, and be less than the years the
person has been alive (calculated from their birthday).

Biography This should be a required field.
Maybe we need a length limit?

> I've decided not to require the years they've been practicing, their birthdate, or a bio. So if someone doesn't want to give that information, they can still sign up. But I've definitely got to have a good first name, last name, and e-mail address.

The owner of the page knows their requirements <u>better</u> than you do.

No matter how good of a programmer you are, you're not an expert in your <u>customer's</u> business. So you probably won't always make good assumptions about things like required fields, the types of data that can be entered, or the format of that data.

For Marcy's site, Marcy is the customer, and you're the programmer.

It's best to come up with some basic ideas about validation, and then confirm and expand those ideas by talking to whomever actually owns the site or business that the site represents.

there are no Dumb Questions

Q: Is this gonna be another one of those, "Not really Ajax" chapters?

A: Yes and no. We'll be spending most of the chapter working on validation, not asynchronous requests. But figuring out how to actually get accurate requirements and validating data for those requirements applies to all software development, not just Ajax apps.

The customer defines the requirements, not the programmer.

The best way to build a site your customer loves is to build the site the your customer actually wants. Don't make assumptions about functionality... instead, ASK the customer how they want things to work.

Validation should work from the web page <u>BACK</u> to the server

Validation is usually a multi-step process. Some things you can catch by using certain controls on your web page, like a select box instead of a text field. You can catch other things with your client-side JavaScript, like the format of an email field. And still other things might need to go to the server to get validated, like seeing if a username's already taken.

The most effective way to handle multi-layered validation like this is to always validate as much as you can on the web page. Then, move to JavaScript, and validate as much as you can there. Finally, involve the server.

enroll.js

Web Server

<u>Web</u> page

A web page can constrain data through specific controls, like length-limited text boxes and select boxes with only a few appropriate options.

Do as much as you can here to constrain data. Don't check for things in your JavaScript that you can restrict with form controls.

JavaScript

Your client-side JavaScript can check data formats, ensure data's entered into fields, and prevent submissions until a group of fields have data in them.

Try and never send the server data that's not formatted correctly. Let the server worry about business logic, not formatting.

Server

The server has access to the business data of your app. So it can check data consistency or perform other business logic that requires interaction with other data in the system.

The server should focus on the <u>correctness</u> of the data: based on existing data, is this new data correct and consistent?

Constraints ➡ Validity ➡ Consistency

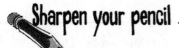

Sharpen your pencil

Below is the XHTML for Marcy's current version of the enrollment form. What changes would you make, based on the things you wrote down on page 412, along with Marcy's comments?

Go ahead and mark your changes directly on the XHTML.

```
<html>
<head>
 <title>Yoga for Programmers</title>
 <link rel="stylesheet" type="text/css" href="css/yoga-enroll.css" />
</head>
<body>
 <div id="background">
  <h1 id="logo">Yoga for Programmers</h1>
  <div id="content">
   <h2>Enroll</h2>
   <form action="process-enrollment.php" method="post">
    <fieldset><label for="firstname">First Name</label>
     <input name="firstname" id="firstname" type="text" /></fieldset>
    <fieldset><label for="lastname">Last Name</label>
     <input name="lastname" id="lastname" type="text" /></fieldset>
    <fieldset><label for="email">Email</label>
     <input name="email" id="email" type="text" /></fieldset>
    <fieldset><label for="birthday">Birthday</label>
     <input name="birthday" id="birthday" type="text" /></fieldset>
    <fieldset><label for="years">Years of Experience</label>
     <input name="years" id="years" type="text" /></fieldset>
    <fieldset><label for="bio">Biography</label>
     <textarea name="bio" id="bio"></textarea></fieldset>
    <fieldset class="nolabel">
     <input type="submit" id="enroll" value="Enroll" />
    </fieldset>
   </form>
  </div>
 </div>
</body>
</html>
```

Sharpen your pencil
Solution

Your job was to add constraints to the data Marcy collects from her customers by changing her XHTML. What did you come up with? Here's what we did.

```
<html>
<head>
 <title>Yoga for Programmers</title>
 <link rel="stylesheet" type="text/css" href="css/yoga-enroll.css" />
</head>
<body>
 <div id="background">
  <h1 id="logo">Yoga for Programmers</h1>
  <div id="content">
   <h2>Enroll</h2>
   <form action="process-enrollment.php" method="post">
    <fieldset><label for="firstname">First Name</label>
     <input name="firstname" id="firstname" type="text" /></fieldset>
    <fieldset><label for="lastname">Last Name</label>
     <input name="lastname" id="lastname" type="text" /></fieldset>
    <fieldset><label for="email">Email</label>
     <input name="email" id="email" type="text" /></fieldset>
    <fieldset><label for="birthday">Birthday</label>
     <input name="birthday" id="birthday" type="text" />
     <select name="month" id="month">
         <option value="">--</option>
         <option value="january">January</option>
         <option value="february">February</option>
         <!-- ... etc... -->
       </select>
      <select name="day" id="day">
        <option value="">--</option>
        <option value="1">1</option>
        <option value="2">2</option>
        <option value="3">3</option>
        <!-- ... etc... -->
```

There are a fixed number of values for birthday, so let's not use a text box, which allows bad entries.

Instead, we can use a select box for the month, and list the 12 possible month values...

...and another select for the day of the month, with all the possible day values.

Marcy told us she didn't want a birth year, so we didn't need to worry about that.

```
    </select>
    </fieldset>
    <fieldset><label for="years">Years of Experience</label>
     <input name="years" id="years" type="text" />
        <select name="years" id="years">
          <option value="">--</option>
          <option>none</option>
          <option>less than 1</option>
          <option>1-2</option>
          <option>3-5</option>
          <option>more than 5</option>
        </select>
    </fieldset>
    <fieldset><label for="bio">Biography</label>
     <textarea name="bio" id="bio"></textarea></fieldset>
    <fieldset class="nolabel">
     <input type="submit" id="enroll" value="Enroll" disabled="disabled" />
    </fieldset>
   </form>
  </div>
 </div>
</body>
</html>
```

We can group the years of experience into useful ranges, and simplify things here, too.

We're going to need some JavaScript validation, so let's disable the Enroll button... we know people can't enroll without filling out some fields, so this protects the form from being submitted too soon.

TEST DRIVE

See how many errors we can catch now...

Download or type in `signup.html`, and make the changes from page 416 and 417. Then load the page up in your browser. We've already knocked out a few of the problems Marcy was having:

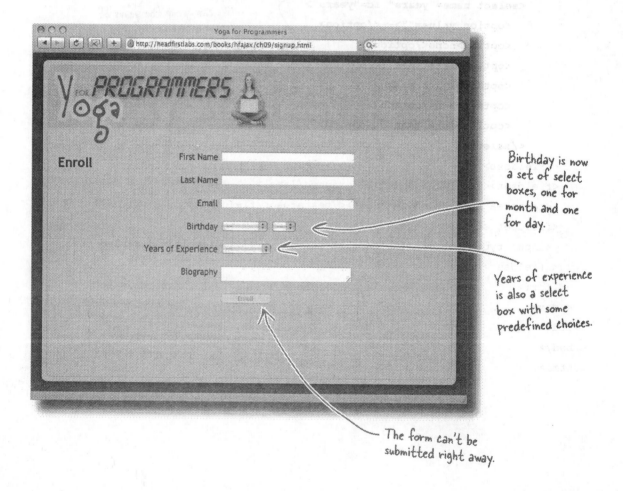

Birthday is now a set of select boxes, one for month and one for day.

Years of experience is also a select box with some predefined choices.

The form can't be submitted right away.

there are no
Dumb Questions

Q: Are you kidding? This isn't even JavaScript... it's just HTML. What gives?

A: It can definitely be a little boring to dig into XHTML if you'd rather be writing JavaScript and asynchronous requests. Then again, your coding gets a lot easier if you've got a good web page doing its job.

Q: So I should use select boxes whenever possible?

A: When it comes to data entry, that's a good principle. The more invalid or poorly formatted data that comes to your JavaScript, the more work your JavaScript has to do.

Q: What's the big deal with doing all of this in my JavaScript, and not messing with the XHTML web page?

A: Impatient customers are the big deal. It's often easy for you to code validation in your scripts, but customers don't like error messages. If you can make sure they enter data by using good controls, customers are less likely to need error messages from your validation code. That makes for a happier user experience, and that's always a good thing.

Q: Why did you disable the Enroll button in the HTML? Haven't we usually been doing that in an initPage() function, and calling initPage() from window.onload?

A: In earlier chapters, we've used initPage() to disable buttons, yes. You can certainly do the same thing here, or you can set the button to disabled in the XHTML. There's not a big difference in either approach, really.

One slight advantage to disabling the Enroll button in your XHTML, though, is that the XHTML now really does represent the initial state of the page. In other words, initPage() doesn't change the form as soon as it loads. That makes the XHTML a more accurate representation of the form at load-time. Still, it's not a big deal if you'd rather disable the button in an initPage() function.

Nobody enjoys an error message that says, "Hey, you screwed that up. Try again."

You can validate the **FORMAT** of data, and you can validate the **CONTENT** of data

We've been using the term validation pretty loosely. At the user's browser, we might make sure that the user enters their first name and birthday. That's one form of validation. At the server, we might make sure that the user's username isn't already taken. That's another form of validation.

In the first case, you're validating a data *format*. You might make sure that a username is at least six characters long, or that there's a value for the first name field, or that an email address has an @ sign and a `.com` or `.org` in it. When you're validating a data format, you're usually working with client-side code.

Validate the _format_ of user data with JavaScript.
By using client-side code to validate data formats, you can let users know of problems quickly, without waiting on a server response.

Sometimes you've got to do more than just see how many characters a string is, or make sure an entry is really a month of the year. You may need to check data against your database to prevent duplicate entries, or run a computation that involves other programs on your network.

In those cases, you're validating the content of user data. And that's not something you can usually do at the client. You'll need to send the data to your server, and let programs on the server check out the data for validity.

Validate the _content_ of user data on the server.
You'll need your app's business logic to see if the content of user data is acceptable. Use server-side programs to let users know of problems with what they've entered.

Well-designed applications validate both the FORMAT and the CONTENT of user data.

You need BOTH types of validation to keep bad data out of your apps and databases.

We need to validate the <u>FORMAT</u> of the data from Marcy's enrollment page

Let's take another look at what we need to do to validate Marcy's page. For each field, we're actually just validating the format of the data. That means we should be able to do pretty much everything we need using JavaScript:

Here's our list of validation requirements.

First name   This should be a required field................................
               Names should only have letters.................................

Last name   This should be a required field................................
              Names should only have letters.................................

E-Mail   This should be a required field.................................
           We also need to make sure it's.................................
             formatted like an e-mail.................................

Birthday   ~~This should be a required field.~~................................
         ~~This should be some sort of consistent format.~~................

We've got birthday in a consistent format by using XHTML select boxes.

Years of Yoga   ~~This should be a required field.~~
            ~~This should be a number.~~................

This isn't a number, but it's in a format we control via select boxes.

Biography   ~~This should be a required field.~~
          Maybe we need a length limit?................................

Marcy said we don't need to require a birthday, bio, or the years they've been practicing yoga.

Exercise

We can use JavaScript to validate the format of all of these fields, but what *exactly* would you do next?

....
....
....

> So I've been looking through these validation requirements, and I don't think this should be too hard. We just need to build a bunch of event handlers, one for each field on the page.

Frank

Jim

Joe

Joe: Like `checkFirstname()` and `checkLastname()`, right?.

Jim: Right. Then we just register each event handler to the right field, and boom, we're good to go.

Joe: Perfect. So let's—

Frank: Hang on a second, guys. I'm not sure that's such a good idea. Aren't we doing the same checks on several different fields?

Jim: You mean like making sure a field has a non-empty value? Yeah, that's... ummm... first name, last name, and email.

Frank: Right. But aren't we going to be repeating code in each one of those event handlers if we're doing the same checks for different fields?

Joe: You know, he's right. So maybe we need to have utility functions, like `fieldIsFilled()`, and we can call those from each event handler. So `checkFirstname()` and `checkLastname()` could just call `fieldIsFilled()` to see if those fields are empty.

Jim: Oh, that is better. So come one, let's get—

Frank: Wait a second. I still think we can do better. Why do we even need a `checkFirstname()` function?

Jim: Well, duh, that's got to call all the utility functions.

Joe: Hey, hang on, I think I see what Frank's getting at. What if we built the utilities to take in a field, and do their check?

Jim: But you'd still need something to call all the checks for each field. Like I said, `checkFirstname()`, or whatever...

Joe: But can't you assign multiple handlers to a single field?

Frank: That's it! So you could just assign each validation function to the field it applies to. Like this...

Don't Repeat Yourself: DRY

One of the core principles in software design is called DRY: don't repeat yourself. In other words, if you write a piece of code once, in one place, try to avoid writing that piece of code again in some other place.

When it comes to validation, that means we shouldn't write code that checks to see if a field is empty in two (or more!) places. Let's write one utility function, and then use that function over and over again:

This function is generic. It can be applied as an event handler to any field.

```
function fieldIsFilled() {

   if (this.value == "") {

      // Display an error message

   } else {

      // No problems; we're good to go

   }

}
```

Check to see if the field has no value...

...and then display an error or let the user continue.

Now you can assign this handler to several fields, for instance in an `initPage()` function:

```
document.getElementById("firstname").onblur = fieldIsFilled;

document.getElementById("lastname").onblur = fieldIsFilled;

document.getElementById("email").onblur = fieldIsFilled;
```

Because fieldIsFilled() isn't tied to a particular field, it can be used as a handler for multiple fields.

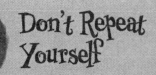

Don't Repeat Yourself

If the same code exists in two places, it's easy to change one bit of code and forget to change the other. By only writing code once, your app will be easier to maintain, as well as more modular. Don't repeat yourself!

Exercise

There's a pretty big problem with fieldIsFilled(). Can you figure out what it is, and fix it?

Hint: You might need another JavaScript file to correct the problems with fieldIsFilled().

This looks good, Jim, but I think there might be problems down the line, especially when you start assigning multiple handlers like this to the same object on a page.

Jim: What do you mean? I tried it out, everything works great.

Frank: But you're only assigning a single event handler to each field, right?

Jim: Right. And we've got our utility function, `addEventHandler()`, ready for when we need to add more handlers. So I'm all ready to handle multiple browsers and that whole `addEventListener`/ `attachEvent` thing.

Frank: But you're using `this` in `fieldIsFilled()`...

Jim: Sure. What's the big... oh. Once we use `addEventHandler()`—

Frank: —`this` stops working. That's the problem.

EXERCISE SOLUTION

Did you find the problem in fieldIsFilled()? If you assign multiple handlers to a field, you'll need to use addEventHandler()... and as soon as you use that function, the "this" keyword no longer works in your handlers. Here's how we fixed the problem.

We'll get an event object when our utility function, addEventHandler(), is used.

```
function fieldIsFilled(e) {
    var me = getActivatedObject(e);
    if (me.value == "") {
        // Display an error message
    } else {
        // No problems; we're good to go
    }
}
```

We need to get the activated object since "this" isn't reliable with multiple handlers registered to the same field.

This code will require utils.js, which is where we have getActivatedObject() and addEventHandler() coded.

there are no
Dumb Questions

Q: Why do we need to use multiple event handlers again?

A: Because we're building a handler for each type of validation function, like checking to see if a field's value is empty or if a value is in an email format.

So for a single field, there might be several of those utility functions that should be assigned. For example, the firstname field shouldn't be empty, but it also should only contain alphabetic characters.

Q: So since we're using more than one event handler, we can't use this?

A: Indirectly, yes. Beceause we need multiple event handlers on some fields, we'll need to use the addEventHandler() utility method we wrote in utils.js earlier. And since we're using that approach to register handlers, we can't use this in those handlers.

Q: Wouldn't it be easier to use a shell function for each field, like checkFirstname(), and then call each individual validation function from that?

A: Not really. Switching from this to getActivatedObject() isn't a big deal (especially if you've got a set of helper functions, like we do in utils.js). Besides, we'd need even more functions. In addition to the validation functions, we'd need a wrapper for each field that just connected the field to all of its handlers.

Q: I don't think I got that DRY thing. Can you explain that again?

A: Sure. DRY stands for "Don't Repeat Yourself." DRY is a pretty well-known software design principle. DRY just means that you want a single piece of code appearing in one single place. So if you're checking a field for an empty value, you should have that code in one place, and other pieces of code that need that functionality then call that single bit of code.

If you follow DRY, you never have to change one piece of code in *more* than one place in your scripts. That means your code ends up being easier to change, maintain, and debug.

You can check out *Head First Object-Oriented Analysis and Design* for a lot more on DRY and other design principles.

Q: And how does DRY fit into Marcy's Yoga app?

A: Well, each of our validation functions is a single bit of code, in a single function. If we put that code into individual handlers, we might have duplicate code. So checkFirstname() might have code that checks for an empty field, but checkLastname() might have the same code. If you found a better way to do that bit of functionality, you'd have to make a change in two places—and that violates DRY.

Q: So you never repeat code, no matter what?

A: Every once in a while you'll have to violate DRY, but it's pretty rare. As a general rule, if you work really hard to follow DRY, you'll have better designed code. If you've tried but can't manage it, then don't worry too much. The point is to *try your best* to not repeat code, as that makes you design and write better code in the long run.

Code that doesn't repeat itself is easier to change, maintain, and debug.

Always try and write DRY code!

Let's build some more event handlers

`fieldIsFilled()` was pretty simple. Let's go ahead and write code
for the other event handlers we'll need. We can build each just like
`fieldIsFilled()`: using `getActivatedObject()`, we can figure
out the activated object, and then validate the format of the field.

```
function fieldIsFilled(e) {
  var me = getActivatedObject(e);
  if (me.value == "") {
    // Display an error message
  } else {
    // No problems; we're good to go
  }
}

function emailIsProper(e) {
  var me = getActivatedObject(e);
  if (!/^[\w.-_\+]+@[\w-]+(\.\w{2,4})+$/.test(me.value)) {
    // Display an error message
  } else {
    // No problems; we're good to go
  }
}
```

*This handler checks an email format to make
sure it's name@domain.com (or .org, .gov, etc.)*

*This is the regular expression
for checking email formats from
Head First JavaScript.*

*We'll work out what code we
need for when there are errors
and when there aren't any
problems in just a little bit. For
now, we can use these comments.*

This handler checks a field to see if it only contains letters: from a–z, case-insensitive.

```
function fieldIsLetters(e) {
  var me = getActivatedObject(e);
  var nonAlphaChars = /[^a-zA-Z]/;
  if (nonAlphaChars.test(me.value)) {
    // Display an error message
  } else {
    // No problems; we're good to go
  }
}

function fieldIsNumbers(e) {
  var me = getActivatedObject(e);
  var nonNumericChars = /[^0-9]/;
  if (nonNumericChars.test(me.value)) {
    // Display an error message
  } else {
    // No problems; we're good to go
  }
}
```

Here's another regular expression. It represents all characters that are NOT between a to z, or A to Z. So all non-alphabetic characters.

If any of these non-alphabetic characters are in the field's value, the value isn't all letters.

fieldIsNumbers() ensures a field has only numeric values in its value.

This expression grabs all characters NOT (using the ^ symbol) in the numbers 0 through 9.

For a lot more on regular expressions, check out Head First JavaScript

Sharpen your pencil

Now that you've got event handlers, can you write initPage() for Marcy's app? Create a new script and save it as enroll.js. Add the event handlers above and your version of initPage(). Then reference enroll.js and utils.js in Marcy's XHTML.

Try and load the enrollment page. Does it validate your entries?

Sharpen your pencil
Solution

Your job was to build an initPage() function for Marcy's yoga page, and use the handlers on the last two pages to validate user entry.

```
window.onload = initPage;

function initPage() {
    addEventHandler(document.getElementById("firstname"), "blur", fieldIsFilled);
    addEventHandler(document.getElementById("firstname"), "blur", fieldIsLetters);
    addEventHandler(document.getElementById("lastname"), "blur", fieldIsFilled);
    addEventHandler(document.getElementById("lastname"), "blur", fieldIsLetters);
    addEventHandler(document.getElementById("email"), "blur", fieldIsFilled);
    addEventHandler(document.getElementById("email"), "blur", emailIsProper);
}
```

We get each field...

...we want to validate when users move out of the field...

...and finally, we assign the handler for the field.

Several fields have multiple handlers assigned.

> You said to test these, but how? Right now, we just have comments for when there's a problem... should we put in alert() statements to let the user know when there's a problem?

An alert() stops <u>EVERYTHING</u>... and users don't like to stop.

Using an `alert()` is pretty heavy-handed. That little popup brings everything on the page to a crashing halt. Earlier, we used some icons to let the user know what's going on. But there was a problem with that approach, especially if you try and apply it to what we're doing with Marcy's page.

Why doesn't a simple approved or denied icon work for Marcy's page? What would you do differently?

> I think we need to tell users what the problem is with their entries. There's a big difference between not entering anything into a field, and not using the right format, like for an email. A big red "X" doesn't help much in figuring out what's wrong.

Jim: That makes sense. So for each error, we can just display a message related to that error. Like, "Please enter a first name" or "E-mails should be in the format name@domain.com".

Frank: Yeah. That seems a lot more user-friendly.

Joe: But that won't be so easy—.

Frank: Right, you see it, don't you?

Jim: What?

Joe: Well, we moved to generic handler functions. Those functions don't know about which field they're testing, so they won't know what error message to display.

Frank: Yeah. We need some way to have a set of error messages associated with each field. And then figure out a way to look up the right error message.

Joe: What about the activated object? We've got that in our handlers, so what if we use the object to look up an error message?

Jim: Hey, I've got an idea. Can we just have some sort of name/value thing, where there's a name of a field, and the value for that field is an error message?

Frank: I like that... I think that would work. So we lookup the error based on the name of the field, which we've got from the activated object.

Joe: But aren't there multiple problems that can occur for each field? We need more than one error message per field.

Frank: Hmmm. So we need a key for each field, and then a set of errors and corresponding messages for that. Right?

Jim: How the heck do we do that in JavaScript?

RETURN of SON of JavaScript

In the last chapter, server-side programs used JSON to represent complex object structures. But JSON isn't just for the server-side! Anytime you need to represent name-to-value mappings, JSON is a great solution:

This is the variable name
for this object.

The value for itemDetails.
id is "itemShades."

```
itemDetails = {
    "id" : "itemShades",
    "description" : "Yoko Ono's sunglasses. ...",
    "price" : 258.99,
    "urls" : ["http://www.beatles.com/",
              "http://www.johnlennon.com/",
              "http://www.yoko-ono.com/"]
}
```

The value for itemDetails.
urls is an array of values.

The value of a property can be another JavaScript object

You've already seen properties have string values, integer values, and array values. But a property can also have *another* object as its value, again represented in JSON:

```
itemDetails = {
    "id" : "itemShades",
    "description" : "Yoko Ono's sunglasses. ...",
    "price" : 258.99,
    "urls" : {
        "band-url": "http://www.beatles.com/",
        "singer-url": "http://www.johnlennon.com/",
        "owner-url": "http://www.yoko-ono.com/"
    }
}
```

This time, the value of the
urls property is another
JSON-represented object.

itemDetails.urls.band-url

itemDetails.urls.singer-url

itemDetails.urls.owner-url

Curly braces signal
another object value.

You can just "tack on"
another dot operator to
get to these nested values.

JSON Magnets

Can you use all the magnets below to build a set of mappings?
You should have each field represented, and for each field, a set of
mappings from a specific type of error to a message for that error.

```
var _____ = {
    "_____" : {
        "_____" : "_____",
        "_____" : "_____"
    },
    "_____" : {
        "_____" : "_____",
        "_____" : "_____"
    },
    "_____" : {
        "_____" : "_____",
        "_____" : "_____"
    }
}
```

required

Only letters are allowed in a first name.

firstname

lastname

letters

Please enter in your e-mail address.

Please enter in your first name.

letters

email

Please enter your e-mail in the form 'name@domain.com'.

required

Only letters are allowed in a last name.

required

Please enter in your last name.

format

warnings

JSON Magnet Solutions

Can you use all the magnets below to build a set of mappings?
You should have each field represented, and for each field, a set of
mappings from a specific type of error to a message for that error.

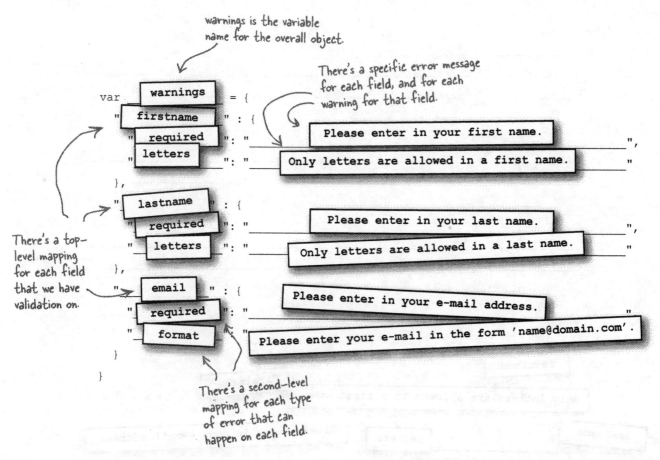

warnings is the variable
name for the overall object.

There's a specific error message
for each field, and for each
warning for that field.

```
var  warnings  = {
  " firstname " : {
    " required " : " Please enter in your first name. ",
    " letters " : " Only letters are allowed in a first name. "
  },
  " lastname " : {
    " required " : " Please enter in your last name. ",
    " letters " : " Only letters are allowed in a last name. "
  },
  " email " : {
    " required " : " Please enter in your e-mail address. ",
    " format " : " Please enter your e-mail in the form 'name@domain.com'. "
  }
}
```

There's a top-
level mapping
for each field
that we have
validation on.

There's a second-level
mapping for each type
of error that can
happen on each field.

Let's warn Marcy's customers when there's a problem with their entry

With a warnings object full of useful messages, we can add warnings to Marcy's page. Here's what we've got in each event handler validation function:

1 The field, via an activated object, that we need to validate.

2 A specific type of problem that occurred (for example, we know whether a field was empty or invalidly formatted).

Based on that information, here's what we need to do in our warning:

1 Figure out the parent node of the field that there's a problem with.

2 Create a new <p> and add it as a child of that field's parent node.

3 Look up the right warning, and add that warning as text to the new <p>, which will cause the browser to display the warning on the form..

Here's a warn() function that handles this for Marcy's form:

In our handler functions, we can pass in the field and type of problem.

This evaluates the string that matches the field and warning type.

```
function warn(field, warningType) {
  var parentNode = field.parentNode;
  var warning = eval('warnings.' + field.id + '.' + warningType);
  if (parentNode.getElementsByTagName("p").length == 0) {
    var p = document.createElement("p");
    field.parentNode.appendChild(p);
    var warningNode = document.createTextNode(warning);
    p.appendChild(warningNode);
  } else {
    var p = parentNode.getElementsByTagName("p")[0];
    p.childNodes[0].nodeValue = warning;
  }
  document.getElementById("submit").disabled = true;
}
```

This check is to see if there's already a <p> that we can add the warning to.

If not, create a new <p> and text node with the right warning.

This "else" is for when there's already a <p> to add the warning to.

If there's a problem, make sure the "Enroll" button can't be clicked.

Exercise

We've done a lot over the last few pages, and before you test everything out, there are several steps you need to make sure you've taken. Here's what you need to do:

☐ Add the warnings variable from page 432 into your enroll.js script. You can put the variable anywhere outside of your functions, at the same "level" as your window.onload event handler assignment.

☐ Add the warn() function from page 433 into enroll.js, as well.

☐ Update each of your validation functions, like fieldIsFilled() and fieldIsLetters(), to call warn() when there's a problem. You should pass the warn() function the activated object, and a string, like "required" or "format." You can figure out which strings to use for the warning type by looking at the values in the warnings variable on page 432.

there are no Dumb Questions

Q: How does warn() know what field it's adding a warning message to?

A: Each validation function knows what field it's validating, because of getActivatedObject(). So when the handler function calls warn(), that function passes the activated object on to warn().

Q: And what about the warning type? Where does that come from?

A: The warning type is specific to the event handler function. fieldIsFilled() would have a warning type of "required," because that's what that function is essentially checking for: to see if a required field has a value.

Each handler should pass on a warning type that matches one of the pre-defined values from the warnings variable, like "required" or "letters" or "format."

Q: What's all that parentNode stuff?

A: We want to add the warning just *under* the actual input box. If we get the parent of the input box (the field), then we can add another child of that same node with the warning. The result is that the warning message becomes a sibling of the input field itself... and displays right under the field.

Q: And the warning message is from the warnings variable?

A: Exactly. We put that message in a <p>, as a child of the field's parent node.

Q: What's going on with that eval() line? That's a little confusing to me...

A: First, look at what's being evaluated: 'warnings.' + field + '.' + warningType. That might come out to 'warnings.firstname.required' or warnings.email.format'. Each of those maps to an error message, which is what we want.

So to evaluate the expression 'warnings.firstname.required', we run eval() on that expression. The result is the matching error message, which we can then show on the enrollment form.

TEST DRIVE

It's time for more error counting.

Make sure you've done everything on the checklist on page 434, and then reload Marcy's enrollment page. Try out several "bad" combinations of data: skip entering a value for a few fields, enter in a bad email address, try numbers in the name fields. What happpens?

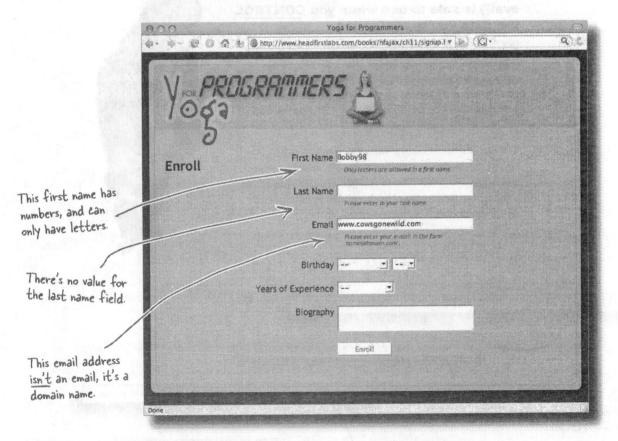

This first name has numbers, and can only have letters.

There's no value for the last name field.

This email address isn't an email, it's a domain name.

BRAIN POWER

How can we figure out when all fields are valid, and it's safe to allow users to click "Enroll"?

Wait a second... we spent all that time last chapter talking about how dangerous eval() is. And now we're using it again? Haven't you been paying attention?

eval() is safe to use when you <u>CONTROL</u> the data you're evaluating.

In Chapter 10, we were evaluating data from a server-side program. We didn't write that program, and weren't even able to look at the source code. That makes that code unsafe to evaluate. We just weren't sure that the code would be valid JSON, and would be safe to run on a user's browser.

But with the warnings variable, we *created* the code we're evaluating. So there's no danger. In fact, we can test things out, and if there is a problem, we just make a change to warnings. So it's perfectly safe to run eval() on code you're in control of.

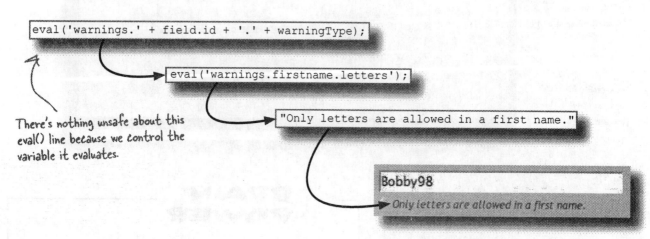

```
eval('warnings.' + field.id + '.' + warningType);
```

```
eval('warnings.firstname.letters');
```

```
"Only letters are allowed in a first name."
```

Bobby98
> Only letters are allowed in a first name.

There's nothing unsafe about this eval() line because we control the variable it evaluates.

If you don't warn(), you have to unwarn()

There's one big problem with Marcy's enrollment page: how do we get rid of those error messages when there's *not* a problem? Here's what our error handlers look like right now:

```
function fieldIsFilled(e) {
  var me = getActivatedObject(e);
  if (me.value == "") {
    // Display an error message
    warn(me, "required");
  } else {
    // No problems; we're good to go
  }
}
```

The warn() function takes care of displaying errors on the form.

```
Bobby98
Only letters are allowed in a first name.
```

If there's not a problem, we need to remove any error messages.

IF there's a warning, get rid of it

Let's build an unwarn() function. The first part is pretty simple: for the field that's passed in, we just need to see if there's a warning. If so, we can get rid of the warning. If there's not a warning, we don't need to do anything:

```
function unwarn(field, warningType) {
  if (field.parentNode.getElementsByTagName("p").length > 0) {
    var p = field.parentNode.getElementsByTagName("p")[0];
    var currentWarning = p.childNodes[0].nodeValue;
    var warning = eval('warnings.' + field.id + '.' + warningType);
    if (currentWarning == warning) {
      field.parentNode.removeChild(p);
    }
  }
}
```

We only need to remove a warning if there's at least one <p> with a warning already in place.

Figure out which warning type we're unwarning for.

We only remove a warning if it matches the warningType passed in to unwarn().

If the warning types match, remove the warning.

Exercise

unwarn() isn't complete yet. The function still needs to figure out if the Enroll button should be enabled or disabled. Can you write code that figures out if there are any warnings being displayed? If so, Enroll should be disabled; otherwise, users can click Enroll to submit the form.

Hint: if you need a refresher, the XHTML for the enrollment page is on page 416.

Exercise Solution

unwarn() isn't complete yet. The function still need to figure out if the Enroll button should be enabled or disabled. Your job was to write code that figures out if there are any warnings being displayed? If so, Enroll should be disabled; otherwise, users can click Enroll to submit the form.

```javascript
function unwarn(field, warningType) {
  if (field.parentNode.getElementsByTagName("p").length > 0) {
    var p = field.parentNode.getElementsByTagName("p")[0];
    var currentWarning = p.childNodes[0].nodeValue;
    var warning = eval('warnings.' + field.id + '.' + warningType);
    if (currentWarning == warning) {
      field.parentNode.removeChild(p);
    }
  }
  var fieldsets =
    document.getElementById("content").getElementsByTagName("fieldset");
  for (var i=0; i<fieldsets.length; i++) {
    var fieldWarnings = fieldsets[i].getElementsByTagName("p").length;
    if (fieldWarnings > 0) {
      document.getElementById("enroll").disabled = true;
      return;
    }
  }
  document.getElementById("enroll").disabled = false;
}
```

All the <p> warnings are children of <fieldset> elements, so let's get all those <fieldset>'s.

For each <fieldset>, we can see if there are any <p> child elements.

If there are any warnings, disable Enroll and return.

This is equivalent to seeing if there are any warnings since each warning is in a <p>.

If there aren't any warnings, the form is okay... enable Enroll.

Test Drive

Turn warnings on AND off.

Time to take the enrollment form for another test drive. In each of your validation handlers, add a line that calls `unwarn(me);` if there's not a validation problem. Looking pretty good, right?

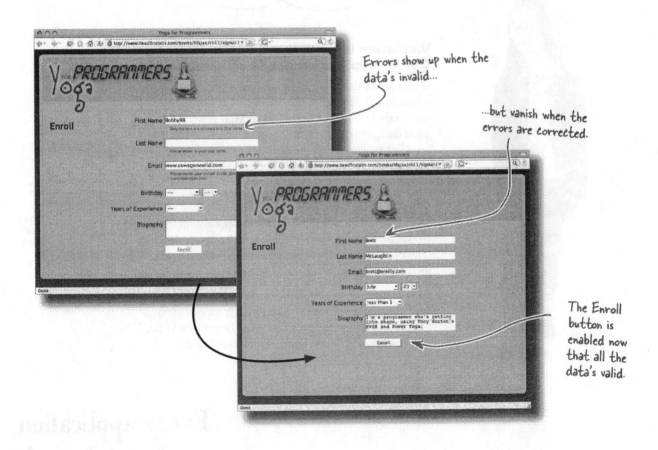

Errors show up when the data's invalid...

...but vanish when the errors are corrected.

The Enroll button is enabled now that all the data's valid.

> Are you kidding me? All this for a little validation on the client-side? This is a little ridiculous, isn't it? Besides, where the heck is the Ajax?

Validation is hard, thankless work... and <u>EVERY</u> application needs validation.

Getting data right on a form is often boring, and takes a long time to get right. But, validation is incredibly important to most customers. Take Marcy: without good data, she can't enroll people in classes, she can't send out mailings, and she can't get new business.

Multiply that by all the web apps that you're getting paid to develop, and validation becomes critical. And while Marcy's enrollment form isn't making asynchronous requests, it's still a web application that's typical of the things you'll have to work on as a web developer. Not many programmers can make a living *only* working on asynchronous requests.

So take the time to get validation on your pages right. Your customers will love you and their businesses will flourish... and that means more work, better paychecks, and less middle-of-the-night, "It's broken!" calls.

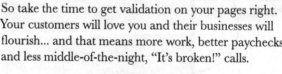

Every application needs validation!

Sharpen your pencil

Below is Marcy's database and the problems we found way back on page 410. Next to each problem, make a note about whether your changes to the enrollment form have fixed that problem yet.

firstname	lastname	email	bday	yrs	bio
Susan	Smith	ss@myjob.com	1 January	0	I'm a systems analyst
Bob	Brown		August 300	5	
Susan	Smith	ss@myjob.com	1 January	0	I'm a systems analyst
F0b#2938					View my porn for free!!!! 192.72.90.234
Jones	Jane	www.myjob.com			
Gerry	MacGregor	mac@myjob	March 23, 1972	99	
Mary		mw@myjob.com			I've been doing yoga for 12 years
Bill	Bainfield	bb@myjob.com	5-27-69		

1. Susan Smith is registered twice. ....

2. Bob Brown didn't give his email address. ....

3. The F0b#2938 entry is spam, not a real client. ....

4. Jane Jones entered in a website URL, not an email address. ....

5. Gerry MacGregor's email isn't valid... he probably left off .com or .org. ....

6. Gerry MacGregor couldn't have been practicing yoga for 99 years. ....

7. Mary didn't enter in a last name. ....

8. Everyone's using a different format for their birthday. ....

9. There's information missing for Jane Jones, Bob Brown, and Bill Bainfield. ....

10. ....

Sharpen your pencil
Solution

We've added a lot of validation... but what problems have we really solved? Your job was to figure out what problems our validation is preventing.

firstname	lastname	email	bday	yrs	bio
Susan	Smith	ss@myjob.com	1 January	0	I'm a systems analyst
Bob	Brown		August 300	5	
Susan	Smith	ss@myjob.com	1 January	0	I'm a systems analyst
F0b#2938					View my porn for free!!!! 192.72.90.234
Jones	Jane	www.myjob.com			
Gerry	MacGregor	mac@myjob	March 23, 1972	99	
Mary		mw@myjob.com			I've been doing yoga for 12 years
Bill	Bainfield	bb@myjob.com	5-27-69		

We don't have anything to handle this yet.

1. Susan Smith is registered twice.......................................

2. Bob Brown didn't give his email address............................ *Required fields are handled now.*

3. The F0b#2938 entry is spam, not a real client.

4. Jane Jones entered in a website URL, not an email address...... *Our formatting requirements for names and emails take care of this.*

5. Gerry MacGregor's email isn't valid... he probably left off .com or .org.

6. Gerry MacGregor couldn't have been practicing yoga for 99 years......

7. Mary didn't enter in a last name.....................................

8. Everyone's using a different format for their birthday................ *The XHTML changes to the page keep these from occurring.*

9. There's information missing for Jane Jones, Bob Brown, and Bill Bainfield...............

10. ....

Between Marcy's updated requirements and our validation, this is no longer a problem.

Duplicate data is a <u>SERVER</u> problem

The only problem we've got left is when someone enters in their information twice, like Susan Smith on the last page. But it's going to take a server-side program to handle that sort of problem... the server would need to take an entry, and compare it with existing entries in Marcy's customer database.

Web Page   **Web Server**   **Database**

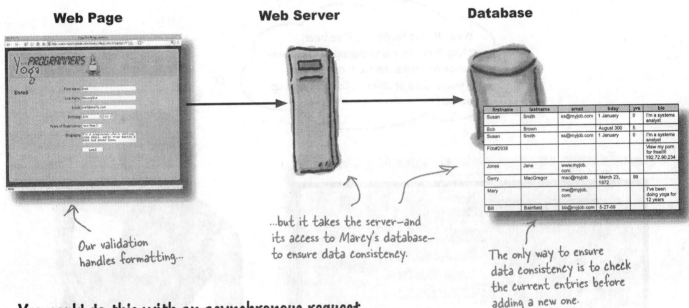

Our validation handles formatting...

...but it takes the server—and its access to Marcy's database—to ensure data consistency.

The only way to ensure data consistency is to check the current entries before adding a new one.

You <u>could</u> do this with an asynchronous request...

Suppose we build a server-side program to take a user's information, and check Marcy's customer database to see if that user already existed. We could request that program using an asynchronous request in our JavaScript. Then, once the server returned a response, we could let the user know that their data's been accepted.

...but what's the benefit?

The only problem is that there's nothinig for the user to do while they're waiting. We're probably using at least their first name, last name, and email to check against the database, so at most, a user could keep entering in their birthdate and bio. But even those aren't required fields...

It's really better to let the server check the user's information when the user tries to enroll, and issue an error then. Since duplicate users aren't a huge problem right now, you're better off saving a ton of extra code, and simply letting the server handle reporting a problem to the user.

Sometimes, it's best to let the server handle problems synchronously.

Not every web app needs asynchronous requests and responses!

So we're done now, right?

That's right. We've handled all of Marcy's validation problems, and she's going to have her server-side guys take a look at preventing duplicate data. In fact, let's see how Marcy likes her new enrollment page...

> Wow, this is fantastic. I've been getting twice as many signups every week since going online, and I'm not getting any weird data problems. Care to sign up yourself?

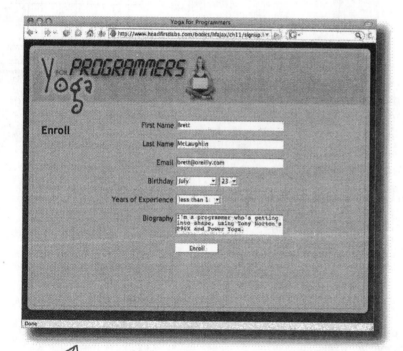

Another web programming success story to add to your portfolio.

12 post requests

Paranoia: It's your friend

Someone's watching you. Right now. Seriously.

Freedom of Information Act? Isn't that called the Internet? These days, anything a user types into a form or clicks on a web page is subject to **inspection**. Whether it's a network admin, a software company trying to learn about your trends, or a malicious hacker or spammer, your *information isn't safe unless you make it safe*. When it comes to web pages, you've got to **protect your users' data** when they click Submit.

There's a villain in the movies

Just when we thought that we'd solved all of the web world's problems, it looks like one of our earlier customers is back... and he's not happy.

> I've got issues. I'm starting to get customer complaints... they're all getting spammed, and they think it's because they registered for my movie review site. This is your code... you better fix it!

Your code... your problem!

Mike, of Mike's Movies fame, has another problem. It doesn't seem like his customers getting spammed is really related to the registration form we built for Mike, but since we built that form, he's blaming us. Welcome to web development.

So what do you think is going on? Is it possible that spammers are getting Mike's customer email addresses because of something we did—or didn't do—on the enrollment form?

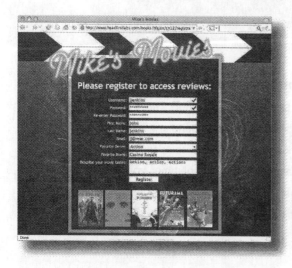

Remember Mike? We built his movie review registration page.

Sharpen your pencil

What's going on with Mike's registration page? Do we have anything to do with his customers getting spammed?

Below is Mike's page and server. Your job is to draw all the interactions between them. Be sure to include what's passing between the web page and the server.

Don't worry about the specifics of any particular user. Just write what fields and data is being sent back and forth.

Registration page

Web server

Do you think we have anything to do with the problems that Mike's customers are complaining about?

....

....

....

Sharpen your pencil
Solution

Your job was to draw all the interactions between Mike's page and server. Be sure to include what's passing between the web page and the server. Here's what we came up with.

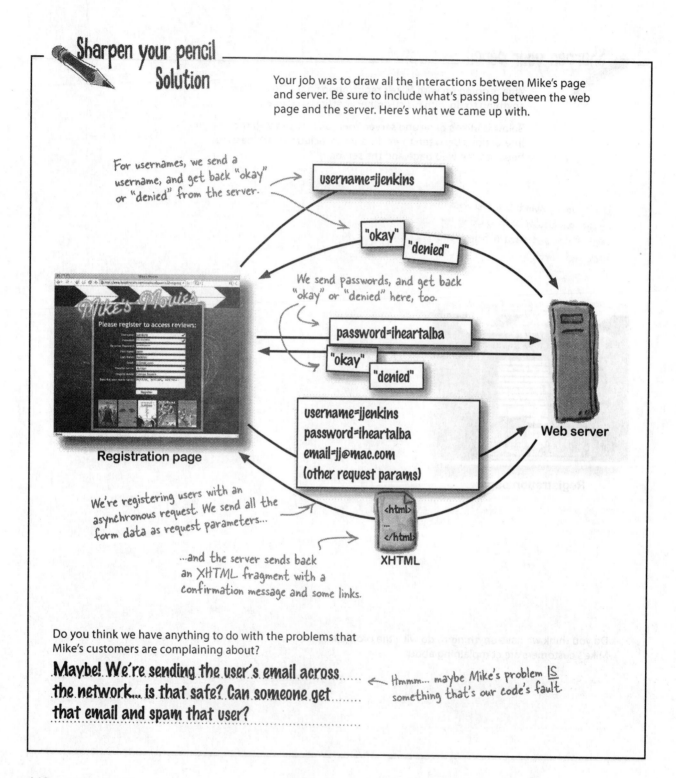

For usernames, we send a username, and get back "okay" or "denied" from the server.

username=jjenkins

"okay" "denied"

We send passwords, and get back "okay" or "denied" here, too.

password=iheartalba

"okay" "denied"

Registration page

username=jjenkins
password=iheartalba
email=jj@mac.com
(other request params)

Web server

We're registering users with an asynchronous request. We send all the form data as request parameters...

<html>
...
</html>

XHTML

...and the server sends back an XHTML fragment with a confirmation message and some links.

Do you think we have anything to do with the problems that Mike's customers are complaining about?

Maybe! We're sending the user's email across the network... is that safe? Can someone get that email and spam that user?

← Hmmm... maybe Mike's problem IS something that's our code's fault.

GET requests send request parameters across the network as clear text

We're using a GET request to send all of a user's information to the server:

registerUser() sends a user's information using an asynchronous request.

```
function registerUser() {
  t = setInterval("scrollImages()", 50);
  document.getElementById("register").value = "Processing...";
  registerRequest = createRequest();
  if (registerRequest == null) {
    alert("Unable to create request.");
  } else {
    var url = "register.php?username=" +
      escape(document.getElementById("username").value) + "&password=" +
      other request parameters...;
    registerRequest.onreadystatechange = registrationProcessed;
    registerRequest.open("GET", url, true);
    registerRequest.send(null);
  }
}
```

Here's where we tell the request object to use a GET method for sending the request.

Clear text is text... in the clear!

When parameters are sent using a GET request, those parameters are just text moving across the network. And that text is sent *in the clear*. In other words, anyone listening to your network can pick up that text.

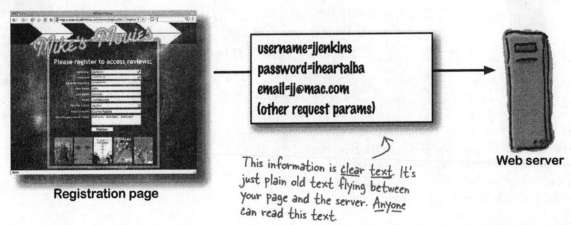

Registration page

username=jjenkins
password=iheartalba
email=jj@mac.com
(other request params)

This information is clear text. It's just plain old text flying between your page and the server. Anyone can read this text.

Web server

POST requests <u>DON'T</u> send clear text

What we need is a way to send that same data, but to avoid the data going across the network as clear text. That way, people can't snoop around and find Mike's customers' email addresses. That should take care of his spam problem once and for all.

Fortunately, that's just what POST requests do. They send their request data in a ***different way*** than GET does. Let's take a look:

GET requests send data <u>in</u> the request URL

GET requests send data to the server as part of the request URL, using request parameters that are part of the actual URL.

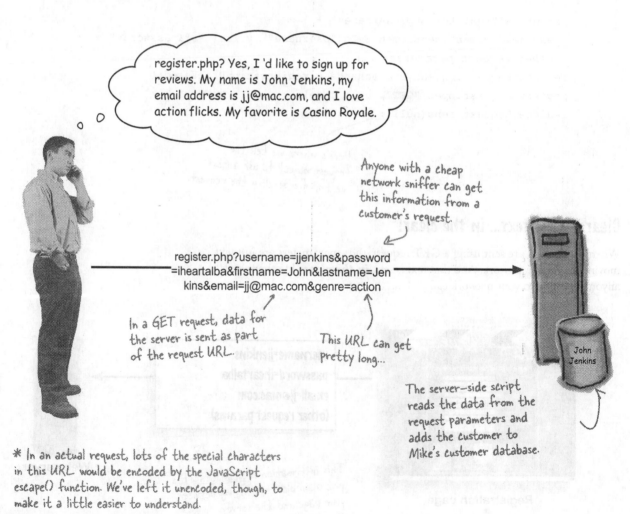

register.php? Yes, I'd like to sign up for reviews. My name is John Jenkins, my email address is jj@mac.com, and I love action flicks. My favorite is Casino Royale.

Anyone with a cheap network sniffer can get this information from a customer's request.

register.php?username=jjenkins&password=iheartalba&firstname=John&lastname=Jenkins&email=jj@mac.com&genre=action

In a GET request, data for the server is sent as part of the request URL.

This URL can get pretty long...

John Jenkins

The server-side script reads the data from the request parameters and adds the customer to Mike's customer database.

* In an actual request, lots of the special characters in this URL would be encoded by the JavaScript escape() function. We've left it unencoded, though, to make it a little easier to understand.

POST requests send data <u>separate</u> from the request URL

In a POST request, data that has to be sent to the server is kept separate from the URL. So there's no lengthy URL with data in it, and no clear text customer data is sent over the network.

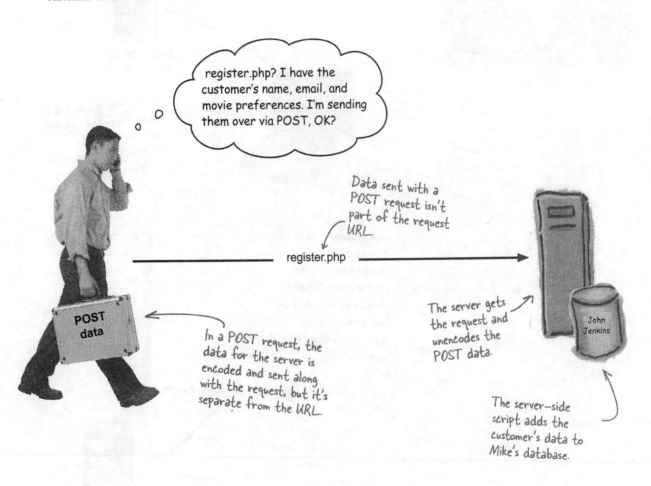

register.php? I have the customer's name, email, and movie preferences. I'm sending them over via POST, OK?

Data sent with a POST request isn't part of the request URL.

register.php

The server gets the request and unencodes the POST data.

POST data

In a POST request, the data for the server is encoded and sent along with the request, but it's separate from the URL.

John Jenkins

The server-side script adds the customer's data to Mike's database.

The data in a POST request is
<u>ENCODED</u> until it reaches the server

Once a web server gets a POST request, it figures out what type of data it has received, and then passes that information on to the program in the request URL.

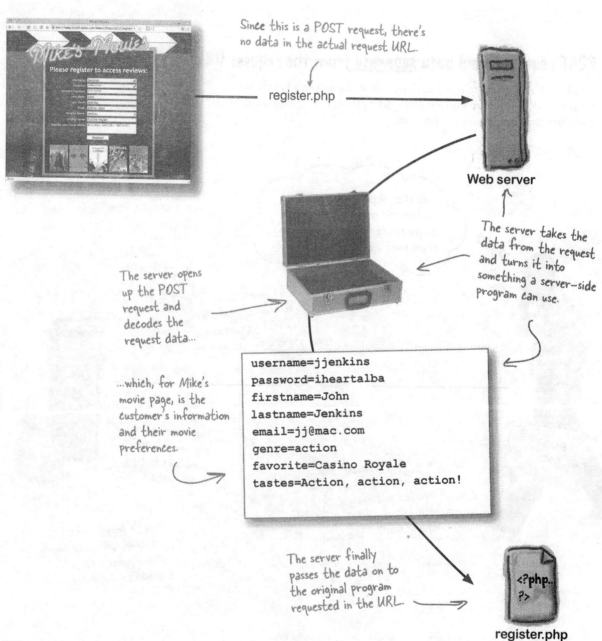

Since this is a POST request, there's no data in the actual request URL.

register.php

Web server

The server takes the data from the request and turns it into something a server-side program can use.

The server opens up the POST request and decodes the request data...

...which, for Mike's movie page, is the customer's information and their movie preferences.

```
username=jjenkins
password=iheartalba
firstname=John
lastname=Jenkins
email=jj@mac.com
genre=action
favorite=Casino Royale
tastes=Action, action, action!
```

The server finally passes the data on to the original program requested in the URL.

<?php...
?>

register.php

there are no
Dumb Questions

Q: So POST requests are more secure than GET requests?

A: Yes. There's one additional step that goes into packaging up POST data: the data is encoded in the browser and decoded on the server. Still, decrypting POST data isn't foolproof. Determined hackers can unencode your POST data, although it takes a lot more work than grabbing request parameters from the URL of a GET request.

If you really want to secure your request, you'll have to use a secure network connection, like SSL. But that's a little beyond what we're covering in this book.

Q: So if POST is still insecure, how will that help Mike's customers?

A: Most spammers are looking for the easiest targets possible. Most of the time, a single bit of trouble—like unencoding POST data—is all it takes to send spammers and hackers looking for an easier target. With Mike's site, moving to POST takes a little bit of effort, but will probably protect his site from the majority of malicious attacks.

A little bit of security on the Internet goes a long way.

Encoding your request data will cause most hackers to look for an easier target somewhere **OTHER** than on your web site.

Q: So are you saying that POST is safe and GET is unsafe?

A: Not really. "Safe" and "unsafe" are pretty relative terms, and it's impossible to predict all the ways something can go wrong. But sending data to the server using POST takes an extra step to protect that data. Sometimes that one step is the difference between your users getting your monthly newsletter, and those same users getting a spammer's porn mail.

Q: So why not send every request using POST?

A: There's really no need to. For one thing, encoding and unencoding data takes a bit of processing time. Besides that, GET is fine for sending shorter, non-private data. Also, if you use POST for everything, your users won't benefit from tools like Google Accelerator, and some search engine spiders might not pick up your links.

Q: And to send a POST request, all we have to do is put the request data in the send() method instead of the URL?

A: Exactly. You send the data in exactly the same format. You can pass name/value pairs to the request object's send() method, almost exactly like you did when you were sending a GET request.

Q: That's it? There's nothing else to do?

A: Well, let's try it out on Mike's page and see what happens...

send() your request data in a POST request

In a GET request, all the request data is sent as part of the request URL. So you build long URLs, like `register.php?username=jjenkins&password=...` But since request data isn't sent as part of the URL for a POST request, you can put all the data directly into the `send()` method of yor request object:

```
function registerUser() {
  t = setInterval("scrollImages()", 50);
  document.getElementById("register").value = "Processing...";
  registerRequest = createRequest();
  if (registerRequest == null) {
    alert("Unable to create request.");
  } else {
    var url = "register.php";
    var requestData = "username=" +
      escape(document.getElementById("username").value) + "&password=" +
      escape(document.getElementById("password1").value) + "&firstname=" +
      escape(document.getElementById("firstname").value) + "&lastname=" +
      escape(document.getElementById("lastname").value) + "&email=" +
      escape(document.getElementById("email").value) + "&genre=" +
      escape(document.getElementById("genre").value) + "&favorite=" +
      escape(document.getElementById("favorite").value) + "&tastes=" +
      escape(document.getElementById("tastes").value);
    registerRequest.onreadystatechange = registrationProcessed;
    registerRequest.open("POST", url, true);
    registerRequest.send(requestData);
  }
}
```

The request URL is just the name of the program on the server. No request parameters.

You don't need to precede yor request data with a question mark (?) in a POST request.

Instead of adding this data to the request URL, let's store it in a string variable.

Use the same ampersand character (&) to separate parameters.

This is a POST request now.

The request data is sent as a string and passed to the send() method of the request object.

---

there are no Dumb Questions

Q: Why don't I need a question mark?

A: The question mark (?) separated a server-side program name, like register.php, from the request data name/value pairs. Since you're not appending the request data to the program name, you don't need that question mark anymore.

Q: But I still do need an ampersand?

A: Yes. The ampersand (&) separates different pieces of data. That tells the server where one name/value pair ends, and where the next one starts.

TEST DRIVE

Secure Mike's app with a POST request.

Change your version of registerUser() in validation.js to match the version on page 454. Then reload Mike's registration page, and enter in some data. Try and submit the registration... does everything work like it should?

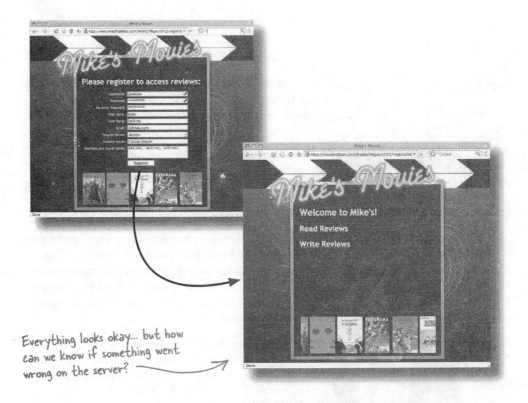

Everything looks okay... but how can we know if something went wrong on the server?

BRAIN POWER

Would any of the other requests on the registration page be good candidates for POST requests?

Always check to make sure your request data was <u>RECEIVED</u>.

It seems like we're sending a valid POST request, and we know that the request data's right from when we built Mike's registration page using GET. But we really don't know for sure that our request is getting handled.

In cases like this, where you don't get direct feedback from a server, you need to check that your request data got sent to the server and was properly received. Otherwise, you could find out there's a problem much later. And problems like that are hard to debug... who remembers the code they wrote three months ago, anyway?

Why don't I jsut ask the guys to add a few lines to register.php? It's probably a good idea to let Mike's new customer know what they submitted, anyway.

This is Jill... she's been hanging out with Mike's server-side guys lately.

Good server-side programs <u>CONFIRM</u> the data you sent.

The server-side programs that verified usernames and passwords gave you direct feedback. That made it easy to confirm that your request data was received. In fact, most server-side programs respond to your request data and give you some sort of feedback.

But a few programs—like Mike's server-side registration page—don't let you know what data they've received. Work with the programmers writing those programs. Often, it's easy to add a few lines and at least echo back what request data was received. Then, you can ensure the data you sent is the data that those programs received.

Test Drive (again)

Let's see what the **SERVER** says.

If you haven't already, download the example files for Chapter 12 from Head First Labs. There's an updated version of register.php called register-feedback.php that gives you some visual feedback when a new user submits their registration data.

Update the request URL in registerUser(), in validation.js, to use this new script. Then, try Mike's registration page again.

Uh oh... this doesn't look too good. There's no username, name, or email address...

Why didn't the POST request work?

Jim

> It's got to be the register.php script. We did everything right on our end, so it's got to be a server problem.

> I don't think so... those server-side guys say nothing's wrong with their end.

This is Jill... she's been hanging out with Mike's server–side guys lately.

Jim: Are you sure? I'll bet someone forgot to change the script to accept POST parameters. Come on, that's got to be it! Fix the thing, and we can get on with it...

Jill: No, I asked him about that specifically. The script accepts GET and POST parameters. Are you sure you sent the customer's details over?

Jim: I'm positive. `registerUser()` uses a POST request, and I know the request object works from when I was still using GET.

Jill: Well, you must have made a mistake somewhere.

Jim: No way. All the data's in the `send()` method of my request object... I even double-checked. So I know the data's getting to the web server.

Jill: Well, it's not getting to the script. Look at the output page! There's nothing for username, firstname, or lastname, or anything.

Jim: Wait a second. If I'm sending the data to the server correctly...

Jill: ...and the script's asking the server for the data and getting nothing...

Together: *The problem must be the server!*

The server unencodes POST data

Our script is sending a request to the server with the right request data. But somehow, the server's not getting that data to the server-side program, `register-feedback.php`. So what's going on between the server and `register-feedback.php`?

We know the server is supposed to take our POST data and unencode it. But the server has to know *how* to unencode that data... and that means knowing what *type* of data it's receiving.

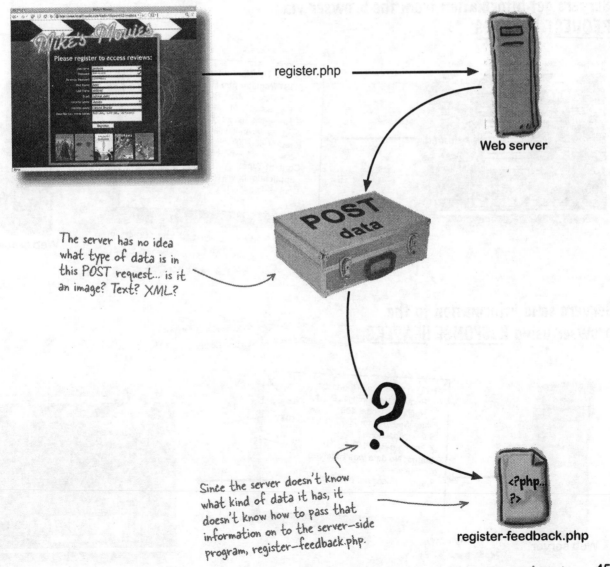

register.php

Web server

The server has no idea what type of data is in this POST request... is it an image? Text? XML?

POST data

Since the server doesn't know what kind of data it has, it doesn't know how to pass that information on to the server-side program, register-feedback.php.

```
<?php...
?>
```

register-feedback.php

We need to **TELL** the server what we're sending

We need to let the server know exactly what type of data we're sending it. But that information can't be part of the request data itself, so we need another way to tell the server.

Anytime you need to talk to the server about a request, you use a **request header**. A request header is information that's sent along with the request and the server can read right away. The server can also send back **response headers**, which are pieces of information about that server's response:

Servers get information from the browser via REQUEST HEADERS.

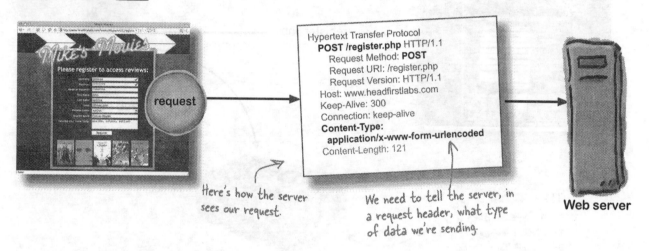

Hypertext Transfer Protocol
POST /register.php HTTP/1.1
    Request Method: **POST**
    Request URI: /register.php
    Request Version: HTTP/1.1
Host: www.headfirstlabs.com
Keep-Alive: 300
Connection: keep-alive
Content-Type:
    application/x-www-form-urlencoded
Content-Length: 121

Here's how the server sees our request.

We need to tell the server, in a request header, what type of data we're sending.

Web server

Servers send information to the browser using RESPONSE HEADERS.

The server sends back a response header and status code.

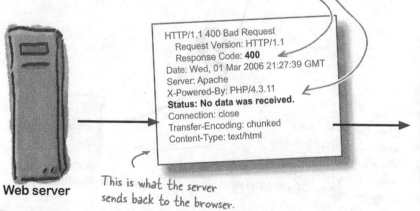

HTTP/1.1 400 Bad Request
    Request Version: HTTP/1.1
    Response Code: **400**
Date: Wed, 01 Mar 2006 21:27:39 GMT
Server: Apache
X-Powered-By: PHP/4.3.11
Status: No data was received.
Connection: close
Transfer-Encoding: chunked
Content-Type: text/html

Web server

This is what the server sends back to the browser.

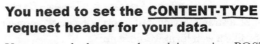

OK, I get it. In a GET request, the data is part of the request URL, so it has to be just text. But in a POST request, we have to explicitly tell the server what to expect.

You need to set the <u>CONTENT-TYPE</u> request header for your data.

You can send a lot more than plain text in a POST request. When a server receives your POST request, it won't know what kind of data it's dealing with unless you **tell the server what to expect**.

Once the server knows what kind of data you're sending, it can decode the POST data and handle it properly. For Mike's registration page, we need to tell the server we're sending it name/value pairs. We can do this by setting a request header called `Content-Type`.

register.php? I have the customer's name, email, and movie preferences. I'm sending them over **as name/value pairs** via POST, OK?

This time, the request includes a content type along with the request URL and POST data.

register.php

The POST data is the same as before...

...but with a content type, the server knows what kind of data to expect, and it can figure out how to unencode that data.

POST data

Set a request header using setRequestHeader() on your request object

Once you know what request header to set, it's easy to do. Just call setRequestHeader() on your request object, and pass in the name of the request header and the value for that header.

For name/value pairs, we want to set the Content-Type request header. We need to set the value of that header as application/x-www-form-urlencoded. That's a bit of a strange string, but it just tells the server we're sending it name/value pairs, like a web form would send:

```
function registerUser() {
  t = setInterval("scrollImages()", 50);
  document.getElementById("register").value = "Processing...";
  registerRequest = createRequest();
  if (registerRequest == null) {
    alert("Unable to create request.");
  } else {
  var url = "register.php";
  var requestData = "username=" +
    escape(document.getElementById("username").value) + "&password=" +
    escape(document.getElementById("password1").value) + "&firstname=" +
    escape(document.getElementById("firstname").value) + "&lastname=" +
    escape(document.getElementById("lastname").value) + "&email=" +
    escape(document.getElementById("email").value) + "&genre=" +
    escape(document.getElementById("genre").value) + "&favorite=" +
    escape(document.getElementById("favorite").value) + "&tastes=" +
    escape(document.getElementById("tastes").value);
  registerRequest.onreadystatechange = registrationProcessed;
  registerRequest.open("POST", url, true);
  registerRequest.setRequestHeader("Content-Type",
    "application/x-www-form-urlencoded");
  registerRequest.send(requestData);
  }
}
```

This sets the Content-Type request header...

...and tells the server to expect name/value pairs, like a web form would send in a submission.

Q: So a request header is sent to the server along with the request?

A: Yes. All request headers are part of the request. In fact, the browser sets some request headers automatically, so you're really just adding a request header to the existing ones.

Q: Have we been getting response headers all along, too?

A: Yup. The browser and server always generate headers. You only have to worry about them if there's information you need to work with, like setting the content type or retrieving a status from a response header.

Q: So "Content-Type" is used to tell the server what kind of POST data we're sending?

A: Exactly. In this case, we're using name/value pairs, and the content type for that is "application/x-www-form-urlencoded." That particular type tells the server to look for values like those it would get from a normal form submission.

Q: Are there other content types?

A: Tons. To find out about the rest of them, try searching for "HTTP Content-Type" in your favorite search engine.

BRAIN BARBELL

Suppose you wanted to send XML data to a server-side program. What do you think you'd need to do in order for the web server to unencode that data properly?

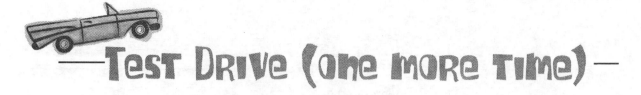

TEST DRIVE (one more time)

Did it work? Did it work?

Update your request to include a `Content-Type` request header, and try Mike's registration page again. Submit your information, and see what the server says.

The server unencoded our request data and passed it on to the server-side program.

Nice work! You knocked that out in no time. Is there anything else you need to fix while you're here?

POST secure data.

What other secure data does Mike pass between his registration page and the server? Should the username request be POST? What about the password request?

It's up to you to figure out which requests are best sent as POSTs, and which ones are fine as GET requests. Go ahead and update Mike's page to make it safer. When you're done, flip the page for a few more exercises.

Word Search

```
X  A  R  S  Y  R  O  T  A  D  N  A  M
A  C  L  V  V  R  E  T  N  I  T  E  S
A  V  I  O  A  S  B  A  L  T  R  S  V
Q  S  L  X  H  L  N  D  L  E  R  S  L
C  U  Y  O  R  S  I  A  E  A  Y  A  R
A  C  N  N  E  U  T  D  Y  N  S  R  A
L  O  E  C  C  B  T  U  A  D  N  E  S
L  P  U  K  A  M  A  N  N  T  O  L  N
G  R  Y  C  C  I  S  E  O  X  I  B  R
E  N  I  A  H  T  E  N  A  U  T  O  R
T  U  N  B  A  D  Q  C  N  R  P  A  N
K  N  G  T  F  A  P  O  S  T  O  S  A
N  D  U  L  R  I  E  D  R  I  U  D  Y
A  S  E  R  E  D  A  E  H  T  E  S  D
J  E  R  C  I  C  T  H  R  I  Z  A  R
```

Word list:

Get
Post
Validation
Submit
Mandatory
Options
Secure
Unencode
Header
Status

GET **or** POST?

It's time for another episode of "GET or POST?" It's up to you to decide which request method is best for each of the following web apps.

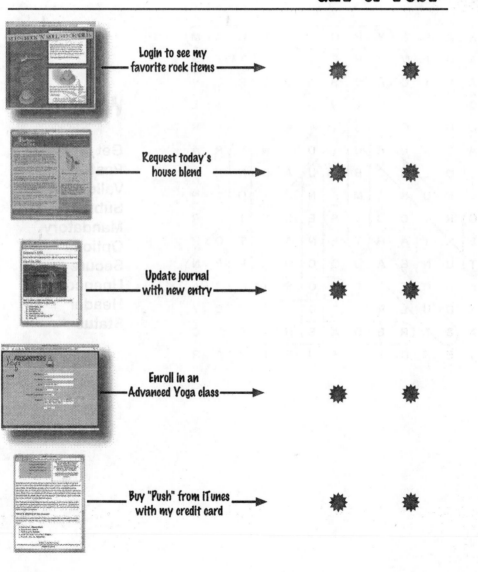

GET or POST

Login to see my favorite rock items ——————▶   ✹   ✹

Request today's house blend ——————▶   ✹   ✹

Update journal with new entry——————▶   ✹   ✹

Enroll in an Advanced Yoga class——————▶   ✹   ✹

Buy "Push" from iTunes with my credit card ——————▶   ✹   ✹

Word Search Solution

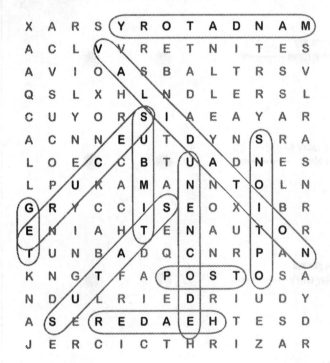

```
X  A  R  S (Y  R  O  T  A  D  N  A  M)
A  C  L (V  V  R  E  T  N  I  T  E  S
A  V  I  O  A  S  B  A  L  T  R  S  V
Q  S  L  X  H  L  N  D  L  E  R  S  L
C  U  Y  O  R (S) I  A  E  A  Y  A  R
A  C  N  N  E  U  T  D  Y  N (S) R  A
L  O  E  C  C  B  T  U  A  D  N  E  S
L  P  U  K  A  M  A  N  N  T  O  L  N
(G  R  Y  C  C  I  S) E  O  X  I  B  R
(E) N  I  A  H (T) E  N  A  U (T) O  R
(T) U  N  B  A  D  Q  C  N  R  P  A  N
K  N  G  T  F  A (P  O  S  T) O  S  A
N  D  U  L  R  I  E  D  R  I  U  D  Y
A (S  E  R  E  D  A  E  H) T  E  S  D
J  E  R  C  I  C  T  H  R  I  Z  A  R
```

Word list:

Get
Post
Validation
Submit
Mandatory
Options
Secure
Unencode
Header
Status

GET OR POST?
SOLUTIONS

It's time for another episode of "GET or POST?" It's up to you to decide which request method is best for each of the following web apps.

GET or POST

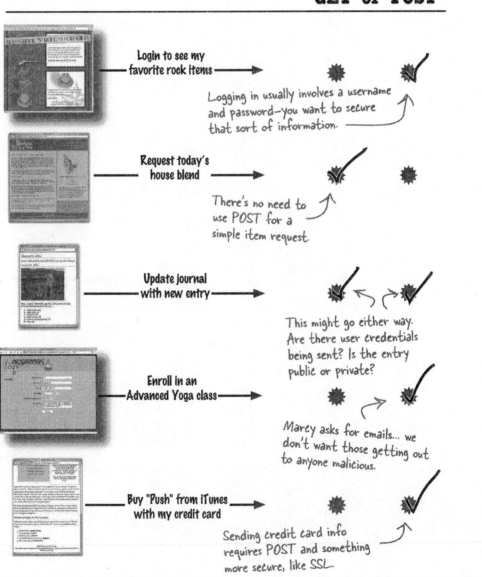

Login to see my favorite rock items →

Logging in usually involves a username and password—you want to secure that sort of information.

Request today's house blend →

There's no need to use POST for a simple item request.

Update journal with new entry →

This might go either way. Are there user credentials being sent? Is the entry public or private?

Enroll in an Advanced Yoga class →

Marcy asks for emails... we don't want those getting out to anyone malicious.

Buy "Push" from iTunes with my credit card →

Sending credit card info requires POST and something more secure, like SSL.

appendix i: leftovers

The Top Five Topics
(we didn't cover)

It's been a long ride... and you're almost to the end.

We can barely stand to let you go, but before you do, there's still a few things left
to cover. We can't possibly fit everything about Ajax into one 600-page book. Well,
actually, we *tried* that... but marketing felt that a 28-pound technical book wouldn't do
too well on the shelves. So we threw out everything you didn't really need to know
and kept the last few important bits in this appendix.

That's right... this really is the end. Well, except for one more short appendix... and the
index (truly, a must-read). Oh, and a few ads in the back... well, you get the idea.

#1 Inspecting the DOM

By now, you're a pro at using the Document Object Model to update your web pages on the fly. But once you've used the DOM to make changes to your page, how can you see exactly what the web browser sees? The answer is to use a DOM inspector:

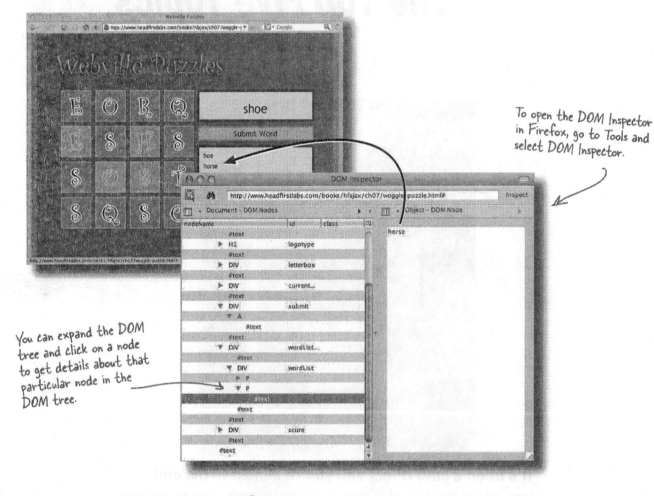

To open the DOM Inspector in Firefox, go to Tools and select DOM Inspector.

You can expand the DOM tree and click on a node to get details about that particular node in the DOM tree.

Watch it!

You have to request that the DOM inspector be installed on Windows.

When you're installing Firefox, select Custom Install, and then Web Developer Tools. That will get the DOM inspector running on Windows machines.

Inspecting the DOM in Internet Explorer

You'll need to download and install a separate tool for inspecting the DOM on Windows, using Internet Explorer. IEInspector is a tool that includes a DOM inspector for Internet Explorer as well as an HTTP Analyzer tool). Here's exactly what you need to do:.

Where to get it: http://www.ieinspector.com/dominspector/

How to use it: Download and install the .EXE for IEInspector. You can then launch the tool and view a page, its markup, and its DOM tree all in a single window.

IE WebDeveloper is shareware. It will cost $59 to purchase, but it's got a lot more than just DOM inspection and comes with a 30-day money-back guarantee.

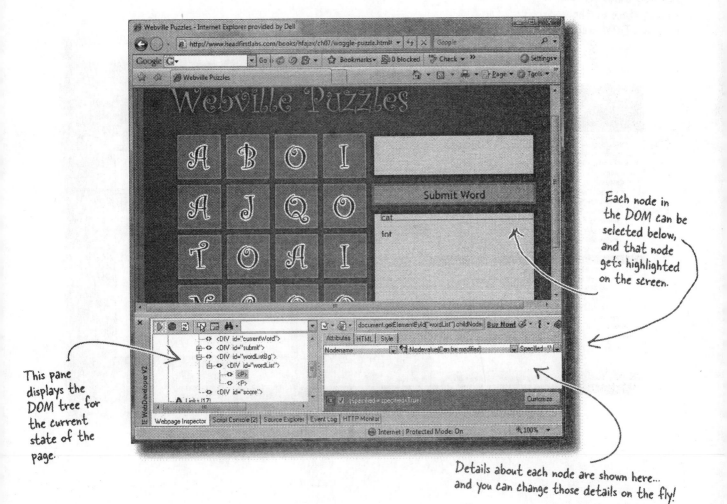

This pane displays the DOM tree for the current state of the page.

Each node in the DOM can be selected below, and that node gets highlighted on the screen.

Details about each node are shown here... and you can change those details on the fly!

Inspecting the DOM in Safari

To inspect the DOM in Safari, you'll need to use WebKit. WebKit is
the open-source system framework used by Mac OS X apps like Safari,
Dashboard, and Mail. You can get it from http://webkit.opendarwin.org/.

Once you've downloaded WebKit, drag it into your Applications folder. Then
you'll need to run the following command in a terminal window:

```
defaults write com.apple.Safari WebKitDeveloperExtras -bool true
```

Now go to your Applications folder and open WebKit. Right-
click anywhere on your page, and select "Inspect Element:"

This pane shows you the
current state of the
browser's DOM tree.

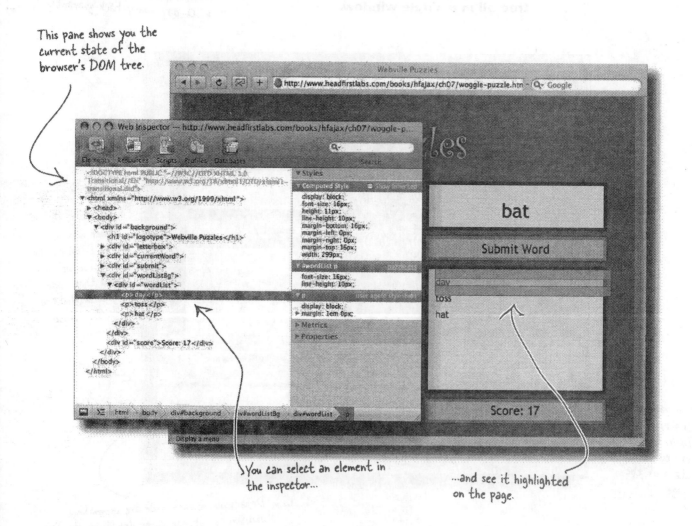

You can select an element in
the inspector...

...and see it highlighted
on the page.

#2 Graceful degradation

One of the thorniest issues in Ajax is **graceful degradation**: how do you ensure that your app works for browsers *without* JavaScript enabled (or with a *really* old version of JavaScript). Since this is such a tricky topic, and lots of folks are designing apps targeted specifically at modern browsers, we've had to leave the topic for an appendix.

Still, if you're interested in creating a user experience for every possible visitor, here's what you'll need to do:

1 **Start out by designing a JavaScript-free site.**
This is the biggest difference in building degradable sites. You can't start with an Ajaxian site and then create code to "fall back" to a non-Ajax site; there's no code that runs on a non-JavaScript browser.

So you've got to create a site that works well **without any JavaScript**. This is why most designers simply ignore non-JavaScript browsers.

This isn't a great way to please a really wide customer-base, but we can understand why most people go that route.

2 **Use <a> elements and Submit buttons liberally.**
No JavaScript means no event handlers. When you're stripped of `onBlur` and `onClick`, the only markup you can use to trigger action is an <a> element (a link) and a form submit button. You should use those elements a *lot* since they're the only way to initiate server-side processing from a non-JavaScript page.

Here's another reason to use <a> elements for any sort of links in your page.

3 **Write server-side programs that don't assume Ajaxian requests.**
Writing a server-side program that responds to an asynchronous request isn't fundamentally different from writing a program that responds to a form submit. The big difference, though, is in what that server-side program *returns*. The response to a validation request from an Ajax page might be "okay"; but how can a non-JavaScript page interpret "okay"?

Instead, your server-side programs usually need to figure out, based on request parameters, what's making a request. Then, based on that, your programs will need to return different data. So for an Ajax request, your program might return a short response; for a non-Ajax request, the response might be a new XHTML page or redirect.

4 **Test, test, test... and then test some more.**
The biggest issue in graceful degradation is testing. Even if you build a non-JavaScript version of your page and use the right elements and server-side programs, you've got to test your pages on every browser you can think of. In particular, once you've added in an Ajax version of the page, test on those non-JavaScript browsers a few more times. You never know what's crept in as you've added interactivity.

#3 script.aculo.us and the Yahoo UI libraries

You've already seen a bit about some of the cool Ajax toolkits and frameworks out there, and we mentioned script.aculo.us as one of those. Really, though, script.aculo.us is more of a user interface (UI) toolkit. There are more UI libraries out there, too. All of them are focused on making it easy to build nice, user-friendly, and sometimes visually amazing user interfaces.

These libraries are usually just JavaScript files you can download and then reference in your XHTML pages, whether the page is connected to asynchronous JavaScript or not.

script.aculo.us

Where to get it: **http://script.aculo.us/**

How to use it:

```
<head>

  <title>Webville Puzzles</title>

  <link rel="stylesheet" href="css/puzzle.css" type="text/css" />

  <script type="text/javascript" src="http://script.aculo.us/prototype.js"></script>

  <script type="text/javascript" src="http://script.aculo.us/scriptaculous.js"></script>

  <script type="text/javascript" src="utils.js"> </script>

  ... etc ...
```

You can even use script.aculo.us without downloading anything... just reference these URLs.

script.aculo.us uses the Prototype library for its server interaction and some lower-level JavaScript functions.

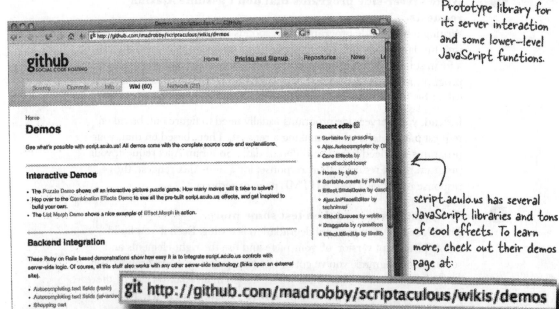

script.aculo.us has several JavaScript libraries and tons of cool effects. To learn more, check out their demos page at:

git http://github.com/madrobby/scriptaculous/wikis/demos

Yahoo UI (YUI)

Where to get it: **http://developer.yahoo.com/yui/**

How to use it:

> YUI breaks things up into lots of different scripts... you would probably only use a few of these for most pages.

```
<head>
 <title>Webville Puzzles</title>
 <link rel="stylesheet" href="css/puzzle.css" type="text/css" />
 <script type="text/javascript"
    src="http://yui.yahooapis.com/2.5.2/build/yuiloader/yuiloader-beta-min.js"></script>
 <script type="text/javascript"
    src="http://yui.yahooapis.com/2.5.2/build/dom/dom-min.js"></script>
 <script type="text/javascript"
    src="http://yui.yahooapis.com/2.5.2/build/event/event-min.js"></script>
 <script type="text/javascript"
    src="http://yui.yahooapis.com/2.5.2/build/animation/animation-min.js"></script>
 <script type="text/javascript"
    src="http://yui.yahooapis.com/2.5.2/build/dragdrop/dragdrop-min.js"></script>
 <script type="text/javascript"
    src="http://yui.yahooapis.com/2.5.2/build/element/element-beta-min.js"></script>
 <script type="text/javascript" src="http://yui.yahooapis.com/2.5.2/build/button/button-
 min.js"></script>
 <script type="text/javascript" src="utils.js"> </script>
 ... etc ...
```

> Each script does one thing: drag-and-drop, or DOM, or event handling.

> Like script.aculo.us, YUI has lots of great UI features, notably some really cool drag-and-drop functionality.

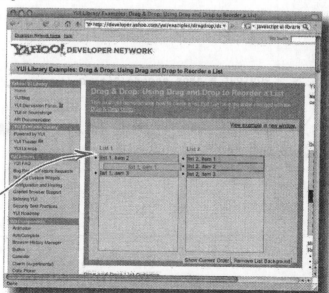

> Here, we're dragging an item from the top of the list to a lower position... all without page reloading or server interaction!

#4 Using JSON libraries in your PHP code

You've already seen how JSON can help you send and receive complex objects in your Java apps. But for PHP scripts, you're going to need a library if you don't want to type in your JSON-formatted data manually. That's a pain, so having a JSON library is a big deal for server-side JSON interaction.

Here's how you can use JSON in your PHP scripts, without getting into lots of JSON-specific syntax in your PHP:

Where to get it: **It's included with PHP 5.2.0 and later**

JSON support is now part of PHP, so you don't have to do anything to access JSON-specific functions in your PHP scripts.

How to use it: **Call `json_encode()` and pass in your PHP variables and data.**

You can create arrays and variables just as you normally would in your PHP code.

```
$itemGuitar = array(
 'id' => 'itemGuitar',
    'description' => 'Pete Townshend once played this
             guitar while his own axe was in the shop having
             bits of drumkit removed from it.',
    'price' => 5695.99,
    'urls' => array('http://www.thewho.com/',
                    'http://en.wikipedia.org/wiki/Pete_Townshend')
);


$output = json_encode($itemGuitar);
print($output);
```

All you need to do to convert your PHP data into JSON is call json_encode() and pass in the PHP variables or data.

Using JSON in PHP 5.1 and earlier

Say you're not using PHP 5.2, and you can't get your system upgraded (or don't want to). In that case, you'll need to download a library to get PHP working with JSON on your server.

This library is robust, easy to use, and packaged up through PEAR for easy access.

Where to get it: http://pear.php.net/pepr/pepr-proposal-show.php?id=198

How to use it: **Create a new `Services_JSON` object, and pass your PHP data to the `encode()` method on that object.**

You'll need to require() or require_once() the downloaded library, since it's not included as part of PHP automatically.

First, create a new object of type Services_JSON.

Your PHP data is created normally. Nothing JSON-specific here.

```php
require_once('JSON.php');
$json = new Services_JSON();


$itemGuitar = array(
  'id' => 'itemGuitar',
  'description' => 'Pete Townshend once played this
        guitar while his own axe was in the shop having
        bits of drumkit removed from it.',
  'price' => 5695.99,
  'urls' => array('http://www.thewho.com/',
                  'http://en.wikipedia.org/wiki/Pete_Townshend')
);


$output = $json->encode($itemGuitar);

print($output);
```

Finally, call encode() on your data, using the Services_JSON object you created earlier.

#5 Ajax and ASP.NET

If you're frequently working with Microsoft technologies, you may want to look into ASP.NET Ajax. ASP.NET Ajax is Microsoft's free, proprietary version of Ajax that hooks into Visual Studio 2008 and the rest of the Microsoft technology stack.

Because ASP.NET Ajax is built to work with Microsoft's visual products, it's more of a drag-and-drop set of front end controls, along with the ability to build code to "back" those controls.

You can find out all you ever wanted to know about ASP.NET Ajax at http://www.asp.net/ajax.

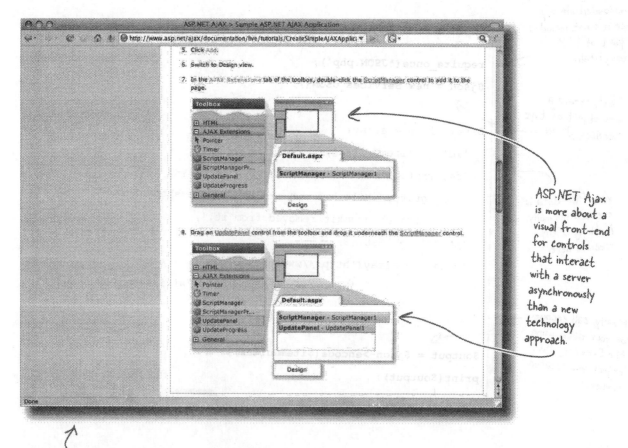

ASP.NET Ajax is more about a visual front—end for controls that interact with a server asynchronously than a new technology approach.

Microsoft has a ton of online documentation for ASP.NET Ajax... it's easy to learn a lot by just surfing the asp.net/ajax web pages.

You don't <u>NEED</u> ASP.NET Ajax to build Internet Explorer-compatible web apps

There are a lot of good reasons to dig into ASP.NET Ajax if you're working on or for a hardcore Microsoft product or shop. And if you're already building apps using Visual Studio, then ASP.NET Ajax will drop right in with what you're already doing.

But if you're just building web apps that you want to work on Internet Explorer—as well as other browsers like Firefox and Safari—then you don't need ASP.NET Ajax. You can use the techniques you've already learned, along with the DOM and request creation utility methods, to get your apps working on all major browsers.

Marcy's Yoga for Programmers site worked great on IE as well as other browsers, using standard Ajax techniques. So for most public-facing web development, what you already know will work just fine.

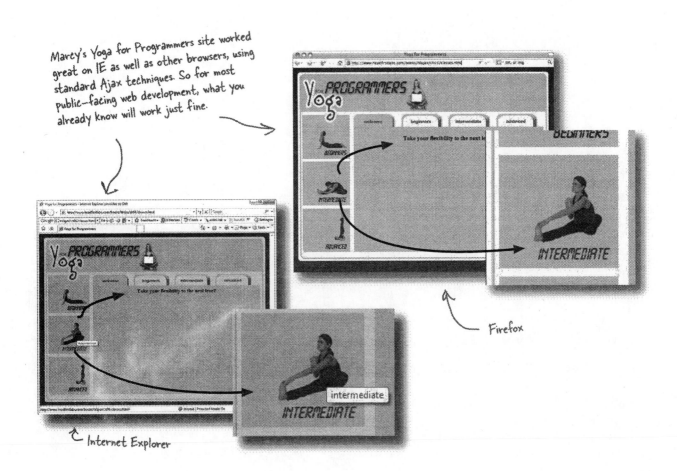

Firefox

Internet Explorer

appendix ii: utility functions

Just Gimme the Code

> There's nothing better than rewriting my favorite code fragments... it really helps me get my head around all the tricky abstractions.

Sometimes you just want everything in one place.

You've spent a lot of time using utils.js, our little utility class of Ajax, DOM, and event utility functions. Inside these pages, you'll get all those functions in one place, ready to put into your own utility scripts and applications. Take one last chance to familiarize yourself with these functions, and then get to work on your own utilities!

utils.js: a work in progress

Here's the code we've got so far for `utils.js`. But why stop here? You should add your own functions into `utils.js`. Need a handy reusable function for getting the text out of a node? Put that function in `utils.js`.

Over time, `utils.js` should become your own personal framework.

```
function createRequest() {
  try {
    request = new XMLHttpRequest();
  } catch (tryMS) {
    try {
      request = new ActiveXObject("Msxml2.XMLHTTP");
    } catch (otherMS) {
      try {
        request = new ActiveXObject("Microsoft.XMLHTTP");
      } catch (failed) {
        request = null;
      }
    }
  }
  return request;
}

function isArray(arg) {
  if (typeof arg == 'object') {
    var criteria = arg.constructor.toString().match(/array/i);
    return (criteria != null);
  }
  return false;
}
```

This works in Safari, Firefox, Opera, etc. Everything but IE, more or less.

This is one version of Microsoft's request object...

...and here's the other.

We return null, so the calling program can figure out how to report or handle an error.

Try not to use alert() in utility functions. You need to let the function caller decide how to handle problems.

We moved isArray() into utils.js because it's a general function, not specific to a particular app.

This checks the constructor of the supplied object for the string "array," regardless of case.

If the constructor contains array, criteria won't be null, and this will return true. Otherwise, return false.

This takes an Event object and returns the object that triggered that event.

```
function getActivatedObject(e) {
  var obj;
  if (!e) {
    // early version of IE
    obj = window.event.srcElement;
  } else if (e.srcElement) {
    // IE 7 or later
    obj = e.srcElement;
  } else {
    // DOM Level 2 browser
    obj = e.target;
  }
  return obj;
}
```

Early IE stores the activated object in the window object.

Modern versions of IE use the srcElement property on the Event object.

Non-Microsoft browsers like Firefox, Opera, and Safari store the activated object in the target property of the Event object.

```
function addEventHandler(obj, eventName, handler) {
  if (document.attachEvent) {
    obj.attachEvent("on" + eventName, handler);
  } else if (document.addEventListener) {
    obj.addEventListener(eventName, handler, false);
  }
}
```

attachEvent() is Microsoft-specific syntax.

addEventListener() is for DOM Level 2 browsers.

This one's all about syntax. We need to register an event handler, but do it in a browser-independent manner.

Index

Symbols & Numbers

Shroff / O'Reilly

Titles at Reduced Prices

ISBN	Title	Author	Year	Price
9788184043099	A+, Network+, Security+ Exams in a Nutshell (Cover Essentials 220-602,220-603,220-604 N10-00), 826 Pgs	Bhardwaj	2007	150.00
9788173661990	Access 2003 Personal Trainer **(B/CD)**, (2 Color book), 372 Pages	Custom Guide	2005	150.00
9788184042573	Access 2007: The Missing Manual, 776 Pages	MacDonald	2006	100.00
9788173665769	ActionScript for Flash MX: The Definitive Guide, 2/ed, 904 Pgs	Colin Moock	2003	150.00
9788173667350	Active Directory Cookbook for Windows Server 2003 and Windows 2000, 632 Pages	Allen	1993	150.00
9788173666568	Active Directory for Windows Server 2003, 2/ed, 692 Pages	Allen	2003	150.00
9788173668203	AI for Game Developers, 400 Pages	Bourg	2004	100.00
9788173667442	Apache Cookbook (Covers Apache 2.0 & 1.3), 264 Pages	Coar	2003	75.00
9788184041026	ASP .NET 2.0 Cookbook (Cover ASP .NET 2.0), 1,028 Pages	Kittel	2005	150.00
9788184040012	Asterisk: The Future of Telephony, 414 Pages	Meggelen	2005	50.00
9788173662348	AutoCAD 2000 In a Nutshell: A Command Reference Guide, 592 Pgs	Kent	1999	75.00
9788173668982	Better, Faster, Lighter Java, 270 Pages	Tate	2004	75.00
9788173666582	BGP, 292 Pages	van Beijnum	2002	100.00
9788184040548	Blackberry Hacks: Tips & Tools for Your Mobile Office, 350 Pages	Mabe	2005	75.00
9788173665127	BLAST, 372 Pages	Korf	2003	100.00
9788173668999	BSD Hacks:100 Industrial-Strength Tips & Tools, 458 Pages	Lavigne	2004	75.00
9788173662287	Building Java Enterprise Applications: Vol. 1 - Architecture, 324 Pages	McLaughlin	2002	75.00
9788173662881	Building Oracle XML Applications **(B/CD)**, 824 Pages	Muench	2000	100.00
9788173665622	Building Secure Servers with Linux, 454 Pages	Bauer	2003	100.00
9788173664250	Building Wireless Community Networks, 144 Pages	Flickenger	2002	50.00
9788184043846	C# 3.0 in a Nutshell: A Desktop Quick Reference, 3/ed, 874 Pgs	Albahari	2007	150.00
9788184040937	C# Cookbook, 2/ed 1,196 Pages	Hilyard	2006	150.00
9788173662263	CDO & MAPI Programming with Visual Basic, 388 Pages	Grundgeiger	2002	75.00
9788173663659	COM & .NET Component Services, 390 Pages	Lowy	2001	75.00
9788184040197	Computer Privacy Annoyances, 218 Pages	Tynan	2005	50.00
9788184042658	CSS Pocket Reference, 2/ed, 142 Pages	Meyer	2007	25.00
9788173669163	CSS Cookbook (Cover CSS 2.1), 280 Pages	Schmitt	2004	75.00
9788184042733	CSS Cookbook, 2/ed, 552 Pages	Schmitt	2006	150.00
9788173667800	Database In Depth: The Relational Model for Practitioners, 250 Pgs	C.J.Date	2005	75.00
9788173663888	Designing Large Scale LANs, 408 Pages	Dooley	2002	75.00
9788173662874	Developing ASP Components 2/ed, 864 Pages	Powers	1998	100.00
9788173663789	DNS on Windows 2000, 2/ed, 376 Pages	Larson	2001	50.00
9788173662997	Dreamweaver MX: The Missing Manual, 750 Pages	McFarland	2003	150.00
9788173665288	Dynamic HTML: The Definitive Reference, 2/ed, 1,428 Pages	Goodman	2006	150.00
9788173668166	Enterprise Service Architecture - O'Reilly SAP Series, 236 Pages	Woods	2003	50.00
9788173669439	Essentail SharePoint, 338 Pages	Webb	2005	50.00
9788184040920	Essential Microsoft Operation Manager, 400 Pages	Fox	2006	75.00

ISBN	Title	Author	Year	Price
9788173663581	Essential SNMP, 338 Pages	Mauro	2001	75.00
9788173669613	Excel 2003 Personal Trainer **(B/CD)**, (2 Color book) 490 Pgs	CustomGuide	2004	200.00
9788173668296	Excel 2003 Programming: A Developer's Notebook, 330 Pages	Webb	2004	100.00
9788184042955	Excel 2007 for Starters: The Missing Manual, 408 Pages	MacDonald	2005	150.00
9788173669408	Excel Annoyances: How to Fix the Most Annoying Things about Your Favorite Spreadsheet , 266 Pages	Frye	2004	75.00
9788184040845	Excel Scientific and Engineering Cookbook, 442 Pages	Bourg	2006	100.00
9788173663598	Exim: The Mail Transport Agent, 638 Pages	Hazel	2001	75.00
9788173665257	Exploring the JDS Linux Desktop **(B/CD)**, 418 Pages	Adelstein	2004	100.00
9788184042177	Fedora Linux, 672 Pages	Tyler	2006	150.00
9788184043488	Flash CS3 the Missing Manual, 542 Pages	Veer	2007	100.00
9788184040500	FrontPage 2003: The Missing Manual, 446 Pages	Mantaro	2005	150.00
9788184040852	Google Advertising Tools, 366 Pages	Davis	2006	150.00
9788173669491	Google Hacks: Tips & Tools for Smarter Searching 2/ed, 496 Pgs	Calishain	2005	100.00
9788173663420	Hardening Cisco Routers, 196 Pages	Akin	2002	50.00
9788173668210	Hardware Hacking Projects for Geeks, 358 Pages	Fullam	2004	100.00
9788173663161	Home Hacking Projects for Geeks, 346 Pages	Faulkner	2004	75.00
9788173669446	Home Networking Annoyances: How to Fix the Most Annoying Things About Your Home Network, 234 Pages	Ivens	2005	50.00
9788184040203	Home Networking: The Missing Manual, 263 Pages	Lowe	2005	75.00
9788173669415	Internet Annoyances: How to Fix the Most Annoying Things about Going Online, 266 Pages	Gralla	2005	75.00
9788184040159	Internet Forensics, 250 Pages	Jones	2005	75.00
9788173664489	IPv6 Essentials, 362 Pages	Hagen	2002	75.00
9788173667480	IRC Hack: 100 Industrial-Strength Tips & Tools, 442 Pages	Mutton	2004	75.00
9788173664496	Java & XML Data Binding, 224 Pages	McLaughlin	2002	75.00
9788173666674	Java Data Objects, 568 Pages	Jordan	2003	100.00
9788173666681	Java Extreme Programming Cookbook, 296 Pages	Burke	2003	75.00
9788173664403	Java Management Extensions, 318 Pages	Perry	2002	75.00
9788173665783	Java Performance Tuning, 2/ed, 600 Pages	Shirazi	2003	150.00
9788173660573	Java Threads, 2/ed, 336 Pages	Oaks	1999	100.00
9788173661105	JavaScript Application Cookbook, 512 Pages	Bradenbaugh	1999	75.00
9788184040128	Learning SQL, 290 Pages	Beaulieu	2005	75.00
9788173664441	Learning the Korn Shell, 2/ed, 438 Pages	Rosenblett	2002	100.00
9788173665639	Learning Visual Basic .NET, 326 Pages	Liberty	2002	100.00
9788173669422	Learning Windows Server 2003, 682 Pages	Hassell	2006	150.00
9788173663178	Learning WML & WMLScript, 204 Pages	Frost	2002	50.00
9788184041439	Linux Annoyances for Geeks, 516 Pages	Jang	2006	100.00
9788173663604	Linux Device Drivers, 2/ed, 650 Pages	Rubini	2002	150.00
9788173669620	Linux in a Nutshell, 5/ed, 954 Pages	Siever	2005	150.00
9788173669453	Linux in a Windows World, 504 Pages	Smith	2005	125.00
9788184040319	Linux Multimedia Hacks, 342 Pages	Rankin	2005	100.00
9788173666759	Linux Server Hacks: 100 Industrial - Strength Tips & Tools, 240 Pages	Flickenger	2003	75.00
9788184040517	Linux Server Hacks: Volume 2, 490 Pages	Hagen	2005	100.00
9788173662560	Lotus Domino in a Nutshell, 374 Pages	Neilson	2000	50.00
9788184041781	LPI Linux Certification in a Nutshell, 2/ed, 996 Pages	Pritchard	2006	150.00
9788173663611	Managing NFS & NIS, 2/ed, 518 Pages	Stern	2001	100.00

ISBN	Title	Author	Year	Price
9788173665233	Managing RAID on Linux, 268 Pages	Vadala	2002	100.00
9788173668654	Managing Security with Snort & IDS Tools, 296 Pages	Cox Ph.D.	2004	100.00
9788173662805	Managing the Windows 2000 Registry, 564 Pages	Robicheaux	2000	100.00
9788173664458	Mastering FreeBSD and OpenBSD Security, 472 Pages	Korff	2005	100.00
9788173665707	Mastering Visual Studio .NET 2003, 420 Pages	Flanders	2003	100.00
9788184040524	Monad, 218 Pages	Oakley	2005	75.00
9788173667497	Mono: A Developer's Notebook, 312 Pages	Dumbill	2004	100.00
9788173665646	MySQL Cookbook (Covers MySQL 4.0), 1,028 Pages	DuBois	2003	150.00
9788173666773	MySQL Pocket Reference, 94 Pages	Reese	2003	25.00
9788173663529	Network Security Hacks: 100 Industrial-Strength Tips & Tools, 328 Pages	Lockhart	2004	100.00
9788173665615	Object-Oriented Programming with Visual Basic .NET, 306 Pgs	Hamilton	2003	50.00
9788173667510	OpenOffice.org Writer (B/CD), 234 Pages	Weber	2004	75.00
9788173660672	Oracle Database Administration: The Essential Reference, 552 Pages	Kreines	1999	50.00
9788173660689	Oracle Distributed Systems (Book / DISK), 552 Pages	Dye	2000	75.00
9788173669354	Oracle Essentials: Oracle Database 10g, 3/ed, 368 Pages	Greenwald	2004	100.00
9788173664113	Oracle Essentials: Oracle9i, Oracle8i & Oracle8, 2/ed, 382 Pgs	Greenwald	2001	50.00
9788173663246	Oracle Net8 Configuration & Troubleshooting, 412 Pages	Toledo	1998	75.00
9788173663628	Oracle PL/SQL Best Practices, 208 Pages	Feuerstein	2001	50.00
9788184042542	Oracle PL/SQL Language Pocket Reference, 3/ed, 140 Pages	Feuerstein	2006	25.00
9788184040487	Oracle PL/SQL Programming, 4/ed, 1,210 Pages	Feuerstein	2005	200.00
9788173661198	Oracle PL/SQL Programming: Guide to Oracle8i Features (Book / DISK), 264 Pages	Feuerstein	1999	50.00
9788173660290	Oracle Scripts (B/CD), 208 Pages	Lomansky	1998	50.00
9788173660719	Oracle Security, 448 Pages	Theriault	1998	75.00
9788173662911	Oracle SQL: The Essential Reference, 424 Pages	Kreines	2000	75.00
9788173661211	Oracle Web Applications: PL/SQL Developer's Intro, 264 Pages	Odewahn	1999	75.00
9788173660283	Oracle8 Design Tips, 136 Pages	Ensor	1997	50.00
9788173668029	PC Annoyances: How to Fix the Most Annoying Things about your Personal Computer, 236 Pages	Bass	2003	75.00
9788173668272	PC Pest Control, 296 Pages	Gralla	2005	75.00
9788184041392	PC's: The Missing Manual, 612 Pages	Rathbone	2005	100.00
9788173661228	Perl 5 Pocket Reference, 2/ed, 96 Pages	Vromans	2002	25.00
9788173667190	Perl 6 Essentials, 208 Pages	Randal	2003	75.00
9788173668043	Perl Template Toolkit, 600 Pages	Chamberlain	2003	150.00
9788173661242	Perl/Tk Pocket Reference, 104 Pages	Lidie	1998	25.00
9788173662690	PHP Pocket Reference, 124 Pages	Lerdorf	2000	25.00
9788173669804	Powerpoint 2003 Personal Trainer (B/CD), (2 Color Book) 242 Pages	CustomGuide	2004	150.00
9788173661266	Practical Internet Groupware, 520 Pages	Udell	1999	75.00
9788173667114	Practical mod_perl, 932 Pages	Bekman	2003	150.00
9788184040326	Practical Perforce, 370 Pages	Wingerd	2005	100.00
9788173666735	Practical RDF, 360 Pages	Powers	2003	100.00
9788184040098	Prefactoring, 248 Pages	Pugh	2005	100.00
9788184047226	Programming Entity Framework, 844 Pages	Lerman	2009	150.00
9788173661273	Programming Internet E-mail, 384 Pages	Wood	1999	50.00
9788184040791	Programming MapPoint in .NET (B/CD), 400 Pages	Thota	2005	100.00

ISBN	Title	Author	Year	Price
9788173667060	Programming Visual Basic .NET 2003, 2/ed, 564 Pages	Liberty	2003	100.00
9788184040371	Programming Visual Basic 2005, 580 Pages	Liberty	2005	100.00
9788173662072	Programming Web Services with XML-RPC, 240 Pages	St.Laurent	2001	50.00
9788173668173	Programming with QT (Covers Qt 3), 2/ed, 532 Pages	Dalheimer	2002	125.00
9788184041507	Project 2003 Personal Trainer, **(B/CD)**, 246 Pages	CustomGuide	2005	100.00
9788173660191	QuarkXPress in a Nutshell, 552 Pages	O'Quinn	1998	50.00
9788173669682	RT Essentials, 228 Pages	Vincent	2005	75.00
9788173664229	SAX2 (Simple API for XML), 248 Pages	Brownell	2002	50.00
9788173667282	Secure Programming Cookbook for C and C++, 800 Pages	Viega	2003	150.00
9788173663260	Securing Windows NT/2000 Servers for the Internet, 200 Pages	Norberg	1998	50.00
9788173669378	Securing Windows Server 2003, 456 Pages	Danseglio	2004	100.00
9788173662485	sed & awk Pocket Reference, 60 Pages	Robbins	1998	25.00
9788173661297	sendmail Desktop Reference, 74 Pages	Costales	1997	25.00
9788173665837	sendmail, 3/ed, 1,238 Pages	Costales	2002	150.00
9788184040678	Skype Hacks: Tips & Tools for Cheap, Fun, Innovative Phone Service, 354 Pages	Sheppard	2005	75.00
9788173663864	Solaris 8 Administrator's Guide, 308 Pages	Watters	2002	100.00
9788173669194	SpamAssassin (Covers 3.0), 232 Pages	Schwartz	2004	100.00
9788173668418	Squid: The Definitive Guide, 472 Pages	Wessels	2004	100.00
9788173662928	SSH: The Secure Shell: The Definitive Guide, 564 Pages	Barrett	2001	75.00
9788184042634	Statistics Hacks, 380 Pages	Frey	2006	100.00
9788184041798	SUSE Linux, 460 Pages	Brown	2006	100.00
9788173669514	SWT: A Developer's Notebook, 330 Pages	Hatton	2004	100.00
9788173663253	T1: A Survival Guide, 312 Pages	Gast	2001	50.00
9788184040531	Talk is Cheap: Switching to Internet Telephones, 278 Pages	Gaskin	2005	100.00
9788173662607	Tcl/Tk Pocket Reference, 100 Pages	Raines	1998	25.00
9788173666872	Tomcat: The Definitive Guide (Cover Tomcat 4), 336 Pages	Brittain	2004	100.00
9788184040210	Twisted Network Programming Essentials, 210 Pages	Fettig	2005	100.00
9788173665844	Using Samba, 2/ed, 568 Pages	Eckstein	2003	100.00
9788173663307	VBScript Pocket Reference, 118 Pages	Childs	2000	25.00
9788173661341	Virtual Private Networks, 2/ed, 228 Pages	Scott	1998	50.00
9788184042092	Visual Basic 2005 Cookbook, 754 Pages	Craig	2006	150.00
9788184040913	Visual Basic 2005 in a Nutshell 3/ed, 766 Pages	Patrick	2006	150.00
9788184040067	Visual Basic 2005 Jumpstart, 226 Pages	Lee	2005	75.00
9788173666162	Visual Basic 2005: A Developer's Notebook, 272 Pages	MacDonald	2005	100.00
9788173669743	Visual C# 2005: A Developer's Notebook, 250 Pages	Liberty	2005	100.00
9788173665011	Visual Studio Hacks: Tips & Tools for Turbo charging the IDE, 304 Pages	Avery	2005	75.00
9788173663475	Web Database Applications with PHP & MySQL, 600 Pages	Williams	2002	75.00
9788173664410	Web Performance Tuning, 2/ed, 488 Pages	Killelea	2002	75.00
9788173665219	Web Privacy with P3P, 350 Pages	Cranor	2002	100.00
9788184046151	Web Security Testing Cookbook, 328 Pages	Hope	2008	100.00
9788173669675	Web Site Measurement Hacks: Tips & Tools to Help Optimize Your Online Business, 442 Pages	Peterson	2005	75.00
9788173665936	WebLogic Server 6.1 Workbook for Enterprise JavaBeans, 3/ed, 264 Pages	Nyberg	2001	50.00
9788173662638	Windows 2000 Active Directory, 624 Pages	Lowe-Norris	2002	75.00

ISBN	Title	Author	Year	Price
9788173662782	Windows 2000 Administration in a Nutshell: A Desktop Quick Reference, 1,000 Pages	Tulloch	2001	50.00
9788173663314	Windows 2000 Commands Pocket Reference, 122 Pages	Frisch	2001	25.00
9788173663321	Windows 2000 Performance Guide, 650 Pages	Friedman	2002	75.00
9788173660740	Windows 2000 Quick Fixes, 304 Pages	Boyce	2001	50.00
9788184042603	Windows Developers Power Tools, 1,322 Pages	Avery	2006	250.00
9788173660887	Windows NT TCP/IP Network Administration, 512 Pages	Hunt	1999	100.00
9788184040777	Windows Server 2003 Security Cookbook, 522 Pages	Danseglio	2005	150.00
9788184042986	Windows Vista In A Nutshell, 766 Pages	Gralla	2006	100.00
9788184043075	Windows Vista Pocket Reference, 208 Pages	Gralla	2007	50.00
9788184042139	Windows Vista: The Definitive Guide, 958 Pages	Stanek	2007	150.00
9788184042580	Windows Vista: The Missing Manual, 860 Pages	Pogue	2006	150.00
9788173669644	Windows XP Personal Trainer **(B/CD)**, 480 Pages	Custom Guide	2004	150.00
9788173665912	Windows XP Unwired: A Guide for Home, Office, and the Road, 316 Pages	Lee	2003	75.00
9788173667466	Wireless Hacks: 100 Industrial-Strength Tips & Tools, 424 Pages	Flickenger	2003	100.00
9788184043020	Wireless Hacks, 2/ed: Tips & Tools For Building, Extending & Securing Your Network 2/ed, 480 Pages	Flickenger	2005	100.00
9788173666117	Word Annoyances, 218 Pages	Hart	2005	75.00
9788184041422	XAML in a Nutshell, 316 Pages	MacVittie	2006	100.00
9788184045574	XSLT, 2/ed (Now Covers XSLT 2.0), 1,002 Pages	Tidwell	2008	150.00
9788184040074	Yahoo! Hacks: Tips & Tools for Living on the Web Frontier, 504 Pgs	Bausch	2005	75.00
9788184040883	Zero Configuration Networking: The Definitive Guide, 252 Pages	Cheshire	2005	50.00

Current Titles

ISBN	Title	Author	Year	Price
9788173666537	.NET and XML, 484 Pages	Bornstein	2004	425.00
9788173669200	.NET Compact Framework Pocket Guide, 122 Pages	Lee	2004	125.00
9788173665721	.NET Gotchas: 75 Ways to Improve Your C# and VB.NET Programs, 402 Pages	Subramaniam	2005	300.00
9789350234051	**21 Recipes for Mining Twitter, 96 Pages**	**Russell**	**2011**	**150.00**
9789350233993	**50 Tips and Tricks for MongoDB Developers, 88 Pages**	**Chodorow**	**2011**	**125.00**
9788184041637	802.11 Wireless Networks: The Definitive Guide, 2nd/ed (Covers 802.11a, g, n & i), 668 Pages	Gast	2005	550.00
9788184049510	**97 Things Every Programmer Should Know, 272 Pages**	**Henney**	**2010**	**350.00**
9788184048131	97 Things Every Project Manager Should Know, 268 Pages	Davis	2009	350.00
9788184046892	97 Things Every Software Architect Should Know, 236 Pages	Monson	2009	300.00
9788184042924	Access 2007 For Starters: The Missing Manual, 426 Pages	MacDonald	2007	400.00
9789350230503	**Access 2010: The Missing Manual, 852 Pages**	**MacDonald**	**2010**	**950.00**
9788184043334	Access Data Analysis Cookbook, 384 Pages	Bluttman	2007	375.00
9788173664281	Access Database Design & Programming, 3/ed, 454 Pages	Roman	2002	375.00
9788173666377	Access Hacks: Tips & Tools for Wrangling Your Data, 362 Pages	Bluttman	2005	325.00
9788184042832	ActionScript 3.0 Cookbook, 600 Pages	Lott	2006	475.00
9788173667237	ActionScript Cookbook, 904 Pages	Lott	2003	675.00
9788184043747	ActionScript 3.0 Design Patterns: Object Oriented Programming Techniques (Adobe Developer Library), 552 Pages	Sanders	2007	500.00
9788184046120	ActionScript 3.0 Quick Reference Guide, The, 508 Pages	Stiller	2008	425.00
9788173666551	ActionScript for Flash MX Pocket Reference, 152 Pages	Moock	2003	125.00

ISBN	Title	Author	Year	Price
8184046496496	Active Directory: Designing, Deploying, and Running Active Directory, 4/ed, 876 Pages	Desmond	2008	800.00
9788184047103	Active Directory Cookbook, 3/ed: Solutions for Administrators & Developers, 1104 Pages	Hunter	2009	750.00
9788184045390	Adobe AIR for JavaScript Developers Pocket Guide, 220 Pages	Chambers	2008	150.00
9788184043501	Adding Ajax, 418 Pages	Power	2007	400.00
9788184044980	ADO.NET 3.5 Cookbook, 2/ed (Updated for .NET 3.5, LINQ, and SQL Server 2008), 1,098 Pages	Hamilton	2008	750.00
8184046446441	Adobe AIR 1.5 Cookbook: Solutions and Examples for Rich Internet Application Developers, 460 Pages	Tucker	2008	500.00
9789350231197	**Adobe InDesign CS4 One-on-One, 580 Pages**	**McClelland**	**2010**	**875.00**
9788184043563	Adobe Integrated Runtime(AIR) for JavaScript Developers Pocket Reference, 192 Pages	Dura	2007	150.00
9788173668302	Advanced Perl Programming, 2/ed, 308 Pages	Cozens	2005	325.00
9788184044409	Advanced Rails, 374 Pages	Ediger	2008	375.00
9788184046083	Algorithms in a Nutshell: A Desktop Quick Reference, 376 Pages	Heineman	2008	250.00
9788184041576	Ajax Design Patterns, 668 Pages	Mahemoff	2006	500.00
9788184041064	Ajax Hacks: Tips & Tools for Creating Responsive Web Sites, 304 Pages	Perry	2006	350.00
9788184043082	Ajax on Java, 176 Pages	Olson	2007	250.00
9788184042610	Ajax on Rails, 364 Pages	Raymond	2007	350.00
9788184044898	Ajax: The Definitive Guide, 996 Pages	Holdener	2008	800.00
9788173667299	Amazon Hacks: 100 Industrial Strength Tips & Tricks, 312 Pages	Bausch	2003	250.00
9788173667794	Analyzing Business Data with Excel, 276 Pages	Knight	2006	300.00
9788184047332	Android Application Development, 354 Pages	Rogers	2009	425.00
9788184040807	ANT: The Definitive Guide, 2/ed (Cover ANT 1.6), 346 Pages	Holzner	2005	375.00
9788184044416	Apache Cookbook, 2/ed, 322 Pages	Bowen	2008	375.00
9788184046007	Apache 2 Pocket Reference, 230 Pages	Ford	2008	150.00
9788173662270	Apache Security, 428 Pages	Ristic	2005	400.00
9788173665134	Apache: The Definitive Guide, 3/ed, 594 Pages	Laurie	2002	500.00
9788184043549	Apollo for Adobe Flex Developers Pocket Guide, 154 Pages	Dixon	2007	125.00
9789350233962	**App Inventor, 352 Pages**	**Wolber**	**2011**	**625.00**
9788184040395	Applied Software Project Management, 304 Pages	Stellman	2005	350.00
9788184048452	Apprenticeship Patterns: Guidance for the Aspiring Sofware Craftsman, 184 pages	Hoover	2009	275.00
9789350233627	**Arduino Cookbook, 680 Pages**	**Margolis**	**2011**	**850.00**
9788184044232	The Art of Agile Development, 446 Pages	Shore	2007	450.00
9788184045963	The Art of Capacity Planning, 168 Pages	Allspaw	2008	200.00
9788184047370	The Art of Concurrency, 322 Pages	Breshears	2009	575.00
9788173667831	The Art of Project Management, 512 Pages	Berkun	2005	350.00
9788184048513	The Art of SEO, 620 Pages	Enge	2009	925.00
9788184041415	The Art of SQL, 382 Pages	Faroult	2006	400.00
9788173664588	ASP.NET 2.0: Developer's Notebook, 358 Pages	Lee	2005	525.00
9788173669385	AspectJ Cookbook, 364 Pages	Miles	2004	350.00
9788184045468	Asterisk: The Future of Telephony, 2/ed, 618 Pages	Meggelen	2008	575.00
9788184042702	Astronomy Hacks, 420 Pages	Thompson	2005	450.00
9788184047318	Automating System Administration with Perl, 2/ed, 686 Pages	Edelman	2009	600.00
9788184042900	Backup & Recovery, 774 Pages	Preston	2007	600.00

ISBN	Title	Author	Year	Price
9789350234662	Basic Sensors in iOS, 128 Pages	Allan	2011	200.00
9788184043471	Bash Cookbook, 640 Pages	Albing	2007	500.00
9789350230312	Bash Pocket Reference, 148 Pages	Robbins	2010	225.00
9788184043556	Beautiful Code: Leading Programmers Explain How They Think, 634 Pages	Wilson	2007	550.00
9788184046908	Beautiful Architecture, 442 Pages	Gousios	2009	500.00
9788184047967	Beautiful Data, 404 Pages	Segaran	2009	650.00
9788184047110	Beautiful Security, 316 Pages	Oram	2009	350.00
9788184047035	Beautiful Teams, 524 Pages	Stellman	2009	475.00
9788184048650	Beautiful Testing, 358 Pages	Goucher	2009	550.00
9789350230510	Beautiful Visualization, 404 Pages	Steele	2010	600.00
9788173663956	Beginning Perl for Bioinformatics, 390 Pages	Tisdall	2001	375.00
9789350230657	Being Geek: The Software Developer's Career Handbook, 356 Pages	Lopp	2010	450.00
9789350231142	Best iPhone Apps, 2/ed, 272 Pages	Biersdorfer	2010	375.00
9788184040036	Beyond Java, 206 Pages	Tate	2005	200.00
9788184048988	Bioinformatics Programming Using Python, 540 Pages	Model	2010	550.00
9788184044393	Building a Web 2.0 Portal with ASP.NET 3.5, 324 Pages	Zabir	2008	325.00
9789350231173	Building Android Apps with HTML, CSS, & JavaScript, 204 Pgs	Stark	2010	300.00
9789350234488	Building and Testing with Gradle, 136 Pages	Berglund	2011	225.00
9788184047127	Building Embedded Linux Systems, 2/ed: Concepts, techniques, tricks, and traps, 478 Pages	Gerum	2009	450.00
9788173661013	Building Internet Firewalls 2/ed, 904 Pages	Chapman	2000	650.00
9788184049428	Building iPhone Apps with HTML, CSS, & JavaScript, 202 Pgs	Stark	2010	300.00
9788173661396	Building Linux Clusters (B/CD), 360 Pages	Spector	2002	350.00
9788184041545	Building Scalable Web Sites, 362 Pages	Henderson	2006	325.00
9788184048322	Building Social Web Applications, 452 Pages	Bell	2009	675.00
9788173664748	Building the Perfect PC, 360 Pages	Thompson	2004	350.00
9789350231906	Building the Perfect PC, 3/ed, 368 Pages	Thompson	2010	825.00
9789350230527	Building the Realtime User Experience, 344 Pages	Roden	2010	525.00
9789350234525	Building on SugarCRM, 104 Pages	Mertic	2011	175.00
9789350232897	Building Wireless Sensor Networks, 344 Pages	Faludi	2010	525.00
9789350234471	Building Web Apps for Google TV, 140 Pages	Ferrate	2011	225.00
9789350230145	Buying a Home: The Missing Manual, 372 Pages	Conner	2010	550.00
9788184040494	C in a Nutshell, 618 Pages	Prinz	2005	400.00
9788173666605	C Pocket Reference, 142 Pages	Prinz	2002	125.00
9788184044423	C# 3.0 Cookbook, 3/ed, 902 Pages	Hilyard	2008	650.00
9788184044379	C# 3.0 Design Patterns, 338 Pages	Bishop	2008	350.00
9788184049459	C# 4.0 in a Nutshell, 4/ed, 1064 Pages	Albahari	2010	725.00
9788184044911	C# 3.0 Pocket Reference, 2/ed, 258 Pages	Albahari	2008	175.00
9789350230831	C# 4.0 Pocket Reference, 3/ed, 232 Pages	Albahari	2010	225.00
9788173663192	C# Essentials, 2/ed, 224 Pages	Albahari	2002	275.00
9788173664298	C# Essentials, 2/ed, 224 Pages	Albahari	2002	175.00
9788173665196	C# Language Pocket Reference, 132 Pages	Drayton	2002	100.00
9788173664434	C# & VB .NET Conversion Pocket Reference, 156 Pages	Mojica	2002	125.00
9788184040364	C++ Cookbook, 604 Pages	Stephens	2005	400.00
9788173666629	C++ in a Nutshell, (Cover ISO/IEC 14882 STD) 816 Pages	Lischner	2003	500.00

ISBN	Title	Author	Year	Price
9788173667107	C++ Pocket Reference, 148 Pages	Loudon	2003	100.00
9789350232392	**Canvas Pocket Reference, 128 Pages**	**Flanagan**	**2010**	**125.00**
9789350231937	**Cassandra: The Definitive Guide, 352 Pages**	**Hewitt**	**2010**	**525.00**
9788173660450	CGI Programming with Perl 2/ed, 476 Pages	Gundavaram	2000	350.00
9788184042849	Cisco IOS Cookbook, 2/ed, 1,250 Pages	Dooley	2006	900.00
9788173669842	Cisco IOS in a Nutshell, 2/ed: A Desktop Quick Reference for IOS on IP Network, 808 Pages	Boney	2005	500.00
9788184047134	CJKV Information Processing, 2/ed, 916 Pages	Lunde	2009	700.00
9788173668463	Classic Shell Scripting, 568 Pages	Robbins	2005	475.00
9789350231111	**Closure: The Definitive Guide, 616 Pages**	**Bolin**	**2010**	**925.00**
9788184047141	Cloud Application Architectures: Building Applications and Infrastructure in the Cloud, 220 Pages	Reese	2009	300.00
9788184048155	Cloud Security and Privacy, 352 Pages	Mather	2009	450.00
9789350230152	**Cocoa and Objective-C: Up and Running, 436 Pages**	**Stevenson**	**2010**	**650.00**
9788184047455	Complete Web Monitoring, 682 Pages	Croll	2009	975.00
9788184041583	Computer Security Basics, 2/ed, 324 Pages	Lehtinen	2006	325.00
9789350234204	**Concurrent Programming in Mac OS X & iOS, 80 Pages**	**Nahavandipoor**	**2011**	**125.00**
9788184048469	Confessions of a Public Speaker, 256 Pages	Berkun	2009	375.00
9789350231593	**Conversion Optimization: The Art and Science of Converting Prospects to Customers, 292 Pages**	**Saleh**	**2010**	**450.00**
9789350231210	**Cooking for Geeks: Real Science, Great Hacks, & Good Food, 456 Pages**	**Potter**	**2010**	**825.00**
9788184049473	**CouchDB: The Definitive Guide, 288 Pages**	**Anderson**	**2010**	**425.00**
9788184047158	Creating a Web Site: The Missing Manual, 2/ed: 622 Pages	MacDonald	2009	550.00
9789350233955	**Creating a Web Site: The Missing Manual, 3/ed: 604 Pages**	**MacDonald**	**2011**	**550.00**
9788184048971	CSS Cookbook, 3/ed, 746 Pages	Schmitt	2009	850.00
9788184047165	CSS Pocket Reference: Visual Presentation for the Web, 3/ed: 184 Pgs	Meyer	2009	150.00
9788184048124	CSS: The Missing Manual, 2/ed, 580 Pages	McFarland	2009	825.00
9788184042788	CSS: The Definitive Guide, 3/ed, 550 Pages	Meyer	2006	500.00
9789350231777	**Data Analysis with Open Source Tools, 556 Pages**	**Janert**	**2010**	**825.00**
9788173662362	Database Nation: The Death of Privacy in the 21st Century, 336 Pages	Garfinkel	2000	235.00
9788173662898	Database Programming with JDBC & Java 2/ed, 348 Pages	Reese	2000	300.00
9788184046632	Data-Driven Services with Silverlight 2, 372 Pages	Papa	2009	400.00
9789350230992	**Delphi in a Nutshell: A Desktop Quick Reference, 596 Pages**	**Lischner**	**2010**	**825.00**
9788184042597	Designing Embedded Hardware, 2/ed, 406 Pages	Catsoulis	2005	275.00
9789350232408	**Designing Interfaces, 2/ed, 600 Pages**	**Tidwell**	**2011**	**750.00**
9789350234532	**Designing for XOOPS, 148 Pages**	**Ruoyu**	**2011**	**225.00**
9789350234006	**Developing Android Applications with Adobe AIR, 340 Pages**	**Brossier**	**2011**	**500.00**
9789350234129	**Developing Android Applications with Flex 4.5, 136 Pages**	**Tretola**	**2011**	**200.00**
9788173662423	Developing Bio-informatics Computer Skills, 504 Pages	Gibas	2001	225.00
9789350234464	**Developing BlackBerry Tablet Applications with Flex 4.5, 136 Pgs**	**Tretola**	**2011**	**225.00**
9788173669477	Developing Feeds with RSS and Atom, 280 Pages	Hammersley	2005	300.00
9788184049626	**Developing Large Web Applications, 306 Pages**	**Loudon**	**2010**	**475.00**
9788184040111	Digital Identity, 266 Pages	Windley	2005	275.00
9788184041965	DNS & BIND (Covers BIND 9.3), 5/ed, 654 Pages	Albitz	2006	600.00
9788173665677	DNS & BIND Cookbook, 248 Pages	Liu	2002	250.00

ISBN	Title	Author	Year	Price
9789350234112	**DNS and BIND on IPv6, 76 Pages**	**Liu**	**2011**	**100.00**
9789350230374	**DocBook 5: The Definitive Guide, 568 Pages**	**Walsh**	**2010**	**850.00**
9788184045567	Dojo: The Definitive Guide, 502 Pages	Russell	2008	400.00
9788184041200	Dreamweaver 8 Design and Construction, 330 Pages	Campbell	2006	375.00
9788184041033	Dreamweaver 8: The Missing Manual, 964 Pages	David	2005	600.00
9788184046519	Dreamweaver CS4: The Missing Manual, 1,104 Pages	McFarland	2008	850.00
9789350230534	**Dreamweaver CS5: The Missing Manual, 1116 Pages**	**McFarland**	**2010**	**1,225.00**
9789350232958	**Droid 2: The Missing Manual, 414 Pages**	**Gralla**	**2011**	**625.00**
9788184042771	Dynamic HTML: The Definitive Reference, 3/ed, 1,336 Pages	Goodman	2006	800.00
9788184048308	Essential Blogging, 280 Pages	Doctorow	2009	425.00
9788173669019	Eclipse (Coverage of 3.0), 344 Pages	Holzner	2004	325.00
9788173669309	Eclipse Cookbook (Cover 3.0), 372 Pages	Holzner	2004	350.00
9788173669941	Eclipse IDE Pocket Guide, 140 Pages	Burnette	2005	125.00
9788173663017	Effective awk Programming, 3/ed, 454 Pages	Robbins	2001	325.00
9789350234679	**Elastic Beanstalk, 108 Pages**	**Vliet**	**2011**	**175.00**
9788184049886	**Enterprise Development with Flex, 700 Pages**	**Fain**	**2010**	**850.00**
9788184041194	Enterprise JavaBeans 3.0, 5/ed, 774 Pages	Monson-Haefel	2006	500.00
9789350231135	**Enterprise JavaBeans 3.1, 6/ed, 788 Pages**	**Rubinger**	**2010**	**525.00**
9788184046137	Enterprise Rails, 366 Pages	Chak	2008	350.00
9788173666780	Enterprise Service Bus, 284 Pages	Chappell	2004	300.00
9788184041446	Enterprise SOA, 468 Pages	Woods	2006	450.00
9788184047493	Erlang Programming, 514 Pages	Cesarini	2009	850.00
9788173669316	Essential ActionScript 2.0, 528 Pages	Moock	2004	475.00
9788184043662	Essential ActionScript 3.0, 962 Pages	Moock	2007	600.00
9788184040104	Essential Business Process Modeling, 362 Pages	Havey	2005	350.00
9788184042757	Essential CVS, 2/ed, 442 Pages	Vesperman	2006	425.00
9788184040241	Essentail PHP Security, 152 Pages	Shiflett	2005	125.00
9788184045437	Essentail SharePoint 2007, 2/ed, 462 Pages	Webb	2008	475.00
9788184042825	Essentail SNMP, 2/ed, 480 Pages	Mauro	2005	400.00
9788184045277	Essential SQLAlchemy, 242 Pages	Copeland	2008	275.00
9788173665295	Essential System Administration, 3/ed, 1,178 Pages	Frisch	2002	650.00
9788173666643	Essential System Administration Pocket Reference, 152 Pages	Frisch	2002	125.00
9788173660252	Essential Windows NT System Administration, 488 Pages	Frisch	1998	225.00
9788173662492	Ethernet: The Definitive Guide, 528 Pages	Spurgeon	2000	300.00
9788184047462	Even Faster Web Sites, 274 Pages	Souders	2009	500.00
9788184044058	Excel 2007 Pocket Guide, 2/ed, 180 Pages	Frye	2007	125.00
9788184042559	Excel 2007: The Missing Manual, 870 Pages	MacDonald	2006	550.00
9789350230541	**Excel 2010: The Missing Manual, 916 Pages**	**MacDonald**	**2010**	**500.00**
9788184043518	Excel Hacks, 2/ed, Tips & Tools for Streamlining Your Spreadsheets, 428 Pages	David	2007	400.00
9789350233764	**Facebook: The Missing Manual, 3rd Edition**	**Veer**	**2011**	**600.00**
9789350230985	**Flash 8: The Missing Manual, 484 Pages**	**Veer**	**2010**	**725.00**
9788184041361	Flash 8 Cookbook, 548 Pages	Lott	2006	400.00
9788184041040	Flash 8 Project for Learning Animation and Interactivity **(B/CD)**, 372 Pages	Shupe	2006	400.00
9788184046502	Flash CS4: The Missing Manual, 768 Pages	Grover	2008	700.00

ISBN	Title	Author	Year	Price
9789350230381	**Flash CS5: The Missing Manual, 796 Pages**	**Grover**	**2010**	**725.00**
9788173667473	Flash Hacks: 100 Industrial Strength Tips & Tools, 504 Pages	Bhangal	2004	400.00
9788173668593	Flash Out of the Box: A User-Centric Beginner's Guide to Flash **(B/CD)**, 264 Pages	Hoekman	2004	300.00
9788173667312	Flash Remoting MX: The Definitive Guide, 652 Pages	Muck	2003	550.00
9788184048162	flex & bison, 310 Pages	Levine	2009	475.00
9788184045246	Flex 3 Cookbook, 798 Pages	Noble	2008	800.00
9789350230428	**Flex 4 Cookbook, 780 Pages**	**Noble**	**2010**	**900.00**
9788184048940	Flex 3 with Java, 309 Pages	Kore	2009	350.00
9789350234686	**Functional Programming for Java Developers, 112 Pages**	**Wampler**	**2011**	**175.00**
9789350234549	**Gamification by Design, Implementing Game Mechanics in Web and Mobile Apps, 232 Pages**	**Zichermann**	**2011**	**350.00**
9789350230664	**Gamestorming: A Playbook for Innovators, Rulebreakers, and Changemakers, 308 Pages**	**Gray**	**2010**	**450.00**
9788173668685	GDB Pocket Reference, 78 Pages	Robbins	2005	75.00
9788184045284	Getting Started with Flex 3: An Adobe Developer Library Pocket Guide, 162 Pages	Herrington	2008	125.00
9789350230596	**Getting Started with Processing, 232 Pages**	**Reas**	**2010**	**300.00**
9789350234136	**Getting Started with the Internet of Things, 212 Pages**	**Pfister**	**2011**	**275.00**
9788184049503	**Google Advertising Tools, 2nd/ed, 452 Pages**	**Davis**	**2010**	**675.00**
9789350230923	**Google Analytics, 240 Pages**	**Cutroni**	**2010**	**350.00**
9788184045079	Google Apps Hacks, 396 Pages	Lenssen	2008	525.00
9788184044942	Google Hacks, 3/ed, Tips & Tools for Finding and Using the World's Information, 558 Pages	Dornfest	2008	400.00
9788184040876	Google Maps Hacks: Tips & Tools for Geographic Searching & Remixing, 366 Pages	Gibson	2006	350.00
9788173667138	Google Pocket Guide, 144 Pages	Calishain	2003	125.00
9789350234556	**Google Power Search, 96 Pages**	**Spencer**	**2011**	**150.00**
9788184048285	Google SketchUp, 616 Pages	Grover	2009	925.00
9788184042856	Google: The Missing Manual, 2/ed, 478 Pages	Milstein	2006	425.00
9789350234013	**Graphics and Animation on iOS, 104 Pages**	**Nahavandipoor**	**2011**	**150.00**
9788184046915	Grep Pocket Reference, 98 Pages	Bambenek	2009	125.00
9789350230398	**Hackers & Painters: Big Ideas from the Computer Age, 292 Pages**	**Graham**	**2010**	**450.00**
9789350230404	**Hackers: Heroes of the Computer Revolution, 540 Pages**	**Levy**	**2010**	**800.00**
9788184048148	Hacking: The Next Generation, 314 Pages	Dhanjani	2009	475.00
9788184048667	Hadoop: The Definitive Guide, 544 Pages	White	2009	550.00
9789350231272	**Hadoop: The Definitive Guide, 2/ed, 648 Pages**	**White**	**2010**	**550.00**
9788173668258	Hardcore Java, 354 Pages	Simmons	2004	300.00
9788184045024	Harnessing Hibernate, 396 Pages	Elliott	2008	400.00
9788184048735	Head First 2D Geometry, 372 Pages	Fallow	2009	525.00
9788184045819	Head First Ajax: A Brain-Friendly Guide, 544 Pages	Riordan	2008	450.00
9788184046595	Head First Algebra: A Brain-Friendly Guide, 576 Pages	Pilone	2009	550.00
9788184044195	Head First C#: A Brain-Friendly Guide, 794 Pages	Stellman	2007	550.00
9789350230350	**Head First C#, 2ed: A Brain-Friendly Guide, 504 Pages**	**Stellman**	**2010**	**650.00**
9788184047998	Head First Data Analysis, 504 Pages	Milton	2009	500.00
9788173664663	Head First Design Patterns, 688 Pages	Sierra	2004	625.00

ISBN	Title	Author	Year	Price
9788173665264	Head First EJB: Passing the Sun Certified Business Component Developer Exam, 744 Pages	Sierra	2003	650.00
9788184049893	**Head First Excel: A Brain-Friendly Guide, 458 Pages**	**Milton**	**2010**	**450.00**
9788184040821	Head First HTML with CSS & XHTML, 694 Pages	Freeman	2005	500.00
9788184048476	Head First iPhone Development, 567 Pages	Pilone	2009	525.00
9788173666025	Head First Java: Your Brain on Java - A Learner's Guide, 2nd/ed (Cover Java 5.0), 730 Pages	Sierra	2005	625.00
9788184044362	Head First JavaScript: A Brain-Friendly Guide, 666 Pages	Morrison	2008	600.00
9788184047301	Head First Networking: A Brain-Friendly Guide, 556 Pages	Anderson	2009	550.00
9788184042214	Head First Object - Oriented Analysis & Design, 648 Pages	McLaughlin	2006	600.00
9788184048001	Head First PMP, 2nd/ed 852 Pages	Greene	2009	700.00
9788184048766	Head First Programming, 460 Pages	Griffiths	2009	450.00
9788184046588	Head First PHP & MySQL : A Brain-Friendly Guide, 828 Pages	Beighley	2009	650.00
9788184045994	Head First Physics: A Learner's Companion to Mechanics and Practical Physics, 956 Pages	Lang	2008	750.00
9789350231883	**Head First Python, 516 Pages**	**Barry**	**2010**	**500.00**
9788184046571	Head First Rails: A learner's companion to Ruby on Rails, 478 Pgs	Griffiths	2009	500.00
9788184044973	Head First Servlets & JSP, 2/ed (COVER J2EE 1.5): Passing the Sun Certified Web Component Developer Exam, 948 Pages	Basham	2008	700.00
9788184044508	Head First Software Development, 512 Pages	Pilone	2008	500.00
9788184043686	Head First SQL: Your Brain on SQL -- A Learner's Guide, 624 Pgs	Beighley	2007	575.00
9788184045826	Head First Statistics: A Brain-Friendly Guide, 732 Pages	Griffiths	2008	650.00
9788184046601	Head First Web Design: A Brain-Friendly Guide, 512 Pages	Watrall	2009	500.00
9789350230671	**Head First WordPress: A Brain-Friendly Guide, 386 Pages**	**Siarto**	**2010**	**450.00**
9788184041057	Head Rush Ajax, 464 Pages	McLaughlin	2006	375.00
9788173669347	Hibernate: A Developer's Notebook, 190 Pages	Elliott	2004	225.00
9788184049909	**High Performance JavaScript, 252 Pages**	**Zakas**	**2010**	**275.00**
9788173669262	High Performance Linux Cluster with OSCAR, Rocks, OpenMosix, and MPI, 380 Pages	Sloan	2004	350.00
9788173669026	High Performance MySQL: Optimization, Backups, Replication & Load Balancing, 304 Pages	Zawodny	2004	300.00
9788184047189	High Performance MySQL: Optimization, Backups, Replication 2/ed, 724 Pages	Schwartz	2009	625.00
9788184043808	High Performance Web Sites: Essential Knowledge for Front-End Engineers, 184 Pages	Souders	2007	200.00
9788184049527	**HTML & CSS: The Good Parts, 368 Pages**	**Henick**	**2010**	**550.00**
9788184042696	HTML & XHTML Pocket Reference, 3/ed, 118 Pages	Robbins	2006	125.00
9788184048995	**HTML & XHTML Pockte Reference, 4/ed, 206 Pages**	**Robbins**	**2010**	**250.00**
9788184042146	HTML & XHTML the Definitive Guide, 6/ed, 692 Pages	Musciano	2006	500.00
9789350234020	**HTML5 Canvas, 676 Pages**	**Fulton**	**2011**	**825.00**
9789350234174	**HTML5 Geolocation, 136 Pages**	**Holdener**	**2011**	**175.00**
9789350230824	**HTML5: Up and Running, 244 Pages**	**Pilgrim**	**2010**	**375.00**
9788184049466	**HTTP: The Definitive Guide, 676 Pages**	**Gourley**	**2010**	**800.00**
9789350233801	**iMovie '11 & iDVD: The Missing Manual, 568 Pages**	**Pogue**	**2011**	**850.00**
9788184042917	Information Architecture for The World Wide Web, 3/ed, 540 Pgs	Morville	2006	500.00
9788184049039	**Inside Cyber Warfare, 252 Pages**	**Carr**	**2010**	**375.00**
9788184040388	Integrating Excel and Access, 232 Pages	Schmalz	2005	250.00

ISBN	Title	Author	Year	Price
9788184043617	Intel Threading Building Blocks Out fitting C++ for Multi-Core Processor Parallelism, 348 Pages	Reinders	2007	350.00
9788184045635	Intellectual Property and Open Source: A Practical Guide to Protecting Code, 406 Pages	Lindberg	2008	450.00
9788184040999	Intermediate Perl, 290 Pages	Schwartz	2006	300.00
9788173661051	Internet Core Protocols: The Definitive Guide **(B/CD)**, 476 Pgs	Hall	2000	375.00
9789350234037	**Introduction to Search with Sphinx, 168 Pages**	**Aksyonoff**	**2011**	**250.00**
9789350232934	**iOS 4 Programming Cookbook, 664 Pages**	**Nahavandipoor**	**2011**	**800.00**
9788173663376	IP Routing, 244 Pages	Malhotra	2002	250.00
9789350233979	**iPad: The Missing Manual, 352 Pages**	**Biersdorfer**	**2011**	**500.00**
9789350230336	**iPhone 3D Programming, 460 Pages**	**Rideout**	**2010**	**700.00**
9789350230329	**iPhone App Development: The Missing Manual, 360 Pgs**	**Hockenberry**	**2010**	**550.00**
9788184048728	iPhone Game Development, 276 Pages	Zirkle	2009	425.00
9788184046922	iPhone SDK Application Development, 408 Pages	Zdziarski	2009	500.00
9788184048742	iPhone The Missing Manual 3/ed, 428 Pages	Pogue	2009	525.00
9789350230848	**iPhone The Missing Manual 4/ed, 466 Pages**	**Pogue**	**2010**	**650.00**
9789350233818	**iPhoto '11: The Missing Manual, 408 Pages**	**Pogue**	**2011**	**600.00**
9788184042818	IPv6 Essentials, 2/ed, 450 Pages	Hagen	2006	450.00
9788173663024	IPv6 Network Administration, 316 Pages	Murphy	2005	325.00
9788173667374	J2EE Design Patterns, 390 Pages	Crawford	2003	400.00
9788173663437	J2ME in a Nutshell, 474 Pages	Topley	2002	450.00
9788173669293	Jakarta Commons Cookbook, 412 Pages	O'Brien	2004	375.00
9788173669484	Jakarta Struts Cookbook, 536 Pages	Siggelkow	2005	400.00
9788173667145	Jakarta Struts Pocket Reference, 142 Pages	Cavaness	2003	125.00
9788173664472	Java & SOAP, 286 Pages	Englander	2002	275.00
9788184043068	Java & XML, 3/ed, 496 Pages	McLaughlin	2006	450.00
9788173663796	Java & XSLT, 534 Pages	Burke	2001	350.00
9788173668470	Java 1.5 Tiger: A Developer's Notebook, 210 Pages	McLaughlin	2004	175.00
9788173669361	Java Cookbook (Coverage of 1.5), 2/ed, 872 Pages	Darwin	2004	600.00
9789350232903	**Java Cryptography, 388 Pages**	**Knudsen**	**2011**	**575.00**
9788173666667	Java Database Best Practices, 304 Pages	Eckstein	2003	275.00
9789350233610	**Java Distributed Computing, 408 Pages**	**Farley**	**2011**	**600.00**
9788173665776	Java Enterprise Best Practices, 296 Pages	Eckstein	2002	275.00
9788184042870	Java Enterprise in a Nutshell, 3/ed, 906 Pages	Farley	2005	600.00
9788173668630	Java Examples in a Nutshell: A Tutorial Companion to Java in a Nutshell, 3/ed, 728 Pages	Flanagan	2004	400.00
9788184042160	Java Generics and Collections, 308 Pages	Naftalin	2006	350.00
9788184042665	Java in a Nutshell, 5/ed, 1,266 Pages	Flanagan	2005	650.00
9788184041187	Java I/O, 2/ed, 740 Pages	Harold	2006	650.00
9788184047349	Java Message Service, 2/ed, 348 Pages	Richards	2009	350.00
9788173663536	Java Network Programming, 3/ed, 770 Pages	Harold	2004	500.00
9788173665110	Java NIO, 308 Pages	Hitchens	2002	275.00
9788184044881	Java Pocket Guide, 208 Pages	Liguori	2008	150.00
9788184045031	Java Power Tools, 926 Pages	Smart	2008	775.00
9788173663901	Java Programming with Oracle JDBC, 504 Pages	Bales	2001	300.00
9788173663819	Java RMI, 578 Pages	Grosso	2001	450.00
9788173664120	Java Security, 2/ed, 624 Pages	Oaks	2001	500.00
9788173668227	Java Servlet & JSP Cookbook, 756 Pages	Perry	2004	600.00

ISBN	Title	Author	Year	Price
9788173662850	Java Servlet Programming 2/ed, 786 Pages	Hunter	2001	600.00
9788173665684	Java Swing, 2/ed, 1,288 Pages	Loy	2002	750.00
9788173665929	Java Threads (Covers J2SE 5.0), 3/ed, 368 Pages	Oaks	2004	400.00
9788173663444	Java Web Services, 286 Pages	Chappell	2002	300.00
9788173666698	Java Web Services in a Nutshell: A Desktop Quick Reference (Covers J2EE 1.4 & JWSDP), 696 Pages	Topley	2003	500.00
9788184047196	Java Web Services: Up and Running, 332 Pages	Kalin	2009	325.00
9789350230138	**Java: The Good Parts, 212 Pages**	**Waldo**	**2010**	**325.00**
9788184045222	JavaScript: The Good Parts, 186 Pages	Crockford	2008	200.00
9788184041941	JavaScript: The Definitive Guide, 5/ed, 1,032 Pages	Flanagan	2006	775.00
9789350233948	**JavaScript: The Definitive Guide, 6/ed, 1,120 Pages**	**Flanagan**	**2011**	**825.00**
9788184045659	JavaScript: The Missing Manual, 560 Pages	McFarland	2008	500.00
9788184045451	JavaScript and DHTML Cookbook, 2/ed, 620 Pages	Goodman	2008	475.00
9789350230688	**JavaScript Cookbook, 574 Pages**	**Powers**	**2010**	**725.00**
9789350231159	**JavaScript Patterns, 260 Pages**	**Stefanov**	**2010**	**400.00**
9788173669033	JavaServer Faces, 614 Pages	Bergsten	2004	450.00
9788173663833	JavaServer Pages Pocket Reference, 96 Pages	Bergsten	2001	65.00
9788173665301	JavaServer Pages (Covers JSP 2.0 & JSTL 1.1), 3/ed, 762 Pgs	Bergsten	2003	550.00
9788184047011	Java SOA Cookbook, 756 Pages	Hewitt	2009	600.00
9788173669460	JBoss: A Developer's Notebook, 182 Pages	Richards	2005	225.00
9788184040173	JBoss at Work: A Practical Guide, 318 Pages	Marrs	2005	325.00
9788173666711	JDBC Pocket Reference, 160 Pages	Bales	2003	100.00
9788173662508	Jini in a Nutshell, 340 Pages	Oaks	2000	425.00
9789350234563	**Jenkins: The Definitive Guide, 428 Pages**	**Smart**	**2011**	**650.00**
9788173668609	JUnit Pocket Guide, 100 Pages	Beck	2004	100.00
9788184041163	JUNOS Cookbook, 682 Pages	Garrett	2006	450.00
9788184044997	JUNOS Enterprise Routing, 828 Pages	Marschke	2008	800.00
9788184047974	JUNOS Enterprise Switching, 772 Pages	Marschke	2009	1,150.00
9788184048193	JUNOS High Availability, 704 Pages	Sonderegger	2009	1,050.00
9789350231104	**Junos Security, 872 Pages**	**Cameron**	**2010**	**1,300.00**
9788184048018	Just a Geek, 316 Pages	Wheaton	2009	350.00
9789350234716	**Just Spring, 84 Pages**	**Konda**	**2011**	**125.00**
9788184048759	jQuery Cookbook, 594 Pages	Experts	2009	550.00
9789350234570	**jQuery Mobile, 152 Pages**	**Reid**	**2011**	**250.00**
9789350232385	**jQuery Pocket Reference, 176 Pages**	**Flanagan**	**2010**	**175.00**
9788184046427	JRuby Cookbook, 238 Pages	Edelson	2008	300.00
9788173665158	JXTA in a Nutshell: A Desktop Quick Reference, 422 Pages	Oaks	2002	225.00
9788173665608	Kerberos: The Definitive Guide, 280 Pages	Garman	2003	275.00
9788173669729	Killer Game Programming in Java, 986 Pages	Davison	2005	675.00
9788184040265	Knoppix Pocket Reference, 104 Pages	Rankin	2005	100.00
9788173666728	LDAP System Administration, 318 Pages	Carter	2003	400.00
9789350231364	**Learning ActionScript 3.0: A Beginner's Guide, 2/ed, 480 Pages**	**Shupe**	**2010**	**1,075.00**
9789350233788	**Learning Android, 292 Pages**	**Gargenta**	**2011**	**450.00**
9788184040456	Learning ASP.NET 2.0 with AJAX, 536 Pgs	Liberty	2007	400.00
9788184045666	Learning ASP.NET 3.5, 2/ed, 624 Pages	Liberty	2008	400.00
9788184046465	Learning C# 3.0, 708 Pages	Liberty	2008	450.00
9789350231890	**Learning Flex 4: Getting Up to Speed with Rich Internet Application Design and Development, 500 Pages**	**Cole**	**2010**	**1,125.00**

ISBN	Title	Author	Year	Price
9788173669637	Learning GNU Emacs, 3/ed, 544 Pages	Cameron	2004	450.00
9788184049718	**Learning iPhone Programming, 396 Pages**	**Allan**	**2010**	**600.00**
9788184040333	Learning Java,3/ed **(B/CD)** (Cover J2SE 5.0), 986 Pages	Niemeyer	2005	650.00
9788184047202	Learning JavaScript 2/ed, 412 Pages	Powers	2009	400.00
9788184042672	Learning MySQL, 632 Pages	Tahaghoghi	2006	575.00
9788184045970	Learning OpenCV: Computer Vision with the OpenCV Library, 592 Pages	Dr. Bradski	2008	525.00
9788173663918	Learning Oracle PL/SQL (Covers Oracle9i), 452 Pages	Pribyl	2001	325.00
9788184044263	Learning Perl, 5/ed (Covers Perl 5.10), 364 Pages	Schwartz	2008	325.00
9788184043716	Learning PHP & MySQL, 2/ed: Step-by-Step Guide to Creating Database-Driven Web Sites, 444 Pages	Davis	2007	400.00
9788184047943	Learning PHP, MySQL, and JavaScript, 548 Pages	Nixon	2009	675.00
9788173667329	Learning PHP 5, 378 Pages	Sklar	2004	350.00
9788184048261	Learning Python, 4/ed, 1,230 Pages	Lutz	2009	750.00
9788184046458	Learning Rails, 458 Pages	St. Laurent	2008	500.00
9788184043341	Learning Ruby, 272 Pages	Fitzgerald	2007	300.00
9789350234594	**Learning SPARQL, 280 Pages**	**DuCharme**	**2011**	**400.00**
9788184047219	Learning SQL 2/ed, 352 Pages	Beaulieu	2009	325.00
9788184043044	Learning SQL on SQL Server 2005, 342 Pages	Bagui	2006	350.00
9788173668050	Learning the Bash Shell, 3/ed, 362 Pages	Newham	2005	375.00
9788173664236	Learning the UNIX Operating System, 5/ed, 174 Pages	Peek	2001	150.00
9788173660610	Learning the vi Editor 6/ed, 352 Pages	Lamb	1998	250.00
9788184045840	Learning the vi and Vim Editors, 7th/ed, 508 Pages	Robbins	2008	400.00
9788184042689	Learning UML 2.0, 300 Pages	Miles	2006	275.00
9788184040906	Learning Web Design, 2nd/ed, 484 Pages	Robbins	2003	750.00
9788184049381	**Learning Web Design, 3rd/ed, 500 Pages**	**Robbins**	**2010**	**750.00**
9788184043495	Learning WCF, 624 Pages	Bustamante	2007	550.00
9788184048964	Learning XML, 2nd/ed, 436 Pages	Ray	2009	650.00
8184046476472	Learning XNA 3.0: XNA 3.0 Game Development for the PC, Xbox 360, and Zune, 506 Pages	Reed	2008	500.00
9789350232415	**Learning XNA 4.0: Game Development for the PC, Xbox 360, and Windows Phone 7, 558 Pages**	**Reed**	**2011**	**850.00**
9788173660627	lex & yacc 2/ed, 392 Pages	Levine	1992	250.00
9788184044904	LINQ Pocket Reference, 188 Pages	Albahari	2008	150.00
9788173668449	Linux Cookbook, 590 Pages	Schroder	2004	525.00
9788184040166	Linux Desktop Pocket Guide, 202 Pages	Brickner	2005	150.00
9788173668494	Linux Device Drivers, 3/ed, 646 Pgs	Rubini	2005	450.00
9788184048278	Linux in a Nutshell 6/ed, 960 Pages	Siever	2009	600.00
9788173668500	Linux iptables Pocket Reference, 106 Pages	Purdy	2004	100.00
9788184043525	Linux Kernel In A Nutshell, 216 Pages	Kroah	2006	225.00
9788173664540	Linux Network Administrator's Guide, 3/ed, 372 Pages	Kirch	2005	350.00
9788184044218	Linux Networking Cookbook, 654 Pages	Schroder	2007	575.00
9788173668647	Linux Pocket Guide, 212 Pages	Barrett	2004	150.00
9788173667183	Linux Security Cookbook, 340 Pages	Barrett	2003	325.00
9788184042887	Linux Server Security, 2/ed, 556 Pages	Bauer	2005	450.00
9788184043105	Linux System Administration, 310 Pages	Adelstein	2007	300.00
9788184043815	Linux System Programming: Talking Directly to the Kernel and C Library, 404 Pages	Love	2007	375.00

ISBN	Title	Author	Year	Price
9788173668432	Linux Unwired, 322 Pages	Weeks	2004	300.00
9788184048216	Living Green: The Missing Manual, 332 Pages	Conner	2009	475.00
9789350230558	**LPI Linux Certification in a Nutshell, 3/ed, 540 Pages**	**Haeder**	**2010**	**750.00**
9788184048483	Mac OS X Snow Leopard: The Missing Manual, 924 Pages	Pogue	2009	1,375.00
9788184048704	Mac OS X Snow Leopard: Pocket Guide, 252 Pages	Seibold	2009	250.00
9789350233740	**Make: Arduino Bots and Gadgets, 320 Pages**	**Karvinen**	**2011**	**650.00**
9789350233207	**Make: Electronics, 376 Pages**	**Platt**	**2011**	**450.00**
9789350231401	**Making Software:**			
	What Really Works, and Why We Believe It, 644 Pages	**Oram**	**2010**	**750.00**
9788173664656	Managing & Using MySQL, 2/ed, 448 Pages	Reese	2002	325.00
9789350234365	**Managing Infrastructure with Puppet, 68 Pages**	**Loope**	**2011**	**100.00**
9788173660276	Managing IP Networks with Cisco Routers, 352 Pages	Ballew	1997	200.00
9788173669583	Managing Projects with GNU Make, 3/ed, 310 Pages	Mecklenburg	2004	325.00
9788184047028	Masterminds of Programming, 510 Pages	Biancuzzi	2009	450.00
9788173661167	Mastering Algorithms with C **(B/CD)**, 572 Pages	Loudon	1999	400.00
9788173664618	Mastering Oracle SQL, 2/ed, 504 Pages	Mishra	2004	400.00
9788184043648	Mastering Perl, 458 Pages	Foy	2007	400.00
9788173666766	Mastering Perl for Bioinformatics, 406 Pages	Tisdall	2003	300.00
9788184043013	Mastering Regular Expressions, 3/ed, 556 Pages	Friedl	2006	450.00
9789350230305	**Mathematica Cookbook, 848 Pages**	**Mangano**	**2010**	**1,275.00**
9788173667916	Maven: A Developer's Notebook, 232 Pages	Massol	2005	250.00
9788184045987	Maven: The Definitive Guide, 484 Pages	Sonatype	2008	450.00
9788184042184	MCSE Core Elective Exams in a Nutshell, 604 Pages	Bhardwaj	2006	500.00
9788184041552	MCSE Core Required Exams in a Nutshell, 3/ed, 750 Pages	Stanek	2006	450.00
9788184043730	Microsoft Project 2007: The Missing Manual, 720 Pages	Biafore	2007	625.00
9789350230565	**Microsoft Project 2010: The Missing Manual, 788 Pages**	**Biafore**	**2010**	**1,175.00**
9789350234372	**Migrating Applications to IPv6, 72 Pages**	**York**	**2011**	**100.00**
9789350232941	**Mining the Social Web, 378 Pages**	**Russell**	**2011**	**575.00**
9788184047479	Mercurial: The Definitive Guide, 300 Pages	O'Sullivan	2009	550.00
9788184048179	Mobile Design and Development, 352 Pages	Fling	2009	525.00
9789350231128	**MongoDB: The Definitive Guide, 240 Pages**	**Chodorow**	**2010**	**350.00**
9789350234143	**Motorola Xoom: The Missing Manual, 444 Pages**	**Gralla**	**2011**	**625.00**
9788184042801	MySQL Cookbook, 2/ed, 990 Pages	DuBois	2006	900.00
9789350230695	**MySQL High Availability, 644 Pages**	**Bell**	**2010**	**800.00**
9788173668067	MySQL in a Nutshell, 358 Pages	Dyer	2005	325.00
9788184045444	MySQL Pocket Reference, 2/ed 148 Pages	Reese	2008	125.00
9788184041408	MySQL Stored Procedure Programming, 650 Pages	Harrison	2006	450.00
9788184047486	Natural Language Processing with Python, 522 Pages	Bird	2009	850.00
9788173665240	NetBeans: The Definitive Guide, 662 Pages	Boudreau	2002	500.00
9788184044256	Network Security Assessment: Know Your Network, 2/ed, 520 Pgs	McNab	2007	450.00
9788184042740	Network Security Hacks, 2/ed, 492 Pages	Lockhart	2006	425.00
9788173668395	Network Security Tools: Writing, Hacking,			
	and Modifying Security Tools , 350 Pages	Dhanjani	2005	350.00
9788173663680	Network Troubleshooting Tools, 370 Pages	Sloan	2005	250.00
9789350234150	**Network Warrior, 2nd Edition, 808 Pages**	**Donahue**	**2011**	**975.00**
9788184043532	Network Warrior, 614 Pages	Donahue	2007	450.00
9788173667923	Nokia Smartphone Hacks: Tips & Tools for Your Smallest			
	Computer, 418 Pages	Yuan	2005	400.00

ISBN	Title	Author	Year	Price
9788173667848	NUnit Pocket Reference, 100 Pages	Hamilton	2004	100.00
9788173668265	Office 2003 XML, 596 Pages	Lenz	2004	450.00
9788184043303	Office 2007: the Missing Manual, 890 Pages	Grover	2007	550.00
9789350230701	**Office 2010: The Missing Manual, 976 Pages**	**Conner**	**2010**	**800.00**
9789350232880	**Office 2011 for Macintosh: The Missing Manual, 840 Pages**	**Grover**	**2010**	**1,250.00**
9788184049534	**Open Government, 452 Pages**	**Lathrop**	**2010**	**675.00**
9788173667725	Open Source for the Enterprise, 246 Pages	Woods	2005	250.00
9788184040296	Open Sources 2.0, 488 Pages	DiBona	2005	425.00
9788173667404	Optimizing Oracle Performance, 426 Pages	Milsap	2003	375.00
9788173669286	Oracle Applications Server 10g Essentials, 292 Pages	Greenwald	2004	275.00
9788173661174	Oracle Built-in Packages **(Book/Disk)**, 956 Pages	Feuerstein	1998	475.00
9788173667077	Oracle Data Dictionary Pocket Reference, 150 Pages	Kreines	2003	125.00
9788173664175	Oracle DBA Checklist Pocket Reference, 88 Pages	RevealNet	2001	65.00
9788184040005	Oracle DBA Pocket Guide, 164 Pages	Kreines	2005	125.00
9788184044201	Oracle Essentials: Oracle Database 11g, 4/ed,422 Pages	Greenwald	2007	400.00
9788173665806	Oracle in a Nutshell: A Desktop Quick Reference, 934 Pages	Greenwald	2002	600.00
9788173664564	Oracle Initialization Parameters Pocket Reference (Oracle Database 10g), 128 Pages	Kreines	2004	125.00
9788184045413	Oracle PL/SQL Best Practices, 2/ed, 308 Pages	Feuerstein	2008	325.00
9788173661181	Oracle PL/SQL Built-ins Pocket Reference, 78 Pages	Feuerstein	1998	60.00
9788184040357	Oracle PL/SQL for DBAs: Security, Scheduling, Performance & More Includes Oracle Database 10g, 466 Pages	Feuerstein	2005	425.00
9788184045420	Oracle PL/SQL Language Pocket Reference, 4/ed, 194 Pages	Feuerstein	2008	125.00
9788184049497	**Oracle PL/SQL Programming, 5/ed, 1,246 Pages**	**Feuerstein**	**2010**	**650.00**
9788173662409	Oracle PL/SQL Programming: A Developer's Workbook, 576 Pages	Feuerstein	2000	575.00
9788173668111	Oracle Regular Expression Pocket Reference, 74 Pages	Burcham	2003	75.00
9788173661204	Oracle SAP Administration, 208 Pages	Burleson	1999	175.00
9788173663635	Oracle SQL* Loader: The Definitive Guide, 278 Pages	Gennick	2001	175.00
9788173669330	Oracle SQL*Plus Pocket Reference, 3/ed, 160 Pages	Gennick	2004	125.00
9788173666063	Oracle SQL*Plus: The Definitive Guide, 2/ed, 592 Pages	Gennick	2004	400.00
9788173661846	Oracle Utilities Pocket Reference, 136 Pages	Mishra	2003	100.00
9789350233771	**PayPal APIs: Up and Running, 148 Pages**	**Balderas**	**2011**	**250.00**
9789350234358	**Packet Guide to Core Network Protocols, 180 Pages**	**Hartpence**	**2011**	**275.00**
9788184042528	PC Annoyances, 2/ed: How To Fix The Most Annoying Things About Your Personal Computer, Wind & More, 268 Pages	Bass	2005	300.00
9788173667152	PC Hacks: 100 Industrial-Strength Tips & Tools, 316 Pages	Aspinwall	2004	300.00
9788173669736	PC Hardware Annoyances: How to Fix the Most ANNOYING Things About Your Computer Hardware, 276 Pages	Bigelow	2004	275.00
9788173665325	PC Hardware in a Nutshell: A Desktop Quick Reference, 3/ed, 848 Pgs	Thompson	2003	325.00
9788173667121	PDF Hacks: 100 Industrial-Strength Tips & Tools, 308 Pages	Steward	2004	300.00
9789350230169	**Perl & LWP, 280 Pages**	**Burke**	**2010**	**350.00**
9788173664465	Perl & XML, 224 Pages	Ray	2002	175.00
9788173661075	Perl 5 Pocket Reference, 3/ed, 96 Pages	Vromans	2001	70.00
9788184042764	Perl 6 and Parrot Essentials, 2/ed, 304 Pages	Randal	2004	325.00
9788173668289	Perl Best Practices, 554 Pages	Conway	2005	425.00
9789350230183	**Perl Graphics Programming, 498 Pages**	**Wallace**	**2010**	**750.00**

ISBN	Title	Author	Year	Price
9788173667336	Perl Cookbook, 2/ed, 976 Pages	Christiansen	2003	675.00
9788184041385	Perl Hacks, 310 Pages	Chromatic	2006	325.00
9789350234587	**Perl Pocket Reference, 5/ed, 120 Pages**	**Vromans**	**2011**	**125.00**
9788173668364	Perl Testing: A Developer's Notebook, 212 Pages	Langworth	2005	225.00
9789350230411	**Personal Investing: The Missing Manual, 268 Pages**	**Biafore**	**2010**	**400.00**
9788184046625	Photoshop CS4: The Missing Manual, 804 Pages	King	2008	725.00
9789350230343	**Photoshop CS5: The Missing Manual, 836 Pages**	**Snider**	**2010**	**1,250.00**
9788184043006	PHP Cookbook, 2/ed, 842 Pages	Sklar	2006	750.00
9788184040814	PHP Hacks: Tips & Tools for Creating Dynamic Web Sites, 468 Pages	Herrington	2005	400.00
9788184040234	PHP in a Nutshell, 370 Pages	Hudson	2005	350.00
9789350230176	**PHP: The Good Parts, 194 Pages**	**MacIntyre**	**2010**	**300.00**
9788184040258	PHPUnit Pocket Guide, 88 Pages	Bergmann	2005	100.00
9788173668715	Postfix: The Definitive Guide, 288 Pages	Dent	2003	275.00
9788184042948	PowerPoint 2007 For Starters: The Missing Manual, 325 Pages	Vander	2007	325.00
9788184042566	Powerpoint 2007: The Missing Manual, 502 Pages	Veer	2006	450.00
9788173660306	Practical C Programming 3/ed, 456 Pages	Oualline	1997	275.00
9788173666827	Practical C++ Programming, 2/ed, 582 Pages	Oualline	2002	225.00
9788184040050	Practical Development Environments, 340 Pages	Doar	2005	325.00
9789350234211	**Practical JIRA Administration, 116 Pages**	**Doar**	**2011**	**175.00**
9789350234693	**Practical JIRA Plugins, 136 Pages**	**Doar**	**2011**	**200.00**
9788173663925	Practical PostgreSQL (B/CD), 642 Pages	Command Prompt Inc.	2002	450.00
9788173666834	Practical Unix & Internet Security, 3/ed, 994 Pages	Garfinkel	2003	650.00
9788173664397	Practical VoIP Using VOCAL, 532 Pages	Dang	2002	450.00
9788184042108	Process Improvement Essentials, 364 Pages	Persse, PhD	2006	400.00
9788184040227	Producing Open Sources Software, 302 Pages	Fogel	2005	325.00
9788184045581	The Productive Programmer, 238 Pages	Ford	2008	275.00
9788184040340	Programming .NET Components, 2/ed (Covers .NET 2.0 & Visual Studio 2005), 656 Pages	Lowy	2005	425.00
9788184045673	Programming .NET 3.5, 492 Pgs	Liberty	2008	400.00
9788173667206	Programming .NET Security, 704 Pages	Freeman	2003	550.00
9788173664380	Programming .NET Web Services, 500 Pages	Ferrara	2002	375.00
9788173667411	Programming .NET Windows Applications (Covers .NET 1.1, & Visual Studio .NET 2003), 1,316 Pages	Liberty	2003	750.00
9789350233757	**Programming Amazon EC2, 208 Pages**	**Vliet**	**2011**	**325.00**
9788184045055	Programming Amazon Web Services: S3, EC2, SQS, FPS, and SimpleDB, 624 Pages	Murty	2008	600.00
9789350234495	**Programming Android, 524 Pages**	**Mednieks**	**2011**	**500.00**
9788184043839	Programming ASP.NET AJAX: Build rich, Web 2.0-style UI with ASP.NET AJAX, 490 Pages	Wenz	2007	400.00
9788184046113	Programming ASP.NET 3.5, 4/ed, 1,178 Pages	Liberty	2008	750.00
9788184042085	Programming Atlas, 418 Pages	Wenz	2006	375.00
9788184044386	Programming C# 3.0, 5/ed, (Cover Visual Studio 2008, LINQ, .NET 3.5 & More), 624 Pages	Liberty	2008	525.00
9789350230855	**Programming C# 4.0, 6/ed, 880 Pages**	**Griffiths**	**2010**	**575.00**
9788184043709	Programming Collective Intelligence: Building Smart Web 2.0 Applications, 376 Pages	Segaran	2007	375.00
9788173660764	Programming Embedded Systems in C & C++, 198 Pages	Barr	1999	175.00

ISBN	Title	Author	Year	Price
9788184042627	Programming Embedded Systems with C and GNU Development Tools, 2/ed, 340 Pages	Barr	2006	250.00
9789350230862	**Programming Entity Framework, 2/ed, 936 Pages**	**Lerman**	**2010**	**1,075.00**
9788184041453	Programming Excel with VBA and .NET, 1,128 Pages	Webb	2006	750.00
9788184048490	Programming F#, 424 Pages	Smith	2009	625.00
9788173669699	Programming Flash Communication Server, 842 Pages	Lesser	2005	600.00
9788184043358	Programming Flex 2, 520 Pages	Kazoun	2007	250.00
9788184047233	Programming Flex 3, 674 Pages	Kazoun	2009	600.00
9789350233214	**Programming Google App Engine, 416 Pages**	**Sanderson**	**2011**	**625.00**
9788184047981	Programming Interactivity, 756 Pages	Noble	2009	1,125.00
9789350234198	**Programming iOS 4, 856 Pages**	**Neuburg**	**2011**	**1,000.00**
9789350230572	**Programming Jabber, 500 Pages**	**Adams**	**2010**	**750.00**
9788173668180	Programming Jakarta Struts 2/ed, 470 Pages	Cavaness	2004	400.00
9788173662652	Programming Perl 3/ed, 1,116 Pages	Wall	2000	750.00
9788184042719	Programming PHP, 2/ed, 425 Pages	Lerdorf	2006	425.00
9788184043792	Programming Python (Covers Python 2) **(B/CD)**, 3/ed, 1,582 Pgs	Lutz	2006	875.00
9789350232873	**Programming Python, 4/ed, 1,652 Pages**	**Lutz**	**2011**	**800.00**
9788173667862	Programming SQL Server 2005, 600 Pages	Wildermuth	2006	400.00
9788184048247	Programming Scala, 464 Pages	Qampler	2009	700.00
9788184048186	Programming the iPhone User Experience, 208 Pages	Boudreaux	2009	300.00
9789350230718	**Programming the Mobile Web, 532 Pages**	**Firtman**	**2010**	**675.00**
9788173662379	Programming the Perl DBI, 372 Pages	Descartes	2000	350.00
9788184047950	Programming the Semantic Web, 320 Pages	Segaran	2009	475.00
9788184045253	Programming Visual Basic 2008, 798 Pages	Patrick	2008	550.00
9788184047004	Programming WCF Services, 2/ed, 800 Pages	Löwy	2009	725.00
9789350230947	**Programming WCF Services, 3/ed, 936 Pages**	**Löwy**	**2010**	**600.00**
9788173665738	Programming Web Services with Perl, 492 Pages	Ray	2002	400.00
9788173662041	Programming Web Services with SOAP, 268 Pages	Snell	2001	200.00
9789350230367	**Programming Windows Azure, 388 Pages**	**Krishnan**	**2010**	**575.00**
9788184043723	Programming WPF, 2/ed, 880 Pages	Sells	2007	725.00
9788173664793	Python Cookbook (Covers Python 2.3 & 2.4), 2/ed, 852 Pages	Martelli	2005	600.00
9788184045833	Python for Unix and Linux System Administration, 472 Pages	Gift	2008	450.00
9788184045406	Python in a Nutshell 2/ed, 726 Pages	Martelli	2008	500.00
9788173669705	Python Pocket Reference (Covers Python 2.4), 3/ed, 168 Pages	Lutz	2005	125.00
9788184048506	Python Pocket Reference, 4/ed, 226 Pages	Lutz	2009	275.00
9788173668487	qmail, 268 Pages	Levine	2004	275.00
9789350233795	**R Cookbook, 460 Pages**	**Teetor**	**2011**	**700.00**
9788184049015	**R IN A NUTSHELL, 652 Pages**	**Adler**	**2010**	**775.00**
9788184049435	**RADIUS, 224 Pages**	**Hassell**	**2010**	**325.00**
9788184042962	Rail Cookbook, 600 Pages	Orsini	2007	500.00
9788184046090	Rails: Up and Running, 2/ed, 232 Pages	Tate	2008	300.00
9788184045956	Rails Pocket Reference, 212 Pages	Berry	2008	150.00
9788184046489	Real World Haskell: Code You Can Believe In, 710 Pages	O'Sullivan	2008	600.00
9789350231913	**Real World Instrumentation with Python: Automated Data Acquisition and Control Systems, 644 Pages**	**Hughes**	**2010**	**975.00**
9788173666896	Real World Web Services, 230 Pages	Iverson	2004	225.00
9788184045857	Refactoring SQL Applications, 372 Pages	Faroult	2008	350.00
9788184043761	Regular Expression Pocket Reference, 2/ed, 126 Pages	Stubblebine	2007	150.00

ISBN	Title	Author	Year	Price
9788184047172	Regular Expressions Cookbook, 530 Pages	Goyvaerts	2009	800.00
9788184041989	The Relational Database Dictionary, 126 Pages	Date	2006	150.00
9788184041378	Repairing and Upgrading Your PC, 462 Pages	Thompson	2006	450.00
9788184048698	RESTful Java with JAX-RS, 328 Pages	Burke	2009	500.00
9788184043327	Restful Web Services, 462 Pages	Richardson	2007	425.00
9788184049558	**RESTful Web Services Cookbook, 332 Pages**	**Allamaraju**	**2010**	**500.00**
9789350231166	**REST in Practice, 472 Pages**	**Webber**	**2010**	**700.00**
9788184040869	RFID Essentials, 276 Pages	Glover	2006	275.00
9788184047509	Ruby Best Practices, 347 Pages	Brown	2009	550.00
9788184041804	Ruby Cookbook, 920 Pages	Carlson	2006	650.00
9788184041996	Ruby on Rails: Up and Running, 196 Pages	Tate	2006	225.00
9788184043624	Ruby Pocket Reference, 182 Pages	Fitzgerald	2007	150.00
9788184044928	The Ruby Programming Language, 460 Pages	Flanagan	2008	425.00
9788184042726	Running Linux, 5/ed, 986 Pages	Welsh	2005	600.00
9788173667053	Samba Pocket Reference, 2/ed, 146 Pages	Eckstein	2003	125.00
9789350234600	**Scaling CouchDB, 92 Pages**	**Holt**	**2011**	**150.00**
9788184044935	ScreenOS Cookbook, 854 Pages	Brunner	2008	600.00
9788173667213	Secure Coding: Principles & Practices, 200 Pages	Graff	2003	225.00
9788184047240	Search Engine Optimization for Flash, 294 Pages	Perkins	2009	350.00
9788184043600	Securing Ajax Applications, 266 Pages	Wells	2007	275.00
9788184047257	Security Monitoring, 262 Pages	Fry	2009	300.00
9788184040081	Security and Usability, 748 Pages	Cranor	2005	550.00
9788184043754	Security Power Tools, 872 Pages	Burns	2007	650.00
9788173668401	Security Warrior, 562 Pages	Peikari	2004	500.00
9788173660788	sed and awk, 2/ed, 440 Pages	Dougherty	1997	375.00
9788184049572	**sed and awk Pocket Reference, 2/ed, 64 Pages**	**Robbins**	**2010**	**100.00**
9788173669187	SELINUX NSA's Open Source Security Enhanced Linux, 264 Pgs	McCarty	2004	275.00
9788173668234	sendmail Cookbook, 418 Pages	Hunt	2003	400.00
9788184044225	sendmail, 4/ed, 1,324 Pages	Costales	2007	850.00
9788184048674	SEO Warrior, 512 Pages	Jerkovic	2009	775.00
9788173666865	Sequence Analysis in a Nutshell: A Guide to Common Tools & Databases (Covers EMBOSS 2.5.0), 310 Pages	Markel	2003	275.00
9788184040449	SharePoint 2007: The Definitive Guide, 836 Pages	Pyles	2007	600.00
9788184046144	SharePoint for Project Management, 266 Pages	Raymond	2008	300.00
9788173669835	SharePoint Office Pocket Guide, 94 Pages	Webb	2005	100.00
9788173667398	SharePoint User's Guide, 158 Pages	IDC	2005	150.00
9788173669507	Snort Cookbook, 296 Pages	Orebaugh	2005	300.00
9788184043693	SOA in Practice: The Art of Distributed System Design, 358 Pgs	Josuttis	2007	375.00
9788173668197	Spidering Hacks: 100 Industrial - Strength Tips & Tools, 436 Pages	Hemenway	2003	350.00
9788173668371	Spring: A Developer's Notebook, 202 Pages	Tate	2005	225.00
9788184046939	SQL and Relational Theory: How to Write Accurate SQL Code, 442 Pages	Date	2009	350.00
9788184040685	SQL Cookbook, 640 Pages	Molinaro	2005	475.00
9788184042207	SQL Hacks, 424 Pages	Cumming	2006	400.00
9788184047264	SQL IN A NUTSHELL 3/ed, 606 Pages	Kline	2009	500.00
9788173667435	SQL Pocket Guide (Cover Oracle. DB2, SQL Server & MySQL), 170 Pgs	Gennick	2006	125.00

ISBN	Title	Author	Year	Price
9788184046649	Using Drupal, 504 Pages	Byron	2009	525.00
9788184047363	Using Google App Engine, 282 Pages	Severance	2009	350.00
9789350234709	**Using the HTML5 Filesystem API, 96 Pages**	**Bidelman**	**2011**	**125.00**
9788184049008	**Using Joomla, 428 Pages**	**Severdia**	**2010**	**650.00**
9788184043037	Using Samba, 3/ed, 464 Pages	Carter	2007	450.00
9789350233191	**Using SANs and NAS, 248 Pages**	**Preston**	**2011**	**375.00**
9788173665943	VB .NET Language Pocket Reference, 160 Pages	Roman	2002	125.00
9788173666889	VBScript in a Nutshell: A Desktop Quick Reference, 2/e, 528 Pages	Lomax	2003	400.00
9788184047325	Version Control with Git, 348 Pages	Loeliger	2009	400.00
9788184047288	Version Control with Subversion 2/ed, 446 Pages	Pilato	2009	475.00
9788173662621	vi Editor Pocket Reference, 76 Pages	Robbins	1999	60.00
9789350234396	**Virtualization: A Manager's Guide, 96 Pages**	**Kusnetzky**	**2011**	**150.00**
9788173660962	Visual Basic Controls in a Nutshell, 512 Pages	Dictor	1999	310.00
9788184048681	VMware Cookbook, 316 Pages	Troy	2009	475.00
9788184040692	VOIP Hacks: Tips & Tools for Internet Telephony, 326 Pages	Wallingford	2006	325.00
9788184045062	Web 2.0: A Strategy Guide: Business thinking and strategies behind successful Web 2.0 implementations, 302 Pages	Shuen	2008	350.00
9788184047356	Web 2.0 Architectures: What entrepreneurs and information architects need to know, 292 Pages	Nickull	2009	550.00
9788173669057	Web Database Application with PHP & MySQL (Covers PEAR, PHP 5 & MySQL 4.1), 2/ed, 828 Pages	Willaims	2004	600.00
9788184040982	Web Design in a Nutshell: A Desktop Quick Reference, 3/ed, 826 Pages	Niederst	2006	450.00
9788184049046	Web Mapping Illustrated, 388 Pages	Mitchell	2005	575.00
9789350230589	**Web Operations, 360 Pages**	**Allspaw**	**2010**	**550.00**
9788173663949	Web Security, Privacy & Commerce, 2/ed, 768 Pages	Garfinkel	2001	500.00
9788173663390	Web Services Essentials, 320 Pages	Cerami	2002	275.00
9788173667626	Web Site Cookbook, 262 Pages	Addison	2006	300.00
9788184045628	Website Optimization, 408 Pages	King	2008	450.00
9788173663093	WebLogic 8.1: The Definitive Guide, 860 Pages	Mountjoy	2004	650.00
9788173661303	The Whole Internet: The Next Generation, 576 Pages	Conner/Krol	1999	425.00
9788173661365	Win32 API Programming with Visual Basic **(B/CD)**, 534 Pages	Roman	1999	400.00
9789350230299	**Windows 7 Annoyances, 740 Pages**	**Karp**	**2010**	**900.00**
9788184048339	Windows 7: Up and Running, 220 Pages	Wei-Meng Lee	2009	450.00
9788184048537	Windows 7: The Definitive Guide, 1008 Pages	Stanek	2009	925.00
9788184049916	**Windows 7: The Missing Manual, 924 Pages**	**Pogue**	**2010**	**450.00**
9788184044034	Windows PowerShell Cookbook: for Windows, Exchange 2007, and MOM V3, 600 Pages	Holmes	2007	800.00
9789350230930	**Windows PowerShell Cookbook, 2/ed, 904 Pages**	**Holmes**	**2010**	**600.00**
9788184045239	Windows PowerShell Pocket Reference, 182 Pages	Holmes	2008	150.00
9788184045000	Windows Server 2008: The Definitive Guide, 508 Pages	Hassell	2008	475.00
9788173668838	Windows Server Hacks: 100 Industrial-Strength Tips & Tools , 328 Pages	Tulloch	2004	325.00
9788184042979	Windows Vista For Starters: The Missing Manual, 493 Pages	Pogue	2007	325.00
9788173669668	Windows XP Cookbook, 690 Pages	Allen	2005	500.00
9788173667459	Windows XP Hacks: 100 Industrial-Strength Tips & Tools, 294 Pages	Gralla	2003	350.00
9788173666919	Windows XP Pocket Reference, 196 Pages	Karp	2002	125.00
9788184042931	Word 2007 For Starters: The Missing Manual, 372 Pages	Grover	2007	350.00

ISBN	Title	Author	Year	Price
9788173666926	Word Pocket Guide, 160 Pages	Glenn	2003	125.00
9789350234068	**Writing and Querying MapReduce Views in CouchDB, 100 Pages**	**Holt**	**2011**	**150.00**
9788173665356	Writing Excel Macros with VBA, 2/ed, 580 Pages	Roman	2002	500.00
9789350234044	**Writing Game Center Apps in iOS, 100 Pages**	**Nahavandipoor**	**2011**	**150.00**
9788184044430	X Power Tools, 286 Pages	Tyler	2008	325.00
9788173666155	XML Hacks: 100 Industrial-Strength Tips & Tools, 490 Pages	Fitzgerald	2004	425.00
9788173668456	XML in a Nutshell (Covers XML 1.1 & XInclude), 3/ed, 724 Pgs	Harold	2005	500.00
9788184042641	XML Pocket Reference, 3/ed, 198 Pages	Laurent	2005	125.00
9788184047295	XMPP: The Definitive Guide, 324 Pages	Saint	2009	375.00
9788184043181	XQuery, 528 Pages	Walmsley	2007	500.00
9788173664908	XSLT 1.0 Pocket Reference, 188 Pages	Lenz	2005	150.00
9788184040784	XSLT Cookbook (Cover XSLT 1.0 & 2.0, 2/ed, 786 Pages	Mangano	2005	500.00

US EDITION AVAILABLE AT SPECIAL PRICE:

ISBN	Title	Author	Year	Price
9780596102364	Adobe Creative Suite 2 Workflow, 634 Pages	Alspach	2005	1,625.00
9780596006006	Adobe Encore DVD: In the Studio, 336 Pages	Dixon	2004	1,225.00
9780596529765	Adobe InDesign CS3 One-On-One (Book / DVD), 560 Pages	McClelland	2007	$44.00
9780596529758	Adobe Photoshop CS3 One-On-One (Book / DVD), 544 Pages	McClelland	2007	$40.00
9780596807979	**Adobe Photoshop CS5 One-on-One, 544 Pages**	**McClelland**	**2010**	**$49.99**
9781449382551	**Best Android Apps: The Guide for Discriminating Downloaders, 240 Pages**	**Hendrickson**	**2010**	**$19.99**
9780596101367	Building Extreme PCs, 192 Pages	Hardwidge	2006	1,200.00
9780596520748	Coding4Fun: 10 .NET Programming Projects for Wiimote, YouTube, World of Warcraft, and More, 512 Pages	Fernandez	2008	$39.00
9780596008499	Commercial Photoshop Retouching: In The Studio, 410 Pages	Honiball	2005	1,425.00
9780596008581	Creating Photomontages with Photoshop: A Designer's Notebook, 96 Pages	Collandre	2005	800.00
9780596008031	Designing Interfaces, 352 Pages	Tidwell	2005	$49.95
9780596528102	Designing Web Navigation: Optimizing the User Experience, 456 Pgs	Kalbach	2007	$40.00
9780596526801	Devices of the Soul Batting for Our Selves in an Age of Machines, 302 Pages	Talbott	2007	$18.00
9780596006662	Digital Photography Hacks: 100 Industrial - Strength Tips & Tools, 336 Pages	Story	2004	800.00
9780596100155	Digital Photography Pocket Guide, 3/ed, 160 Pages	Story	2005	450.00
9780596005474	Digital Photography: Expert Techniques, 496 Pages	Milburn	2003	1,375.00
9780596008413	Digital Photography: The Missing Manual, 432 Pages	Grover	2006	1,200.00
9780596009465	Digital Video Hacks: Tips & Tools for Shooting, Editing & Sharing, 426 Pages	Paul	2005	800.00
9780596005238	Digital Video Pocket Guide, 474 Pages	Story	2003	500.00
9780596510572	Dynamic Learning Dreamweaver CS3 (Book / DVD), 416 Pgs	Gerantabee	2007	$36.00
9780596510589	Dynamic Learning Flash CS3 (Book / DVD), 456 Pages	Gerantabee	2007	$36.00
9780596510619	Dynamic Learning: Photoshop CS3 (Book / DVD), 360 Pages	Smith	2007	$36.00
9780596102425	Fonts & Encodings, 1,037 Pages	Haralambous	2007	$48.00
9780596002879	Free As In Freedom: Richard Stallman's Crusade for Free Software, 243 Pages	Williams	2002	750.00
9780596006624	Hackers & Painters: Big Ideas From the Computer Age, 276 Pgs	Graham	2004	700.00

ISBN	Title	Author	Year	Price
9780596526856	Illustrated Guide to Astronomical Wonders: From Novice to Master Observer (DIY Science), 519 Pages	Thompson	2007	$24.00
9780596008598	Illustrations with Photoshop: A Designer's Notebook, 96 Pages	Rodarmor	2004	775.00
9780596100483	InDesign Production Cookbook, 224 Pages	Dabbs	2005	1,200.00
9780596007683	Just A Geek, 296 Pages	Wheaton	2004	700.00
9780596527877	Learning ActionScript 3.0: A Beginner's Guide, 382 Pages	Shupe	2008	$32.00
9780596517328	Learning Flex 3: Getting up to Speed with Rich Internet Applications (Adobe Developer Library), 304 Pages	Cole	2008	$32.00
9780596527525	Learning Web Design: A Beginner's Guide to (X)HTML, StyleSheets, and Web Graphics, 3/ed, 479 Pages	Robbins	2007	$36.00
9780596517717	Making Things Happen: Mastering Project Management (Theory in Practice), 408 Pages	Berkun	2008	$32.00
9780596007034	Mapping Hacks: Tips & Tools for Electronic Cartography, 574 Pgs	Erle	2005	900.00
9780596527051	Myths of Innovation, 196 Pages	Berkun	2007	$20.00
9780596002688	Oracle SQL Tuning Pocket Reference, 112 Pages	Gurry	2002	$9.95
9780596008604	Photo Retouching with Photoshop: A Designer's Notebook, 96 Pgs	CLEC'H	2004	775.00
9780596100209	Photoshop Blending Modes Cookbook for Digital Photographers, 176 Pages	Beardsworth	2005	1,025.00
9780596008512	Photoshop CS2 Raw: Using Adobe Camera Raw, Bridge, and Photoshop to Get the Most Out of Your Digital Camera, 206 Pgs	Aaland	2006	1,075.00
9780596515041	Photoshop CS3 Photo Effects Cookbook: 53 Easy-to-Follow Recipes for Digital Photographers, Designers, & Artists, 176 Pgs	Shelbourne	2007	$24.00
9780596510527	Photoshop CS3 Raw: Get the Most Out of the Raw Format with Adobe Photoshop, Camera Raw, and Bridge, 272 Pages	Aaland	2008	$28.00
9780596100216	Photoshop Filter Effects Encyclopedia, 176 Pages	Pring	2005	1,050.00
9780596100629	Photoshop Fine Art Effects Cookbook, 176 Pages	Beardsworth	2006	1,050.00
9780596100995	Photoshop Lightroom Adventure: Mastering Adobe's next-generation tool for digital photographers, 350 Pages	Aaland	2007	$32.00
9780596100223	Photoshop Photo Effects Cookbook, 176 Pages	Shelbourne	2005	1,025.00
9780596100308	Photoshop Retouching Cookbook for Digital Photographers, 176 Pages	Huggins	2005	1,025.00
9780596101138	Programming Windows Presentation Foundation, 430 Pages	Sells	2005	1,100.00
9780596007195	Revolution in the Valley, 324 Pages	Hertzfeld	2004	775.00
9780596523701	Stephen Johnson on Digital Photography, 320 Pages	Johnson	2006	1,500.00
9780596001087	The Cathedral & The Bazaar, 256 Pages	Raymond	2001	525.00
9780596100476	The Creative Digital Darkroom, 429 Pages	Eismann	2008	$40.00
9780596007331	We the Media: Grassroots Journalism by the People, for the People, 320 Pages	Gillmor	2004	775.00
9780596100834	Windows Seat, 152 Pages	Kost	2006	1,600.00

- Prices are subject to change without notice.
- All Prices are in Indian Rupees except where indicated in € (Euro Dollar) $ (US Dollar) and £ (Pound)
- **Titles Released after January 2010 are marked in Bold.**